LITERATURE AS CONDUCT

Literature as Conduct

SPEECH ACTS IN HENRY JAMES

J. HILLIS MILLER

FORDHAM UNIVERSITY PRESS

New York 2005

Copyright © 2005 Fordham University Press

Library of Congress Cataloging-in-Publication Data

Miller, J. Hillis (Joseph Hillis), 1928–
Literature as conduct : speech acts in Henry James / J. Hillis
Miller.—1st ed.
p.   cm.
Includes bibliographical references and index.
ISBN 0-8232-2537-2 (hardcover) — ISBN 0-8232-2538-0
(pbk.)
1. James, Henry, 1843–1916—Criticism and
interpretation.   2. Speech in literature.   3. Oral
communication in literature.   4. Conduct of life in
literature.   5. Speech acts (Linguistics)   I. Title.
PS2127.S73.m55   2005
813'.4—dc22
2005015743

Printed in the United States of America
07 06 05   5 4 3 2 1
First edition

the whole conduct of life consists of things done, which do other things in their turn. . . . we recognize betimes that to "put" things is very exactly and responsibly and interminably to do them.

HENRY JAMES,
Preface to *The Golden Bowl*

In Memory of Jacques Derrida

CONTENTS

ix

ACKNOWLEDGMENTS

I thank all those students and colleagues who listened to oral presentations of parts of this book in seminars, lectures, and conferences in the United States, in Europe, and in the People's Republic of China. I learned much from their responses. I thank also the journals and publishers who brought out preliminary versions of some chapter sections. I thank them for granting me permission to reuse this material in revised form:

"History, Narrative, and Responsibility: Speech Acts in Henry James's 'The Aspern Papers,'" *Textual Practice* 9, no. 2 (Summer 1995): 243–67.
"Reference in *The Wings of the Dove*: Literature as Speech Act," Graat No. 20, *Ré-Inventer le Réel* (Tours: Université de Tours, 1999), 165–77.
"Lying against Death: Out of the Loop," *Arbejdspapir*, 26–99. Pamphlet published by the Department of Comparative Literature, University of Aarhus.
"The Story of a Kiss: Isabel's Decisions in *The Portrait of a Lady*," *American Vistas and Beyond: A Festschrift for Roland Hagenbüchle*, ed. Marietta Messmer and Josef Raab (Trier: Wissenschaftlicher Verlag, 2002), 95–108.
"Lying against Death: Out of the Loop," *Acts of Narrative*, ed. Carol Jacobs and Henry Sussman (Stanford: Stanford University Press, 2003), 15–30.
"The 'Quasi-Turn-of-Screw Effect': How to Raise a Ghost with Words," *The Oxford Literary Review* 25 (2003): 121–37.
"What Is a Kiss? Isabel's Moments of Decision," *Critical Inquiry* 31, no. 3 (Spring 2005): 722–46.

I have silently changed James's spelling from English to United States practice. I hope his hovering ghost will forgive me for thereby appropriating him for American literature.

J. Hillis Miller
Sedgwick, Maine
April 7, 2005

xi

With a few exceptions, as stated in the notes, the novels and stories of Henry James are cited from the reprint of the New York Edition of *The Novels and Tales of Henry James*, 26 vols. (Fairfield, N.J.: Augustus M. Kelley, 1971–79). References are given by volume and page of this edition. The following abbreviations have been used in the text and notes.

AR   Paul de Man, *Allegories of Reading* (New Haven: Yale University Press, 1979).

HT   J. L. Austin, *How to Do Things with Words*, 2d ed., ed. J. O. Urmson and Marina Sbisà (Oxford: Oxford University Press, 1980).

IC   Jean-Luc Nancy, *The Inoperative Community*, ed. Peter Connor, trans. Peter Connor, Lisa Garbus, Michael Holland, and Simona Sawhney (Minneapolis: University of Minnesota Press, 1991).

LITERATURE AS CONDUCT

Introduction

A phrase in my epigraph, "the . . . conduct of life," is the title of a high-minded book by Ralph Waldo Emerson. James may have intended a reference to Emerson's book when he wrote those words. They are part of the eloquent affirmations in the final paragraph of the last preface to the New York Edition, the preface to *The Golden Bowl*.[1] James claims that "putting" things, that is, saying or writing them, for example in those fictions he wrote, is as much a form of doing, and therefore of conduct, as any other act. *Conduct*: the word is defined by the *Pocket Oxford Dictionary* as a noun meaning "one's actions, the way one acquits oneself (esp. as concrete counterpart of character)," and as a verb (with the accent on the second syllable) meaning "lead or guide or escort, direct or control or manage." James wants to stress the way "putting things" in speech or writing is a counterpart of character. "Conduct," one might say, "conducts" one toward the manifestation of character as it is oriented toward some goal.

James emphasizes the superiority of putting things in words, as a form of doing, over other forms of social behavior. The latter are often dispersed or forgotten, while the former leave traces behind, for example, all those printed pages in the New York Edition. Such enduring words, putting as doing, their author can, or even must, acknowledge: "Yes, I wrote that. I take responsibility for it, and for whatever effects it may have had on my readers." Here is James's way of putting this:

> Our expression of them [i.e., "things"], and the terms on which we understand that, belong as nearly to our conduct and our life as every other feature of our freedom; these things yield in fact some of its most exquisite material to the religion of doing. More than that, our literary deeds enjoy this marked advantage over many of our acts, that, though they go forth into the world and stray even in the desert, they don't to the same extent lose themselves; their attachment and reference to us, however strained, needn't necessarily lapse—while of the tie that binds us to *them* we may make almost anything we like. (23: xxiv–xv)

I claim that each such putting/doing is what recent philosophers call a speech act. Putting things in words is speech that acts. It does something that may do other things in its turn. It is a way of doing things with words. Three forms of this may be identified in connection with literature as conduct. (1) The author's act of writing is a doing that takes the form of putting things in this way or that. This, James claims, is part of the conduct of life. (2) The narrators and characters in a work of fiction may utter speech acts that are a form of doing things with words—promises, declarations, excuses, denials, acts of bearing witness, lies, decisions publicly attested, and the like. Such speech acts make up crucial moments in the narrator's or the characters' conduct of life. (3) The reader, in his or her turn, in acts of teaching, criticism, or informal comment, may do things by putting a reading into words. Doing that may have an effect on students, readers, or acquaintances. Teaching, or writing criticism, or just talking about a book is a doing that may do other things in its turn. My title, "Literature as Conduct," can refer to the way writing literature is a form of conduct, or to the representation of conduct within literary fictions, or, using *conduct* as a verb, to the way literature may conduct its readers to believe or to behave in new ways. This book explores the relations of literature to conduct by reading Henry James's work.

Literature as Conduct has been an absurdly long time in the making. My only excuse (a speech act there!) is that, though I have always been fascinated by Henry James's work, I have also always doubted my ability to do it full justice. It may, I have thought, be beyond me. I have, nevertheless, through all the time spent writing these chapters, stuck to my original project. This was to read a representative group of Henry James's major works in the light of speech act theory. Can any group, however, be said to be representative of so abundant and diverse an oeuvre? Nevertheless,

I was forced to choose. To attempt discussion of all James's works would have been, so I thought and still think, impossibly diffuse and superficial. James wrote over one hundred short stories alone, for example, each one deserving an extended analysis. Many admirable short fictions are not even included in the New York Edition. James also published many wonderful volumes of nonfictional prose. Four volumes of his letters have been collected in the standard edition of those. A volume of his plays has been published.

I wanted to allow myself space in each chapter for a detailed reading of a single work by James. My plan was to choose examples from early, middle, late, and very late James fictions. In each case I would, in the act of reading, keep a sharp eye out for speech acts uttered by the characters or by the narrator. I would try to see just how they function inside the work. I also hypothesized that James's prefaces to the New York Edition might not only contain speech acts but also indicate ways in which a whole literary work by James might function as a speech act. I was also mindful that reading a literary work confers a responsibility on the reader to make an accounting of his or her act of reading. Such an accounting has a performative as well as a constative dimension. A reading, as I have said, is, to some degree, a doing that may do other things in its turn.

I had at first intended to begin with a brief introduction to speech act theory as it might be related to literature, but this got longer and longer until it became a separate book, *Speech Acts in Literature*.[2] The present introduction contains a brief summary of speech act theory in its relation to literature. Since this book depends on a certain version of speech act theory, a word about that seems necessary. I say "a word" because a full account would be a long story indeed, as my *Speech Acts in Literature* suggests. Speech act theory, moreover, remains controversial. No account of it can be merely factual or, as Austin would say, "constative." An example of the continuing controversy is an essay in which Stanley Cavell takes it upon himself to defend Austin once more from Derrida's supposed misunderstanding of him.[3]

After a brief first chapter making use of speech act theory to read "The Aspern Papers" (1888), successive chapters of this book are more extended exploitations of speech act theory's interpretative power in readings of James's sometimes exorbitant longer novels. I chose, not quite arbitrarily, *The Portrait of a Lady* (1881) as my early work, *The Awkward Age* (1899) for my middle work, *The Wings of the Dove* (1902) and *The Golden Bowl* (1904) as my late works, and the unfinished *The Sense of the Past* (1917) as my late late work. When I got down to the business of carefully reading these novels, I found the presence and function within them of speech acts—promises, lies, declarations, decisions, excuses, testimonies, legacies, and so on—a fascinating and rich field for analysis and understanding. I found also that each novel differed sharply from the others in the kinds of speech acts that are most important and in the way they function. Each chapter therefore differs from the others in focusing on a different region of the immense field of speech acts and in obeying the specific interpretative exigencies of a given novel. I have taken hold of each novel by whatever speech act handle seemed best for that particular work.

Just what is a speech act? It is an utterance that does not name something but makes something happen. A speech act, unlike a constative statement, cannot be either true or false. It can either work to make something happen or it can fail to do that. A paradigmatic example is the minister's "I pronounce you man and wife." That sentence does not describe anything. Uttered in the right circumstances, the sentence brings it about that the couple is married. The reader should remember that my central concern in this book is not with speech act theory as such. I am anxious, of course, to get that right. My focus, however, is on the permeable frontier—the overlapping, intersection, collision, or confrontation—between speech act theory and literary works, specifically works by Henry James.

No doubt people have long known that language can make something happen. Nevertheless, the publication in 1962 of J. L. Austin's *How to Do Things with Words* marked a watershed in speech act theory.[4] Austin himself had developed his ideas as early as 1939. He had published one essay using these ideas in 1946, had lectured at Oxford in 1952 and thereafter on "Words and Deeds," and had delivered the lectures on which *How to Do Things with Words* is based at Harvard in 1955. In spite of these preliminaries, *How to Do Things with Words* is the basic speech act (though Austin perhaps would not have called it that) from which speech act theory in all its contradictory complexity has sprung. I call the book a speech act because it was inaugural. It used words to make something happen, though not quite what Austin may have intended or foreseen. It may have been anxiety about this, as well as a conviction that he had not quite worked things out to his satisfaction, that led Austin to withhold the lectures from publication during his lifetime, even though his agreement with Harvard involved a contractual promise (a speech act!) to let the Harvard University Press publish the lectures. Whatever may have been the reasons for delay, Austin was dead by the time *How to Do Things with Words* was published. That did not deprive the book of performative force, any more than does the death of someone who has made a will deprive that will of force. I shall return to this point in my reading of *The Wings of the Dove*.

Austin's book has engendered two radically different forms of appropriation and development. One has remained within linguistics, pragmatics, and analytical philosophy. This branch of speech act theory has minimized what is problematic or contradictory in Austin's work on speech acts, for example, his shifts in terminology,[5] or the multitude of contradictory examples of speech acts he gives, or his admission in various places that the clarity about speech acts he is seeking is eluding him. The swarm of examples suggests that each speech act may function according to its own laws. An excuse is different from a promise, Both are different from a bet or a bequeathing. The standard works on speech act theory also tend to underemphasize Austin's gift, a gift he shares with every great philosopher, for choosing examples that put the greatest pressure on the conceptual formulations they seem meant simply to exemplify. *How to Do Things with Words* is a wonderfully witty and ironic book. It is full of splendid formulations that show a great command of the complexities of ordinary language. These formulations often also twist that language in strange ways, as when Austin says, "here I must let some of my cats on the table" (*HT*, 20).

The first way of thinking about speech acts has attempted to develop a coherent theory of speech acts, with clear and reasonable distinctions among different kinds of speech acts, a standard terminology, and a more or less infallible set of rules for distinguishing between speech acts and other uses of language, between one kind of speech act and another, as well as between "felicitous" and "infelicitous" speech acts. The work of John Searle and the discussion of speech acts in a book by Jacob Mey are salient points within this tradition.[6] The title of one of Searle's essays, "A Classification of Illocutionary Acts,"[7] indicates the bent of this sort of work. It assumes that speech acts can be classified and analyzed. They can be dominated by philosophical or linguistic reasoning. Austin died young, before he had time to put the finishing touches on a coherent theory of speech acts. It remains, such scholars assume, only to tidy things up a bit, and then such a theory can be established.

The other branch of thinking about speech acts is best represented by the work of Paul de Man, Jacques Derrida, Shoshana Felman, Werner Hamacher, Judith Butler, and others, that is, by an important strand within so-called "deconstruction."[8] This strand recognizes, at least implicitly, that, far from being the development of a watertight theory of how to do things with words, Austin's book is what he himself calls, in a characteristically ironic phrase, a demonstration of how "to bog, by logical stages, down" (*HT*, 13). Derrida's discussion of Austin in "Signature Event Context" (original French version: 1971) elicited a vigorous reply from Searle in 1977. That in turn led to Derrida's response in "Limited Inc abc . . ." (1977).[9] Meanwhile, in *Allegories of Reading* (1979) and other later essays, as well as in his teaching, Paul de Man appropriated speech act theory for his own way of reading reading.

What is the difference between these two ways of taking up Austin's legacy? For the first way, the different kinds of speech acts all in one way or another depend on the presence of the thinking, self-aware "I." This ego is in full possession of itself and of what it does with words. In a speech act it utters or writes with conscious intention a set of words meant to have a certain result. The predictable efficacy of such an utterance is controlled and delimited by a clear context of rules, regulations, conventions, laws, and institutions. These ensure the felicity of a good speech act. The minister, in the appropriate circumstances, says, "I pronounce you man and wife," and behold! the couple is married, before God and man and in the eyes of the law. Yet no one thinks an actor and actress performing a marriage on the stage are married when another actor playing the minister utters the same words. (The example is Austin's.[10])

For de Man and Derrida, in slightly different ways, all these assumptions are profoundly problematic. Rather than multiplying distinctions among different kinds of speech acts, they tend to use, as I do in this book, the term *performative* as an all-inclusive term naming the general power of words to do something, though with a recognition that each performative is to some degree unique. In an explicit challenge to Searle, Derrida argues in "Signature Event Context" that the context of a performative utterance can never be "saturated." The context cannot be identified and controlled enough to ensure the distinction between a felicitous and an infelicitous speech act. Derrida and de Man tend, as I do and as Austin himself did, to see a swarming of speech acts even in language that does not fit the delimited notion of speech acts, as opposed to other uses of language, as defined in Searle's work or in work by others of that ilk. Austin saw, for example, that explicit speech is not necessary to make a speech act, or what might better be called a "sign act." "In very many cases," says Austin,

> it is possible to perform an act of exactly the same kind [as a speech act] *not* by uttering words, whether written or spoken, but in some other way. For example, I may in some places effect marriage by cohabiting, or I may bet with a totalisator machine by putting a coin in a slot. . . . [W]e can for example warn or order or appoint or give or protest or apologize by non-

verbal means. . . . Thus we may cock a snook[11] or hurl a tomato by way of protest. (*HT*, 8, 119).

Austin also recognizes, giving a characteristically witty example, the implicit ambiguity in such sign acts or gesture acts: "suppose I bow deeply before you; it might not be clear whether I am doing obeisance to you or, say, stooping to observe the flora or to ease my indigestion" (*HT*, 69). The possibility of sign acts that work like speech acts is important for me in this book, for example, in my analysis in chapter 2 of Caspar Goodwood's kiss of Isabel in James's *The Portrait of a Lady*.

Apparent constatives often work performatively. When a conservative politician in the United States says, "The American people do not want universal health care run by the government," or "The American people wanted Saddam Hussein removed from power," each sentence looks like a statement of fact. It is actually a performative utterance tending to bring about the situation it pretends only to describe. Soon such politicians and their hacks in the media will be saying: "The American people do not want evolution, multiculturalism, queer theory, minority discourse, or cultural studies taught." In fact they *have* said it. Performative signs (including pictures, moving and still, as well as oral speech, written language, and music) masking as constative assertions generate what we call ideology.

No form of words, moreover, is ever wholly performative or wholly constative, as Austin already recognized, though the cognitive and performative functions of a given piece of language can never be reconciled fully or made to jibe. "[W]e are," says Austin in one place, "assimilating the supposed constative utterance to the performative" (*HT*, 52). In another place he says that the distinction between "doing" and "saying," which he has been using "as a means of distinguishing performatives from constatives," seems to be breaking down: "If we are in general always doing both things, how can our distinction survive?" (*HT*, 133). In "Psyché: Inventions of the Other," Derrida speaks of this as "the infinitely rapid oscillation between the performative and constative." He goes on to say: "This instability constitutes that very event—let us say, the work—whose invention disturbs normally, as it were, the norms, the statutes, and the rules. It calls for a new theory and for the constitution of new statutes and conventions that, capable of recording the possibility of such events, would be able to account for them. I am not sure that speech act theory, in its present state and dominant form, is capable of this."[12]

This constant contamination of the performative by the constative and of the constative by the performative means that we are surrounded by language that is to some degree performative. It also means that it is not so certain, for example, that a marriage on the stage does not make *something* happen. Austin's attempt to exclude literature generally from the realm of speech acts fails to recognize, according to de Man and Derrida, the many ways in which literature makes something happen, as well as the many ways in which nonliterature is infected by the literary. A Searlean speech act, moreover, leaves intact the rules and conventions that enabled it, whereas for de Man and Derrida, in somewhat different ways, each performative, even though it may repeat a form of words used perhaps innumerable times before, is radically singular and inaugural. It changes the rules and institutions themselves, as well as the surrounding context, rather than simply depending on them to get something efficiently done.

For both Derrida and de Man, the efficacy of a performative does not depend on the conscious intention of the speaking or writing subject. The "author" of the words does not even need to be still alive for his or her words to be effective. In a certain sense, the moment of performative efficacy is always the death of the author, as de Man implies in words I am about to cite. De Man is at his most radical in insisting that words in themselves have a performative effect that may go counter to the intention of the speaker or writer and that does not depend on his or her continued existence as a conscious "I" for their power. We intend to do one thing or intend to do nothing at all, and something we had neither foreseen nor intended happens anyway, as a result of the words. As de Man says (in one of the essays on Rousseau in *Allegories of Reading* that makes explicit reference to Austin):

> writing always includes the moment of dispossession in favor of the arbitrary power play of the signifier and from the point of view of the subject, this can only be experienced as a dismemberment, a beheading, or a castration. . . . It is no longer certain that language, as excuse, exists because of a prior guilt but just as possible that since language, as a machine, performs anyway, we have to produce guilt (and all its train of psychic consequences) in order to make the excuse meaningful. . . . The narrative [of Rousseau's *Confessions*] begins to vacillate only when it appears that these (negative) cognitions fail to make the performative function of the discourse predictable and that, consequently, the linguistic model cannot be reduced to a mere system of tropes. Performative rhetoric and cognitive rhetoric, the rhetoric of tropes, fail to converge.[13]

This means that we are always likely to be doing things with words whenever we speak or write, but that full understanding of what we are doing is forbidden—before, during, and after. Human temporality may be another name for the impossibility of bringing together the cognitive and performative functions of language. We die with an unappeased desire to know.

Such language as that in my last sentence, however, would also, with a different twist, be characteristic of Derrida, for example, in *Aporias*.[14] Derrida's more recent work, in published essays and books as well as in spoken seminars—his work on gifts, on the force of law, on witnessing, on friendship, on sexual difference, on responsiveness and responsibility, on ghosts in Marx, on capital punishment, on animal rights—could be said to be a long exploration of the performative efficacy of language and other signs. Derrida keeps returning in one way or another to an aporia whereby a form of words works performatively, on its own, to bring something singular and unheard of, something not amenable to any law, into the open, while after the fact seeming to be a response to something that was already there. The United States Declaration of Independence is paradigmatic of this aporia. The Declaration speaks "in the Name and by the Authority of the good people of these Colonies," and it calls them "these united Colonies." But the document itself brings that people, as a unified people, into existence, just as it functions to unite the thirteen separate colonies. The people must pre-exist the declaration for it to be efficacious, but the people in the sense that we now speak of "the American people" did not exist before the declaration called that people into being.[15]

Derrida says something similar about a speech act in the form of an apostrophe that brings sexual difference into being. Here is his characteristically scrupulous formulation in *Fourmis*," by way of a discussion of Hélène Cixous's work:

> All of that *seems* to institute sexual difference in the most pragmatic, the most performative, *act* of reading/writing, here the experience of an originary apostrophe also recalling the origin of the apostrophe, the "you" which, interrupting the silence of what is hidden and does not speak [*le "tu" qui, interrompant le silence de ce qui est tu*], brings to birth, engenders, and provokes, calls but in truth *recalls* [*appelle mais en vérité* rappelle] the "he" into being. For that act is not only an appearance that *seems to give rise to* [semble se donner] sexual difference, it is not simply active or decisive, creative or productive. Reading as much as it writes, deciphering or citing as much as it inscribes, this act is also an act of memory (the other is already there, irreducibly), this act enacts [*cet acte prend acte*]. In calling you back, it remembers. [*En te rappelant, il se rappelle.*][16]

It is a matter of great delicacy and intellectual tact to distinguish rightly between de Man and Derrida. Distinguishing between them involves getting right the deepest and most obscure bases of their thought, no easy task. Such a distinction, however, might focus on the way de Man's notion of performative language is associated with two central and difficult ideas in his work: his particular concept of irony and his concept (if that is the right word for it) of the nonphenomenal materiality of language. Because language is material, it has force. It can make things happen. Because this materiality is nonphenomenal, not open to sense perception, its effects are not open to verification or prediction, just as irony is a pervasive force in language that makes it potentially, or in fact inevitably, unreadable, unintelligible. Performativity, prosopopoeia, irony, and nonphenomenal materiality—these in their intertwining form a knot or node in de Man's work, especially in his last essays.

For Derrida, by contrast, the performative force of language is characteristically associated with what he calls the "other" of language. He would not be likely to use the term "materiality" to name this otherness. In an interview with Richard Kearney published in 1984, Derrida responded sharply to the charge that deconstruction sees language as referring only to itself: "It is totally false to suggest that deconstruction is a suspension of reference. Deconstruction is always concerned with the 'other' of language. I never cease to be surprised by critics who see my work as a declaration that there is nothing beyond language, that we are imprisoned in language; it is, in fact, saying the exact opposite."[17] The other in question here is something radically other, not a social, psychological, material, or phenomenal other. As Derrida puts this in *Aporias*, "Every other is wholly other [*Tout autre est tout autre*]."[18] A performative speech act, for Derrida, is a response to the call of this wholly other. A performative calls or invokes, while at the same time itself being called. It is a use of language "to give a place to the other, to let the other come [*donner lieu à l'autre, laisser venir l'autre*]."[19] Such a performative does not fit the paradigm of the lawful, rule-obeying speech act as defined by Austin or Searle. Passages at the end of "Psyché: l'invention de l'autre" (not included in Peggy Kamuf's partial translation) state succinctly the relation of the Derridean performative to the wholly other. Speaking of the repetition of the word *par* ("by") in the first line of Francis Ponge's little poem "Fable" ("Par le mot *par* . . ."), Derrida says:

The very movement of this fabulous repetition can, according to a crossing of chance and necessity, produce the novelty of an event. Not just the singular invention of a performative, since every performative assumes conventions and institutional rules; but in twisting those rules through respect for those very rules [*mais en tournant ces règles dans le respect de ces règles mêmes*] in order to let the other come or announce itself in the opening of this dehiscence [*dans l'ouverture de cette déhiscence*].[20] This is perhaps what one calls deconstruction. . . . The deconstruction about which I speak does not invent and does not affirm, it does not let the other come, except to the degree in which, performative, it is not solely that but continues to perturb the conditions of the performative and of what distinguishes it peacefully from the constative.[21]

It may be, however, that what de Man calls the nonphenomenal materiality of language, the feature that gives it performative force, is another name for what Derrida calls "the other of language," since both of these names are themselves performative catachreses, figurative names for what has no proper name and is, strictly speaking, unknown and unknowable. As Derrida says, the other always comes in "multiple voices."[22] De Man's and Derrida's "callings," in the sense that they give names to this other of language, are themselves examples of what they name.

I conclude this introduction with the claim (another performative there!) that the concept of performative language, more in the Derridean or de Manian than in the Searlean sense, is an indispensable tool in the right reading of literary works. This book will attempt to make good on that claim. My dedication is a gesture not only toward the relation of this book to Derrida's books and seminars, but also toward the memory of my almost forty years of unclouded friendship with Jacques Derrida.

CHAPTER I

History, Narrative, Responsibility: "The Aspern Papers"

The Introduction identifies speech act theory as a tool of analysis for prose fiction. Of course matters are not quite so simple. A literary work is not a machine that can be dismantled with this or that tool, its workings exposed. In reading literature, the tool turns into the machine and vice versa. To put this less metaphorically, both speech act theory and James's fiction are made of language. Nothing is more problematic and tricky than the intersection of theory and literature in an act of reading the latter. In this chapter I shall attempt to bring together speech act theory and James's characteristically brilliant and puzzling novella "The Aspern Papers" (1888).

The relation between history and narrative seems at first glance fairly straightforward. Adding to the mix the role of speech acts in generating history complicates things quite a bit. History and narration have been inseparably associated in literary theory and in our everyday assumptions at least since Aristotle. In the *Poetics* Aristotle prefers a probable fiction to an improbable history as the plot for a tragedy. Though narration is not the only way to represent history, it is certainly one of the major ways. We tend to assume that historical events occurred as a concatenated sequence that can be retold now as a story of some kind: first this happened, and then that happened, and so on. Some form of causal connection is presumed. The earlier event will explain the later event and make it understandable, because the earlier caused the later. Post hoc propter hoc. Narrative will tell the truth about history. Both narrative and history belong to the regime of truth.

Narration is one of the chief ways to account for history, to take account of it, to rationalize it and explain it, to find out its reason or ground. Fictional narrations, at least in the West, have tended to present themselves in the guise of histories, as in Fielding's title *The History of Tom Jones*, or in Thackeray's full title for *Henry Esmond: The History of Henry Esmond, Esq., a Colonel in the Service of Her Majesty Q. Anne, Written by Himself.* Henry James remarks in his essay on Anthony Trollope that unless a fictional narration maintains the illusion of its historicity, it has no ground to stand on: "It is impossible to imagine what a novelist takes himself to be unless he regards himself as an historian and his narrative as history. It is only as an historian that he has the smallest *locus standi.*"[1] The figure of the *locus standi* returns in "The Aspern Papers." The motif appears there, as I shall show, in various figures, arguing that biographical knowledge forms an indispensable ground for measuring literature's value. This intimate and unbreakable connection between narrative and history in the Western tradition seems unproblematic enough.

Raising questions about "responsibility," however, adds a complication. This further wrinkle may upset the presumed symmetry between narrative and history. If both narrative and history are of the order of truth, responsibility is of the order of doing, of ethics, of the conduct of life. Responsibility invokes performative rather than of constative uses of language. Do narrative and history in any way involve issues of ethical response to an imperative demand? I shall explore this question in a reading of "The Aspern Papers."

To whom is the narrator of this story talking or writing? As in all first person narrations, it is not easy to answer that question. Third person narration depends on the convention of an often anonymous narrating voice. In the case of a first person narration like "The Aspern Papers," however, it is as though we as readers, or, better, I as reader, since it is an intimate and singular experience, have been made to overhear a murmuring internal voice of narration. The narration is spoken by an imaginary "I" that is going over and over the facts of the case as remembered, trying to put them in order, trying above all to justify itself. This voice seemingly speaks in response to a demand for an accounting. Someone, it seems, has said to the storyteller: "Account for yourself." The narrator of "The Aspern Papers" speaks as a witness. As James's preface to *The Golden Bowl* says, he is "witness of the destruction of 'The Aspern Papers'" (23:vii). James's odd capitalization and punctuation here identifies the Aspern papers themselves and the story of that title. In what way the story itself is "destroyed" or what that might mean remains to be seen. The reader, in any case, is put by the narrator's deposition in the position of the conscience, the judge or jury. It is as if we had demanded this accounting and had taken upon ourselves the responsibility of evaluating it for plausibility and credibility, then judging it. We have to pronounce "Guilty" or "Innocent." If the verdict is "Guilty," we must decide what punishment should be meted out.

Or, rather, "I" am put in that position. The call is addressed to me, personally. I alone must act, must respond. I cannot let anyone else read for me. Perhaps, for example, I might think the narrator is punished enough by being forced to think over and over what he has done, for the story ends with his statement of suffering: "When I look at it [the picture of Jeffrey Aspern] I can scarcely bear my loss—I mean of the precious papers" (12:143).[2] Or the reader might be led to ask whether the narrator must be held responsible for moral stupidity, for not having understood correctly the relation between narration and history. What is the proper punishment for that crime? I must carefully sift the evidence, read between the lines, put two and two together. The effect of this is to make me read carefully (or it should be). I must pay attention to tiny details of language, to any other clues the narrator may give, perhaps in spite of himself. If he is that notorious personage the "unreliable narrator," then James may be speaking to me, ironically, through gaps and lapses in the narrator's language.

As in all such cases, I am myself on trial. I am in danger of being unjust, insensitive, or inattentive. I may have missed something crucial. James excels in putting the reader in that situation. If the narrator has, it may be, treated Juliana and Tina badly, I may be in danger of treating *him* badly, of judging him wrongly. If he behaved badly, how should he have behaved? Where did he go wrong? How would I have behaved in his place? And of course beneath all that, or around it, I am judging James, who I know is the author of the tale I am reading. Can I trust him as a moral guide, as someone who tells the truth about the human situation?

Is this putting of the reader on trial characteristic of James's stories and novels, or is it peculiar to this one or to a group like this one? Do all James's works put on the reader this heavy responsibility of judging, with an implied penalty if he or she makes an error? I think it can be said to be a general characteristic. In each story by James the characters behave in a certain way and the story comes out in a certain way. The reader is asked to evaluate that behavior and that outcome. I must then pass ethical judgment. Usually the reader is asked especially to judge some climactic decision and act, almost always some act of (apparent) renunciation, of giving up, almost always a sexual renunciation. In "The Aspern Papers" the narrator refuses Miss Tina's offer of herself in marriage. That precipitates the dénouement. In *The Portrait of a Lady*, the heroine, Isabel Archer, returns to her cruel and egotistical husband, Gilbert Osmond. In *The Ambassadors* Strether refuses to get anything out of it for himself. He refuses Maria Gostrey's offer of herself. In *The Awkward Age* Vanderbank refuses to marry Nanda. In *The Wings of the Dove*, Densher refuses the immense legacy Millie Theale has left him and thereby loses Kate Croy. In *The Golden Bowl* Maggie does not act to expose her husband's adultery with her stepmother. In all these diverse cases the reader must pass judgment on the protagonist's decisive, life-determining act, or, one might better call it, death-in-life-determining act.

James always gives the reader abundant, even superabundant, evidence, lots of rope with which to hang himself or herself. Unfortunately, the evidence is always in one way or another indirect. It is problematic or ambiguous. The rule is that James never tells me in so many words what I should conclude, how I should evaluate and judge the characters. This exasperates some readers, for example, Wayne Booth in *The Rhetoric of Fiction*. It is as though James were saying, with a faint, ironic smile, "Here is all the evidence. I have kept nothing back. I have even given you, it may sometimes seem to you, a tedious superfluity of evidence. Now it is up to you to judge." This is analogous to one of the imaginary visions the narrator of "The Aspern Papers" has when he looks at the portrait of the dead poet Jeffrey Aspern, whose life so obsesses him: "I but privately consulted Jeffrey Aspern's delightful eyes with my own—they were so young and brilliant and yet so wise and so deep. . . . He seemed to smile at me with friendly mockery; he might have been amused at my case. I had got into a pickle for him—as if he needed it! He was unsatisfactory for the only moment since I had known him" (12:130–31). Many readers have found James himself elusive and mocking. To read James is to be put in the pickle of being made responsible for judgment when the grounds for judgment are not entirely certain. The reader is put on trial in a way that is not wholly pleasant. Certainly it is not relaxed or merely receptive. The reader's state is not consonant with the idea that the pleasures of reading James are pure, irresponsible pleasures of aesthetic form, the pleasures of passive admiration. This is the case even though James himself, in the prefaces to his work, often seems to promise just that, in the form of what he calls "amusement."[3]

Well, what is the evidence on which to base a properly responsive, responsible judgment of what "The Aspern Papers" has to say about history, narration, and responsibility?

The preface to this story, written for the New York Edition, stresses in several ways the relation of the story to history. Thinking about its genesis brings back to James the history of his own past life in Italy, "the inexhaustible charm of Roman and Florentine memories," not to speak of the "old Venice" of the story itself (12:vi). Moreover, the story had its genesis, James says, in the way "history, 'literary history' we in this connection call it, had in an out-of-the-way corner of the great garden of life thrown off a curious flower that I was to feel worth gathering as soon as I saw it" (12:v). This is James's characteristically oblique way of saying that "The Aspern Papers" is based on a historical episode. This was the survival into the mid-nineteenth century in Florence of Jane Clairmont, "for a while the intimate friend of Byron and the mother of his daughter" (12:vii), and the attempt by a man from Boston, Captain Edward Silsbee, to become a lodger in her house and thereby get hold of documents about Shelley and Byron she was thought to possess.

James's account of how he came to write "The Aspern Papers" leads him to make some general reflections about history and narrative. The anecdote about Jane Clairmont appealed to him as the subject of a story, he says, because it was just far enough in the past, but not too far: "And then the case had the air of the past just in the degree in which that air, I confess, most appeals to me—when the region over which it hangs is far enough away without being too far" (12:ix). The eloquent passage that follows develops and explains this appeal. Such a nearby past is visitable, recoverable. It combines strangeness and familiarity in just the right proportions, whereas a more distant past cannot be visited and reappropriated by the writer, thereby made into a narrative. Too many other historical periods intervene. These baffle the imaginative writer's attempts at an intimate recovery:

> I delight in a palpable imaginable *visitable* past—in the nearer distances and the clearer mysteries, the marks and signs of a world we may reach over to as by making a long arm we grasp an object at the other end of our own table. The table is the one, the common expanse, and where we lean, so stretching, we find it firm and continuous. That, to my imagination, is the past fragrant of all, or of almost all, the poetry of the thing outlived and

lost and gone, and yet in which the precious element of closeness, telling so of connections but tasting so of differences, remains appreciable. With more moves back the element of the appreciable shrinks—just as the charm of looking over a garden-wall into another garden breaks down when successions of walls appear. The other gardens, those still beyond, may be there, but even by use of our longest ladder we are baffled and bewildered—the view is mainly a view of barriers. The one partition makes the place we have wondered about *other*, both richly and recognizably so; but who shall pretend to impute an effect of composition to the twenty? We are divided of course between liking to feel the past strange and liking to feel it familiar; the difficulty is, for intensity, to catch it at the moment when the scales of the balance hang with the right evenness. (12:x)

The figure of peeping over a garden wall suggests that the act of recovering history is a slightly furtive act of voyeurism, as indeed it is for the narrator. He wants to learn about Aspern's private life. The passage seems to promise that "The Aspern Papers" will be a narrative about a successful visiting of the early nineteenth century, the time when Byron and Shelley lived in Italy. That James's definition of such a past (familiar and yet strange) corresponds exactly to Freud's definition of the uncanny (*das Unheimlich*) might give the reader pause. It would define such a recovery of the past as a raising of ghosts, would be the return of something repressed, something exposed and yet hidden, something known that nevertheless ought to be kept secret. This definition of the near past as an uncanny mixture of familiarity and strangeness may connect this story in some obscure way with James's ghost stories, such as "The Jolly Corner" and *The Turn of the Screw*. That, however, may be a false association, since what James here emphasizes is the possible successful recovery of history through narration. There seems nothing uncanny about this process.

The image of the ghostly resurrected revenant has, however, already appeared early in the preface when James speaks of his memories of Italy as "haunting presences" (12:vi). The figure of the ghost is also present in the story itself. Juliana Bordereau, the old woman in the story who corresponds to Jane Clairmont in the "real life" historical events, seems to the unnamed narrator who has designs on her papers "too strange, too literally resurgent" (12:23). "[A]s she sat there before me," he says, "my heart beat as fast as if the miracle of resurrection had taken place for my benefit. Her presence seemed somehow to contain and express his own, and I felt nearer to him at that first moment of seeing her than I ever had been before or ever have been since" (12:23). The resurrection of Juliana Bordereau is in a manner of speaking the resurrection of Jeffrey Aspern himself, James's fictional equivalent of Byron. Juliana's "literal" resurgence generates Aspern's figurative resurrection. The narrator at various crucial moments in the story imagines himself confronting Aspern face to face, even talking with him and hearing his voice:

> That spirit [of Venice] kept me perpetual company and seemed to look out at me from the revived immortal face—in which all his genius shone—of the great poet who was my prompter. I had invoked him and he had come; he hovered before me half the time; it was as if his bright ghost had returned to earth to assure me he regarded the affair as his own no less than as mine and that we should see it fraternally and fondly to a conclusion. It was as if he had said, "Poor dear, be easy with her; she has some natural prejudices; only give her time. Strange as it may appear to you she was very attractive in 1820." (12:42–43)

What the narrator says here employs language that is ordinarily used to describe the invocation of a spirit. The rhetorical name for this is apostrophic prosopopoeia, the ascription of a name, a voice, or a face to the absent, inanimate, or dead. To ascribe or inscribe a name or a voice to the dead is performatively to recall the dead into being, to invoke, to resurrect. It is to utter a new version of Jesus' "Lazarus, come forth!" All historical story-telling depends on the efficacy of such performative prosopopoeias. These figures raise by way of the words on the page the illusions of the various personae, including the narrator. In that sense all historical stories are ghost stories. I shall return to James's ghost stories in the last chapter of this book.

One function of James's ghost stories proper, it might be argued, is to bring into the open this basic aspect of historical narration. "I had invoked him and he had come." The one who raises a ghost must then take responsibility for his or her act. That responsibility is most accurately figured in some demand the resurrected ghost makes on the one to whom he appears. The ghost of Hamlet's father demands that Hamlet revenge his murder. The narrator of "The Aspern Papers" incurs a responsibility, by way of Aspern's ghost, for Juliana and Tina. The narrator wants knowledge. He does not get the knowledge he wants, but he does get responsibility. Is it possible that our situation as readers may parallel that of the narrator? We have been taught to read literary works, for example "The Aspern Papers," in order to understand them. Reading may rather put an unforeseen burden of obligation on our shoulders. The story, it may be, demands not that we know but that we do.

The narrator's failure to know is paralleled by the way the story by no means fulfills the retrospective promise of the preface to give the reader knowledge of history, of "a palpable . . . visitable past." "The Aspern Papers" is rather a story of the impossibility of knowing and possessing the historical past through narrative.

Why is this? Why is it that "The Aspern Papers" is a narrative of the failure of narrative to reach and possess history, even that charmingly close period of the early nineteenth century the preface promises the story will visit? The story is a brilliant putting into question of just those hermeneutic assumptions about the relation between narrative and history I began by describing. These are the assumptions taken for granted, for the most part, in our intellectual tradition. Those preconceptions are also just the ones apparently assumed in James's preface when he talks about a "visitable past." By "hermeneutic" I mean the presupposition that the truth about a set of historical events, like the truth about a document or set of documents, for example, a work of literature like "The Aspern Papers," is inside the evidence. That truth can by proper procedures be penetrated, reached, decoded, revealed, and unveiled. It can then be triumphantly brought out into the open where all may see it and where it may be told as a coherent narrative. Joseph Conrad expresses this assumption when he has the primary narrator in *Heart of Darkness* say that "The yarns of seamen have a direct simplicity, the whole meaning of which lies within the shell of a cracked nut."[4]

The narrator of "The Aspern Papers" is a literary scholar who specializes in the work of an American poet of the early nineteenth century, Jeffrey Aspern. The narrator's basic professional assumption is that biographical facts will explain Aspern's poetry. He immensely admires the poetry. James does not, however, allow him the slightest insight into the possibility that the poetry might be worth reading for its own sake or that it might have any meaning that would exceed its biographical references. He assumes that the more he knows about Aspern's life the more he will have established solid grounds for decoding the poetry. In explaining this, the narrator uses a religious metaphor that recurs in the story. The figure provides another version of the hermeneutic structure. In one place, for example, the narrator says Juliana represented "esoteric knowledge" about Aspern's life (12:44). Earlier he asserts, "One doesn't defend one's god: one's god is in himself a defense" (12:5). This desire to get at the hidden facts of Aspern's life outweighs any compunction the narrator might have about lying to Juliana and about forcing his way into her intimacy, even though he says at one point, when he is trying to worm information out of Juliana's niece (or daughter by Jeffrey Aspern), Tina: "I felt almost as base as the reporter of a newspaper who forces his way into a house of mourning" (12:82).

Later on, in a crucial discussion with Juliana, the narrator tells her he is "a critic, a commentator, an historian" (12:89). He writes, he says, about "the great philosophers and poets of the past; those who are dead and gone and can't, poor darlings, speak for themselves" (12:89). The interchange that follows identifies just what form the narrator's interpretative assumptions take. The narrator believes that getting the full biographical facts about Jeffrey Aspern and then narrating them as a full history of his life will serve as a solid ground by which to measure his works. He defends himself to Juliana by asking: "What becomes of the work I just mentioned, that of the great philosophers and poets? It is all vain words if there is nothing to measure it by" (12:90). Juliana pours scorn on this idea by saying it is like applying a measuring tape to someone in order to make him a suit. "You talk as if you were a tailor," she says (12:89). The truth, for Juliana, is inaccessible by the narrator's kind of search for historical truth.

Why Juliana is right and the narrator wrong, the working out of the story makes clear. Juliana is so appalled when she catches the narrator in the act of trying to break into her secretary desk to steal the papers that she dies of the shock. The narrator has in a manner of speaking killed her. Tina reports that Juliana believed that the narrator would have been capable of "violating a tomb" (12:134). Juliana was right. Tina has functioned throughout as an intermediary and go-between. She gives the narrator indirect access to Juliana, just as Juliana will give him indirect access, he hopes, to Aspern. After Juliana's death Tina offers to give him the papers if he will marry her: "What in the name of the preposterous did she mean if she did not mean to offer me her hand? That was the price—that was the price!" (12:136). The narrator refuses to marry her and leaves. Tina then burns all the papers. She tells him when he returns, with her inadvertently comic literalism: "It took a long time—there were so many" (12:143). The narrator says "a real darkness descended for a moment on my eyes" (12:143). He is left with the portrait of Aspern and with his chagrin: "[I]t hangs above my writing-table. When I look at it I can scarcely bear my loss—I mean of the precious papers" (12:143).

What does this dénouement mean? As many critics have noted, the unnamed teller of this story is unreliable not because he deliberately lies but because, though he is intelligent, he fails more or less completely to understand what has happened to him. The "real darkness" that descends on him when he learns the papers are burned is the correlative of the figurative darkness that has afflicted him all along: his failure to understand. That other blindness keeps him permanently in the dark about the meaning of his experience. When he identifies his unbearable loss as being that of the precious papers, he almost recognizes, in the pause indicated by the dash, that he has brought on himself another worse and unrecognized loss. It is worse in part because it is unrecognized. "The Aspern Papers" parallels in this ending another celebrated story by James, "The Beast in the Jungle." In that tale, however, the protagonist gets clear insight at the end of the story, when it is already too late.

The narrator of "The Aspern Papers" has assumed that his only responsibility is to the historical truth about Aspern. Any means, even a theft that is presented as a figurative sexual assault, even as a kind of necrophilia, "violating a tomb," are justified in the name of finding out that truth. The narrator's responsibility to this kind of truth is underwritten by the institutional apparatus of literary history as a discursive practice in our culture. It is not an accident that *The New York Times Book Review*, for example, routinely reviews literary biographies, good or bad, while passing by even distinguished critical readings of the same authors. This notion of literary history is also institutionalized in the university study of literature. The search for literary historical truth is one version of the university's commitment to a selfless search for the bringing to light of knowledge. The motto of Yale University is "Lux et Veritas." The motto of Harvard is "Veritas." The motto of the University of California is "Let There Be Light." The university assumes that everything has its reason, its underlying explanatory *Grund*, its measure, its *logos*. Our primary and exclusive responsibility as academics is to bring that truth to light. The commitment to the search for a narratable historical truth is one version of the commitment to truth-seeking in our culture. The university is one of this commitment's main institutional guardians.

What the narrator does not see and what his narration allows the reader to glimpse indirectly, to "read between the lines," as one says, is that historical events are not open to this kind of knowledge and therefore cannot be narrated. All that can be narrated is the failure to see, know, possess, or uncover the actual events of the historical past. The paradigmatic example of a historical event in the story is the presumed love affair between Juliana Bordereau and Jeffrey Aspern that apparently resulted in Tina's birth, though that remains an unverified hint. Such an event, the story implies, cannot be known from the outside. It is not something that could ever have been known through research and then told in a narration. It can only be "known," without being known, in an event that repeats it, that bears witness to it by doing something like it again.

Why can a historical event like the presumed lovemaking of Juliana and Aspern not be known? A true historical event, the story indicates, does not belong to the order of cognition. It belongs to the order of performative acts, speech acts or acts employing other kinds of signs in a performative way. Such an event makes something happen. It leaves traces on the world that might be known—for example, the Aspern papers if they were published and read—but in itself it cannot be known. Even if the narrator had taken possession of the papers and read them, he would not have known what he wanted to know.

Two kinds of knowledge may be distinguished. One is the kind obtained from historical research or from seeing something with one's own eyes. That kind can be narrated. The other is the blind, bodily, material kind that cannot be narrated. We can only witness to it, in another speech act. This kind is expressed in the biblical formula "Adam knew his wife and she conceived." The sex act is paradigmatic of this other kind of knowledge. All speech acts, for example, promises, are of the same order, as is the unknowable event of my own death. The connection among these three forms of nonnarratable historical events is indicated in the way the three crucial moments in Hyacinth Robinson's life, in James's great political novel, *The Princess Casamassima* (1886), are not directly narrated. They are blanks in the text. These events are Hyacinth's promise to the revolutionaries that he will commit a terrorist act, Hyacinth's experience of sleeping with the Princess, and Hyacinth's suicide—a vocational commitment, sex, and death.

In "The Aspern Papers" the narrator can only "know" what he wants to know by a present performative that repeats the earlier one. That "knowledge" will not be the sort of clear, transmissible cognition that we usually mean when we think of historical knowledge. It will be the sort of knowledge Adam had of his wife, an unknowing knowing. Such an event is unavailable to clear cognition in the same way as the performative side of speech acts cannot be known, or as the materiality of any inscription is not phenomenal, since it is instantly seen as a sign, or as the rhetorical dimension of language as it interferes with clear grammatical and logical meaning makes that language what theorists call "unreadable."

To repeat what Aspern did by marrying Tina, as the story makes clear, would put the narrator in a double bind. It would be a double bind at least from the point of view of his goal of revealing history through narration. In order to get possession of the papers the narrator must marry Tina.

That this would repeat what Jeffrey Aspern did is made clear earlier in the
story when the narrator says of Aspern:

> Half the women of his time, to speak liberally, had flung themselves at his
> head, and while the fury raged—the more that it was very catching—
> accidents, some of them grave, had not failed to occur. . . . "Orpheus and
> the Mænads!" had been of course my foreseen judgment when first I turned
> over his correspondence. Almost all the Mænads were unreasonable and
> many of them unbearable; it struck me that he had been kinder and more
> considerate than in his place—if I could imagine myself in any such box—I
> should have found the trick of. (12:7)

Orpheus was torn to pieces by the Mænads. The narrator, in his misogyny,
blames not Aspern himself but the women Aspern betrayed, for example,
as is hinted, by the "grave accident" of making them pregnant. Miss Tina
is apparently the result of such an accident.

The narrator is infatuated with Jeffrey Aspern and jealous of all those
lovers he had, in a way that is homosocial if not straightforwardly homosexual. Recent work by queer theorists has made readers sensitive to this
dimension of James's work. The narrator sees the living women as no
more than means of access to Aspern, whom he really loves, though without, apparently, being at all aware of the nature of that love. He is fascinated by Juliana Bordereau because, so he thinks, she has slept with Jeffrey
Aspern, with Miss Tina as living evidence of that liaison. The narrator's
love for Aspern, the love that dare not speak its name, is covertly and
unintentionally revealed by what the narrator says about his feelings for
Aspern, for example, when he looks at Aspern's portrait. No evidence that
I know of exists to indicate that James himself was aware of this dimension
of his story, or that he felt he had given this secret away.

By grounding a reading of "The Aspern Papers" on James's presumed
homosexuality, however, the critic repeats the disastrous error the story
warns against, that is, seeing literature as no more than a species of covert
autobiography. Literature, "The Aspern Papers" forcefully implies, is its
own ground. It does not need to be grounded in the biography of its author. The reader or critic should be careful not to repeat the narrator's
catastrophic mistake. Who would want to be a "publishing scoundrel"
(12:118), as Juliana calls the narrator when she catches him trying to steal
the Aspern papers? How can I be sure I am not becoming such a scoundrel
by publishing this book?

One odd, one might even say queer, form James's work takes is the way
so many of his fictions—all those discussed in this book, for example—

turn on a strange variation of Freud's Oedipal paradigm. All men, according to Freud, would like to have been present at the "primal" scene of their own conception in the sex act performed by their parents, most often lawfully wedded parents. In Freud's view this is because all men would like to have replaced their fathers in the marriage bed. In James's case this takes the queer form of the way so many of his stories and novels presuppose an illicit sex act, not a lawful one. This act, in James's work, most often took place long before the story proper begins. The story moves forward to lead the protagonist (and the reader) to knowledge, though problematic and often unverifiable knowledge, of this inaugural event. This is James's strange version of the primal scene. I call it "queer" because it so saliently presupposes that heterosexual sex is illicit, guilty. Such sex is like the story of Orpheus and the Mænads. It is something that is thought of with fascination but also with a measure of distaste. It is not viewed with Freudian Oedipal desire. The narrator of "The Aspern Papers" discovers, or thinks he discovers, that Miss Bordereau had been Jeffrey Aspern's mistress. Isabel, in *The Portrait of a Lady*, discovers that Madame Merle has been her husband's mistress and that Pansy is their daughter. Maggie, in *The Golden Bowl*, discovers that her husband has had an affair long before with her stepmother and that this liaison has been recently renewed. Strether, in *The Ambassadors*, finds out about Chad's affair with Madame de Vionnet. The list of examples in James's work of this motif could be more or less indefinitely extended.

The narrator of "The Aspern Papers," as he says, "had not the tradition of personal conquest" (12:22). He means he has not been successful with women, unlike Aspern. He is not the marrying sort, though he has been encouraged in his literary historical quest by a woman friend, Mrs. Prest, with whom he has cordial relations. In spite of this failure with women, the narrator finds himself, in a manner of speaking, in Jeffrey Aspern's place before the story is done. Tina "throws herself at his head." He does get into a grave situation with her. The difference is that Aspern did apparently sleep with at least some of the women who threw themselves at him. The grave accidents that followed were, so the narrator hints, results of that. The narrator, however, refuses Tina, even though for a moment what the original version of 1888 calls his "literary concupiscence"[5] leads him to think he might marry her: "I heard a whisper in the depths of my conscience: 'Why not, after all—why not?' It seemed to me I *could* pay the price" (12:142). His delay in deciding about that costs him the papers, since by the time he is ready to marry Tina, to "pay the price," she has already burned them.

If he had married Tina, however, he would have become, as she says, "a relation." "Then," she says, "it would be the same for you as for me. Anything that's mine would be yours, and you could do what you like. I shouldn't be able to prevent you—and you would have no responsibility" (12:133). If, on the one hand, he would have no responsibility of the sort he would have incurred if he had stolen the papers, rapt them away, on the other hand, he would have the infinite responsibility Juliana incurred toward Jeffrey Aspern by becoming his mistress (if she did in fact do that, which can never be known for certain). Juliana assumed a responsibility to keep her liaison with Aspern secret. Married to Tina, the narrator would have had a husband's obligation to keep his wife's family secrets. He cannot have the papers if he remains an outsider, so cannot publish them. He can have them if he becomes an insider, but then he cannot publish them. He will have incurred a family duty that will far outweigh his responsibility as a literary historian. Either way he will be baulked.[6]

The knowledge the narrator would have as Tina's husband would repeat the knowledge Jeffrey Aspern had. It is not, however, the kind of knowledge that can or should be narrated in a cognizable historical text. Such an event can only be repeated in another performative act. An example is the way Aspern's presumed affair with Juliana appears to be repeated in the poetry that Jeffrey Aspern wrote about her. The reader is given not one single word of that poetry. All we know is that the narrator wants to go straight through it to reach the biographical facts that will explain and "measure" it. That poetry is both intimately connected to the historical events that "generated" it and at the same time disconnected from them by an uncrossable breach. This is a chasm as wide as that between the "sources" of James's story and the story itself. To understand "The Aspern Papers," or to find out if it is intelligible, you have no recourse but to read it. Reading it, as I shall argue, may be another kind of performative repetition. The narrator's story in "The Aspern Papers" is a parody of this kind of repetition. It repeats as a narrative of nonknowledge the event/ nonevent of the narrator's refusal to marry Tina. The narrator does indeed unwittingly bear witness to the destruction of "The Aspern Papers" as a truth-telling historical narrative, as well as to the destruction of the Aspern papers.

The line of analysis I have been following would seem to put the canny reader in a position of superiority to the unperceptive narrator. The narrator cannot read the data with which he is confronted, but the reader can at every point second-guess him. He or she can do this thanks to the abundant clues for the reader's enlightenment James has strewn throughout the story. Is this really the case? For one thing it would appear to reaffirm for the perceptive reader, the reader in depth, just that hermeneutic model of penetration within or behind or below the data to reach a hidden meaning that has been discredited in the story itself. It has been discredited as the mistaken paradigm that not only prevents the narrator from achieving real knowledge but also makes him responsible for despicable acts toward Juliana and Tina, not to mention his desecration of the grave, so to speak, of Jeffrey Aspern.

The answer to this apparent contradiction is that what the reader learns is not definite knowledge. It is at most a bodily understanding of why he or she cannot in principle objectively and impersonally know, but can only do, perform, act. The new act in question would be an interventionist reading. Such a reading might possibly repeat James's story in another mode, but it would certainly not give definitive knowledge of the meaning of James's tale. Or, in a better formulation, the reader does not even understand that, since it cannot be understood in the ordinary sense of the term. The story suggests that even if the narrator had got hold of the Aspern Papers he would not have got the knowledge he wanted. The irony, of course, is that we are "learning" this through an act of reading, that is, reading "The Aspern Papers." Reading, it may be, however, is a mode of doing, not a mode of knowing. I say "may be" because there is no way in principle to know whether a given reading works in that way. If it does work that way, it belongs not to the order of truth and knowledge, but to the order of unknowable speech acts. If it were a speech act, it would be a new historical event repeating the previous one of James's writing the tale, just as the narrator of "The Aspern Papers" would by marrying Tina have repeated Jeffrey Aspern's liaison with Juliana Bordereau, if that liaison did in fact exist. That the story keeps eternally secret, just as I cannot in principle have knowledge of the efficacy of speech acts I perform, such as an act of literary criticism, since such acts are a doing not a knowing. They are part of the conduct of life, like James's writing of the story. They are a doing that does other things in turn.

Let me try to explain this further, in conclusion, by a brief discussion of four views of history that parallel, to some degree, the relation between narrative and historical events I have identified in James's "The Aspern Papers." The idea that history may be unknowable and nonnarratable is difficult to grasp, understand, or accept. Four authors may help to approach apprehension of it. Friedrich Nietzsche distinguishes in "On the Uses and Disadvantages of History for Life" ("Vom Nutzen und Nachtheil der Historie für das Leben") between two relations to history. On the one hand, there is the relation of those who write academic history, for example, the institutionalized literary history that the narrator of "The Aspern Papers" wants to practice. On the other hand, there is a paradoxical relation of forgetting to the historical past. It must be forgotten, Nietzsche argues, in order to make a space for present action. To turn history into the object of scientific knowledge is to neutralize it and to neutralize ourselves, too, to make us all like university professors in the humanities (Nietzsche's main polemical target in this essay). Such professors are learned men whose learning has no effect on the world. The paradox, as Nietzsche recognizes, is that we are what history has made us. To expunge our memory of the historical past in order to act freely in the present would be to expunge ourselves, to wipe the slate clean. The past must be forgotten as objective narratable knowledge in order not so much to be remembered as to be repeated in vigorous inaugural present action that gives birth to the future. "We need history, certainly," Nietzsche says, "but we need it for reasons different from those for which the idler in the garden of knowledge [*der verwöhnte Müssiggänger im Garten des Wissens*] needs it. . . . We need it, that is to say, for the sake of life and action [*zum Leben und zur That*], not so as to turn comfortably away from life and action."[7]

In one way or another both Jacques Derrida and Paul de Man hold that historical events cannot be known in the way academic historians claim to know and narrate them. For Derrida and de Man, the performative, therefore the nonphenomenal and nonknowable, aspect of literature, philosophy, and criticism, of language and other signs generally, makes history. This distinction between cognitive statements and performative speech acts has been the basis of my reading here, though it must be remembered that the separation can never be made absolute. As J. L. Austin recognized repeatedly in *How to Do Things with Words*, there is always a cognitive side to performatives, and vice versa, even though these two sides of language can never be reconciled. The performative side of language is not something that can be known, even though there is an imperative need to know it in order to find out what we have done with words and to take responsibility for that doing. This impossibility of knowing speech acts is part of what Derrida means in recent seminars when he says "the gift, if there is such a thing," "the secret, if there is such a thing," "witnessing, if there is such a thing." Since the gift, the secret, and witnessing are kinds of speech acts or sign acts, they are not the objects of a possible, verifiable cognition. They must remain a matter of "if."

Paul de Man's way of putting this is to say that the performative force of language, its power to make something happen in history and society, is linked to its materiality, that is, to a nonreferential, noncognitive side of language. In "Kant and Schiller," given at Cornell University a few months before his death, de Man discusses the sequence in Kant's *Third Critique* from "the cognitive discourse of trope" to "the materiality of the inscribed signifier."[8] He argues that only the latter is historical, a historical event. The regressive misreading of Kant initiated by Schiller is not historical. The misreadings of Kant are not a series of historical events. There is in Kant, says de Man,

> a movement, from cognition, from acts of knowledge, from states of cognition, to something which is no longer a cognition but which is to some extent an *occurrence*, which has the materiality of something that actually happens, that actually occurs. And there, the thought of material occurrence, something that occurs materially, that leaves a trace on the world, that does something to the world as such—that notion of occurrence is not opposed in any sense to the notion of writing. . . . There is history from the moment that words such as "power" and "battle" and so on emerge on the scene; at that moment things *happen*, there is *occurrence*, there is *event*. History is therefore not a temporal notion, it has nothing to do with temporality, but it is the emergence of a language of power out of the language of cognition.[9]

De Man, I believe, means by "language of power" not just language that names, constatively, aspects of power, but language that has power. He means language that does what it names, as "I pronounce you man and wife," spoken in the right circumstances, brings it about that the couple is married. This conception of the materiality of inscription is worked out by de Man in "Shelley Disfigured," in "Aesthetic Formalization: Kleist's *Über das Marionettentheater*," and in "Hypogram and Inscription," as well as in his late essays on Kant and Hegel.

De Man, like Derrida or Nietzsche, argues for a potential performative, history-making power in language, including the language of literature, philosophy, and even "practical criticism." This potential power may or may not be actualized or effective in a given case. It would be a foolhardy person who would claim that what he or she writes is a historical event. It is in any case not of the order of cognition. To put this in de Manian terms, the "linguistics of literariness" includes the performative dimension of literary language. Understanding it will help account for the occurrence of ideological aberrations, but knowing those aberrations will not change them.[10] Only the performative, material, "word-thing" side of language will do that. A rhetorical reading, registered in the most responsible critical terms, may actively liberate a past text for present uses. This new act is not engineered by a previously existing, self-conscious "I," the sovereign reader in full control of his or her knowledge of a text. The reading is constitutive of the "I" that enunciates it.

Walter Benjamin describes, in somewhat consonant terms, in the seventeenth of the "Theses on the Philosophy of History," the way a "historical materialist" sees "a revolutionary chance in the fight for the oppressed past" when he finds a way to "blast [*herauszusprengen*] a specific era out of the homogeneous course of history—blasting a specific life out of the era or a specific work out of the lifework."[11] *Herauszusprengen* names here a speech act that has effects on the future, not a historical cognition that tells something true about the past. A historical event, as all these authors, including James in "The Aspern Papers," posit, cannot be known through narration. It can only be performatively repeated, since it was a speech act in the first place. For that repetition the one who repeats must take responsibility. The doer must take responsibility, that is, for what he or she does not know, but can only perhaps succeed in reinscribing. He or she reinscribes it in a new, singular, unheard-of way, with incalculable effects on the future.

I turn now, in the next chapter, to a much more extended narration of a decision to renounce, *The Portrait of a Lady*. My focus remains on the efficacy of speech acts, or of "sign acts" that work like speech acts. J. L. Austin recognized the latter to be often the case, as when, to recall his examples, I protest not by shouting something but by "cocking a snook," that is, by thumbing my nose, or by hurling a tomato.[12]

CHAPTER 2

The Story of a Kiss: Isabel's Decisions in
The Portrait of a Lady

Foreplay

A recent popular romance by Danielle Steel, whose books are read by
millions worldwide, is entitled *The Kiss*. The cover blurb says: "a single
shattering moment can change lives forever. . . ." Almost the last thing
that happens in *The Portrait of a Lady* is Caspar Goodwood's kiss of Isabel.
The last thing of all is Caspar's discovery from Henrietta Stackpole that
his kiss has precipitated Isabel's decision to return to Rome and to her
despicable husband. Caspar "averts" himself to hide his dismay at this
news (4:437).[1] He then walks away with Henrietta, thereby completing the
series of "turnings" that are executed at the end of the novel, primarily by
Isabel. My goal in this chapter is to account for Caspar's kiss. I want to
"read" the narrator's account of it and of its effect on Isabel Archer, now
Mrs. Osmond. The kiss makes her turn away from Caspar and turn toward
her husband, Gilbert Osmond. I take this kiss to be an exemplary case of
a "sign act" that functions "felicitously" in lieu of a speech act. It makes
something happen, though not what Caspar intends.

More than one kiss punctuates *The Portrait of a Lady*, at irregular intervals. These kisses mark decisive turns in the action. They are mostly kisses
between women, such as Isabel's kiss of Madame Merle. This is a kind of

Judas kiss in reverse. It seals their one-sided, or at any rate asymmetrical compact, since Isabel does not know what Madame Merle knows. Madame Merle says: "one doesn't make new friends at my age. I've made a great exception for you. You must remember that and must think as well of me as possible. You must reward me by believing in me" (3:298). Believing in her is one of Isabel's biggest mistakes, since Madame Merle's appeal is based on a lie. She is asking Isabel to believe in an integrity and good will that are missing. Madame Merle's appeal, however, is answered by a kiss: "By way of answer Isabel kissed her, and, though some women kiss with facility, there are kisses and kisses, and this embrace was satisfactory to Madame Merle" (3:290–91). Another important kiss is the one Isabel exchanges with Pansy, her stepdaughter, to seal her promise to return when she leaves Pansy. When Isabel goes to England to be at the bedside of the dying Ralph Touchett, in defiance of her husband's express prohibition, she leaves Pansy immured by her father's cruelty in a Roman convent. Other kisses are Henrietta Stackpole's kiss of greeting when Isabel arrives in London on her way to Ralph: "Henrietta kissed her, as Henrietta usually kissed, as if she were afraid she should be caught doing it" (4:303), or Mrs. Touchett's thin-lipped kiss of Isabel when she arrives at Gardencourt to be with Ralph as he dies: "Her lips felt very thin indeed on Isabel's hot cheek" (4:404). The kiss Madame Merle and Isabel exchange anticipates Maggie's "prodigious kiss" of Charlotte before her husband and father in James's final masterpiece, *The Golden Bowl*. "Prodigious" has there its etymological sense of "ominous," "full of omens," "prophetic." Maggie's kiss signals publicly her decision not to take her prerogative as an injured wife and accuse Charlotte of adultery with her husband, Prince Amerigo. As I shall show in my chapter on *The Golden Bowl*, this refraining is the cruelest thing she can do to Charlotte, or to her husband. It separates them for good when her father and Charlotte leave Europe permanently for "American City," leaving Maggie behind in Europe to enjoy her husband in peace. Maggie loses her beloved father but gains unshared possession of her husband.

Not all the kisses in *The Portrait of a Lady* are between women. Old Mr. Touchett gallantly kisses his niece, Isabel, when she first arrives at Gardencourt, at the beginning of the novel. Isabel kisses Ralph good-bye when, mortally ill, he is leaving Rome for Gardencourt in England, to die there in the same bed in which his father died. She thinks she will never see him again. She returns, however, to Gardencourt to kiss his hand as he lies on his deathbed. She tells him overtly, for the first time, that she loves him. This is the only time in the novel she is representing as saying

"I love you" to a man, in so many words, though plenty of men say that to her.

All these kisses function as efficacious speech acts, or rather as mute gestures that stand in place of speech acts. Their peculiarity is that kisses on the lips preclude speech while they are taking place. They nevertheless function as effective performatives, in lieu of speech. A kiss is a way of doing things not with words but with signs. As I have said earlier in this book, there is nothing particularly against standard speech act theory in saying this. Austin in *How to Do Things with Words* allows for the possibility of such wordless words, as when a judge condemns a man with a gesture rather than with speech, for example, by donning a black hood, or as when the audience in the Roman Colosseum doomed a gladiator by turning thumbs down. The most decisive of such kisses, historically, is Judas's kiss of Jesus, which marked him as the one to be arrested, tried, and crucified.

What Is a Kiss?

Caspar Goodwood's kiss of Isabel takes place not only as the last in the long line of kisses in *The Portrait of a Lady*, but also in the context of the tradition in our culture that makes kisses: an expression of love; a form of greeting, whether a kiss on the cheek or a kiss to the other's hand; an act of obeisance, as when a Catholic believer kisses the Pope's ring; a way to seal a compact; a way of saying yes, or of making a promise, or of taking responsibility, as when the bride and groom kiss as a signal that the marriage ceremony is complete and that the couple is now lawfully free to kiss and to consummate the marriage. "You may kiss your bride," says the minister, in a sexist assertion that the marriage gives the bridegroom the right of mastery over the bride. A kiss may be an act of magically asserting religious fidelity and appealing to God, that is, a kiss may be a form of prayer, as when a believer kisses the Torah, or the Bible, or the toe of Saint Peter's statue in Saint Peter's in Rome. A kiss may also, paradoxically, signal an act of betraying a promise or of breaking an engagement. When Søren Kierkegaard ended his engagement to Regina Olsen, her father insisted that Kierkegaard meet with her, which he did. He writes of that meeting:

> She asked me: Will you never marry? I answered: Yes, in ten years time, when I have had my fling, I will need a lusty girl to rejuvenate me. It was a necessary cruelty. Then she said to me: Forgive me for what I have done to

you. I answered: I'm the one, after all, who should be asking that. She said: Promise to think of me. I did. She said: Kiss me. I did—but without passion—Merciful God![2]

A kiss may even be the beginning of an artistic vocation, if Benjamin West is to be believed: "Sir Benjamin West relates that his mother kissed him eagerly when he showed her a likeness he had sketched of his baby-sister, and he adds, '*That kiss made me a painter!*'"[3]

The abundant naming of kisses in literature, for example, in the Western tradition, where literary kisses are legion, is not universal. When I was about to give a version of part of this chapter as a lecture in the People's Republic of China, I checked Stephen Owen's magisterial anthology in English translation of Chinese literature from the beginning to 1911.[4] I did not find one single kiss, though Owen includes numerous explicitly erotic texts. Probably the Chinese kiss one another, but until Western influences became strong, for example, by way of Western films, kisses were apparently not something one mentioned in a poem. I have never, in numerous visits, seen people kiss in public in China.

What is a kiss? That is not as easy to say as it might seem, though most people bestow and receive kisses all the time. Stephen Dedalus as a child asked himself just that question in Joyce's *A Portrait of the Artist as a Young Man*: "He still tried to think what was the right answer. Was it right to kiss his mother or wrong to kiss his mother? What did that mean, to kiss? You put your face up like that to say goodnight and then his mother put her face down. That was to kiss. His mother put her lips on his cheek; her lips were soft and they wetted his cheek; and they made a tiny little noise: kiss. Why did people do that with their two faces?"[5] A kiss always has an erotic dimension, no doubt, but a kiss on the lips makes this more obvious than a kiss on the hand or the cheek of the other. A real kiss is on the lips, an exchange of bodily fluids that is an exposure of intimacy by a touch between two erogenous zones. Such a kiss often anticipates the greater intimacy of sexual intercourse. For Freud, in a somewhat puritanical passage in Lecture 21 of the *Introductory Lectures on Psychoanalysis*, "The Development of the Libido and the Sexual Organization," the kiss is the first perversion. It is the prelude to all other perversions, since it is a use of erogenous zones with the aim of pure pleasure, separated from the goal of reproduction. Kissing is all right if it is a prelude to sexual intercourse:

There is something else that I must add in order to complete our view of sexual perversions. However infamous they may be, however sharply they may be contrasted with normal sexual activity, quiet consideration will show that some perverse trait or other is seldom absent from the sexual life of normal people. Even a kiss can claim to be described as a perverse act, since it consists in the bringing together of two oral erotogenic zones instead of two genitals. Yet no one rejects it as perverse; on the contrary, it is permitted in theatrical performances as a softened hint at the sexual act. But precisely kissing can easily turn into a complete perversion—if, that is to say, it becomes so intense that a genital discharge and orgasm follow upon it directly, an event far from rare. . . . [W]e shall recognize more and more clearly that the essence of the perversions lies not in the extension of the sexual aim, not in the replacement of the genitals, not even always in the variant choice of the object, but solely in the exclusiveness with which these deviations are carried out and as a result of which the sexual act serving the purpose of reproduction is put on one side. In so far as the perverse actions are inserted in the performance of the normal sexual act as preparatory or intensifying contributions, they are in reality not perversions at all. The gulf between normal and perverse sexuality is of course very much narrowed by facts of this kind. It is an easy conclusion that normal sexuality has emerged out of something that was in existence before it, by weeding out certain features of that material as unserviceable and collecting together the rest in order to subordinate them to a new aim, that of reproduction. . . . Indeed, Gentlemen, I have no objection to all organ-pleasure.[6]

Thank you, Dr. Freud! A Freudian might argue that calling some kisses perversions is no more than an objective, scientific, clinical description. Perhaps. Nevertheless, it is hard, for me at least, to eliminate the moral judgment that in common parlance accompanies the word *perversion*. The passage on kissing in the *Introductory Lectures* echoes the discussions of kisses in the much earlier *Three Essays on the Theory of Sexuality*. These essays were originally published, in German, in 1905. Freud several times mentions kisses there in more or less the same way as in the *Introductory Lectures*. In one passage, for example, in a section called "Deviations in Respect of the Sexual Aim," Freud says: "Moreover, the kiss, one particular contact of this kind [the kind accompanied by pleasure "which should persist until the final sexual aim is attained"], between the mucous membrane of the lips of the two people concerned, is held in high sexual esteem among many nations (including the most highly civilized ones), in spite of the fact that the parts of the body involved do not form part of the sexual apparatus but constitute the entrance to the digestive tract."[7] Am I wrong to detect a faint disgust in Freud's phrasing? Who, when kissing one's beloved, would want to remember that her or his lips are no more than the entrance to the stomach and intestines? Though Freud does not say so, at least not here, something similar can be said of genital lovemaking. As Yeats puts it in "Crazy Jane Talks with the Bishop": "But Love has pitched his mansion in / The place of excrement."[8]

A kiss may be an expression of mastery, not pure pleasure at all. It can be a taking possession of the other in an act that always has an element of violence, of taking by force, even of a kind of rape. The lips are the most intimate part of the body that is not generally covered, hidden in shame, except in Moslem countries where women veil their faces except the eyes, or sometimes just one eye is exposed. The lips are a boundary. They are portals where the inside is exposed to the outside, where the breath of life passes in and out, where food is taken in and speech breathed forth. It is impossible to kiss one's own lips, and even kissing another part of one's body does not seem to work as a form of auto-affection, though George Eliot, in a brilliant moment of psychological insight, represents the narcissistic Hetty Sorrel, in *Adam Bede*, passionately kissing her own arms when she cannot bring herself to drown herself: "The very consciousness of her own limbs was a delight to her: she turned up her sleeves, and kissed her arms with the passionate love of life."[9] A Western tradition affirms that you must touch your lips with your fingers in order to initiate speech. A children's myth in the United States, however, asserts that if you succeed in kissing your own elbow (which you cannot do) you will change sexes magically. You will become a girl if you are a boy, a boy if you are a girl, in a satisfaction of the curiosity children (and adults) have to know what it would be like to be of the other sex. In any case, you need the other for a kiss to be a real kiss. A kiss can be a greeting between friends or family members, or it may be a good-bye kiss. Intimate family members, and others, too, characteristically kiss one another goodnight, in implicit recognition that sleep is a little death. The goodnight kiss may always be the last kiss. The invitation to a kiss can also be an insult, as in the gesture of thumbing one's nose, which means "Kiss my ass" or, as James Joyce puts it in the Aeolus section of *Ulysses*, "K. M. R. I. A.," which stands for "Kiss my royal Irish Arse."[10] *Finnegans Wake* contains a little drawing of a nose being thumbed.[11] The "kiss of death" is a modern form of the Judas kiss. The mafia capo kisses the subordinate or rival whom he marks for execution. In an episode in *The Simpsons*, "Fat Tony" kisses a character and tells him to transmit that kiss as a gift to another character. The recipient is horrified to receive the relayed kiss, since he knows it is the kiss of death.

Marcel Proust, by contrast, gives the reader three kinds of apparently more benign, though still not entirely benign, kisses to think about: the goodnight kiss that the narrator's mother used to give him when he was a child and that he could not go to sleep without receiving; the loss of his grandmother's kiss when he talks to her on the telephone, a premonition of her death; and the kisses he exchanges with his mistress, Albertine.[12]

Kissing, it is worth noting, by no means differentiates human beings from animals, as philosophers used to think thinking, tool using, or language does. Chimpanzees kiss, as do other animals.

Well, what is a kiss? Jacques Derrida asks just this question, or a version of it, toward the beginning of *Le toucher, Jean-Luc Nancy* (*Touch, to Touch Him, Jean-Luc Nancy*): "The kiss, is it a caress among others? And the kiss on the mouth? And the biting kiss, like all that can then be exchanged between the lips, the tongues, and the teeth?"[13] This question precedes a long section on Emmanuel Levinas's theory of the caress. It introduces further discussions of touching as thematized in Edmund Husserl, Jean-Louis Chrétien, the New Testament, Aristotle, and many others, along with, chiefly, Nancy himself.

Almost at the end of *Le toucher*, in a characteristically brilliant and provocative three pages, Derrida analyzes the kiss as an extreme form of touching, contact, the tactile. These pages have as their context all that has come before on touching and on the caress as a touching without touching that undoes basic phenomenological assumptions. Derrida cites a passage from Novalis's *Fragments* in which Novalis asserts that "One can never avow that one loves oneself. The secret of this vow is the vivifying principle of the only true and eternal love. The first kiss, according to this understanding of it, is the principle of philosophy—the origin of a new world—the beginning of an absolute era—the act that fulfills an alliance with the self (*Selbstbund*). Whom would a philosophy whose germ is a first kiss not to some degree please?" (cited on 327). The germ in question is not the female egg but the male fructifying pollen or sperm, as the title of Novalis's set of fragments, "Blütenstaub," "Grains of Pollen," suggests. As Derrida observes, moreover, a principle or germ is not the thing itself. If the life-giving principle of philosophy is a first kiss, then philosophy may be defined as haunted by the attempt both to remember and at the same time to forget, as something a little shameful or undignified, that first, initiatory kiss.

What in the world does it mean to say that philosophy starts, is given life, by a first kiss? What Novalis asserts is a little odd, to say the least. That first kiss is the beginning of a new world, an absolute era ("absolute" in the Hegelian sense of completed, no longer tied to any partiality, in a final dialectical *Aufhebung* or sublation), not because it signals an alliance or openness to the other, as one might expect, but because it accomplishes an alliance with oneself, a *Selbstbund*. It appears that for Novalis I need the other to attain a narcissistic alliance with myself. How could that be? Does the kiss of Isabel by Caspar Goodwood, which I am about to cite (if one can cite a kiss; that is one of my questions), accomplish anything like that for Isabel? Does it do anything for Caspar, the kisser, not the kissed? That remains to be seen. Derrida, in any case, proposes not that a kiss gives self-possession but that it functions precisely to break "the reappropriation or the absolute reflection of self-presence" (326).

If philosophical dialectical thinking presupposes a going forth from the self in order to return to the self, now, ultimately, enriched by absolute knowledge and the liberation this gives, the first kiss interrupts that dialectical movement once and for all. It makes a permanent break or fissure in the self, a wound in self-presence that can never be healed. Whatever Novalis may have meant, Derrida wants to claim that this rupture in dialectical thinking is the germ of philosophy, or, one might better say, though it is another way of saying the same thing, of the deconstruction of philosophy:

> The interruption of dialectic (which does not exclude dialectic . . .), it is you, when I touch myself in touching you [*c'est toi, quand je me touche toi*]. It is for that that I love you, and often so unhappily, in the heart of extreme pleasure [*la jouissance même*]. And if I insist here on that interruption of reflexivity as absolute specularity at the heart of the "to touch oneself," it is because only touching (contact, the caress, the kiss) can, as "touching oneself touching you," interrupt the reflection in the mirror in its visual dimension. (326)

The act of touching, especially the touch of two pairs of lips that meet, breaks for good the specularity whereby I see myself in the eyes of another, as if they were my own eyes looking back at me, as Narcissus loved his own face reflected in the water, or as Willoughby, the egoist in George Meredith's novel of that name, sees his own image in miniature in Laetitia's eyes and is appeased: "The anxious question allowed him to read deeply in her eyes. He found the man he sought there, squeezed him passionately, and let her go." Willoughby's relation to Clara Middleton, in the main action of the novel, is less satisfactory, since if she can, Echolike, return his mirror image to him as a new Narcissus, she can also destroy him by refusing the reciprocity he seeks: "Clara let her eyes rest on his, and without turning or dropping, shut them."[14] I shall return to the relation of the look to the kiss. For Derrida, following Novalis, in that first kiss I encounter the wholly other, perhaps even a wholly other that is lodged somewhere within myself. In that encounter I leave myself or exit from myself, never to return to masterful self-possession.

Derrida plays in these pages on a more or less untranslatable possibility in the French language, namely, using a reflexive in a transitive way, for example, in saying *se toucher toi*, to touch myself touching you, to touch you touching myself—no English formula does justice to the reflexive-transitive force of this French locution. "But surely," says Derrida, "it is necessary in order that I be touched in this way by you that I must be able to touch myself. In the 'to touch oneself touching you' [*se toucher toi*], the 'oneself' is just as indispensable as the 'you.' . . . That it is necessary to love oneself is said by every 'I love you' . . . : another lucky feature of French grammar, which says the transitive in the reflexive, even or especially in the reflexive, and dissociates them for good)" (327). A little later Derrida defines such touching oneself in the reflexive-transitive act of "to love oneself loving you [*s'aimer toi*]" as "auto-hetero-affection" (328).

Derrida also observes, correctly, I believe, that the intimate touching of a kiss that permanently breaks open the self can also occur virtually—by a touching at a distance, through a reciprocal look, through words exchanged, or even through some form of telecommunication: "When I talk to you, I touch you, and you touch me when I hear you, from however far away that reaches me, were it by telephone, by the memory of an inflection of voice on the telephone, by letter also or by e-mail" (326–27). An e-mail kiss, I must say, seems to me lacking in substance, though many of them, one may imagine, have had earthshaking effects for both kisser and kissed. Franz Kafka, however, was less sanguine than Derrida about the possibility of kissing at a distance. In the *Letters to Milena* he laments that his written kisses never reach their goal because they are intercepted along the way by a thirsty horde of ghosts waiting for just this sustenance: "Written kisses don't reach their destination, rather, they are drunk on the way by the ghosts. It is on this ample nourishment that they multiply so enormously. . . . The ghosts won't starve, but we will perish."[15]

Derrida's *Le toucher* begins with a discussion of a form of kissing at a distance, that is, the "touching" of an intense look exchanged, in an expression based on Aristotle's *De anima*: "When our eyes touch, is it day or night?" (11). *Le toucher* returns again to the question of the kiss, by the mouth or by a look, in its last section, "Salve" ("Hail, Salut, Salutation, Salvo"). There Derrida describes, in a remarkable passage, a dream he had after his friend Jean-Luc Nancy had survived a heart-transplant operation: "One day, I have never said this to him, but to Hélène Nancy on the telephone, I dreamed that I kissed him on the mouth. It was a little after the transplantation of his new heart, when I came back from seeing him again and in fact from kissing him on the cheeks, for the first time. Like after a resurrection. And not only his" (339). A little later, Derrida observes, "With the exception of Novalis, people have rarely tried, to my knowledge, to *think*, what one would call think [the reference is to Heidegger's *What Is Called Thinking?*], the kiss. It is already very difficult to think what happens, and no doubt to think at all (but perhaps 'thinking' begins there) when a mouth comes in contact with another mouth and lips, sometimes the tongue and teeth mingle" (343).

If the first kiss was, for Novalis, the beginning of philosophy, the last kiss was, for Immanuel Kant, the end of philosophy and of life itself. Thomas de Quincey, in "The Last Days of Immanuel Kant," tells how Kant on his deathbed, no longer able to speak, signaled to the young disciple who had cared for him in his mortal illness to kiss him on the lips. If it is hard (for me) to think of kissing Freud, it is even harder to think of kissing or being kissed by Immanuel Kant. De Quincey got this anecdote from the memoirs of the young disciple who had kissed Kant.[16]

Kisses are conventionally indicated in a letter by a series of *X*'s: XXXXX, since no accepted form of letters phonetically corresponds to the sound or the feel of a kiss, as Joyce recognizes when he has the young Stephen Dedalus reflect on the oddness of kissing. No one can doubt, however, that the words for "kiss," for example in French, German, or English, sound or seem to sound "motivated," onomatopoeic, however much we post-Cratyleans know that to think so is a fallacy. All these words have *s*'s that sound a little like the noise a kiss makes or may make: *kiss, küssen, Kuß, embrasser, baiser. Baiser* is sounded with the tongue further forward in the mouth than *kiss*. It is a two-syllable word, long drawn out and with the tongue ready, in short, a "French kiss." *Baiser*, I am told, is slang for "to copulate," "to fuck." A French film was entitled *Baise moi*, where *baise* did not mean "kiss." The German version was called *Fichte Mich*. How Germans kiss I do not know, but presumably *küssen* names what one must assume is a German kiss. The Germans even have a word *kußecht*, "kiss-proof," as in a kiss-proof lipstick. Is Isabel Archer "kiss-proof," *kußecht*? Would it be a good thing or a bad thing if she were?

The onomatopoeic aspects of the German word for "kiss," along with, perhaps, German ways of kissing, are used in a savagely ironic wordplay almost at the end of Heinrich von Kleist's *Penthesilea*. Penthesilea has bitten her lover, Achilles, to death. "Küßt ich ihn tot?" she asks in her delirium, "Did I kiss him to death?" She says this happened by a slip of the tongue, so to speak:

So war es ein Versehen. Küsse, Bisse,
Das reimt sich, und wer recht vom Herzen liebt,
Kann schon das eine für das andre greifen.

It was a mistake. Kisses, bites,
They rhyme, and whoever rightly loves from the heart,
Can easily take one for the other.[17]

Henry James confirms Derrida's assertion that eyes, too, are an erogenous zone. Both know that a look exchanged between two people, where
a mutual otherness is recognized or experienced (as opposed to the blindly
egoistic self-reflection of Willoughby's narcissistic gaze in Clara's eyes)
may function like a touch or a kiss. In the scene in *The Portrait of a Lady*
in which Isabel discusses with Lord Warburton his almost-made decision
to propose marriage to Pansy, Isabel's step-daughter, Isabel half-suspects
that Warburton thinks of doing this only because he still loves her, Isabel.
She thinks this even though she has repeatedly rejected him and though
she is now married to Osmond. Warburton, Isabel thinks, may possibly
imagine that by marrying Pansy he can be nearer to Isabel. They exchange
a look that is extremely intimate. It is a kind of ultimate mutual contact or
confession, a touching if not a kissing:

> She met his eyes, and for a moment they looked straight at each other. If
> she wished to be satisfied she saw something that satisfied her; she saw in
> his expression the gleam of an idea that she was uneasy on her own ac-
> count—that she was perhaps even in fear [fear, presumably, that she might
> be tempted to betray her bad husband]. It showed a suspicion, not a hope,
> but such as it was it told her what she wanted to know. Not for an instant
> should he suspect her of detecting in his proposal of marrying her step-
> daughter an implication of increased nearness to herself, or of thinking it,
> on such a betrayal, ominous. In that brief, extremely personal gaze, how-
> ever, deeper meanings passed between them than they were conscious of at
> the moment. (4:221)

If for Freud a kiss may be a perversion, if for Novalis the first kiss is the
beginning of philosophy, in the apocryphal gnostic gospel by Philip, Peter
is shown as jealous of the way Jesus kisses Mary Magdalen on the mouth:

> And the companion of the [Saviour was] Mary Magdalene. He loved her
> more than [all] the disciples [and used to] kiss her often on her [mouth].
> The rest of the disciples [were offended and] said to him: "Why do you
> love her more than all of us?" The Savior answered and said to them, "Why
> do I not love you like her? When a blind man and one who sees are both

together in darkness, they are no different from one another. When the
light comes, then he who sees will see the light, and he who is blind will
remain in darkness."[18]

I take it Jesus is saying, in effect, "If you don't see the difference, I'm not
going to tell you. I could not explain it to you." The parallel in the canonical New Testament is the Parable of the Sower, and Jesus' explanation of
why he speaks to the multitude in parables: "because they seeing see not:
and hearing they hear not, nether do they understand" (Matt. 13:13).

A Decisive Kiss

Here, at last, is the kiss at the end of *The Portrait of a Lady* between Isabel
and Caspar Goodwood. Goodwood, along with Warburton, is another of
Isabel's unsuccessful suitors who keeps coming back again and again and
will not take no for an answer. This literal kiss is a much more overtly
physical, even violent, exchange of "deeper meanings" than the look between Isabel and Lord Warburton, but in both cases it can be said that
Isabel's separate and untouched integrity, or her sovereign freedom, or
even what one might call her still virginal narcissism, is violated. The section in brackets was added in the 1908 revision for the New York Edition.
It replaces the much milder "His kiss was like a flash of lightning; when it
was dark again she was free" in the original 1880 version. Over a thousand
changes were made when James revised the novel for the 1908 version,
many small, but some extensive and significant, as is the case with this
one. A number of secondary works have discussed the revisions and their
significance, stressing, for example, the greater emphasis on the body and
on carnal sexual feelings in the revised version. I shall base my reading
on the 1908 version but indicate, where it seems important to do so, the
differences from the 1880 version:

> He glared at her a moment through the dusk, and the next instant she felt
> his arms about her and his lips on her own lips. [His kiss was like white
> lightning, a flash that spread, and spread again, and stayed; and it was ex-
> traordinarily as if, while she took it, she felt each thing in his hard manhood
> that had least pleased her, each aggressive fact of his face, his figure, his
> presence, justified of its intense identity and made one with the act of pos-
> session. So had she heard of those wrecked and under water following a
> train of images before they sink. But when darkness returned she was free.]
> She never looked about her; she only darted from the spot. There were

lights in the windows of the house; they shone far across the lawn. In an extraordinarily short time—for the distance was considerable—she had moved through the darkness (for she saw nothing) and reached the door. Here only she paused. She looked all about her; she listened a little; then she put her hand on the latch. She had not known where to turn; but she knew now. There was a very straight path. (4:436)

All *The Portrait of a Lady*, it might be said, has been written to make the decision Isabel makes on the basis of the knowledge Caspar's kiss gives her plausible and perspicuous, though I do not know, even so, that Isabel's decision is all that easy to understand. Why does Caspar's kiss tell Isabel that she must return to her odious husband and to a miserably unhappy marriage? She has disobeyed her husband's express injunction to return to Gardencourt to see her cousin Ralph Touchett one last time before he dies. After his death she remains in indecision at Gardencourt: "Isabel thought of her husband as little as might be; but now that she was at a distance, beyond its spell, she thought with a kind of spiritual shudder of Rome. There was a penetrating chill in the image, and she drew back into the deepest shade of Gardencourt. She lived from day to day, postponing, closing her eyes, trying not to think. She knew she must decide, but she decided nothing; her coming itself had not been a decision. On that occasion she had simply started" (4:421). She had simply started, without reflection, from Rome, under the impetus of the news that Ralph was near death and, along with that, the impetus, almost a physical force, of the revelation from the Countess Gemini that her husband and Madame Merle had been lovers and that Madame Merle is Pansy's mother.

Now she must decide, weighing the pros and cons, and balancing her competing obligations: to her marriage vows and to Pansy, on one side, and to her vision and project for herself, on the other. That project her marriage irrevocably violates. She does not know which way to turn. She is visited then first by Lord Warburton, who is now engaged to an English titled lady but makes one last embarrassed, highly indirect approach to Isabel, married though she is, and then by Caspar Goodwood, whose approach is anything but indirect. He finds her in the garden, by the same bench where Lord Warburton had found her when *he* first proposed to her. Caspar takes her by the wrist, forces her to sit down, and then proposes that they should run away together. "There was indeed something really formidable in his resolution" (4:430). Imploring her to "trust me" (4:431), telling her that "You don't know where to turn. I want to persuade you to trust me" (4:433), "that a woman deliberately made to suffer is

justified in anything in life—in going down into the streets if that will help
her!" (4: 434), and, echoing Milton, that "The world's all before us—and
the world's very big. I know something about that" (4:435), he ends his
appeal by taking Isabel in his arms and forcibly kissing her, as described
in the passage cited above. The narrator tells us that she is tempted, before
the kiss: "I know not whether she believed everything he said; but she
believed just then that to let him take her in his arms would be the next
best thing to her dying. This belief, for a moment, was a kind of rapture,
in which she felt herself sink and sink" (4:435).

Two contrary figures govern the description of the kiss. More precisely,
they are catachreses, words drawn from the observable and namable physical world to denominate the effects of an act that generates within Isabel
violent bodily interior experiences that have no proper names. One catachresis James uses is the figure of the drowning person before whose eyes,
at the moment of death, his or her whole life flashes in a series of vivid
images, all in a moment: "The world, in truth, had never seemed so large"
the reader is told a few moments before the kiss; "it seemed to open out,
all round her, to take the form of a mighty sea, where she floated in fathomless waters" (4:435). The kiss itself makes her feel as if she were drowning in those fathomless waters. It makes her think of "those wrecked and
under water following a train of images before they sink." The kiss, however, in a contrary catachrestic image, is also "like white lightning, a flash
that spread, and spread again, and stayed." The kiss makes her whole
body, and her mind too, incandescent, illuminated, but at the same time
it enforces her submission to "an act of possession."

The flash of penetrating illumination passes, and darkness returns,
since it is after dark in the garden when Caspar kisses her. She turns away
from Caspar, "darts" back to the house, and now knows which way to
turn, not away from her husband, but straight onto the road back to Rome
and to that awful husband, in fulfillment of the adage that all roads lead to
Rome: "She had not known where to turn; but she knew now. There was
a very straight path" (4:436).

Why does she make this decision? Is it the right one? Many readers
have so powerfully felt that it is the wrong decision that they have doubted
James means the reader to understand that Isabel has decided to return to
Osmond. The long notebook entry written when James was halfway
through the writing of *Portrait*, however, leaves no doubt about that. On
what basis does she make the lifelong decision to immure herself again in
her husband's house? Why is it that Caspar's kiss gives her the knowledge
that she did not have before? She had not known where to turn; but she

knew now. The whole long novel leads up to this kiss and to the decision
it precipitates. That context ought to make it possible to answer the questions I have raised. In order to see if it does, it will be necessary to read
that context with care, both for the knowledge it gives and to understand,
if it can be understood, the decision that knowledge commands. It will
have been necessary, that is, to read the novel.

Is Close Reading (of a Kiss) Possible? Methodological Excursus

First, however, before trying to do that, I need to present, if the reader
will permit me to do so, a methodological detour. I want to indicate what
it might mean to "read" the novel and to read Caspar's kiss, as the narrator
registers Isabel's experience of it.

In "The Return to Philology," a late essay by Paul de Man, written in
the shadow of his impending death, de Man has this to say about "close
reading":

> [Reuben] Brower, however, believed in and effectively conveyed what ap-
> pears to be an entirely innocuous and pragmatic concept, founded on Rich-
> ards's "practical criticism." Students, as they began to write on the writings
> of others, were not to say anything that was not derived from the text they
> were considering. They were not to make any statements that they could
> not support by a specific use of language that actually occurred in the text.
> They were asked, in other words, to begin by reading texts closely as texts
> and not to move at once into the general context of human experience or
> history. Much more humbly or modestly, they were to start out from the
> bafflement that such singular turns of tone, phrase, and figure were bound
> to produce in readers attentive enough to notice them and honest enough
> not to hide their non-understanding behind the screen of received ideas
> that often passes, in literary instruction, for humanistic knowledge.
>
> This very simple rule, surprisingly enough, had far-reaching didactic
> consequences. . . . Mere reading, it turns out, prior to any theory, is able to
> transform critical discourse in a manner that would appear deeply subver-
> sive to those who think of the teaching of literature as a substitute for the
> teaching of theology, ethics, psychology, or intellectual history. [Today we
> would add: anthropology, political science, cultural studies, and the study
> of gender, race, and class.] Close reading accomplishes this often in spite
> of itself because it cannot fail to respond to structures of language which it
> is the more or less secret aim of literary teaching to keep hidden.[19]

Is, however, such "close reading" or "mere reading" even possible? Can we believe in that cheerfully optimistic phrase: "cannot fail to respond"? Can we ever read without instantly importing "received ideas" of some sort or another, imposing what in another terminology we might call our inbred, unconscious ideological assumptions? If de Man is right in what he says in other late essays, what is "really there" in any text that falls before our eyes is the senseless "materiality of the letter." That materiality, however, is extremely difficult, perhaps impossible, to see, since we automatically "read" the text, that is, impose a coherent and sequential meaning on it. All sorts of preconceptions inflect that reading.

How [de Man asks in "Shelley Disfigured"] can a positional act [such as the one that laid down segments of the text in the first place, for example, a given sentence in James's *The Portrait of a Lady*, let us say the one that describes Caspar Goodwood's kiss of Isabel], which relates to nothing that comes before or after, become inscribed in a sequential narrative? How does a speech act become a trope, a catachresis which then engenders in its turn the narrative sequence of an allegory? It can only be because we impose, in our turn, on the senseless power of positional language the authority of sense and of meaning. But this is radically inconsistent: language posits and language means (since it articulates) but language cannot posit meaning. It can only reiterate (or reflect) it in its reconfirmed falsehood. Nor does knowledge of this impossibility make it less impossible.[20]

I suppose de Man means that language is initially a speech act, a blind performative. It is blind because it is not governed or validated by any cognition that would guarantee its referential validity. Such positional language is a "trope," not only because it figuratively stands for something absent, but also because it turns away from knowledge of that indirection. It "averts" itself, as Caspar Goodwood does at the end of *The Portrait of a Lady*. The trope is a catachresis because it does not replace any available literal name that is secured by reference to something phenomenally known. The trope is thrown out into the void of nonknowledge. This bleak sequence—the senseless power of performative positing that becomes a trope, that is, a catachresis—is really a simultaneous event. It is followed, or accompanied, by a recuperation that ascribes sense and meaning illicitly on the basis of ideological assumptions that have been previously put in place. Language cannot posit meaning. It can only "reflect" it in its "reconfirmed falsehood." The falsehood was confirmed already, though not known as false, by the initial prior positing of language's false referentiality. The new use of language "reconfirms" that falsehood. This process culminates in an "allegory," in de Man's special and somewhat idiosyncratic use of the word. An allegory is a way of speaking otherwise about something. It names the esoteric exoterically, that is, in public, in the "agora," the public square, as the word's etymology indicates.

All allegories, for de Man, however, are ultimately, or "really," allegories of reading. Or, rather, they are allegories of the aboriginal misreading or "impossibility of reading" that irresistibly and spontaneously inscribes meaning taken from preconceived ideas, *idées reçues*, on the senseless materiality of language or other signs. The ostensible topic, whatever it is, is only a cover or allegory of the actual topic. That topic is always reading itself or rather the "impossibility of reading." Speaking in "Reading (Proust)" about *À la recherche du temps perdu* (*Remembrance of Things Past*), de Man says:

> according to the laws of Proust's own statement it is forever impossible to read Reading. Everything in this novel signifies something other than what it represents, be it love, consciousness, politics, art, sodomy, or gastronomy [a wonderful list!]: it is always something else that is intended. It can be shown that the most adequate term to designate this "something else" is Reading. But one must at the same time "understand" that this word bars access, once and forever, to a meaning that yet can never cease to call out for its understanding.[21]

That close reading or mere reading may be impossible, for the reasons de Man gives, does not mean that "we" should not try to do it, as I shall try to do it with James's *The Portrait of a Lady*. In any case, "we" may hope the optimistic praise of close reading in "The Return to Philology" is right and the bleakness of "Shelley Disfigured" and "Reading (Proust)" wrong.

The task of close reading, however, may be made even more difficult in my attempt to read James's *Portrait* by my focus on the role of speech acts in this novel. Speech acts, if de Man is right in what he says repeatedly elsewhere, as well as in the passage cited above from "Shelley Disfigured," are especially resistant to cognition. Even as early as "Rhetoric of Persuasion (Nietzsche)," in *Allegories of Reading*, de Man was proposing that an inescapable aporia is generated by the relation between constative and performative language:

> Considered as persuasion, rhetoric is performative but when considered as a system of tropes, it deconstructs its own performance. Rhetoric is a *text* in that it allows for two incompatible, mutually self-destructive points of view, and therefore puts an insurmountable obstacle in the way of any reading or understanding. The aporia between performative and constative lan-

guage is merely a version of the aporia between trope and persuasion that both generates and paralyzes rhetoric and thus gives it the appearance of a history. (*AR*, 131)

Other essays in *Allegories of Reading* have equally intransigent formulations. These formulations, it should be noted, grow, for example, in the Nietzsche essay already cited or in the Rousseau essays in *Allegories of Reading*, out of an effort of close or "mere" reading:

> A text is defined by the necessity of considering a statement, at the same time, as performative and constative, and the logical tension between figure and grammar is repeated in the impossibility of distinguishing between two linguistic functions which are not necessarily compatible. ("Promises [*Social Contract*]," *AR*, 270)

> Performative rhetoric and cognitive rhetoric, the rhetoric of tropes, fail to converge. The chain of substitutions [that would be "cognitive rhetoric"] functions next to another, differently structured system [the performative one] that exists independently of referential determination, in a system that is both entirely arbitrary and entirely repeatable, like a grammar. ("Excuses [*Confessions*]," *AR*, 300)

Just what these somewhat forbidding formulations mean in practical terms, or as they might be exemplified in trying to read a novel, de Man made clear in remarks in a seminar. Since no written record exists of those remarks, you will need to believe or not believe my testimony concerning what he said. This requires a tacit speech act of your own, following my performative bearing witness. I say, "I swear this is what he said," and you, I hope, say, "I believe you." De Man affirmed that the aporia, or lack of convergence, or possible incompatibility between performative and cognitive language means that you can make a constative or cognitive statement that is able to be tested for its referential validity, its truth or falsehood, and you can utter a performative speech act that works to do something with words, but you can never know for sure just what has been done, and you cannot predict with certainty or verifiability just what your performative utterance will bring about. Knowing and doing (with words) are (possibly) incompatible. One must say "possibly" because you can never know for sure. Since doing something with words involves the performative power of language, it is not open to cognition. As de Man said in that seminar, using a figure he was perhaps too prudent ever to use in a published essay, you aim at a bear and an innocent bird falls out of the sky. The figure suggests that performative utterances are always in one way or another violent, unjust, and unjustified, a case of what Walter Benjamin, in a celebrated essay, "Zur Kritik der Gewalt" ("Critique of Violence"), called *Gewalt*. *Gewalt* in German means "force" and "authority" as well as "violence."

De Man's figure also suggests that all performatives are in one way or another what Austin called "infelicities," "misfires." It is not the case that infelicities are, as Austin wanted to believe, special cases within the larger domain of generally felicitous performatives. Performative infelicity is an injustice, but that infelicity is also, paradoxically, performatives' chance to be just, as opposed to simply lawful, This is so because rendering justice is always a specific act oriented toward a singular case, therefore outside general law, whereas felicitous speech acts, as Austin defines them, are always endorsed by prior convention or law.

The violence inherent in speech acts is spelled out explicitly in de Man's "Excuses (*Confessions*)" apropos of the way Rousseau's *Fourth Revery* demonstrates that "Excuses generate the very guilt they exonerate, though always by excess or by default" (*AR*, 299). What this means, de Man asserts, is that "Since guilt, in this description, is a cognitive and excuse a performative function of language, we are [he means 'I am'] restating the disjunction of the performative from the cognitive: any speech act produces an excess of cognition, but it can never hope to know the process of its own production (the only thing worth knowing). Just as the text [of the *Fourth Revery*] can never stop apologizing for the suppression of guilt that it performs, there is never enough knowledge available to account for the delusion of knowing" (*AR*, 299–300).

Whether *The Portrait of a Lady* will confirm or disconfirm such rather grim formulations remains to be seen. My focus is on Isabel's decisions. A decision is a special kind of performative utterance. I shall therefore not be able, in my reading, to avoid confronting the dissonance between performative and constative language, if indeed such a dissonance obtains.

A final difficulty: *The Portrait of a Lady*, as James specifies in the preface to the New York Edition, is made up of more or less innumerable small verbal details, discrete performative positings, as de Man might have called them. James's figure for this, picking up a figure he says Turgenev used in conversation with him, is a spacious architectural structure made of innumerable small bricks: "On one thing I was determined; that, though I should clearly have to pile brick upon brick for the creation of an interest, I would leave no pretext for saying that anything is out of line, scale or perspective. I would build large—in fine embossed vaults and painted arches, as who should say, and yet never let it appear that the chequered pavement, the ground under the reader's feet, fails to stretch at every point to the base of the walls" (3:xvi). Though the *Portrait* has a large architectural form, it is made of thousands and thousands of individual details, just as a great portrait painting is made of thousands of tiny brush strokes. No single brush stroke is all that meaningful in itself taken in isolation, but each gains meaning from its juxtaposition to all the others in a painterly construction. The difficulty for a written reading that follows what might be called Brower's Law is that it is impossible in reasonable compass to cite all the relevant evidence. Nevertheless, it all counts. As James puts this in the preface, speaking of his "solicitude" for his "relation with the reader":

> That solicitude was to be accordingly expressed in the artful patience with which, as I have said, I piled brick upon brick. The bricks, for the whole counting-over—putting for bricks little touches and inventions and enhancements by the way—affect me in truth as well-nigh innumerable and as ever so scrupulously fitted together and packed-in. It is an effect of detail, of the minutest; though, if one were in this connection to say all, one would express the hope that the general, the ampler air of the modest monument still survives. (3:xix)

The reader must simultaneously pay attention to innumerable minute details and at the same time be aware of the shape and proportions of the large architectural construction those multitudinous bricks constitute. This is an exceedingly difficult prescription to fulfill.

The *Portrait* employs two forms of this micro-meaning or miniaturization: (1) the ramified subtlety of indirect discourse as it registers the complexity of Isabel Archer's interiority or, less often, that of other characters, and (2) the nuance of conversational give and take, or, more often, wary fencing with language, among characters who are granted (most of them) much irony, evasion, and indirection, not to speak of high intelligence. Each detail merits individual attention. It is difficult to measure the exact purport of each in relation to that spacious architectural whole. To bear testimony to the "close reading" of such a large-scale verbal construction is extremely difficult. The whole is made of so many small but individually significant parts, each contributing to the whole. Any writing down of a reading necessarily involves synecdoche, part for whole, the insolence of choice in the selection of details to cite and single out for comment. For that choice the commentator must take responsibility. The reader can only hope he or she has not missed something among all those details that has an important bearing on the reading proposed. The genius is in the details with a vengeance in this particular case.

After such warnings it takes some courage to begin an act of the close reading de Man advocates. Here goes, though with considerable trepidation. James's *Portrait* makes a demand on me to read it, but how can I be sure I am doing it justice?

Performative speech acts occur in at least four registers in *The Portrait of a Lady*. (1) In the positing of the story by the author in the act of writing it, on the basis of who knows what authority or inspiration. James is remarkably evasive about that in the preface, as I shall show. (2) In the testimony of the imagined narrator to the events and to the speech, feelings, and thoughts of the characters. These are now spoken of as having a "real," objective existence, apart from any sovereign act of authorial invention. The narrator knows the characters intimately, knows all their secrets, but they do not know they are under surveillance. They do not know they are being "bugged." This happens according to the extremely peculiar conventions of "omniscient narration," or, as Nicholas Royle has recently argued, in a brilliant essay, under the aegis of telepathy.[22] (3) In performative utterances or writings by characters within the story, for example, promises, lies, wills, declarations, oaths, proposals, and the like. (4) In the response of any reader, for example, in teaching the novel or in writing an essay about it, such as this chapter. Such writing is another form of testimony: "I swear this is what I found when I read *The Portrait of a Lady*." I shall exemplify the last kind of performative in this chapter, as well as reflect a little about it. I shall also have something to say about the first two, but my primary focus will be on performative utterances *within* the novel and, especially, on that peculiar form of speech act we call a decision.

Prefatory Evasions

I begin with the preface to the New York Edition of 1908. It is the first thing many readers encounter these days, in many modern editions of the novel, after the editor's introduction and other "front matter." The preface of 1908 is remarkable in many ways. It is one of the most brilliant of the amazing prefaces James wrote for the New York Edition. Taken together, they constitute the greatest treatise on the art of the novel in English. They are, individually, so powerful a reading of the work or works they preface that the reader, however canny and suspicious, has difficulty keeping his or her balance. The reader may not notice things a given preface does not mention or even distorts. These omissions and distortions challenge the reader to notice them and to try to do better, even if that means putting in question what the author says about his own work. The reader must constantly check his or her own reading of the novel against the almost too persuasive one presented by the preface. This is one of the special difficulties in reading James—reading, that is, the works he chose to include in the New York Edition.

The 1908 preface to *The Portrait of a Lady* is the primary evidence the reader has for the "source" of the novel in James's imagination or experience. Of course, it is not the only evidence. James's notebooks, letters, and autobiographies are additional testimony. The preface tells the reader something about how James decided to write this particular novel. It tells the reader where he was living when he wrote it (Florence and Venice).

The preface begins with an eloquent description of the way James's attempt in his rooms in Venice to get on with the writing of *The Portrait of a Lady* was interrupted by the beguiling view of Venice outside his window. Far from giving him inspiration, this view seduced him away from his task. This is analogous, the reader might reflect, to the way Isabel Archer, in the novel, is seduced away from her project to see the world and to exercise her limitless freedom, now that she is rich. The successful plot by Madame Merle and Gilbert Osmond to entice Isabel into falling in love with Osmond deflects Isabel from her original goal. James's seduction by Venice, however, as he affirms, had its long-term "fertilizing" value. This is presumably because it stored up knowledge or sources of inspiration: "Strangely fertilizing, in the long run, does a wasted effort of attention often prove. It all depends on *how* the attention has been cheated, has been squandered. There are high-handed insolent frauds, and there are insidious sneaking ones. And there is, I fear, even on the most designing artist's part, always witless enough good faith, always anxious enough desire, to fail to guard him against their deceits" (3:vi). The reader who has become wise in the ways of James's indirections will be tempted to read this passage, with its mixture of sexual ("fertilizing," "desire") and economic ("cheated," "squandered," "frauds") terminology converging on "deceits," which belongs to both registers, as an anticipatory-retrospective allegory of Isabel's defrauding by Osmond. It is anticipatory because the reader encounters it first, but retrospective because it was written after the novel was finished. Is Osmond a high-handed, insolent fraud or an insidious, sneaking one? That is for the reader of the novel to decide.

There would be much to say about each segment of the preface to *The Portrait of a Lady*. The preface is, however, as remarkable for what it leaves out as for what it includes. Its segments include the account of a discussion with Turgenev about the priority of character over plot in the creation of a novel, and about the danger of a resultant "manque . . . d'architecture." James agrees about the priority of character over plot, but he boasts later about the superior architecture of *Portrait*. I have already cited the passage about building a shapely edifice with all those little bricks. The *Portrait* preface also contains some famous phrases asserting that the validity of a literary work, its " 'moral' sense," depends "on the amount of felt life concerned in producing it" (3:x): "is it [a "given subject"] valid, in a word, is it genuine, is it sincere, the result of some direct impression or perception of life?" (3:ix). This appeal is partly a defense against any reproach that a forbidden topic—adultery, for example, arguably James's main subject in all his work—is being dramatized. It also straddles a fence in a way thoroughly characteristic of British nineteenth-century literary theory as James had inherited it. A valid work, a sincere work, a "moral" work is validated simultaneously (and inconsistently) by its referential accuracy and by its dependence on the idiosyncratic point of view of the writer. This double assertion gives rise to the celebrated image of the spacious "house of fiction," fenestrated by innumerable windows. In each window sits a novelist with a unique perspective on the real social world:

> The house of fiction has in short not one window, but a million—a number of possible windows not to be reckoned, rather; every one of which has been pierced, or is still pierceable, in its vast front, by the need of the individual vision and by the pressure of the individual will. . . . But they have this mark of their own that at each of them stands a figure with a pair of eyes, or at least with a field-glass, which forms, again and again, for observation, a unique instrument, insuring to the person making use of it an impression distinct from every other. (3:x–xi)

One idiosyncrasy of *The Portrait of a Lady* is James's choice of its central character. Who but James would have thought of Isabel Archer? An extended sequence in the preface discusses the propriety of "endowing" "the mere slim shade of an intelligent but presumptuous girl" "with the high attributes of a Subject" (3:xiii). James justifies himself by citing George Eliot's remark about Gwendolen Harleth in *Daniel Deronda*: "In these frail vessels is borne onward through the ages the treasure of human affection" (3:xiii). He goes on to identify Shakespeare's Juliet and Cleopatra and Portia, George Eliot's Hetty Sorrel in *Adam Bede*, Maggie Tulliver in *The Mill on the Floss* and Rosamond Vincy in *Middlemarch*, as well as Gwendolen, as antecedents and models for making "an ado" about "the mere young thing" (3:xiii, xiv).

James moves triumphantly, in his joyous embrace of difficulty, toward the assertion of the central formal device of *The Portrait of a Lady*. This is the structuring choice that generated the whole novel: " 'Place the center of the subject in the young woman's own consciousness,' I said to myself, 'and you get as interesting and as beautiful a difficulty as you could wish. Stick to *that*—for the center; put the heaviest weight into *that* scale, which will be so largely the scale of her relation to herself' " (3:xv). The last paragraph of the preface asserts that prime examples of the representation of Isabel's relation to herself are the moment when she first sees Madame Merle seated at the piano at Gardencourt and her "extraordinary meditative vigil" in Rome, when she stays awake all night by the dying fire in the drawing room of the house she shares with her husband, confronting the fact that her husband hates her and asking herself what she should *do*:

> It is a representation simply of her motionlessly *seeing*, and an attempt withal to make the mere still lucidity of her act as 'interesting' as the surprise of a caravan or the identification of a pirate. [These figures are parallel to Isabel's lucid identification of her husband's malignity.] It represents, for that matter, one of the identifications dear to the novelist, and even indispensable to him; but it all goes on without her being approached by another person and without her leaving her chair. It is obviously the best thing in the book, but it is only a supreme illustration of the general plan. (3:xx–xxi)

James does not mention Dorothea Brooke in George Eliot's *Middlemarch*. Dorothea also has a midnight vigil of recognition. She is a much closer model for Isabel Archer than either Rosamond Vincy or Gwendolen Harleth. By mentioning several of George Eliot's heroines but not his most likely "source," James obliquely confesses to his indebtedness while at the same time putting the reader off the scent. In a similar way, James says nothing at all in this preface about the extensive revision he was making of *The Portrait of a Lady* at the time of the New York Edition. The preface to *The Golden Bowl*, however, though it is a novel that was not extensively revised, discusses eloquently the way revision is re-vision. Revision is a seeing again of what James calls the "the clear matter" of the tale (23:xiii). Revision is a minute reworking of the words already written to make them correspond better to the ideal vision of the matter that he is trying to put into fit words. The *Portrait* preface comments harshly on the way James's reading audience is for the most part without critical subtlety. Most readers are interested only in the author's "having cast a spell upon the simpler, the very simplest, forms of attention" (3:xviii).

Much more could be said about all these segments of the preface. Perhaps most important for my focus in this chapter on decision making is

James's extraordinary evasiveness about the origins of Isabel and of the characters with which he surrounded her. Where did James get his inspiration? What decided him to write this particular novel as opposed to all the others he might have written? Though James says that he finds "quite as interesting as the young woman herself" "this projection of memory upon the whole matter of the growth, in one's imagination, of some such apology for a motive. These are the fascinations of the fabulist's art, these lurking forces of expansion, these necessities of upspringing in the seed, these beautiful determinations, on the part of the idea entertained, to grow as tall as possible, to push into the light and the air and thickly flower there; and, quite as much, these fine possibilities of recovering, from some good standpoint on the ground gained, the intimate history of the business—of retracing and reconstructing its steps and stages" (3:vii). This passage is a wonderful, miniature example of just what it talks about, "these necessities of upspringing in the seed." Each phrase begets another in a potentially endless appositional string and in complex forms of syntactical parallelism. What James says here is all well and good, but it is more cover-up, evasion, and false promise than revelation. Just what does James tell the reader about the seed of the novel and its growth? Exceedingly little. Damn all, one might say. Citing his purported conversation with Turgenev, James reports that distinguished novelist as saying:

> As for the origin of one's wind-blown germs themselves, who shall say, as you ask, where *they* come from? We have to go too far back, too far behind, to say. Isn't it all we can say that they come from every quarter of heaven, that they are *there* at almost any turn of the road? They accumulate, and we are always picking them over, selecting among them. They are the breath of life—by which I mean that life, in its own way, breathes them upon us. They are so, in a manner prescribed and imposed—floated into our minds by the current of life. (3:viii)

This high-faluting appeal to "inspiration" justifies evading the task of retracing the steps of composition. Though James says he is fascinated by the prospect of "retracing and reconstructing [the] steps and stages" of his imagination when he decides to treat a certain "subject," when he actually comes to the point of doing this he repeatedly claims that he cannot remember. The "germ" of *Portrait*, he says, was his "grasp of a single character," but where Isabel came from he cannot or will not say. The equivocation between cannot and will not is blatant: Isabel was "an acquisition I had made, moreover, after a fashion not here to be retraced. Enough that I was, as seemed to me, in complete possession of it, that I had been so for a long time, that this had made it familiar and yet not blurred in its charm" (3:xi). Once he had "grasped" Isabel as the basis for a story, James tells the reader, then his task was to "place" her in circumstances and in relation to other characters.

This leads to one of the most extraordinary figures in this quite extraordinary preface. This is the claim that Isabel was initially "placed," not in relation to other characters or even to a setting, but in James's own imagination. The figure plays on different meanings of "placed." It compares Isabel to a precious object kept in a locked cupboard by an antique dealer. The image strikingly anticipates, or rather recalls, since the preface was written later, the curiosity shop in which, in *The Golden Bowl*, Charlotte and the Prince find the ominous golden bowl with its hidden flaw. James's reuse of this figure has an portentous implication because it recalls the two aesthetes and collectors in *Portrait* itself, Ned Rosier and Gilbert Osmond. The latter is condemned for looking upon Isabel as another object to add to his collection of precious objects. Is James himself not an aesthete who has "collected" Isabel and stored her away in the back-shop of his mind until he decides to write a novel about her, that is, make another aesthetic object, a text something like a painted portrait, in short, *The Portrait of a Lady*?

If the apparition [of Isabel as the "subject" for a novel] was still all to be placed, how came it to be vivid?—since we puzzle such quantities out, mostly, just by the business of placing them. One could answer such a question beautifully, doubtless, if one could do so subtle, if not so monstrous, a thing as to write the history of the growth of one's imagination. One would describe then what, at a given time, had extraordinarily happened to it, and one would so, for instance, be in a position to tell, with an approach to clearness, how, under favor of occasion, it had been able to take over (take over straight from life) such and such a constituted, animated figure or form. The figure has to that extent, as you see, *been* placed—placed in the imagination that detains it, preserves, protects, enjoys it, conscious of its presence in the dusky, crowded, heterogeneous back-shop of the mind very much as a wary dealer in precious odds and ends, competent to make an "advance" on rare objects confided to him, is conscious of the rare little "piece" left in deposit by the reduced, mysterious lady of title or the speculative amateur, and which is already there to disclose its merit afresh as soon as a key shall have clicked in a cupboard-door. (3:xii)

I have dared to cite all of this long passage both because it is all of a piece, not easily truncated, and because it is such a splendid example of

Jamesian evasiveness. James keeps secrets, not by just hiding them, but by talking around and around them until the reader is bewildered by James's eloquence and so led successfully off the track. James's topic here is his responsibility to "place" Isabel, that is, in one at least of the meanings of "place," to tell the reader where he got her as the central protagonist of his novel. It would be nice if he could do this, says James, that is, do such a subtle and monstrous thing as write the history of the growth of his imagination, that is, the story of how a given "figure or form" had been transferred straight from life into his imagination. He does not say he could not do that, but he distinctly refrains from doing it. The possible confession remains a blank place in the passage. It is as though James were hinting, "I could if I would, but I won't." Has he not told the reader that it would be "monstrous" to reveal such an intimate secret? Exactly what would be monstrous about doing that he does not say, unless he means to play on the etymology of the monster as something uncanny, gruesome, or unnatural that is exposed, shown forth, "demonstrated." Instead of the confession or bringing to light of Isabel's "source" in "life," James gives the reader a spectacular extended image. This image displaces the concept of "placing." It so dazzles the reader that, it may be, he or she forgets to notice that James has avoided doing what he says he might have done, something that would have interested the reader greatly, that is, told the reader what real person served as the model for Isabel. The reader, this reader at least, may wonder if that mysterious source may not have been Henry James himself. Isabel is an innocent maiden who reads a lot in a lonely house in Albany, New York, just as young Henry actually did. Isabel is extremely imaginative and has extremely large designs on life, as young Henry also no doubt was and had.

According to the new meaning of placement, Isabel, as a possible protagonist for a fiction, has been "placed" in James's imagination as a precious objet d'art of mysterious provenance is placed in a locked cupboard in an antiquarian's shop. Four observations may be made about this elaborate figure. (1) It serves as a decoy to lead the reader away from the curiosity James himself has aroused about Isabel's origin. (2) It defines the Jamesian imagination as an overcrowded, incoherent superabundance. Isabel as potential subject was sequestered "in the dusky, crowded, heterogeneous back-shop of the mind." (3) The figure makes James not unlike the villain of *The Portrait of a Lady*, Gilbert Osmond, and even a little like the effeminate Ned Rosier, too. Rosier collects bibelots and cares more about them than about anything else. To sell his valuable collection so he can have enough money to marry Osmond's daughter, Pansy, is, for him, a tremendous sacrifice. Osmond's cardinal sin is to treat Isabel as another precious object to add to *his* collection. To treat a person like a thing, what could be more reprehensible?

James, in the sentences just following the long quotation I have made, speaks of his "pious desire but to place my treasure right." "I quite remind myself thus," he continues, "of the dealer resigned not to 'realize,' resigned to keeping the precious object locked up indefinitely rather than commit it, at no matter what price, to vulgar hands. For there *are* dealers in these forms and figures and treasures capable of that refinement" (3:xii). (4) No doubt what James "literally" means is that he was not going to exploit his carefully hoarded "image of the young feminine nature" (3:xii) on anything less than a major novelistic effort. If James is a refined dealer like the kind he claims does exist, his figure irresistibly recalls the central motif of *The Golden Bowl*, written, of course, a few years before this preface. The curious little antique dealer in that novel keeps the golden bowl locked away just as James here expresses it in his extended figure. The dealer in *The Golden Bowl* will also, at least so he says, sell the bowl only to someone able to appreciate it. That it has a fatal crack, as Prince Amerigo observes in an instant when Charlotte is about to buy the bowl, casts a strange shadow on Isabel as fictional motif, if the reader threads his or her way through the labyrinth of displacements, disguises, and deviations back to Isabel herself. In what way, if any, does she have a fatal flaw? This might be posed as a conundrum: "How is Isabel like the golden bowl?" Whether this riddle has an answer can be found only by reading, what is called "really reading," if that can be done, James's first and last masterpieces, *The Portrait of a Lady* and *The Golden Bowl*.

Yet a third meaning of "place" is the placement of Isabel Archer in her social milieu and in relation to the other characters in the novel. Once more James evades specificity. As for the source of the characters that surround Isabel in the novel, James confesses (or at any rate claims) that he cannot remember where they came from any more than he can, or will, tell us where he got Isabel:

> my memory, I confess, is a blank as to how and whence they came. I seem to myself to have waked up one morning in possession of them—of Ralph Touchett and his parents, of Madame Merle, of Gilbert Osmond and his daughter and his sister, of Lord Warburton, Caspar Goodwood and Miss Stackpole, the definite array of contributions to Isabel Archer's history. . . . It was as if they had simply, by an impulse of their own, floated into my ken, and all in response to my primary question: "Well, what will she *do*?" (3:xvii)

The reader, this skeptical reader at any rate, may be permitted to say "Uh *huh*" (with a rising cadence) in response to this further evasion.

James's decision to write about Isabel and the rest, the preface says, was ungrounded and irrecoverable. Suddenly, from nowhere, he had what he needed. He cannot account for his decision. It happened because it happened, out of the blue. The source or ground is a forever impenetrable secret, either because he cannot tell or because he will not. This secret is like the contents of Milly Theale's letter, in *The Wings of the Dove*, which Kate Croy burns. No one will ever know its contents. Whether or not decisions made by the characters within the novel are at all like James's decision to write the novel remains to be seen. The reader can, however, conclude that, dazzlingly eloquent though it is, the preface still leaves the reader with the obligation to read the novel in order to decide its meaning and purport.

Isabel's Decisions

The problematic of decision, the reader will remember, is my primary concern in this chapter. Most of all, I want to understand Isabel's decision to return to Gilbert Osmond. The two most important decisions Isabel makes are to accept Osmond's proposal of marriage and, much later, at the end of the novel, to return to Osmond even though her marriage to him is miserably unhappy. Both decisions are registered in speech acts, though the first, curiously enough, is not reported directly in the novel. The second also has peculiarities, which I shall discuss later. Other crucial decisions are Isabel's repeated rejections of her two other suitors' proposals, those of Caspar Goodwood and Lord Warburton. What the text says about all these speech acts will be my primary data.

What could have brought someone so intelligent, so sensitive, so fond of her liberty to make the disastrous mistake of agreeing to marry a man so awful as Gilbert Osmond? Isabel does not have the excuse of having been bamboozled. Osmond tells her clearly enough what sort of person he is. He informs her, for example, absurdly and as a kind of joke, but with a sinister resonance of truth, that the only person he really envies is the pope. He would like to have been pope (3:382). Nor has Isabel been entrapped by Madame Merle, as she admits to herself at one crucial moment of self-understanding. Apropos of the attractive possibility of blaming Madam Merle, the narrator reports, in indirect discourse, her reflection: "It might feed her sense of bitterness, but it would not loosen her bonds.

It was impossible to pretend that she had not acted with her eyes open; if ever a girl was a free agent she had been. A girl in love was doubtless not a free agent; but the sole source of her mistake had been within herself. There had been no plot, no snare; she had looked and considered and chosen" (4:160–61).

Why did Isabel choose as she did? Does she do the right thing to stick with Osmond even after she knows with full clarity what a mistake she has made, how she has thrown her life away? What brings her to decide to stay with him? On what grounds are her two life-determining decisions made?

The immediate data the novel gives, on the basis of which the reader must decide about Isabel's decisions, can be quickly identified.

Isabel's decision to marry Osmond, her saying "Yes" to his proposal, is not ever given in so many words in the novel. The reader is shown Isabel rejecting Osmond's overtures in Rome and then told that she goes to Greece, Turkey, and Egypt with Madame Merle. The latter, the reader will remember, is Osmond's friend, at one time his mistress and the mother of his daughter Pansy. Madame Merle introduced Isabel to Osmond. Whatever Isabel thinks, Madame Merle has plotted with Osmond to get Isabel to marry Osmond so he can have her money and add another exquisite object to his collection. The reader sees Isabel rejecting Osmond's advances and affirmations of love. Her response when he says, "I find I'm in love with you," and "I'm absolutely in love with you," is to say, "Oh don't say that please." She says this "with an intensity that expressed the dread of having, in this case too, to choose and decide. What made her dread great was precisely the force which, as it would seem, ought to have banished all dread—the sense of something within herself, deep down, that she supposed to be inspired and trustful passion. It was there like a large sum stored in a bank[23]—which there was a terror in having to begin to spend. If she touched it, it would all come out" (2:17–18). Then, after a leap of a whole year, about which remarkably little is narrated, we see Isabel again at the beginning of chapter 32 about to have a painful scene with Caspar Goodwood over her engagement to Osmond, just as she will have equally painful scenes with Mrs. Touchett and Ralph Touchett over the same event. The event itself, however, is not narrated. Nor is her marriage narrated directly. The reader sees her before she is married. The reader then sees her after her marriage. Two decisive events in Isabel's life are blanks in the narration. They are never made present to the reader. The reader learns that the marriage has been consummated only through a brief reference to the fact that Isabel has had a sickly baby who has died after six months. The actual marriage ceremony is referred to much later by Ralph, in a retrospective reminiscence recalling his attendance at the wedding. The wedding, however, is not narrated directly, in that intense past/present of the narration in which much of Isabel's life is recounted so completely and often in such moment to moment detail.

Why is this? Why does James not show directly just what he might have thought the reader would be most interested in seeing? Would it be "monstrous" to do so? In the preface James boasts about the completeness with which he has built this particular "literary monument." Presumably he could have presented the proposal, its acceptance, and the wedding directly if he had wanted to do so. Why this inexplicable hiatus or break in the narration? Why does the narrator keep just these secrets from the reader? Is there perhaps something unspeakable or non-narratable about these two moments of decision? The narrator has no difficulty recounting in detail Isabel's repeated refusals of proposals from Caspar Goodwood and Lord Warburton (though Caspar's first failed proposal is elided, just as is Osmond's successful proposal). It seems that it would have been easy enough to recount in detail the successful proposal and the wedding. The answers to these questions (there *are* answers!) must abide a more exact identification of James's notion of decision.

Isabel's second crucial moment of decision, the one that leads her to return to Osmond, is more circumstantially presented. Here the narrator, so it appears, keeps no secrets from the reader. Isabel has defied her husband's prohibition against returning to Gardencourt. After Ralph's death, Isabel, as I have shown, hovers in indecision about whether to return to Osmond and her abysmally miserable marriage. Caspar Goodwood implores her to "trust me" (4:431), to abandon her marriage and run away with him: "It's too monstrous of you to think of sinking back into that misery, of going to open your mouth to that poisoned air. It's you that are out of your mind. Trust me as if I had the care of you. Why shouldn't we be happy—when it's here before us, when it's so easy? I'm yours for ever— for ever and ever. Here I stand; I'm as firm as a rock. . . . If you'll only trust me, how little you will be disappointed! The world's all before us—and the world's very big" (4:434).

How many men have said something like that to innocent maidens or to not so innocent married women: "Trust me!" The echo of the end of Milton's *Paradise Lost* in "The world's all before us" (echoed once before earlier in the novel to define Isabel's sense of the boundless freedom that she sees in her future when she has inherited a big piece of her uncle's fortune) indicates the nature of this appeal. It is made by one fallen human being to another, in full knowledge of good and evil on both sides. Nevertheless, Goodwood keeps a somewhat charming and beguiling, incorruptible American innocence in thinking Isabel can start over again with him. Isabel's response is immediate: " 'Do me the greatest kindness of all,' she panted. 'I beseech you to go away!' " (4:436). Caspar's response is a kind of virtual rape. He embraces her and kisses her on the lips. I have already cited this textual kiss. The event is recorded in white and black, on the one hand, the brightness of lightning that is, paradoxically, like being drowned and, on the other hand, the darkness both of the actual scene on the lawn at Gardencourt in the dusk and of Isabel's moral darkness.

Goodwood's kiss instantly precipitates moral clarity and Isabel's decision to return to Osmond. Is that the right path for Isabel? On what grounds does she decide to take that path? Those are my basic questions in this chapter. I do not find them all that easy to answer, especially if I follow Reuben Brower's injunction and base my answers on the text, trying my best not to import preconceived ideas into the text.

On What Grounds?

The text ought to be enough. It ought to provide answers to the questions I have asked, since the novel has Isabel's turn away from Goodwood toward the straight path back to Rome as its goal or endpoint. The intelligibility of the novel depends on the intelligibility of Isabel's climactic double turn. Nor does James refrain from claiming that he has ensured this intelligibility. In the passage from the preface already cited, James boasts that he has made "the chequered pavement, the ground under the reader's feet" (presumably meaning by this the reason or ground that explains why things happen as they do happen in the novel's action) cover the whole surface of the floor, from wall to wall under all the overarching vaults of the big structure. Another such claim is made by James's assertion in the preface that he has, in the "anxiety of [his] provision for the reader's amusement," felt that "no such provision could be excessive" (3:xvi). He means presumably by this to justify the great length of the novel, its status as a "literary monument" (3:xvi) made of all those little bricks. The implicit assurance is that he has left nothing out. He has kept no secrets from the reader. He has told the whole story, in perhaps even excessive detail. He has done this so that the reader can not only be "amused," but also can have all the information necessary to pass judgment on Isabel's actions and decisions. We can trust him to have told all. Whether or not this is really the case remains to be seen.

The answers to questions about the grounds and the rightness or rectitude of Isabel's ultimate decision must be sought in the fine grain of the text itself. Or at least an understanding of why such questions cannot be answered must be sought there. To let some of my cats on the table (a metaphor I borrow from J. L. Austin),[24] I do not believe the answer can be given by arguing that *The Portrait of a Lady* in any straightforward way simply reflects the conditions of women and marriage conventions at the time the novel was written (1879). James goes out of his way to assert that neither Isabel Archer nor Gilbert Osmond, nor, indeed, the other characters, are "types." This is asserted in a passage describing Isabel's sense of Osmond's uniqueness. The passage is worth quoting at length. It indicates James's (or at least Isabel's, since there may be some irony at Isabel's expense in the passage) sense of the individuality of the novel's people. They are not representatives of social types or classes. The passage suggests that James intended his characters to appear as more or less singular. They are at most quite idiosyncratic embodiments of types:

> He [Osmond] resembled no one she had ever seen; most of the people she knew might be divided into groups of half a dozen specimens. There were one or two exceptions to this; she could think for instance of no group that would contain her aunt Lydia. There were other people who were, relatively speaking, original—original, as one might say, by courtesy—such as Mr. Goodwood, as her cousin Ralph, as Henrietta Stackpole, as Lord Warburton, as Madame Merle. [This is more or less a complete list of all the major characters in the novel, with the exception of Isabel's uncle, who is by this time dead.] But in essentials, when one came to look at them, these individuals belonged to types already present to her mind. Her mind contained no class offering a natural place to Mr. Osmond—he was a specimen apart. . . . Madame Merle had had that note of rarity, but what quite other power it immediately gained when sounded by a man! It was not so much what he said and did, but rather what he withheld, that marked him for her as by one of those signs of the highly curious that he was showing her on the underside of old plates and in the corner of sixteenth-century drawings: he indulged in no striking deflections from common usage, he was original without being an eccentric. She had never met a person of so fine a grain. (3: 375–76)

The passage hints that Isabel's reasons for falling for Osmond are to some degree aesthetic. She admires him for his rarity, for his fine grain, just as Osmond values Isabel as another item for his collection, and just as James gives his novel a title that suggests the way he has turned his imaginary personage, modeled perhaps, as scholars have claimed, on his cousin Minny Temple, or perhaps, as I have suggested, on aspects of himself, into a work of art, an aesthetic object, a "portrait." Is Isabel, too, an aesthete? I shall return later to the question of aestheticism in this novel. In any case, Isabel herself is quite exceptionally intelligent, sensitive, free-spirited, and beautiful. Her remarkable sexual attractiveness is made clear in the way man after man falls violently and permanently in love with her—Caspar Goodwood, Lord Warburton, Ralph Touchett, even Gilbert Osmond, insofar as he can love any woman. He loves her, that is, or so he says, at least until he finds out his mistake. He comes to hate her because she has ideas and a mind of her own that he cannot control or possess. Osmond loves Isabel as a collector of rare objects loves one he has found but not yet taken possession of: "he [Osmond] perceived a new attraction in the idea of taking to himself a young lady who had qualified herself to figure in his collection of choice objects by declining so noble a hand [i.e., Lord Warburton's]" (4:9). Perhaps even the reader may fall in love with Isabel, as James himself may be imagined to have done. Certainly I have fallen in love with her. That may cloud my vision, since love, as we know, is blind. For me to be able to say that I have fallen in love with Isabel is an indication that the gender of a reader is never without significance. What does that mean, falling in love with an imaginary personage, a personage one has met in a book and can meet in no other way, can never touch or hold? Could it be that James's powerlessness, like the reader's, is represented in the novel itself by Ralph Touchett's mortal illness, which puts him in the situation of loving Isabel, as all the men in the novel do, but loving, as he puts it at one point, "without hope"? James's powerlessness is perhaps compounded by his presumed homosexuality.

Gilbert Osmond, in any case, is presented as quite exceptionally awful. He is not an example of the common run of patriarchal males. It will not do to transfer to him without modification generalizations about nineteenth-century patriarchy and the subordination of women. Osmond and Madame Merle are consummate villains, among the greatest in literature. Osmond is a more or less "motiveless malignity." He matches even Iago in villainy. None of the main characters is "typical," or fully explicable by reference to social and historical conditions of the times and places represented in the novel, though it is certainly significant that they are all, with the exception of Lord Warburton, expatriate Americans.

James, in the preface, says the main question for him once he had conceived Isabel's character was: "What will she 'do'?" (3:xx). Isabel asks herself the same question, with a shift from the cognitive "will" to the performative "ought." This happens in the great chapter of Isabel's midnight vigil, which James in the preface, you will remember, calls "obviously the best thing in the book" (3:xxi): "what ought *she* to do?" (4:202). Isabel is not a passive victim of others or of the social condition of women at the time. She is exceptionally intelligent, beautiful, rich, and free. What happens to her happens because of things she does.

If the text gives little support to a reading based entirely upon cultural generalizations about the situation of women in the West at the time of the novel, it will be necessary to see what the novel does say about her fate if we are to understand what she does and what happens to her as a result of that doing. I have not imposed the portentous word *fate* from outside the novel. James uses the word at one point in the preface. Speaking of his "grasp of a single character," that is, Isabel, as the germ of the novel, James says "all urgently, all tormentingly, I saw [the character] in motion and, so to speak, in transit. That amounts to saying that I saw it as bent upon its fate—some fate or other; *which*, among the possibilities, being precisely the question" (3:xi).

A Tissue of Performatives

The Portrait of a Lady presents social intercourse as a complex integument of performative utterances, gestures, and even thoughts: promises, vows, declarations, decisions, assertions of belief, accusations, excuses, lies, and the like. Each invites commentary. Sometimes three or more instances are recorded on a single page, either in the give and take of conversation or in such forms as the silent promise to oneself as reported by the narrator. Does an interior speech act have any validity? It is not publicly uttered and endorsed by others, but it nevertheless may be binding on the person who makes it. It may decisively determine a person's future action.

Isabel's two decisive speech acts, her saying "Yes" to Osmond and then implicitly renewing her vows to him at the end of the novel, are placed in the context of a long series of what speech act theory would recognize as performatives. These punctuate the novel with moments when someone does something with words. Each of these speech acts deflects the course of the action in ways large or small. An example would be the change in his will old Mr. Touchett makes on his deathbed at his son Ralph's insistence. He alters his will to leave Isabel seventy thousand pounds, a great fortune in those days. Ralph's motive in persuading his father to do that is to give Isabel, whom he so loves and admires, full scope for the exercise of her imaginative freedom. This change in Touchett's will is an explicit legal performative requiring a competent lawyer, witnesses, signatures, and a following of all the proper procedures. The person who makes a will or changes one must, for example, be of sound mind and not coerced. The first example of a performative speech act J. L. Austin gives in *How to Do Things with Words* is "I give and bequeath my watch to my brother." Austin's point is that it is not a "felicitous" performative if all the circumstances are not correct, for example, if your brother is holding a gun to your head when you sign, or if you do not have a watch to bequeath, or if no one witnesses your signature.

Mr. Touchett's performative act of changing his will is really Ralph's act, since it involves Ralph's forswearing half of his own inheritance. The bequest to Isabel, it might be argued, is a good example of the disjunction between performative and constative utterances that de Man hypothesizes. Ralph wants to give Isabel full scope to live according to her remarkable love of liberty. He believes he knows that making her rich will help that. The result is the opposite of what he intends and thinks he knows will happen. He aims at a bear and an innocent bird falls out of the sky. That Isabel is now a rich, unmarried young woman, beautiful and highly intelligent to boot, makes Madame Merle and Gilbert Osmond decide to entrap her so Osmond can get her money. The performative Ralph's father enacts certainly leads Ralph to get more knowledge, but what neither he nor the reader can ever know, what, it may be, is the only thing worth knowing, is why his intentions go wrong, why Isabel made that mistake, and why, therefore, Mr. Touchett's decision to change his will made him "the beneficent author of infinite woe" (4:193), as Isabel until late in the novel mistakenly thinks. Ralph, not his father, was, rather, the author of that woe. Isabel only discovers that Ralph had decided her fate in this way late in the novel. Madame Merle tells her this, in revenge, when Isabel learns that she, Madame Merle, is Pansy's mother. "At bottom it's him [Ralph] you've to thank," says Madame Merle (4:388).

Another example of an explicit performative utterance occurs when Osmond accuses Isabel of preventing Lord Warburton from proposing to his daughter Pansy. "I accuse you" is a paradigmatic performative. "I think you accuse me of something very base," says Isabel. Osmond replies, "I accuse you of not being trustworthy" (4:264). Warburton, the reader is led to believe through various insinuations, has abandoned the idea of marrying Pansy when he realizes clearly, with a little highly indirect help from Isabel, that he wants to do so only so he can be near Isabel, whom he still loves, though she is now a married woman. Isabel has prevented Lord Warburton from marrying Pansy at least in part because she knows Pansy is really in love with Ned Rosier. Isabel is indeed in a way guilty of the "baseness" of which her husband accuses her, though she acts out of the highest motives toward both Pansy and Lord Warburton.

The give and take of interlocution among the characters is often carried on by declarations, promises, accusations, lies, and the like, especially interchanges between two characters who are in one way or another antagonists. A lie works performatively, if it is believed. It is a way of doing things with words. This use of speech acts is most frequent in one-on-one exchanges in this novel, even if the antagonism is not overt or is a concomitant of love. The astute reader needs to become sensitive to these speech acts and learn to notice them. The novel, as I have said, like most nineteenth-century and modernist novels, is carried on for the most part through alternation between the narrator's presentation in indirect discourse of the interiority of one of the characters and scenes in which two characters confront one another in dialogue. The sequence of the latter forms a slow rotation, setting each of the characters, sooner or later, face to face with each of the others in turn. A good example of the tête-à-tête, or what James called, with reference to stage drama, the "scenic," is the encounter between Isabel and Lord Warburton after the former is married and while Lord Warburton is considering a proposal of marriage to Pansy. I have already cited the narrator's description of the long look they exchange. The meanings conveyed back and forth by that look, a constative exchange of information, leads Lord Warburton to a negative speech act, that is, the decision not to send the letter he has written to Gilbert Osmond asking his permission to propose to Osmond's daughter Pansy. Warburton makes a decision not to propose, that is, a decision to abort a speech act, or, rather, writing act, he has already prepared.

What a person *is*, for James, it might be said, is revealed in how he or she talks to others, since talking is acting, doing, as well as in what the narrator, with his or "its" extraordinary power of penetration, can see of the character's feelings and thoughts. *The Portrait of a Lady* is made up of a long series of delicate notations of these two sorts, requiring the reader to keep perpetually alert and vigilant, prepared to read between the lines for meanings that the characters try to hide from one another. The narrator often only intimates these meanings to the reader. They are not said in so many words.

The presupposition throughout the novel is that the narrator has clairvoyance and can see what is going on in the minds and feelings of all the characters, though he (or she, or it) does not always choose to share that clairvoyance with the reader, whereas the characters are opaque to one another. Isabel must take it on faith that the various men who say they love her are not lying. It is a feature of declarations of love that they must be taken on faith, which makes them peculiar forms of speech acts, not verifiable constative statements. In the passage just referred to, Isabel does not have direct access to Lord Warburton's mind and feelings. She must infer and guess, from external signs, facial expressions, gestures, words, often lying or dissembling words. Those facial expressions, gestures, words are more performative than cognitive. They have an effect on their witness or auditor. They make a demand for interpretation and belief. It might be said that the whole novel is a web of innumerable performative signs or utterances, or, more exactly, of signs and utterances that have a performative as well as a cognitive dimension.

Some performatives, however, are more salient than others. These mark turning points in the action. When, at the beginning of the novel, Isabel says "Yes" to her aunt's invitation to accompany her to Europe, her adventure in life begins. Actually, she says, having at first refused to promise to do everything her aunt tells her to do ("I don't think I can promise that"): "And yet, to go to Florence, . . . I'd promise almost anything!" (3:35). This is not so much a promise as the "mention" of a promise, a promise to promise.

Most of Isabel's other crucial, determining moments of decision thereafter involve her saying "No" to someone's proposal of marriage. She repeatedly says "No" to both Caspar Goodwood and Lord Warburton. Her other determining decision, besides saying "Yes" to Osmond and renewing that allegiance at the very end of the novel, is her resolution to defy her husband and return to England to see the dying Ralph Touchett one more time. She says this was not a deliberate, reasoned decision, but a spontaneous act. She just goes to Ralph. But is any true decision, for James, ever deliberate and reasoned? That is a crucial question in any reading of *The Portrait of a Lady*. Isabel's "decision" to return to England leads the Countess Gemini to decide to reveal to Isabel the secret of the old liaison between Osmond and Madame Merle and the fact that Madame Merle is Pansy's mother.

Just Say "No" (or "Yes")

In nineteenth-century Western culture (as opposed to cultures in which marriages are arranged, for example, in Nepal still today), great pressure from family and friends about a marriage choice was seen as legitimate. Nevertheless, the freedom to say "Yes" or "No" to a marriage proposal was generally recognized as an unmarried woman's right. The daughter was "owned" by her father as long as she was unmarried. She was then "given" at the wedding by her father to her husband as her new lord and master. Even so, this transaction was impossible unless the young woman said "Yes," thereby "engaging" herself in a contractual way, and then later said "I do" in the marriage ceremony. These two stages toward wifehood are indubitable performative utterances, with legal or quasi-legal binding force on the one who utters them.

Speaking of Lady Glencora's love for the "worthless" Burgo Fitzgerald and her marriage to Plantagenet Palliser, whom she does not love (in Anthony Trollope's *Can You Forgive Her?*), Trollope comments in *An Autobiography*: "To save a girl from wasting herself, and an heiress from wasting her property on such a scamp was certainly the duty of the girl's friends. But it must ever be wrong to force a girl into a marriage with a man she does not love."[25] The reader will note that Trollope speaks of Glencora's person as a quasi-monetary commodity, not unlike her fortune, something that can be "wasted" and that should not be wasted. Isabel Archer is even less subject to coercion than Glencora. Her parents are dead. Her remaining relatives and friends, Mrs. Touchett (her aunt), Ralph Touchett (her cousin), her two married sisters, her friend Henrietta Stackpole, though in various degrees they strongly disapprove of her marriage to Osmond, make no effective attempt to stop her. Nor do they try to make her accept Caspar Goodwood or Lord Warburton, the two suitors whom she has rejected before accepting Osmond. "I never meddle," says Mrs. Touchett (4:55). Ralph, though he warns Isabel against Osmond, makes a point of giving her freedom to do as she likes. He is sure, wrongly, that she'll "please herself, of course; but she'll do so by studying human nature at close quarters and yet retaining her liberty" (3:396).

Mrs. Touchett, Ralph's mother, tells him: "The two words in the language I most respect are Yes and No. If Isabel wants to marry Mr. Osmond she'll do so in spite of all your comparisons. Let her alone to find a fine one herself for anything she undertakes" (3:395). Mrs. Touchett here distinguishes performative utterances (Yes and No) from tropological comparisons that can always be falsely adduced to justify Yeses or Nos. The latter, Mrs. Touchett implies, are the only things that really matter. They make something happen. They are also arbitrary, capricious, and fortuitous. They are not reasonably justified by any of the precedents or similarities that may be adduced to make them sound logical.

Mrs. Touchett's admiration for Yes and No chimes oddly with its probable source in what Jesus says in Matthew 5:36–37: "Neither shalt thou swear by thy head, because thou canst not make one hair white or black. But let your communication be, Yea, yea; Nay, nay: for whatsoever is more than these cometh of evil." Jesus is preaching against blasphemous or superstitious oaths, for example, "I swear by my head that I shall do it," whereas Mrs. Touchett is arguing against the use of figures (comparisons) to support a decision. In both cases, however, the tropological (a shift from swearing in God's name to swearing by your head; supporting a decision to marry Osmond by a fine analogy) is said to lack efficacy because it is arbitrary and powerless. You cannot make one hair white or black by swearing by your head. Ralph's high-minded comparisons of Isabel's suitors to besiegers at her gate seem valueless to Mrs. Touchett: "He expressed this view, somewhat after this fashion, to his mother, who looked at him as if he had been dancing a jig. He had such a fanciful, pictorial way of saying things that he might as well address her in the deaf-mute's alphabet" (3:395). The astute reader will note that the narrator, in the figures of the jig and the deaf-mute's alphabet, uses the same rhetorical device that Mrs. Touchett deplores and cannot understand. Both Jesus and Mrs. Touchett praise unadorned speech acts that seal a contract or make a promise by a simple Yes or deny one by a simple No. Efficacious performatives, both seem to feel, have no place for the tropological. The tropological is the realm of the constative, in its assertion that this is like that. Nevertheless, the blind positing of a similarity that can never be cognitively demonstrated contaminates the constative in such extravagant figures as those Ralph uses. The extravagance of the tropes calls attention to what is arbitrary about them. Anything can be compared to anything, more or less.

In his own way, and with whatever reserve of irony, James is expressing by way of Mrs. Touchett just the discrepancy between blind performative positing and tropological reasoning or cognition that de Man identifies in passages already cited. You say "Yes" or "No," and you can always justify it with a comparison to some precedent, but the comparison is itself another positing, not an objective parallel. Whatever Isabel decides, says Mrs. Touchett, she'll be able to claim is justified on the authority of some comparison: "Let her alone to find one [a 'comparison'] herself for anything she undertakes."

Madame Merle, as part of her ever so carefully calculated manipulation of Isabel into accepting Gilbert Osmond's proposal, gives Isabel some worldly advice. The advice presupposes Isabel's right to say "No," but also presupposes that the only course open to a young unmarried woman is ultimately to say "Yes." This need sooner or later to use her one moment of freedom was powerfully instilled in a young woman in that culture. This was the case even in young women with so exceptional a desire to be free and autonomous as Isabel. Isabel's freedom is like money in the bank, as is her passion, her capacity to love. Ultimately she is expected to spend it. "It's a very good thing," says Madame Merle, "for a girl to have refused a few good offers—so long of course as they are not the best she's likely to have. Pardon me if my tone seems horribly corrupt; one must take the worldly view sometimes. Only don't keep on refusing for the sake of refusing. It's a pleasant exercise of power; but acccepting's after all an exercise of power as well. There's always the danger of refusing once too often" (3:289–90). If Isabel had really followed these precepts she would certainly have already accepted Lord Warburton's offer. Almost everyone around her, except perhaps Ralph, cannot understand why she has not accepted him. As she thinks to herself, "nineteen women out of twenty would have accommodated themselves to it [the narrowness of being Lady Warburton] without a pang"(3:195), whereas for Isabel the idea of marrying Lord Warburton, in the narrator's faintly ironic, pompous account of her feelings, "failed to support any enlightened prejudice in favor of the free exploration of life that she had hitherto entertained or was now capable of entertaining" (3:155). Isabel sees marriage to Caspar Goodwood or to Lord Warburton as a curtailment of her liberty, whereas marriage to Gilbert Osmond, she very wrongly thinks, will open up endless vistas of freedom combined with specific duties. That combination is what she wants. As Isabel ultimately recognizes, in the midnight vigil that constitutes a central episode in the novel, marriage to Osmond puts her within labyrinthine corridors leading to a dead end, or, rather, within an enclosed room without windows.

The figure of the labyrinth is used in what is surely the suppressed source text for Isabel's vigil, Dorothea Brooke's midnight vigil when she confronts the disaster of her marriage to Edward Casaubon: "Dorothea had not distinctly observed but felt with a stifling depression, that the large vistas and wide fresh air which she had dreamed of finding in her husband's mind were replaced by ante-rooms and winding passages which seemed to lead nowhither. . . . Having once embarked on your marital voyage, it is impossible not to be aware that you make no way and that the sea is not within sight—that, in fact, you are exploring an enclosed basin."[26] James's narrator records with the same grave irony Isabel's sense of enclosure after her marriage:

> She could live it over again, the incredulous terror with which she had taken the measure of her dwelling. Between those four walls she had lived ever since; they were to surround her for the rest of her life. It was the house of darkness, the house of dumbness, the house of suffocation. Osmond's beautiful mind gave it neither light nor air; Osmond's beautiful mind indeed seemed to peep down from a small high window and mock at her. . . . When she saw this rigid system close about her, draped though it was in pictured tapestries, that sense of darkness and suffocation of which I have spoken took possession of her; she seemed shut up with an odor of mould and decay. (4:196, 199)

The attentive reader will note that the figure here echoes the famous passage in the preface, written almost thirty years later, of course, that says the house of fiction has many windows, at each of which "stands a figure with a pair of eyes" (3:x–xi). The echo is more than merely nominal. It tells the reader that, if Osmond's ironic and life-destroying surveillance of Isabel is diabolic, there may be something sinister in the secret surveillance of social life that generates works of fiction—James's, for example. Or Osmond's perpetual spying on Isabel may be compared to that of the narrator, who throughout the novel can see Isabel, see into her most secret thoughts and feelings, without being seen in return. This is the problematic privilege of the so-called omniscient or, to use Royle's better term, *telepathic* narrator. Such mind-reading is, one might argue, even more sinister than Osmond's surveillance of Isabel, since Isabel is at least aware that the latter is taking place, whereas it is a rule of third person telepathic narrations that the characters are never aware of the narrator. Neither Dorothea Brooke in *Middlemarch* nor Isabel Archer in *The Portrait of a Lady* is aware that her story is being told, her most intimate secrets revealed.

Isabel's Anagnorisis in Context

Isabel's disastrous decision to marry Gilbert Osmond leads eventually to new knowledge, knowledge that she has made a big mistake, but also more knowledge of the wickedness in people around her. In order to understand better what is a stake in Isabel's moment of recognition or discovery, it will be helpful to put it in a somewhat wider context. Aristotle called this moment of insight the "anagnorisis," the ending of a specific ignorance. For Aristotle, the revelation of something hitherto secret marks a turning point, or "peripeteia," in the action. That turn, like Isabel's turn back toward Rome, precipitates the denouement of a tragedy. An example is Oedipus's discovery that he has killed his father and married his mother. The denouement involves in one way or another a decision based on the new knowledge. Oedipus decides to take the guilt upon himself and to punish himself by putting out his eyes so that he cannot see his mother-wife or his children-siblings. He condemns himself to wandering and exile. Oedipus pronounces himself a patricide and guilty of mother-son incest. This performative acceptance of guilt follows upon his cognitive illumination. What Isabel ultimately does, the reader knows. She decides to return to Osmond. What basis she has for that decision is not yet clear, nor is it clear whether or not we can approve of it as the right decision.

In order to approach that, I must identify the context of Isabel's moment of discovery or recognition. Her anagnorisis is registered in her midnight self-confrontation. This recognition is precipitated by a particularly cruel turn in Osmond's mistreatment of her. He tells her that he expects her to bring about Lord Warburton's proposal to his daughter Pansy. Warburton has proposed to her (Isabel) and has been refused. That, Osmond holds, gives her power over him: "Well, I hold that it lies in your hands. I shall leave it there. With a little good-will you may manage it. Think that over and remember how much I count on you" (4:185). This puts Isabel in a double bind. She wants to obey and please her husband as much as she can. She makes it a point of honor and duty to do so. At the same time, she suspects that Warburton contemplates marrying Pansy just so he can be near Isabel, whom he still loves as much as ever. What should she *do*?

Isabel's vigil takes place in the context of a long series of similar scenes in Victorian fiction, in which recognition precipitates decision and action. These scenes are peculiar or distinctive in that they do not involve, as in Jane Austin's novels, for example, or in many scenes in Anthony Trollope's novels, the consideration by the heroine of a proposal of marriage. This alternative motif or convention or archetype (one hardly knows what to call it) involves the recognition by a woman who has already engaged herself or has actually been married that she has made a horrible mistake, a lifelong mistake. Divorce in those days, seen as a mortal sin by Catholic dogma, was still extremely difficult and expensive to obtain through legal means in a Protestant country like England. You more or less had to be Henry VIII to do it. The injunction at the end of the marriage service ("Whom God hath joined let no man put asunder") was still taken seriously. Though a woman could break an engagement to marry, this was seen as an act of perjury, a breach of promise, that is, a particularly reprehensible speech act. Such foreswearing branded her as a "jilt." A jilt was, apparently, someone without solid grounds of selfhood allowing her to make a promise and keep it. This is Clara Middleton's fear for herself if she breaks her engagement to Willoughby in Meredith's *The Egoist*. Isabel says at one point that she takes promises seriously, that she always keeps promises once she has made them. The ability to make a promise and keep it, that is, to go on being the same person long enough to be faithful to a commitment once made, is the fundamental basis of morality in Friedrich Nietzsche's *Zur Genealogie der Moral* (*The Genealogy of Morals*). Misogynist fear of the flightiness, instability, and unfaithfulness of women runs all through J. L. Austin's *How to Do Things with Words*. It is seen as one of the chief obstacles to civil law and order, and to the securing of felicitous performatives. It is the woman who, in one of his examples, throws a monkey wrench into a marriage ceremony by saying "I will not" rather than "I will."[27]

Among the most salient scenes in Victorian fiction in which a woman is shown changing her mind when it is already too late is Cathy Earnshaw's confession to Nelly, in Emily Brontë's *Wuthering Heights*. She says that, though it would "degrade" her to marry Heathcliff, it will be wrong to carry out her engagement to Edgar Linton, since she is indissolubly linked to Heathcliff: "He's more myself than I am." Another such scene is Dorothea's all-night meditation in *Middlemarch*, already referred to as James's prime source for Isabel's vigil. Lady Glencora, in Trollope's *Can You Forgive Her?*, is shown trying to decide whether she should leave her husband, whom she does not love, to run away with the worthless Burgo Fitzgerald, whom she does love. In the climactic scene in Meredith's *The Egoist*, the heroine, Clara Middleton, is shown staying awake all night confronting the mistake she has made by engaging herself to Willoughby, the egoist. She asks herself whether breaking the engagement would simply prove that she is another young woman with no solid base in a self capable of making promises and keeping them. If so, she is so worthless that, in an ironical double bind, she might as well marry Willoughby. In all this sequence, James is no doubt most indebted to Dorothea's midnight meditation in *Middlemarch*.

Why Does Isabel Say "No" or "Yes"?

In the preface, the reader will remember, James makes a tacit promise to tell all, at least all about Isabel's consciousness and about other characters by way of her consciousness of their consciousnesses. That ought to make it easy to identify the grounds of Isabel's various decisions. This turns out, however, to be not all that easy. Let me, following Brower's Law, look a little more closely at what the text actually says about Isabel's moments of decision.

Isabel's first refusal of Goodwood is elided in the novel. It not narrated directly, nor is her actual acceptance of Osmond. It seems as if they were in some way impossible to represent. Her refusal of Warburton is made even before he proposes, that is, it is once more not recorded overtly, except after the fact. It is based on no more than what the narrator calls "a certain instinct, not imperious, but persuasive" (3:144). When Isabel has, offstage as it were, affianced herself to Gilbert Osmond, she is asked to explain her decision by Caspar Goodwood, by her aunt, Mrs. Touchett, and then by Ralph Touchett, in three successive painful confrontation scenes. She says the same thing each time. To Caspar: "Do you think I could explain if I would?" (4:51). To Mrs. Touchett: "I don't think it's my duty to explain to you. Even if it were I shouldn't be able. So please don't remonstrate; in talking about it you have me at a disadvantage. I can't talk about it" (4:55). To Ralph: "I can't explain to you what I feel, what I believe, and I wouldn't if I could" (4:72). In all these cases, the moment of decision is skipped over. It is a blank place in the narration. This systematic nonpresentation of Isabel's crucial moments of decision, the moments that would seem most dramatic, most important, and most in need of representation, seems to me exceedingly peculiar and in need of explanation. Perhaps it is the thing most requiring explanation in this novel.

In the prior context of these determining decisions, Isabel, at the very end of the novel, turns from Goodwood and starts for Rome and Osmond. Just why does Isabel go back to Osmond, now that the scales have fallen from her eyes and she "reads Osmond right," to adapt the phrase she employs in her midnight vigil of recognition? She admits to herself, "she had not read him right" (4:192). Several incompatible answers to this question are suggested by the text. After many readings and re-readings, I still do not see how one can with certainty decide among them. The reader should face that fact squarely if he or she wants to avoid Isabel's mistake of not reading right. By calling the reading situation "undecidable" I do not mean you can say anything you like about Isabel's motives, make any decision you like in presenting a reading. I mean that the text is overdetermined. It offers several determinable explanations that are incompatible. Each one of these can be supported by citations. The three chief possible explanations given in the text correspond, in one way or another, to the reigning modes of explaining literary texts these days: (1) textual or linguistic; (2) psychoanalytic; (3) cultural.

 1. Isabel says explicitly more than once that marriage vows are sacred and that she owes allegiance to her husband, even though he is "the deadliest of fiends," as Caspar calls him (4:432). She is, one reading might argue, bound by language, that is, by the promises and vows she has uttered: "He was not one of the best of husbands, but that didn't alter the case. Certain obligations were involved in the very fact of marriage, and were quite independent of the quantity of enjoyment extracted from it" (4:421). Isabel goes back, this reading would in addition claim, so she can help Pansy all she can. Isabel says she has promised Pansy to return, and she always keeps her promises. As Madame Merle says to Isabel on another occasion involving a visit to Pansy, "How much you think of your promises!" To which Isabel responds, "I think a great deal of my promises" (4:24–25). Isabel, according to this reading, has the kind of presumably admirable moral rectitude or "conscience," as Ralph calls it (3:319), that considers itself bound by speech acts and acts in accordance with vows made in the past. Kant, in the *Foundation of the Metaphysics of Morals*, asserts that the keeping of promises, like not telling lies, is the basis of morality. Nietzsche, as I have said, thinks the same in *The Genealogy of Morals*, though of course much more ironically. James seems to belong to this tradition. James's phrase "There was a very straight path" is of course an echo of the biblical injunction to follow the straight and narrow path of moral rectitude, as in Hebrews 12:13: "And make straight paths for your feet."

 2. Though the novel does not exactly say so, it could be argued, in a quite different reading, that Isabel is afraid of Caspar's masculine power. Many critics have taken this tack. Isabel has been attracted to Osmond because he is so little threatening sexually. She has, such a reader might argue, a deep distaste for, or fear of, heterosexual sex. This distaste, it may be, reflects James's own and cannot of course be spoken directly. Sex, for James, is always illicit and dark. An example is the extramarital liaison that produced Pansy and that precedes the novel. An act of adultery or fornication tends to turn out always already to have occurred in James's novels and stories, for example, in "The Aspern Papers," *The Ambassadors*, and *The Golden Bowl*, as well as in *The Portrait of a Lady* itself. Isabel's love

for Ralph is safe because he is dying. She can with security love him like a brother and even affirm that love by kissing his hand. Isabel is shown as resisting direct heterosexual approaches with a kind of fastidious distaste, as when she rejects, repeatedly, Warburton and Goodwood. She even, in a sense, rejects Ralph's love by refusing to be honest with him about her marital misery. Isabel at one point wonders "if she were not a cold, hard, priggish person" (3:157). She seems to have an instinctive resistance to being possessed by the aggressively masculine (in different ways) Warburton and Caspar. She is attracted by the softer and even effeminate Osmond. "She had never met a person of so fine a grain" (3:376). To be masculine, to be sexually assertive, is to have a coarse grain. The reader may guess, though the narrator does not say so, that after their mutual disappointment with one another and after the death of her baby, Isabel and Osmond sleep together rarely if at all. The baby that died after six months is mentioned, the reader may guess, primarily to assure the reader that the marriage was indeed consummated.

A somewhat different version of this particular way of filling in the blank between the kiss and the resolute decision would be Gert Buelens's interesting essay "Henry James's Oblique Possessions: Plottings of Desire and Mastery in *The American Scene*." This essay reads the kiss in *The Portrait of a Lady* in terms of "queer theory." Buelens argues that James posits a diffuse, transgendered sexual energy "saturating social space," as David Puente puts it in a note to me calling my attention to this essay. This energy, Buelens argues, Caspar passes on to Isabel when he kisses her. The power she takes in with the kiss gives her the courage to return to Osmond. Isabel appropriates "the erotic energies created by their contiguity for her own purposes."[28]

3. Ralph, however, in the last interview between him and Isabel, just before he dies, offers yet a third explanation for Isabel's decision to return to Osmond, in this case a cultural one: "I always understood," he says, "though it was so strange—so pitiful. You wanted to look at life for yourself—but you were not allowed; you were punished for your wish. You were ground in the very mill of the conventional!" (4:415). The trans-Atlantic society within which Isabel is embedded does not allow the freedom and openness to experience Isabel desires.

Why Does Isabel Return? Back to That Kiss

Is this the last word? Who or what, exactly, did not "allow" it? Who or what "punished her for her wish"? She says over and over that she has been free, that she decided on her own to marry Osmond, that she was not trapped. Is her problem too deep a sense of duty, as Ralph suggests (4:416) and as others repeatedly tell her?

An answer may be found by asking why Isabel takes promises so seriously. Well, the reader might argue, she has a big New England conscience. She wants to do her duty when she can find one to do. "You've too much power of thought," Ralph Touchett tells Isabel,"—above all too much conscience. . . . It's out of all reason, the number of things you think wrong. Put back your watch. Diet your fever. Spread your wings; rise above the ground. It's never wrong to do that" (3:319). This ideologeme of American puritanical conscience contradicts the contrary American love of limitless liberty, which Isabel also embodies. Her tragedy or her "fate" (James's word in the preface, you will remember, when he says he wanted to see what Isabel would *do*), could be said to be determined by the clash or contradiction between these two ideals. Both were deeply embedded in American culture, and still are. No way can be found to reconcile them. Both are goods, but if you fulfill one you are betraying the other. In Isabel's case, keeping promises wins out over the desire for infinite freedom and disponibility. Why? What possible good can there be in deciding to stick to a decision, commitment, or promise that turns out to have been made on the basis of a false interpretation, a bad reading, a terrible epistemological error? Answers might be phrased in several (incompatible) ways:

1. The necessarily mistaken decision (since you never know enough when you decide) puts Isabel in a new position, namely a position to be able to find out the truth about Osmond. It is out of loyalty to the blind performative making new knowledge possible that Isabel sticks to her promise to love and obey Osmond. She does this even when she knows that he is an egotist and that he hates her, hates her more and more. She honors the bad choice that has made her what she is. Only after you have made a decision that is a leap in the dark can you know what a big mistake you have made, and by then it is too late. You have decided. You have crossed the Rubicon and cannot swim back without drowning. This is the figure George Meredith employs in *The Ordeal of Richard Feverel* for the decisive commitment of Richard's life.[29] Once you have committed yourself, there is no returning to your disponibility, your unused freedom and what was, in a sense, your irresponsibility. How can I be held responsible if I have not yet decided, have not said "Yes" or "No"?

Once Isabel has said "Yes" to Osmond, once she has uttered solemn vows before the altar, she has only two choices. She is in a very different situation from her previous limitless freedom. She can either be true to the decision and the promise she has made or she can be false to them. If she leaves Osmond, there would be no reason why she could not go on changing later, whimsically, for no reason. If she sticks to her promise, she is doomed to a life of misery, yoked to a man who not only hates her for having a mind of her own but also has refined means of torturing her. Nevertheless, she retains her integrity, and in a paradoxical sense she retains her freedom. This would not have been the case if she had married or run away with Warburton or Goodwood. After all, such a reading might argue, the description of the kiss says the kiss made Isabel aware of what she does not like about Caspar Goodwood: "while she took it, she felt each thing in his hard manhood that had least pleased her, each aggressive fact of his face, his figure, his presence, justified of its intense identity and made one with this act of possession." Yielding to Caspar would be subservience worse than marriage to Osmond. The freedom she has, within the imprisonment of her marriage, is, among other things, the freedom to torment Osmond by her independence of mind.

2. Sticking to her promise to Osmond is, for James, for the narrator, and for Isabel, a way to avoid confronting the fact that selfhood is, as Montaigne put it, "wavering and diverse." Subjectivity has no solid basis in a perdurable, pre-existing, and indestructible selfhood. Selfhood is created and created anew from moment to moment by speech acts. You do not have a self first and then decide on the basis of that. You decide, for reasons that remain ineffably mysterious and unaccountable. The decision gives you a self. This means that a new decision will give you a new self, for example, if Isabel is false to her solemn marriage vows and runs off with Caspar Goodwood. Caspar's kiss precipitates instead the reverse result. In *Washington Square*, written at about the same time as *The Portrait of a Lady*, the heroine, Catherine Sloper, sticks to her foolish love for no other apparent reason than consistency. The Morris Townsend she fell in love with turns out to be nonexistent, just as the Gilbert Osmond Isabel was so charmed by turns out to be a phantom. Nevertheless, both Isabel and Catherine remain faithful to the bad commitments they have made.

3. Renunciation, for James, is, for some mysterious reason, the highest virtue. It certainly runs through all his novels, for example, in Maggie's renunciation of her privileges as an injured wife, or in Strether's returning to Woollett, Massachusetts, in *The Ambassadors*, because, as he says, "That, you see, is my only logic. Not, out of the whole affair, to have got anything for myself" (22:326). All James's fiction tells tales of renunciation and loss. These themes are what you come to expect when you have read a fair amount of James. James has an aesthetic resistance to happy endings, as

opposed to Anthony Trollope, for example. The latter takes the same materials (courtship and marriage) and almost always gives the reader the pleasure of a happy ending.

4. James is a sadist or Isabel a sado-masochist. She takes pleasure in suffering, in making herself or others suffer. Returning to Osmond is the cruelest thing Isabel can do to him, since her presence in his house, silently judging him all the time, is a mortal affront to him.

I have given a number of plausible explanations for why Caspar's kiss gives Isabel the knowledge she needs to decide to return to Osmond. I end by formulating the impossibility, in this case, of verifiable judgment or decision by the reader. By "verifiable" I mean a judgment based on what the text says rather than on unfounded hypotheses about the psychologies of the characters. Judith Butler, in a recent brilliant essay, "Values of Difficulty," has argued cogently that not enough textual evidence is available on which to base a judgment of the reasons Catherine Sloper, at the end of *Washington Square*, refuses Morris Townsend when he returns to propose to her at last.[30] I make a similar claim for Isabel's ultimate decision in *The Portrait of a Lady*. The novel does not tell the reader enough to confirm a reading. It leaves the reader unable to understand Isabel's decisions, therefore unable, if the reader does not import something from outside the text, to pass judgment on her decision as good or bad.

Final Return

I return to that kiss. The kiss, James says, gives Isabel knowledge. It tells her that she must return to Osmond. Why it tells her that, however, the novel does not say. The reader is free, of course, to bring in explanations from earlier in the novel, as I have done in the hypothetical explanations I have proposed, or to import explanations from other works by James, or from the surrounding culture, or from James's psychological makeup as we can figure that out from the evidence we have. There are two problems with doing any form of that, however. One is that the possible explanations provided from earlier passages or from elsewhere are contradictory and diverse. They do not make a coherent system. It is logically inconsistent to have all the reasons I have proposed at once, and yet textual citations can be made to support them all. They constitute a genuine "undecidable" reading situation, a nonsystematic system of incompatible possible readings that the text may be cited to support.

The other reason forbidding a judgment based on the text is that the description of the kiss says nothing definitively supporting any of them or authorizing a choice among them. Why Isabel decides, just what knowledge she gets, remains a secret. The text does not provide a textual basis on which to form a judgment, neither a constative one (asserting in so many words that gaining this or that knowledge is why she decided that way) nor a performative one ("I declare she did right [or wrong]," asserted by the narrator or even by Isabel or by some other character).

It is not an accident or an oversight that the narrator (or James himself) does not tell the reader, elides essential information, or keeps the secret. He would tell if he could, the reader may suppose, since he affirms in the preface that he has told everything he can (3:xvii). He cannot in principle, however much he might want to do so, given that the presuppositions that the novel exemplifies about decision, knowledge of the other and of one-self, tell how a performative (Caspar's words "Trust me," followed by a kiss that is an "act of possession") leads to knowledge. The movement from the one to the other is in principle unknowable. The two are incommensurable. It is not a matter of causation, with the performative causing the knowledge in some direct, intelligible line. The kiss in *The Portrait of a Lady* confirms, at least for this case, what Derrida says in *Force de loi* ("Force of Law") about decision. You can know what happens before and after a decision, but the moment of decision itself is unknowable.[31] The reader can fill the hiatus, the elision, with all sorts of unverifiable hypotheses, but the linguistic ligature, the connection, the bridge between the performative speech act, sealed with a kiss that silences speech, and the knowledge the performative gives is missing. It is a blank place in the language. Whereof one cannot speak one perhaps should remain silent.

This failure of knowledge is parallel to the way James, in the preface, cannot or will not tell the reader where he got the inspiration for Isabel and the other characters. It is parallel also to the lack of explanation for why Isabel refused Caspar and Warburton. It is parallel, finally, to Isabel's inability to explain to Caspar, Mrs. Touchett, or Ralph why she accepted Osmond. In all these cases, for the writer, the narrator, the character, and the reader, the basis of decision is hidden. These cases are examples of true secrets that cannot ever be revealed and about which nothing decisive can be verifiably said, not even that they exist. That, however, does not prevent decisions from being made, nor does it even prevent us from saying that they ought to be made, that they must be made. Nor does it prevent the reader from taking upon himself or herself the responsibility for filling in the gap between the kiss and the knowledge that follows it with one or another of the explanations I have proposed. That is your decision, but you are on your own in making it, just as you are on your own in making any decision.

The reader, teacher, or critic is the last in the line of decision makers that goes from the author, who must decide to write a given novel rather than any other, to the narrator, who hypothetically knows everything and must decide what to tell the reader and what to keep secret, to the characters, who must decide and act in all those small and large turning points that make up their lives, to the reader, teacher, or critic who must pass judgment on the work and decide what to say about it. How Isabel got from the kiss to the knowledge remains an impenetrable mystery. The reader must construct a bridge from the kiss to the knowledge and the decision, or to the knowledge-decision. The reader is free to do that and is even enjoined to do so. He or she must choose, however, in the face of the "warning" (another speech act) that Paul de Man reads in Shelley's *The Triumph of Life*. This is the most rigorous statement I know of the absence of the verifiable ligatures the reader would need to fill in with a clear conscience a blank like that between Caspar's kiss and the knowledge it gives: "*The Triumph of Life* warns us that nothing, whether deed, word, thought, or text, ever happens in relation, positive or negative, to anything that precedes, follows, or exists elsewhere, but only as a random event whose power, like the power of death, is due to the randomness of its occurrence." De Man goes on, however, to add another warning he reads in Shelley's poem: "It [*The Triumph of Life*] also warns us why and how these events then have to be reintegrated in a historical and aesthetic system of recuperation that repeats itself regardless of the exposure of its fallacy."[32]

To propose, as I have done, that *The Portrait of a Lady* is incoherently overdetermined and that no evidence exists to support a single, univocal judgment is also to pass judgment and to perform a somewhat idiosyncratic form of the "recuperation" that de Man warns us we cannot avoid performing. The reader may wonder whether I am most interested, in this chapter, in kisses or in undecidability, or whether I perhaps want to relate them in a general phenomenology of the kiss as indeterminate in meaning. Neither is the case. This chapter grew out of a seminar on "moments of decision" in works of fiction. I was interested in the representation of decisions in words, specifically, words in literary works. These were investigated in the context of various theories of decision, in Heidegger's *Sein und Zeit* (*Being and Time*), for example. The kiss in *The Portrait of a Lady*, I decided, is a splendid example of a "moment of decision," but I would not call it "typical" or generalize on its basis. Nor do I have a general theory of kisses. Each kiss, I suspect, is sui generis. I have found the topic fascinating, however, as I have accumulated more and more examples of kisses in literature, philosophy, and psychoanalysis. I am grateful to my many auditors around the world who have listened to parts of this chapter as a lecture and have given me kisses. My focus is on kisses in literature, which is a more restricted topic than kisses in general. The naming of a kiss in words is a quite different thing from a real kiss, as Kafka knew. Nor would I claim that all kisses in literature (however it may be in life) are "indeterminate in meaning." Many kisses in literature, I should think, are more or less decidable in meaning, for example, the kisses Adam and Eve exchange before the Fall in Milton's *Paradise Lost*, however difficult it may be for us now, after the fall, to imagine innocent kisses: "he in delight / . . . press'd her Matron lip / With kisses pure."[33] Caspar's kiss of Isabel is an imaginary historical event in the sense that it intervenes to deflect decisively the course of Isabel's "history." That kiss, however, exists only as words within a fictional story. It operates in that story rather as an irrational interruption of the heroine's course than as a happening that can be incorporated into a coherent, verifiable, rationally comprehensible "history of a kiss."

Paul de Man, in "The Return to Philology," affirms his allegiance to Reuben Brower's pedagogical law. My reading of *The Portrait of a Lady* has indicated that this law perhaps cannot be obeyed except by silence. As soon as you say anything at all about a literary text, you have gone beyond the text and have said something about it that is, strictly speaking, unwarranted. Nevertheless you must take the plunge, or else remain mute, as Penthesileia remains mute in one version of Kleist's play of that name, rather than explaining, in the passage from the version I have cited, that she has confused *küssen* and *bissen* in a slip of the tongue and kissed/bitten Achilles to death.

The "you" is not empty prior to the act of a reading decision. Isabel at the moment of Caspar's kiss is what her "nature" as a lover of liberty with a conscience, plus all her Yeses and Nos, the decisions she has already taken, her refusals of Goodwood and Warburton, her acceptance of Osmond, have made her. In a similar way, no reader is a blank page on which the text as it is read writes itself. The reader always has all sorts of presuppositions and prejudices. But the "irresponsible" and ultimately unjustifiable act of deciding to fill in the missing link with a certain reading is nevertheless a response to the demand the text makes. In this it is like Isabel's decision to return to Osmond. A reading decision changes the reading "you," reconstitutes it, interrupts what it was before, deflects it, turns it around, and heads it in another direction. Such a decision makes the reader thereafter to some degree determined as the "you" that has filled in that blank in a certain way, just as Isabel will be forever after a wife who decided to return to her bad husband. *The Portrait of a Lady* has an ethical lesson. It teaches that ethical decisions, if they are real decisions and not automatic, preprogrammed actions, are never fully justifiable by rational explanations. They are leaps in the dark. The novel teaches also that reading or writing about a literary work is analogous. A reading is a performative intervention, not a cognitive, completely verifiable assertion, though it is a response to the call for a reading that the text makes: "Read me!"

CHAPTER 3

Unworked and Unavowable: Community in *The Awkward Age*

> "I gather from you—I've gathered indeed from Mr.
> Vanderbank—that you're a little sort of a set that hang
> very much together."
> "Oh yes; not a formal association nor a secret society—still less a
> 'dangerous gang' or an organization for any definite end. We're
> simply a collection of natural affinities," Mitchy explained.
>
> —HENRY JAMES, *The Awkward Age*

> The unavowable in community is also a sovereignty that cannot but
> posit itself and impose itself in silence, in the unsaid. [*L'inavouable de
> la communauté, c'est aussi une souveraineté qui ne peut que se poser et
> s'imposer en silence, dans le non-dit.*]
>
> —JACQUES DERRIDA, *Voyous*

According to J. L. Austin, and for standard speech act theory generally, the felicity of speech acts depends on the existence of a viable community. A viable community is one with fixed laws, institutions, and customs, accepted and acted on by all its members. For a performative to work, says Austin in *How to Do Things with Words*, "there must exist an accepted conventional procedure having a certain conventional effect, that procedure to include the uttering of certain words by certain persons in certain circumstances"(*HT*, 14). Later on, speaking of legal decisions, Austin says, "The whole point of having such a procedure [a preordained, ritualized assembly of performative utterances and rules, along with infallible ways to identify who is authorized to use them] is precisely to make certain subsequent conduct in order and other conduct out of order: and of course for many purposes, with, for example, legal formulas, this goal is more and more nearly approached" (*HT*, 44). Who "accepts" the "accepted conventional procedure"? Though Austin does not say so, he must mean "accepted by some working community." This chapter explores the relation of speech acts to community, or the lack of it, in *The Awkward Age*.

What Is a Community?

First, however, I must ask: What is a community? How would you know when you encounter one or live in one? More particularly, for this chapter, what characteristics of a community are necessary to ensure felicitous performatives, to ensure, that is, that members of that community can do things with words and do what they intend the words to do? The word *community* is part of a family of words containing "commun . . .," or "common . . .," or "con . . ." : *communion, communism, communication, commune, commonality, common* itself (as in the phrases *held in common* or *common land*), *condominium*, and so on.

The paradox of community can be indicated by the Greek word for "common" or "shared by the community": *koinē*. Koine names the Hellenistic dialectic of Greek, derived largely from Attic. It became "common," in the centuries just before and after Christ's birth, to the whole Hellenistic world. It replaced local dialectics. The New Testament was written in Koine. That makes it exoteric, accessible to the whole world. Koine was the initial means of the globalization of Christianity. At the same time, the New Testament expresses an esoteric doctrine defining the in-group of those who understand and believe. As Jesus explains in the Parable of the Sower in *Matthew*, if you don't get it, you won't get it. I give his words in what is now our worldwide Koine, English. He answers the disciples who ask why he speaks to the multitude in parables: "Because it is given to you to know the mysteries of the kingdom of heaven, but to them it is not given. For whosoever hath, to him shall be given, and he shall have more abundance: but whosoever hath not, from him shall be taken away even that he hath. Therefore speak I to them in parables: because they seeing see not; and hearing they hear not, neither do they understand" (Matt. 13:11–13). Christianity is at once a worldwide community and at the same time the most exclusive in-group that can be imagined.

The word *community* must be distinguished from such related words as *culture, ethnicity, group, nation, collectivity, in-group, troupe, set, society, association, religion, collection, gang, organization, amalgamation*, and so on. An in-group, for example, is defined by the *American Heritage Dictionary* as "A group united by common beliefs, attitudes, and interests characteristically excluding outsiders." The last eight of the words in my list are used by James in the space of four pages to name what, in the preface to *The Awkward Age* for the New York Edition of 1907–9, he calls the "circle" of personages in the novel (9:xi). *Circle* is a key word in this work. It is used again and again to describe Mrs. Brookenham's "set." *Religion* and *amalgamation* are used to name a compact in admiration of Vanderbank that is shared by two members of the group, Mr. Longdon and Mitchy. The other words name by negation the "set" of which they are members, that is, to say what this set is not. *Troupe* is used in another place in *The Awkward Age*. Mrs. Brookenham speaks of their circle as a circus troupe: "We're all in the troupe now, I suppose, . . . and we must travel with the show" (9:188). *Community* overlaps in meaning with all the words I have listed, but is identical with none of them. A check of the e-text of *The Awkward Age* reveals that the word *community* never appears in that novel. James never calls Mrs. Brookenham's "set" or "circle" a "community."

We use the word *community* all the time in everyday discourse, without thinking much about it. We speak of a "close-knit community," of a "community of believers," of the "local community," of the "Community Center" (meaning a building where community activities take place), of the "European community," of "the Islamic community," of a "community of readers," or even of "cyber-communities," and so on. Scientists speak of "communities of microbes." The meaning of these phrases seems clear enough.

The word *community*, however, as is usually the case with such conceptual terms, becomes problematic as soon as you detach it from such everyday uses and ask, "What is a community?" The word implies beliefs and assumptions shared, held in common, taken for granted, by a group. We normally assume, I think, an upper and lower limit in size for a community. A community or "amalgamation" of two does not quite seem right, though Jean-Luc Nancy proposes to call the duo of two people in love a form of community, as does Blanchot.[1] A community, nevertheless, needs at least a third as witness, *terstis*, in the old Latin word, someone who gives testimony to the transactions between any two. The narrator of *The Awkward Age* might be seen as playing that role in relation to the religion of admiration for Vanderbank made up of Mr. Longdon and Mitchy. In practice, three persons hardly suffice, nor is a single family, even an "extended one," ordinarily thought of as making a community. We commonly think of a community as made up of a fairly large number of people not all related by birth or marriage, sharing certain assumptions, and dwelling together in the same place. My "we" in the previous sentences, however, appeals to a hypothetical community of those who think of community as I do. They hardly need to dwell in the same place. They are the community of my readers who agree with me, if there are any, wherever they may be living.

Even so, an ideal community, if there is such a thing, is, in most people's idea of it, made up of men and women dwelling together in what
W. B. Yeats calls "one dear perpetual place."[2] They live together under
the aegis of shared beliefs, institutions, laws, and assumptions. Examples
would be monks in a monastery or people living together in the same
rural village or (sometimes) city neighborhood. At its upper limit of size a
community frays off into being something else, for example, a nation. The
"American people" hardly form a community, whatever appeals politicians
may make to some imagined community unity. Politicians say, "The
American people do not want universal health care," as if the American
people were a homogeneous group, when what they mean is that the for-
profit Health Management Organizations and pharmaceutical companies
do not want universal health care. The "Arab community" is not really a
community in the sense I am using the word. It is too big, too diverse.
The "American people" is also too big, too diverse, too heterogeneous.
We speak too many different languages, are too much divided between
rich and poor, haves and have nots. We have too many different religious
faiths and ethnic allegiances to be called a "community." The "European
community" is more a metaphor for an assemblage of nations than a name
for a community in the strict sense of people living together and sharing
the same values and assumptions. The term nevertheless may appeal to
that concept as a horizon to be reached when all Europe comes to have
the same laws, currency, and economic system. Economic unity, however,
hardly makes a community in the usual sense of the word.

Each individual member of a community as I have defined it has, as
Louis Althusser would put it, been interpellated to be what he or she is by
the various circumambient local ideological apparatuses—school, church,
laws, the media—that impinge on that person. This assemblage makes
felicitous speech acts possible: marriages that keep the community going,
promises made and kept, the making of contracts to buy, sell, or exchange,
the making of efficacious wills transmitting money and property to the
next generation, the just incarceration of lawbreakers, and so on.

The Commonsense Model of Community

Just how are the people living together in such a community related to
one another? Here one may oppose two models of community. The first
is the ordinary, commonsensical one that most people have in mind, explicitly or implicitly, when they speak of "community." The other is a less

intuitive model of community that is inextricably entwined with the first. One resists taking the second one seriously, since it is hard to think and has disastrous consequences for the first model. The second model of community "unworks" the first. I make up the neologism "unworked" on the basis of Jean-Luc Nancy's *La communauté désoeuvrée*. The English version of this book translates *désoeuvrée* as "inoperative"—*The Inoperative Community*. *Inoperative* has the advantage of being a real English word, but it is hardly an accurate carrying over of the nuances of the French word *désoeuvrée*. The latter contains an implicit reference to Marxist notions of production and of products that are the "works" of the workers' work, just as a common notion of human communities sees them as the work of a group living and working together. They have constructed the community over time. It is the product of their combined and cooperative work, the result of a social contract they have explicitly or implicitly signed. Their collective work has constituted it, sometimes on the basis of an explicit "constitution." Even the community of my university department, if it is a community, is governed by a departmental "constitution."

This commonly accepted model of community sees the individuals within it as pre-existing subjectivities. These subjectivities have bound themselves together with other subjectivities for the common good. Their mode of communication with one another can be called "intersubjectivity." This communication is an interchange between subjectivities. Such an interchange presupposes that the other is like me. Our common language makes it possible for me, in spite of my individuality, to communicate to my neighbor what I am thinking and feeling, what I am, or to understand through language and other signs what the other person is thinking and feeling. These cohabiting subjectivities have made together a language, houses, roads, farms, towns, cities, industries, laws, institutions, religious beliefs, customs, and mythical or religious stories about their origin and destiny that are told communally or written down in some sacred book to be recited to the group. For example, Christian church services include each week readings from the Old and New Testaments. These readings are synecdoches for a recital of the whole Bible. The Bible is the sacred Book that binds the community together.

Literature within such a community is the imitation, or reflection, or representation of community. It is the construction of cunningly verisimilar miniature models of community. *Bleak House* allows you to carry the whole of Dickens's London in your pocket. Literature is to be valued for its truth of correspondence to a community already there, for its constative value, not for any performative function it may have in constituting communities. Valid language—for example, the language of literature—is primarily and fundamentally literal, not, except as embellishment, figurative, just as the conceptual terms describing this model of community are to be taken literally, *à la lettre*. The primary figure employed is the figure of synecdoche. This figure allows a few examples to stand for the whole, as Gridley, the Man from Shropshire, in *Bleak House* stands for the whole class of those whose lives have been destroyed by the Court of Chancery.

Though the individuals living together in such a community no doubt think of themselves as finite, as mortal, and though one of their community places is the cemetery, nevertheless mortality does not, for them, essentially define community life. The community's constant renewal from generation to generation gives it a collective immortality. In a similar way, the living together of individuals in a community tends to project a hypothetical, sempiternal "community consciousness" or "collective consciousness." Each separate individuality is bathed or encompassed in this collective consciousness, as a fish swims in water. Death tends to be covered over, suppressed, quickly forgotten, as is notoriously the case within many American communities, if they can be called that, today.

It is possible (though it would be an error) to see Victorian novels—for example, George Eliot's novels, or Dickens's, or Anthony Trollope's—as straightforwardly based on such a conception of community and as reflecting or imitating such actually existing communities. An example of such fictive communities is the Barsetshire community in Trollope's Barset novels. The omniscient (or telepathic) narrators in such novels are the expression of the collective consciousness of the community that I mentioned above. Victorian multi-plotted novels are, according to this view, "models of community." They are cunning, miniature fictive replicas of communities that actually existed historically. Their object of representation is not one individual life story but a whole community. The existence of such communities, in reality and in fictive simulacra, so this (false or only partially true) story about Victorian novels goes, ensures the execution of felicitous performatives. In Trollope's novels, as in Victorian fiction generally, the most important speech acts or writing acts are the marriage of marriageable young women and the passing on from one generation to another by gifts, wills, and marriage settlements of money, property, and rank. Most often, in Victorian novels, these two themes are combined. The heroine's marriage redistributes property, money, and rank, and carries it on to the next generation.

The Other Model of Community

Another model of community has been articulated in recent years. This has been done in different but more or less consonant ways by such theorists as Georges Bataille, Maurice Blanchot, Jean-Luc Nancy, Giorgio Agamben, and Alphonso Lingis.[3] A widely influential book by Benedict Anderson, *Imagined Communities*, thinks of nations as ideologically fabricated communities. Anderson's book is, on the whole, no more than a subtle, postmodern version of the first model of community, the one whose features I have already sketched out.[4] I shall describe this alternative model primarily in the terms Jean-Luc Nancy uses in *The Inoperative Community*.

Nancy sees persons not as individualities but as "singularities." Each person is an agent fundamentally different from all the others. Each harbors a secret otherness that can by no means be communicated to any other singularity. Each singularity is essentially marked by its finitude or mortality. Each is from moment to moment, from the beginning, defined by the fact that it will die. Here is Nancy's expression of this, in a passage that is cited in part by Blanchot, in *La communauté inavouable* (*The Unavowable Community*). Blanchot says it is the essential affirmation in *The Inoperative Community*:

That which is not a subject opens up and opens onto a community whose conception, in turn, exceeds the resources of a metaphysics of the subject. Community does not weave a superior, immortal, or transmortal life between subjects (no more than it is itself woven of the inferior bonds of a consubstantiality of blood or of an association of needs), but it is constitutively, to the extent that it is a matter of a "constitution" here, calibrated on the death of those whom we call, perhaps wrongly, its "members" (inasmuch as it is not a question of an organism). But it does not make a work of this calibration. Community no more makes a work out of death than it is itself a work. The death upon which community is calibrated does not *operate* the dead being's passage into some communal intimacy, nor does community, for its part, *operate* the transfiguration of its dead into some substance or subject—be these homeland, native soil or blood, nation, a delivered or fulfilled humanity, absolute phalanstery,[5] family, or mystical body. Community is calibrated on death as on that of which it is precisely impossible to *make a work* (other than a work of death, as soon as one tries to make a work of it). Community occurs in order to acknowledge this impossibility, or more exactly—for there is neither function nor finality here—the impossibility of making a work out of death is inscribed and acknowledged as "community."

Community is revealed in the death of others; hence it is always revealed to others. Community is what takes place always through others and for others. It is not the space of the *egos*—subjects and substances that are at bottom immortal—but of the *I*'s, who are always *others* (or else are nothing). If community is revealed in the death of others it is because death itself is the true community of *I*'s that are not *egos*. It is not a communion that fuses the *egos* into an *Ego* or a higher *We*. It is the community of *others*. The genuine community of mortal beings, or death as community, establishes their impossible communion. Community therefore occupies a singular place: it assumes the impossibility of its own immanence, the impossibility of a communitarian being in the form of a subject. In a certain sense community acknowledges and inscribes—this is its peculiar gesture—the impossibility of community. (*IC*, 14–15)

Each singularity, in Nancy's model of community, is not a self-enclosed subjectivity such as the first model assumes. Each singularity is exposed, at its limit, to a limitless or abyssal outside that it shares with the other singularities, from the beginning, by way of their common mortality. Their community is defined by the imminence of death. This death I experience not in my own death, since that cannot be "experienced," but in the death of another, the death of my friend, my neighbor, my relative. The language defining this other model of community is, necessarily, figurative, catachrestic, since no literal language exists for it. Such language use differs fundamentally from language used to name the first kind of community. Even conceptual words are used by Nancy "anasemically," that is, against the grain of their dictionary meanings. They are also used with an implicit or explicit play on their metaphorical roots. Examples of such words in Nancy's book are *singularité* itself, or *désoeuvrée*, or *partagé*, or *com-parution*, or *limite*, or *exposition*, or *interruption*, or even *littérature*. I give the words in the original French, because their nuances are not easily translated.

The first model of community is easy to understand because it is the one most of "us" take for granted. Nancy's model is more difficult to understand or to think. Moreover, as I have said, one resists thinking it or taking it seriously because it is devastating, a disaster, for the other model. Nancy's systematic dismantling of that other model's assumptions confirms that. No subjectivities, no intersubjective communication, no social "bonds," no collective consciousness, exist in Nancy's "unworked community."

Nancy thinks by way of the permutation of certain key terms that recur, that are incorporated again and again in new formulations. These attempt once more to say what cannot be said. They keep trying to say what is, strictly speaking, unsayable. The last sentence of *The Inoperative Community* in the original French form avers just this. (The original version has just the first three chapters of the five chapters in the English version.) "Here I must interrupt myself: it is up to you to allow to be said what no one, no subject, can say, and what exposes us in common" (*IC*, 81). This essential "impossibility of saying" determines several features of Nancy's style. First, the key words he uses are twisted away from their normal or casual use, suspended from everyday discourse. They are, as it were, held out in the open, dangling, unattached, since they tend to detach themselves through their iteration in different syntactic combinations with other key words. A second stylistic feature is outright contradiction, unsaying in the same sentence what has just been said, as in "allow to be said what no one, no subject, can say." Well, if no subject can say it, who or what can be imagined to say it? A third feature is an odd sort of implicit spatialization of the story Nancy tells. The figures of limit, sharing/shearing, articulation, suspension, exposition, and so on are all implicitly spatial. These words invite the reader to think again what Nancy is thinking in terms of a certain weird space, in which the topographical terms are withdrawn as soon as they are proffered. The limit, for example, is not an edge, border, or frontier, since there is nothing that can be confronted beyond it. It is like the edge/nonedge of the cosmologists' finite but unbounded universe. You confront a limit, a boundary, but you cannot get across it because no beyond exists, no transcendent outside. *Partagé*, to give another example, is a double antithetical word meaning both shared and sheared, divided. It is a spatial or topographical word, but you cannot easily map something that is both shared and sheared, *partagé*. Nancy has written a whole book, *Le partage des voix* (*Sharing Voices*), exploiting the contradictory nuances of the French word *partage*.[6]

A final feature of Nancy's style (which is to say, of his "thought") is that the model of community he proposes is explicitly the negation (though that is not quite the right word) of the community model that most people have in mind when one asks, "What is a community?" The two models are not antithetical or negations of one another, in the Hegelian sense of a determinate negation allowing for dialectical sublation. Each presupposes the other, is entangled with the other, is generated by the other as soon as you try to express it alone, for example, in a novel or in a theoretical treatise, such as Nancy's or such as these paragraphs you are now reading. The "commonsense" model presupposes pre-existing, self-enclosed "individuals," "subjectivities," "selves," "persons," finite no doubt, mortal no doubt, but totalizing, and in that sense immortal. These individuals then encounter other individuals and subsequently establish, by intersubjective communication leading to a compact or contract, a society, a community made up of shared stories (myths of origin and end), a language, institutions, laws, customs, family structures with rules for marriage and inheritance, gender roles, and so on, all organically composed and all the combined work of individuals living together. A group of people living and working together establishes a close-knit community, geographically located, closed in on itself. Language is a tool that "works," or makes, produces, the interchanges of community.

Nancy says we now know no such community ever existed, though the first sentence of *The Inoperative Community* reaffirms a familiar historical myth. That myth or ideologeme presumes such communities once existed and that modernity is characterized by their dissolution: "The gravest and most painful testimony of the modern world, the one that possibly involves all other testimonies to which this epoch must answer (by virtue of some unknown decree or necessity, for we bear witness also to the exhaustion of thinking through History), is the testimony of the dissolution, the dislocation, or the conflagration of community" (*IC*, 1) . The commonly presumed model is always already unworked, *désoeuvré*, by the alternative model. That model is a negation, if not in the dialectical sense allowing some synthetic *Aufhebung*, then at least in the sense that it says "no" to the other one. It defines itself point by point as opposed to the "first" model. In place of individuals with self-enclosed subjectivities, Nancy puts singularities that are aboriginally *partagés*, shared, sheared, open to an abyssal outside. Singularities are extroverted, exposed to other singularities at the limit point where everything vanishes. Language in such a community becomes literature, writing, not sacred myth. Literature is the expression of the unworking of community.

Such a community is "unavowable," to borrow the adjective in Blanchot's title. An unworked community does not provide solid ground for any avowals or speech acts. This does not mean that speech acts do not occur within unworked communities, or that they may not be efficacious. What it does mean, however, is that such speech acts are not endorsed by any public laws and institutions. They work by a resolution to go on being true to them that is continuously self-generated and self-sustained. Such speech acts are a kind of lifting oneself by one's own bootstraps over that abyss to which Nancy and Blanchot give the name *death*.

Matthew Arnold expresses something like this form of unavowable vow in the contradictory last stanza of "Dover Beach." Arnold's formulation is

Blanchotian in its positing of a love between singularities that is without grounds in love as a universal, Love with a capital *L*. Nor does it have grounds in any of the other universals—certitude, peace, joy, light, and so on—that would seem necessary prerequisites for felicitous vows of fidelity exchanged between lovers. Arnold's speaker exhorts his beloved to join him in what Blanchot might have called an *amour sans amour*. This would be the only love possible in an unworked community:

> Ah, love, let us be true
> To one another! For the world, which seems
> To lie before us like a land of dreams,
> So various, so beautiful, so new,
> Hath really neither joy, nor love, nor light,
> Nor certitude, nor peace, nor help for pain.[7]

The Awkward Age *as Virtual Reality*

Does what I have said so far have any relevance to a right reading of *The Awkward Age*? It does not by any means go without saying that it does. To get an answer, I must proceed slowly, circumspectly, *lento*, working patiently through the novel and its preface on their own terms. Like most of James's fictions, *The Awkward Age* is hyperbolically subtle and indirect. At least what I have said so far will serve as a warning against taking everyday ideas about community easily for granted in reading this novel. The word should always be accompanied by a mark of interrogation: "Community?"

I may as well admit at once that I find *The Awkward Age* immensely moving, in spite of, or perhaps because of, its artifice and its high degree of what James in the preface calls "finish." If James's intention was to move his readers, this novel is, for me at least, a felicitous performative. It succeeds in doing things with words.

What do I mean by saying I find *The Awkward Age* moving? Let me express this as naively, as innocently, and as straightforwardly as possible. I do not mean that I find its formal beauty, its "finish," moving. I mean that, in spite of my knowledge that the novel is made of words, and in spite of my more or less sophisticated knowledge of narratology and of narrative technique generally, I still think of the characters in the novel as though they were real people. I find their fates moving. That means I am an example of what Simon During calls "literary subjectivity."[8]

Literary subjectivity, I assert, is quite different from the subjectivity of those who are fascinated by stage plays. Stage plays were imitated, James

claims, in *The Awkward Age*. I confess that plays on the stage do not exercise the same power over me as do novels. I keep seeing real people there
in costume on an artificial stage set uttering words they have memorized
and pretending to be people they are not. Novels, on the contrary, carry
me away into a "virtual reality." I can enter that imaginary place only by
yielding to the magic incantation of the words on the page. I know it is all
done with words, this creation of virtual people. I know all the magic tricks
by which it is done. I shall have a lot to say, in this chapter, about those
tricks. That, however, does not keep the magic from working, on me at
least. If that were not the case, I should not think the novel worth writing
about.

The creation of virtual worlds and of virtual people, people in whom
the reader takes the same interest as he or she does in real people, is the
primary social function in our culture of what we call "novels." That function is fading, as the old print media are replaced by cybermedia, but novels still create virtual realities for me. Without that, they are not much
worth bothering about. I must confess I feel some doubts about whether
it is worth bothering about some clever postmodernist fictions. Some of
these spend so much time talking about or revealing their own artifice that
the magic power to create, out of the words on the page, the illusion of
real people is in them disabled. At that point, who cares how clever the
author is? Even the admirable Jorge Luis Borges, perhaps still the best of
that lot, sometimes affects me that way. It's fun, but it's not serious. *The
Awkward Age* is serious play.

It may be that our responsibility as critics is to deconstruct the illusion
of a perdurable, unitary, extra-verbal self, in literature or in life, but there
is not much point in doing that unless one has first yielded to the illusion.
Only then does one have something to deconstruct. On this point I am in
agreement with Henry James himself. James condemned Anthony Trollope for talking in his novels about the way the novel you are reading is
no more than a novel. The reproach was somewhat unjust, since Trollope
rarely commits this sin. A novelist who does commit it, says James, pulls
the rug out from under his own feet. He deprives himself of any solid
foundation and sinks into an abyss. "It is impossible," says James roundly,
in his long obituary essay of 1883 on Trollope's work,

> to imagine what a novelist takes himself to be unless he regards himself as
> an historian and his narrative as a history. It is only as an historian that he
> has the smallest *locus standi*. As a narrator of fictitious events he is nowhere;
> to insert into his attempt a backbone of logic, he must relate events that

are assumed to be real. . . . Therefore, when Trollope suddenly winks at us and reminds us that he is telling us an arbitrary thing, we are startled and shocked in quite the same way as if Macaulay or Motley [distinguished nineteenth-century historians] were to drop the historic mask and intimate that William of Orange was a myth and the Duke of Alva an invention.[9]

To me Nanda Brookenham, Mr. Longdon, Vanderbank, and the rest of James's characters in *The Awkward Age* are as real as the Duke of Alva. That is why I find what happens to them moving.

James uses the figure of solid ground again in the preface to the New York Edition of *The Awkward Age*. There he is speaking of the technical conventions on the basis of which the work was written. It appears that James was a little anxious about whether or not his fictions had solid ground to stand on. "It comes back to me, the whole 'job,'" he says,

> as wonderfully amusing and delightfully difficult from the first; since amusement deeply abides, I think, in any artistic attempt the basis and groundwork of which are conscious of a particular firmness. On that hard fine floor the element of execution feels it may more or less confidently *dance*; in which case puzzling questions, sharp obstacles, dangers of detail, may come up for it by the dozen without breaking its heart or shaking its nerve. It is the difficulty produced by the loose foundation or the vague scheme that breaks the heart—when a luckless fatuity has over-persuaded an author of the "saving" virtue of treatment. (9:xv)

The reader will remember that the same concern to establish a solid ground for the fiction is expressed in the preface to *The Portrait of a Lady*.

Are Readers of The Awkward Age *a Community?*

It would be hard ever to accuse James of a "luckless fatuity." He never believes that he can hide by "treatment" the lack of a solid, presupposed ground. His novels are made on the basis of certain formal laws rigorously obeyed. What do I find when I dance with James on the solid foundation he has established?

I begin the dance with an apparently peripheral question. This question follows from what I have said about the problematic of community. Do the readers of *The Awkward Age* form a community? What does one mean, in this case, by a "community of readers"? One thinks, for example, of Dickens's sense that he had a personal relation to each of the hundreds of thousands of people who read his novels. He often addresses them directly, as in the last two sentences of the preface of August 1853 to the first book edition of *Bleak House*: "I believe I have never had so many readers as in this book. May we meet again!"[10] George Eliot also, notoriously, addresses her readers directly. She thinks of them as the community of those who are made better by reading about the community of Hayslope in *Adam Bede* or about the community of Middlemarch in *Middlemarch*. Eliot allowed visits from admiring readers. Books were published, even in her lifetime, with titles like *Wise, witty and tender sayings in prose and verse, selected from the works of George Eliot by Alexander Main*; *Wit and wisdom of George Eliot*; *A moment each day with George Eliot*; *a quotation for every day in the year selected from the works of George Eliot, by Ella Adams Moore and the students in her classes in literature*.[11]

The reviewers of Anthony Trollope's *The Last Chronicle of Barset*, with a quite extraordinary unanimity, speak of the characters in Trollope's Barset novels as though they were family members or close friends. The reviewers lament the end of the Barset series in terms like those of grief for the deaths of real people, just as they grieve for the deaths within *The Last Chronicle of Barset* of Mrs. Proudie and Septimus Harding. Trollope's readers, in this case, it could be argued, form a community of those in mourning for the dead. The reviewers unanimously condemn Trollope for having killed off his characters.[12]

Since most Victorian novels were published serially before being published in book form, readers often intervened before the book was finished to try to change its direction. The author got "feedback" from a real and palpable "community of readers," while he or she was in the process of writing and publishing the novel. Well-known examples of this include George Eliot's interchanges with her publisher, John Blackwood. He made comments on the manuscript of *Middlemarch* while she was still writing it. Another example is Dickens's careful attention to what his readers said, for example, in his decision to give *Great Expectations* a happy ending at the request of his novelist friend Edward Bulwer-Lytton. A final example is Trollope's decision to kill off Mrs. Proudie when he overheard two clergymen at one of his clubs discussing how tedious they found her. "I got up and standing between them," writes Trollope in *An Autobiography*, "I acknowledged myself to be the culprit. 'As to Mrs. Proudie,' I said, 'I will go home and kill her before the week is over.' And so I did. The two gentlemen were utterly confounded and one of them begged me to forget his frivolous observations."[13]

How different is the case with *The Awkward Age*'s readers and with James's relation to them! In the preface of 1908 James complains, in a characteristically grumpy fashion, that no reader, apparently, understood, much less admired, what he was up to in this novel. For example, he says, no one seems to have recognized that he was imitating the narrative procedures of the French novelist "Gyp." He says he expected his readers would see that. He confesses that on re-reading the novel he is lost in admiration of it, but no one but he seems to have had that experience. "I fail to make out in the event," he says, "that the book succeeded in producing the impression of *any* plan on any person. No hint of that sort of success, or of any critical perception at all in relation to the business, has ever come my way; in spite of which when I speak, as just above, of what was to 'happen' under the law of my ingenious labor, I fairly lose myself in the vision of a hundred bright phenomena" (9:xiv–xv). The preface is a promise. It promises that if you are one of those who have eyes to see and ears to hear and understand you will be rewarded with the pleasure of seeing a hundred bright phenomena. If not, not.

James seems to have felt that he was a community of one, that is, no community at all. He was the sole discriminating reader of *The Awkward Age*. In the preface he ruefully recounts that the editor of the first book edition, published by Heinemann in 1899, informed him that the book had almost totally failed. "I'm sorry to say," the editor told him, "the book has done nothing to speak of; I've never in all my experience seen one treated with more general and complete disrespect" (9:xv). James concludes: "There was thus to be nothing left me for fond subsequent reference—of which I doubtless give even now so adequate an illustration—save the rich reward of the singular interest attaching to the very intimacies of the effort" (9:xv). He means the preface "illustrates" his admiration for the novel and for the remembered subtleties of its composition. The pleasure of the text, in this case, is the narcissistic circulation from author as writer to author as reader, practically the sole reader, of his own work, taking delight in remembering the "intimacies of the effort."

Nor has the subsequent century seen as much attention paid to *The Awkward Age* as has been paid, for example, to *The Portrait of a Lady* or to *The Golden Bowl*. A good many essays and book chapters have been devoted to *The Awkward Age*. Nevertheless, the novel has been to some degree marginalized. It has been made ancillary to discussions of the three great novels that followed it, *The Ambassadors*, *The Wings of the Dove*, and *The Golden Bowl*. Most of the discussions of *The Awkward Age* are more thematic than formal, if I may be permitted that distinction, since James denies it has cogency with this particular work. To read the novel now in the light of James's preface is by no means to feel that one is joining oneself to a "choir invisible" of other readers, such as that George Eliot imagined was formed by the readers of her work.[14] I as reader feel myself to be to some degree alone with the text, though there are fine essays on *The Awkward Age* by Dorothea Krook, Sheila Teahan, Suzie M. Gibson, George Butte, and others.[15]

Perhaps, however, that is the actual condition of readers at any time, however much they may feel themselves to be members of a community of readers. Reading is, for the most part, a lonely, silent business. How could one know what happens when another person reads a book I have read or am reading? How can I be certain that anything like the same thing happens to other readers as happens to me? Even what might seem a true community of readers—for example, a group of students and their teacher sitting around a seminar table with copies of *The Awkward Age* open before them—only brings the problem more into the open. The novel exists as a literary work only when it is read. Unread, it is just a rectangular material lump. But even if all the students have read the book, it seems prima facie unlikely that their responses have been the same or even necessarily similar.

I say this in spite of Paul de Man's cheerfully ironic claim that the text coerces a reader into thinking according to the patterns of meaning it contains. This would mean that no really bad readers exist. That is a reassuring but implausible conviction. De Man claims that Hölderlin's enigmatic aphorism "Es ereignet sich aber das Wahre" can be "freely translated" as "What is true is what is bound to take place." This, says de Man, applies to the act of reading. In reading, what happens is what is bound to happen: "Reading is an argument (which is not necessarily the same as a polemic) because it has to go against the grain of what one would want to happen in the name of what has to happen."[16] Maybe. I wish I could believe that. It may be, pace de Man, that however coercive the words are, the community of readers gathered around a given literary work, at any time and place, form an "unworked" community. This would be a community bound together by the singularity and incommunicability of each reading experience, rather than an organic community sharing similar experiences of the words on the page as constitutive of meaning.

The Preface

So what's the problem? What features of *The Awkward Age* might make it particularly recalcitrant to unanimity among its readers? James's preface gives me various clues. As is always the case with James's prefaces, however, this one is as much misleading as it is helpful. It leaves essential questions unanswered. It puts its readers off the scent as much as it directs them to the quarry of a right reading.

James tells the reader of the preface that he has no difficulty remembering the germ of *The Awkward Age*. That germ was his observation, by way of his circulation as a visitor in various London homes, of the embarrassments brought about when an adolescent daughter in the household was finally allowed to "come down" and be present at adult conversation. "The 'sitting downstairs,' from a given date, of the merciless maiden previously perched aloft," says James, "could easily be felt as a crisis" to someone, as he was, "infinitely addicted to 'noticing'" (9:vi). Later in the preface James speaks of his germ as "the case of the account to be taken, in a circle of free talk, of a new and innocent, a wholly unacclimatised presence, as to which accommodations have never had to come up" (9:vii), or as "the pretty notion of the 'free circle' put about by having, of a sudden, an ingenuous mind and a pair of limpid searching eyes to count with" (9:viii). "Put about" is an odd phrase here. It suggests that the circle is not only disrupted, but also made to turn, to rotate.

It might be worth noticing at this point that James does not choose in *The Awkward Age*, as one might have expected, the inner drama in which an innocent young girl gradually learns the "facts of life," including the adulteries of her elders, by listening to their free talk. *The Portrait of a Lady* is such a drama of initiation or education. Its focus is on Isabel's gradual learning of what the social world is really like now. She learns that that it is a place of selfishness, secrecy, cruelty, infidelity, and illicit sexuality. Another example is *What Maisie Knew*. When the reader of *The Awkward Age* first meets the heroine, Nanda, however, she is already thoroughly initiated. She does not have much more to learn. James attributes to Nanda a power of intelligence and of penetrating sensitivity not unlike his own. That intelligence is a large part of her pathos. She is, unfortunately for her, tremendously smart, "vague slip of a daughter" (9:vi) though she is.

Middle- and upper-class young girls in England, even in the 1890s, were kept upstairs in the charge of a nursemaid or governess. Their coming down, like their putting their hair up, was a signal event. A child can wear her hair long and exposed. A modest grown-up woman must put her hair up, hide its luxuriance, as a sign of modesty. Only prostitutes wear their hair down. It is hard to imagine that a young girl's coming downstairs would be a big event in most households now! Most girls have never been "up." I shall postpone until the appropriate moment discussion of why this coming down brought about such a crisis. I move first to a somewhat different question.

Why Such a Big Book?

If the complication arising from the coming downstairs of "some vague slip of a daughter" was the germ of *The Awkward Age*, why was it that this vague slip of an idea produced such a big book? James called the germs of his novels "données." They were "gifts" arriving gratuitously from the circumambient social air, germs that flowered in his imagination. The tendency of small germs to generate long novels is a recurrent theme of the prefaces, a leitmotif. *The Awkward Age* is a salient example. James thought at first his idea good enough only for a small, ironic, comic, lightly treated short story. He is so embarrassed by the incommensurability between the acorn and the oak that he considers keeping his "small secret undivulged" (9:v), that is, keeping secret the origin of the work. The truth will out, however, partly because James considers the novel so good an example of this general feature of his work, partly, I suppose, because the truth he tells is also a kind of boast, partly because his rereading of the novel places him "on unexpectedly good terms with the work itself" (9:v). In short, he is extremely "proud" (9:vi) of this work, and wants to explain how it came into being:

> I shall encounter, I think, in the course of this copious commentary, no better example, and none on behalf of which I shall venture to invite more interest, of the quite incalculable tendency of a mere grain of subject-matter to expand and develop and cover the ground when conditions happen to favor it. . . . "The Awkward Age" was to belong, in the event, to a group of productions, here re-introduced,[17] which have in common, to their author's eyes, the endearing sign that they asserted in each case an unforeseen principle of growth. They were projected as small things, yet had finally to be provided for as comparative monsters. That is my own title for them, though I should perhaps resent it if applied by another critic—above all in the case of the piece before us. (9: v)

Key words here are *incalculable, unforeseen,* and *monsters.* A monster is something grotesquely unique, inordinately large, something fitting no generic bounds. The word *monster* etymologically means "shown forth," as in modern French *montre,* "to show." The same root is present in *dem-*

onstration. The Awkward Age shows forth, or demonstrates, or exposes, or exhibits, something outrageous, something that can be shown in no other way, something incalculable and unforeseen. This something perhaps might better have been kept secret, as the Minotaur, monstrous birth of Pasiphae's sexual congress with a bull, is kept hidden in the Daedalian labyrinth. Labyrinthine James's narration in *The Awkward Age* certainly is.

Why is it that James cannot foresee how far his little germ will take him? Just what is that germ's incalculable principle of growth? Why does James not have dominion over his own power of writing? Why does this novel so spiral out of control, in labyrinthine complexity? It is not all that easy to answer these questions. The preface ascribes it to the proliferation of "relations" that his small idea developed. As he says in the preface to *Roderick Hudson*, "Really, universally, relations stop nowhere, and the exquisite problem of the artist is eternally but to draw, by a geometry of his own, the circle within which they shall happily *appear* to do so" (1:vii). The author must by a kind of violence draw an arbitrary line around his material, excluding all those relations outside the line that enticingly invite him to treat them. This problem returns in the preface to *The Awkward Age*. There it is expressed explicitly as a problem of framing: "though the relations of a human figure or a social occurrence are what make such objects interesting, they also make them, to the same tune, difficult to isolate, to surround with the sharp black line, to frame in the square, the circle, the charming oval, that helps any arrangement of objects to become a picture" (9:viii).

Even after the most strenuous and cunning efforts of framing, the germ, or something invisibly hidden within it, something that comes from a principle of growth "other" to James's conscious intention, seems to command an unforeseen and incalculable proliferation. It is like a command from before or beyond or after, an anomalous speech act. The expansion comes, not from James as author speaking an "I decide," but from a demand by the other, by the outside, by the "germ" itself. This demand comes as a fortuitous "gift." The same thing may be said of any commentary on the novel that hopes to achieve responsible responsiveness, such as this one. It cannot be foreseen or calculated beforehand just where an attempt to account for the novel is going to lead you or how many pages it will take.

Another reason for the inordinate length of *The Awkward Age* is given elaborate development in the preface. This is James's decision to treat his idea with an unusual amount of finish, as he boasts he has done. The implicit claim, as always, is that his "idea," when he came to put it on paper (or dictate it aloud), demanded unforeseen elaboration. Finish in this case means elaboration, for reasons I shall identify in a moment.

Another more hidden, unexpressed, perhaps even shameful reason for the length of *The Awkward Age* may be tentatively hypothesized. When a man or a woman is embarrassed or is trying to hide something, one strategy is to talk a lot, putting auditors off the scent. An example of that is given in the novel itself. Vanderbank is compulsively talkative when he visits Nanda for the last time. He is deeply embarrassed by his refusal of her love and deeply fearful of what she may say to him: "Had he an inward terror that explained his superficial nervousness, the incoherence of a loquacity designed, it would seem, to check in each direction her advance?" (9:500). Not only James's preface but even the novel itself may have all that finish not to expose the whole "subject," but to cover it up. The elaboration may be a means of hiding what the novel is really about, the Minotaur at the center of the labyrinth. It may not be about what James says it is about at all. The germ (the daughter's coming down) may be a ruse or diversion leading the reader away from some other, more hidden topic. Whether or not that is the case remains to be seen. If that other topic is really hidden, secret, it may be impossible ever to uncover it for certain. My epigraph from Derrida for this chapter posits a certain *inavouable* and *non-dit*, an unavowable or unsaid, at the heart of every community.

Finish and Exposure

Certainly what James calls his high degree of "finish" means that his story is told with the maximum amount of indirection and innuendo. What has he got to hide? What does he fear to expose directly, in so many words? Perhaps nothing. Exposure is in any case a major motif in the story itself. The give and take of "talk" among the members of Mrs. Brookenham's set is for the sake of exposing, while hiding, the sexual misdemeanors of other members of the set or of those at its periphery. One character, Little Aggie, is kept pure by not being exposed to adult talk or by not understanding it, whereas Nanda is made unmarriageable precisely by being too much "exposed" to such talk. "Nanda's retarded, but eventually none the less real, incorporation [in her mother's "circle"]," says James in the preface, "means virtually Nanda's exposure" (9:xi). No respectable or fastidious man—Vanderbank, for instance—will marry such a piece of damaged goods. She knows too much. Knowledge, it appears, is contaminating.

Mrs. Brook tells Mr. Longdon that he'll enjoy talking to the Duchess about "the whole question, don't you know? Of bringing girls forward or not. The question of—well, what do you call it?—their exposure. It's *the* question, it appears—the question of the future; it's awfully interesting and the Duchess at any rate is great on it. Nanda of course is exposed . . . fearfully" (9:195). The word *exposed* reappears much later in the novel in Vanderbank's witty response to Nanda's assertion that she cannot leave Tishy Grendon alone, "dreadfully frightened" as Tishy is. Tishy is afraid that her husband is off having an affair. "[T]hat's a London necessity," says Vanderbank. "You can't leave anybody with nobody—exposed to everybody" (9:385–86). To what the reader of *The Awkward Age* is exposed by reading it is another question, as is the question of whether such exposure is a good thing or a bad thing. I shall return ultimately to this last question.

The word *exposure* is related to another word, exhibition. James highlights that word in the preface. Speaking of the pleasure he got from imitating in *The Awkward Age* the procedures of a playwright, James speaks of his scenes as "exhibitions." In a novel that imitates a play, "the references in one's action can only be, with intensity, to each other, to things exactly on the same plane of exhibition with themselves" (9:xx). Writing a novel is an act of exhibition, as, one might say, thinking of the sexual issues at the center of *The Awkward Age*, some strange people have an impulse to "exhibit themselves" in an indecent exposure. *The Awkward Age*, it may be, is an act of indecent exposure.

In this novel, James says, in a formulation that recalls what Aristotle says about plot in the *Poetics*, the exhibition takes place by way of cross-references from one exhibition to another, except that the whole exhibits some feature of actual social life outside the novel at that historical moment: "We are shut up wholly to cross-relations, relations all within the action itself; no part of which is related to anything but some other part—save of course by the relations of the total to life" (9:xx). In this formulation describing the two "relations" characteristic of realist fiction, James excludes two other forms of relation. One is the relation to anything outside what is textually related (within the novel's fictive world), except by that relation of the total to life. The other is the relation to the hidden interiors of the characters that the telepathic narrator, in most of James's fiction, reveals to the reader, though they are not always fully known by the characters. In *The Awkward Age*, the characters' interiors are not "related" in the sense of narrated. That is James's strict formal law in this case, more or less strictly obeyed. James's insistence on the way meaning is generated by horizontal relations among elements all "on the same plane of exhibition" may remind the reader of Ferdinand de Saussure's famous claim that meaning in language is generated from differences between juxtaposed phonemes.

No "Going Behind"

Of what does the "finish" James says he artfully applied in *The Awkward Age* consist, and what is its function? More time is spent, in the preface, talking about the finish than in talking about the social event, the young girl's coming down, or out, or "forward," that was the germ destined to grow with such unforeseen luxuriance.

The "finish" consists principally in choosing a method of narration used consistently and systematically in no other of James's novels. Most of them, as readers know, unashamedly "go behind" what an outside spectator might have seen. They present the intimate thoughts and feelings of the protagonists. This allows some critics to describe James's novels as "dramas of consciousness." *The Portrait of a Lady* makes extravagant use of this narrative device, as the previous chapter demonstrates, for example, in the admirable account of Isabel Archer's midnight vigil after she realizes that her husband and Madame Merle have been lovers. The chief conventions of such narration are (1) the positing of an omniscient or telepathic narrator, able to enter the minds and feelings of all the characters at will, and (2) the use of free indirect discourse, whereby the narrator speaks in the third person past tense what the characters might have said to themselves in the first person present tense. The narrator or impersonal "narrative voice" can know only what the characters know, think, and feel, but "he" or "it" can represent these as completely as he or it wishes. "I think I should do something about that" becomes "He thought he should do something about that." A rare example from *The Awkward Age* comes in the first episode, in a sentence reporting Vanderbank's thoughts about Mr. Longdon: "He might almost have been a priest of priests, as it occurred to Vanderbank, were ever such dandies" (9:5).

I shall discuss later the significance of this breaking of the rigid formal law James has set for himself. The three great climactic novels of James's last phase, *The Ambassadors*, *The Wings of the Dove*, and *The Golden Bowl*, make elaborate use of various forms of "going behind." Though James of course inherited these two modes of storytelling, the omniscient narrator and indirect discourse, from his Victorian predecessors, from George

Eliot and Anthony Trollope, for example, nevertheless a hyperbolic use of them is what we especially identify as James's habitual narrative procedure.

For some reason, yet to be determined, if it can be determined, James decided in *The Awkward Age* to forego these privileges. *The Awkward Age* is anomalous among James's works if we assume that for him the principle that there must be a "center of consciousness" in order to achieve economy of form was a universal law. The oddness or lawlessness of *The Awkward Age* (1899) is that it eschews both the omniscient narrator and, almost entirely, "going behind" the objective presentation of the characters. This novel has neither an omniscient narrator in the usual sense nor any centers of consciousness or points of view or focalizations in the minds and feelings of the characters. The novel describes objectively what the characters said and did, how they looked, their clothes, faces, gestures, and other behavior, the things with which they have surrounded themselves. The reader must from this "superficial" or manifest evidence figure out what is going on behind the objective signs. His additional resource is cross-references, repetitions, allusions.

"My idea," writes James in the preface,

> was to be treated with light irony—it would be light and ironical or it would be nothing; so that I asked myself, naturally, what might be the least solemn form to give it, among recognized and familiar forms. The question thus at once arose: What form so familiar, so recognized among alert readers, as that in which the ingenious and inexhaustible, the charming philosophic "Gyp" casts most of her social studies? Gyp had long struck me as mistress, in her levity, of one of the happiest of forms—the only objection to my use of which was a certain extraordinary benightedness on the part of the Anglo-Saxon reader. (9:xii)

"Light irony," by the way, seems to me a grossly inaccurate characterization of *The Awkward Age*. Ironic it is, certainly, through and through, but the irony is somber. The catastrophic renunciation and loss at the end, in this case, though they are characteristic of the denouements in all James's fiction, are anything but comic. Nor does the ending have so much the motif of gain in loss that is characteristic of James's acts of renunciation.

Who Was Gyp?

Who was Gyp? The very name *Gyp*, much less her characteristic form, can hardly be said to be all that recognizable even among alert readers

today. Many specialists in modern French literature have never heard of
her, as I have found out by asking around. Nor have recent critics of James
much followed up this precious clue. Gyp was the pseudonym of a nine-
teenth- and twentieth-century French writer with the almost unbelievable
name, so resonant of the Ancien Régime and the French Revolution, of
Sibylle Gabrielle Marie Antoinette Riqueti de Mirabeau, Comtesse de
Martel de Janville (1849–1932). Gyp was the author of many novels, plays,
and other works. Friedrich Nietzsche, of all people, also greatly admired
her. He mentions her in *Ecce Homo* as a model writer.[18] This is about the
only overt connection between James and Nietzsche that I can think of.

That "happiest of forms," of which Gyp was mistress, was the use of
dialogue in novels that dispensed almost altogether with narrative comment or "going behind." Gyp indicates the speakers simply by giving the
characters' names, or by writing "he" or "she," or just by a dash. Gyp's
novels, like James's *The Awkward Age*, are almost like the written form of
a play, with stage directions. Here is one example, the final pages of *Le
Mariage de Chiffon*, translated (falsely) as *A Gallic Girl*:

> Too shortsighted to catch his glance, Darling [the absurd English trans-
> lation of "Chiffon"] asked, after a long reflection:
> —So you are going away from here, according to what the prince has
> said, in order to do beautiful deeds?
> He shrugged his shoulders. The girl continued:
> —Well, I could indicate to you a very beautiful deed, not far off, either.
> And as he made no answer, she whispered:
> —It would be to marry me.
> Become very pale, the Vicomte walked toward her:
> —What did you say?
> —You have heard . . .
> He replied:
> —Your jokes are ferocious . . . and not funny . . .
> —Jokes!—exclaimed Coryse—I love you more than anything, and there
> are moments when it seems to me that you also love me more than all the
> rest . . . and so I tell you: "Marry me."
> —Darling—said Uncle Marc, softly drawing the little girl [*la petite*] to
> his arms—Oh, yes. I love you. I love you. I love you.
> —So you consent?
> He was covering her with kisses. She sighed:
> —Oh, how good it is to be kissed by you. [*Oh! Que c'est bon . . . d'être
> embrassée par toi! . . .*]
> Then, in a burst of laughter:

—What faces they'll make down-stairs when they know this.

Uncle Marc looked at Darling, hesitating to believe that she was his. Bent on her face, he muttered in a kiss:

—Oh, Darling, if you knew how I have been unfortunate, discouraged and jealous.

—Jealous? . . . oh, that . . . you shouldn't have been.

And coming closer to him, she said, caressingly and tenderly [*Et se serrant éperdument contre lui, elle balbutia, câline et tendre*]:

— . . . It would greatly astonish me if I ever deceived you [*si je te trompais jamais . . . toi! . . .*].[19]

Gyp's novels are, at least from the perspective of the ordinary English or American reader of James's time, scandalously indecent and immoral. Chiffon, for example, though she is barely of marriageable age (just over sixteen), knows all about the illicit liaisons of the adults around her. That knowledge does not seem to have harmed her much or interfered with her suitability for marriage. She ends by marrying her forty-year-old step-uncle. She proposes to him rather than he to her, in defiance of propriety and of the marriage plans of her parents. *Le Mariage de Chiffon* has a wonderfully happy ending. It satisfies the middle-aged man's fantasy of marrying a beautiful, intelligent, irreverently lively, and sexually attractive teenager, or, perhaps, since the novel was written by a woman, the young girl's fantasy of being like Chiffon and of marrying a kindly and affectionate man old enough to be her father. The "situation" in *Le Mariage de Chiffon* is somewhat the same as that of *The Awkward Age*, but the outcome, as will not surprise Jamesian adepts, is the reverse, as I shall show. The reader should keep in mind my basic question of the appropriateness of form to substance in James's novel. How could James use Gyp's form for so different a substance?

James's goal in *The Awkward Age*, he says, was to follow the charming philosophic Gyp and make his novel as much like a stage play as possible. He would give only what the characters said to one another plus a notation of what an observant spectator would have seen in the way of facial expression, bodily movement, exchanged looks, and so on. The latter would be like an extended and continuous set of stage directions, but no "going behind" would be allowed.

The Theory of Occasions

James follows his confession that Gyp was his model (though, as he says, no one has noticed the indebtedness) with a long diatribe against the intellectual impoverishment of stage plays and their audiences in England at that time. This gives one possible explanation for James's adaptation of Gyp's form. Earlier in the 1890s James had dreamed of becoming a successful playwright, but his earnestly contrived *Guy Domville* (1895) was hissed off the stage. This was a great humiliation for James, especially since Oscar Wilde's *The Eternal Husband* was at that moment enjoying a great success at a neighboring London theater.[20] Choosing a form modeled on drama for *The Awkward Age* may have been a covert way of trying to demonstrate that he could, after all, write successfully in dramatic form. This is by no means the whole story, however. Later in the preface James describes how he presented to the editors of *Harper's Weekly* (where the novel first appeared in parts in 1898–99), a model for his projected novel:

> I remember that in sketching my project for the conductors of the periodical I have named I drew on a sheet of paper—and possibly with an effect of the cabalistic, it now comes over me, that even anxious amplification may have but vainly attenuated—the neat figure of a circle consisting of a number of small rounds disposed at equal distance about a central object. The central object was my situation, my subject in itself, to which the thing would owe its title, and the small rounds represented so many distinct lamps, as I liked to call them, the function of each of which would be to light with all due intensity one of its aspects. I had divided it, didn't they see? into aspects—uncanny as the little term might sound (though not for a moment did I suggest we should use it for the public), and by that sign we would conquer. . . . Each of my "lamps" would be the light of a single "social occasion" in the history and intercourse of the characters concerned, and would bring out to the full the latent color of the scene in question and cause it to illustrate, to the last drop, its bearing on my theme. I reveled in this notion of the Occasion as a thing by itself, really and completely a scenic thing, and could scarce name it, while crouching amid the thick arcana of my plan, with a large enough O. (9:xvi–xvii)

The reader will note that the "lamps" here are not centers of consciousness, but objectively presented social scenes, the give and take of conversation in a drawing room. It might appear at first that James is presenting the reader with another exclusively visual figure for the procedures of the novelist, another figure like "focalization" or "point of view." A careful reading, however, shows that matters are not quite so simple. James's figure is presented overtly, up front, as a figure, a trope, and an "arcane," "cabalistic," or "uncanny" one, at that. What is cabalistic, arcane, or uncanny about it? The terms refer to a code for something secret and to the experience of something spooky that nevertheless seems somehow familiar, something, in short, in Freud's term, *unheimlich*. The mystery lies in the impossibility of naming, in so many words, the "central object," his "situation." That central object is uncanny because it appears only in ghosts or revenants, doubles of itself, never in itself or as itself. James nowhere says what he put down, as a picture of this central object, on his mystic sheet of paper, over which he "crouched" like some medieval mage. Was it a point, or another circle, or the drawing of some object or other? He does not say. He does not say because he cannot say. He can only shine lamps on the object and reveal its "aspects" one by one through that method. The rhetorical label for this procedure, that is, for the tropological naming of something that does not have a literal name, is *catachresis*. Each of James's "Occasions" is a catachresis for an unnamed central object, the situation, which can be named in no other way.

To call each "Occasion" a "lamp" to "light with due intensity one of its aspects" differs fundamentally, moreover, from the figure of "focalization" used by narratologists. The latter implies that the object of the narration is there to be seen. It is just a matter of getting it into focus. James's figure of "Occasions," by contrast, implies that the object is in the dark, to some degree permanently in the dark. It, or rather just one of its "aspects," can only be brought into the light indirectly, by a given "Occasion," which functions performatively to expose it. *Occasion*: the word names something that happens or befalls, a fortuitous event. It comes from Latin *occidere* (past participle *occasus*), "to fall down." The difference between a lamp and a focalizer is analogous to Meyer Abrams's famous distinction between the mirror and the lamp. Abrams set the mirror of classical theories of mimesis against the quasi-constitutive force of poetic language. The latter is figured in romantic theories as a lamp.

What justifies my implicit claim, when I speak of catachreses, that these Occasions are acts of language figured by the optical images James uses, not literally matters of seeing at all? The answer is that each of these "aspects" is an "Occasion," that is, a scene in which two or more characters confront one another and talk. Of soliloquy, such as Isabel's midnight vigil in *The Portrait of a Lady*, there is none. Most often a scene is made of the confrontation of two characters, or perhaps of three, but at certain crucial moments a whole roomful of personages, Mrs. Brook's whole "set," are presented talking to one another. This, by the way, is something extremely difficult to do successfully in a novel. Even in such "crowd scenes," nevertheless, most of the action is carried forward by the tête-à-tête, the give and take of talk between two characters. What they say may or may not be overheard by anyone other than that ubiquitous witnessing and testifying narrative voice, surrogate for the reader or imagined spectator. The novel advances and its subject is exposed, for the most part, through scenes in which one character confronts another face to face.

James mentions in the preface three of these Occasions as exemplary of his general procedure: "the hour of Mr. Longdon's beautiful and, as it were, mystic attempt at a compact with Vanderbank, late at night, in the billiard-room of the country house at which they are staying," "the other nocturnal passage, under Mr. Longdon's roof, between Vanderbank and Mitchy, where the conduct of so much fine meaning, so many flares of the exhibitory torch through the labyrinth of mere immediate appearances, mere familiar allusions, is successfully and safely effected," and "the general service of co-ordination and vivification rendered, on lines of ferocious, or really quite heroic compression, by the picture of the assembled group at Mrs. Grendon's, where the 'cross-references' of the action are as thick as the green leaves of a garden, but none the less, as they have scenically to be, counted and disposed, weighted with responsibility" (9:xxii–xxiii).

Looks

Though the interchange between the characters is carried on primarily by way of what they say to one another, another extremely important and enigmatic form of communication between two characters recurs often enough to be a leitmotif. This is the reciprocal look of two pairs of eyes. The dialogues between one pair of characters or another that make up most of the novel are always "interviews" in the literal or etymological sense, views exchanged from one to the other, as each, at least intermittently, looks the other in the eye and is looked at in return, in a "meeting of looks":

> She met his look after an instant, and the wan loveliness and vagueness of her own had never been greater. (9:46)

> The two women, on this, exchanged, tacitly and across the room—the Duchess at the door, which a servant had arrived to open for her, and Mrs. Brookenham still at her tea-table—a further stroke of intercourse, over which the latter was not on this occasion the first to lower her lids. (9:65)

Little Aggie had a smile as softly bright as a Southern dawn, and the friends of her relative [the Duchess] looked at each other, according to the fashion frequent in Mrs. Brookenham's drawing-room, in free exchange of their happy impression. (9:94)

It was a place in which, at all times, before interesting objects, the unanimous occupants, almost more concerned for each other's vibrations than for anything else, were apt rather more to exchange sharp and silent searchings than to fix their eyes on the object itself. (9:107)

The two men, on this, exchanged a long regard. (9:128)

On this, with a drop of his mirth, he met her eyes, and for an instant, through the superficial levity of their talk, they might have appeared to sound each other. . . . These remarks were followed on either side by the repetition of a somewhat intenser mutual gaze, though indeed the speaker's eyes had more the air of meeting his friend's than of seeking them. (9:180, 183)

To that in turn, however, he responded only the more completely, taking her hand and holding it, keeping it a long minute during which their eyes met and something seemed to clear up that had been too obscure to be dispelled by words. (9:231–32)

It was a business sometimes really to hold her eyes, but they had, it must be said for her, their steady moments. She exchanged with Vanderbank a somewhat remarkable look, then, with an art of her own, broke short off without appearing to drop him. (9:303)

Their eyes met long on it. (9:358)

Her friend also paused, and it was as if for a little, on either side of a gate on which they might have had their elbows, they remained looking at each other over it and over what was unsaid between them. (9:443)

She made, at this, a movement that drew his eyes to her own, and for a moment she dimly smiled at him. (9:458)

The eyes of the two men met over it . . . (9: 481)

[T]he eyes of the two visitors again met for a minute. (9:486)

Well, that it *was* the right tone a single little minute was sufficient to prove—a minute, I must yet haste to say, big enough in spite of its smallness to contain the longest look on any occasion exchanged between these friends. It was one of those looks—not as frequent, it must be admitted, as the muse of history, dealing at best in short cuts, is often by the conditions of her trade reduced to representing them—which after they have come and gone are felt not only to have changed relations but absolutely to have cleared the air. (9:503–4)

He looked at her with a complexity of communication that no words could have meddled with. (9:536)

[She] could only give her friend one of those looks that expressed: "If I could trust you not to assent even more than I want, I should say 'You know what I mean!'" (9:539)

The adept reader will notice that such passages recur in a string punctuating the novel at intervals. They gain meaning and import from their repetition, according to a general rule presiding over the establishment of meaning in narrative through recurrence. Other examples are the increase in meaning through repetition of the expletive "Oh," uttered on so many different occasions by different characters. I shall have more to say about "Oh" in the chapter about *The Wings of the Dove*, and also about the locution "There you are!," which recurs in both that novel and in *The Awkward Age*. The phrase appears at the very ends of both as a final climax. "There I am," says Nanda to Mr. Longdon as an ultimate sealing of the compact between them, and "There we are," answers Mr. Longdon (9:545). A stylistic consistency relates the two novels to one another.

The exchanged looks in *The Awkward Age* occur with increasing frequency toward the novel's end, in a mild crescendo or cascade. Their significance as a primary means of communication among the characters is made more explicit. What is enigmatic about these "looks" is that the narrator usually does not say in so many words what, if anything, was communicated by the look. It may be a deep form of intersubjective understanding not shared with the reader. It may, however, be an experience, each time, of the inscrutability and impenetrability of the other, the otherness of the other. The narrative voice does not, in many cases, say one way or the other.

As the reader can see from looking in imagination at these looks, they by no means express unequivocally a mutual understanding. They suggest, rather, that the relations among these imaginary persons, in spite of the bonhomie, good humor, unanimity of judgment, apparent frankness, and total openness prevailing in this community, are in fact an implacable battle of wills, a struggle for domination. Mrs. Brook at one point, for example, is unwilling to have her two closest friends in their circle, Mitchy and Vanderbank, leave her to go off together, since they are both "against

her": "What was in her face indeed during this short passage might prove
to have been, should we penetrate, the flicker of a sense that in spite of all
intimacy and amiability they could, at bottom and as things commonly
turned out, only be united against her" (9:311). The narrative voice, James
promises, does not penetrate, but after all it *does* penetrate.

Each character, in the give and take of talk and of portentous looks
exchanged, attempts to hide his or her true motives behind a veil of apparent candor. Each uses language, not primarily as a means of intercommu-
nication, but as a way of coercing the other through language to act in the
way he or she wants. They use language performatively, as a way of doing
something with words. Mrs. Brookenham wants Mitchy to marry Nanda
so she can have Vanderbank for herself, while the Duchess wants Vanderbank to marry Nanda so she can marry little Aggie to the wealthy Mitchy
and be free to carry on her affair with Petherton, who is now too much
preoccupied by his friendship with Mitchy. The Duchess's plan backfires,
to the Duchess's deep chagrin, when the newly initiated Aggie immediately begins betraying her husband Mitchy in an affair with Petherton,
thus depriving the Duchess of unshared possession of the latter. All these
people try to bring about what they want by what they say to one another
and by the coercive force of a look deep into the other's eyes. It is like the
way two animals try to stare one another down, or like the way a direct
look in the other's eyes is, in inner-city America, a physical challenge that
can lead to violence. The inner-city look says, "I dare you!" Do not most
exchanged looks, however, in any social situation, have a similar preverbal
meaning?

One signal example of the attempt to use words, rather than looks, to
force the other to behave or to be in a certain way is a form of locution
The Awkward Age shares with *The Wings of a Dove* and *The Golden Bowl*.
This locution masks itself as a constative statement, but it actually has
performative force. A multitude of examples punctuate the novel, for example, in Vanderbank's or Mitchy's repeatedly calling Mrs. Brookenham
"magnificent." I give, however, as exemplary a series of such locutions in
the final scene between Nanda and Mitchy. "You're complete!," he says
to her, "But you're too wonderful." Later she says to him, "you're wild—
you're wild" (9:519, 523). Still later he says, "You're stupendous, my
dear!" (9:528). Though these statements seem descriptive, they tend to
bring about the thing they name. Certainly this is so for the reader. They
give the reader a possibly adequate adjective for the character they are
used to describe. They bring it about that Nanda, for example, *is* "stupen-

dous." In effect, they are ellipses for what would be an explicit performative utterance: "I declare you to be stupendous."

Occasions Are Acts

Each scene or Occasion, James says, would be like an act in a play. He would scrupulously obey in each Occasion the formal limitations he had established for himself:

> The beauty of the conception was in the approximation of the respective divisions of my form to the successive Acts of a Play—as to which it was more than ever a case for charmed capitals. [He means just as he capitalized "Occasion" in a previous sentence, so he now capitalizes "Acts of a Play" to emphasize its importance as a formal principle.] The divine distinction of the act of a play—and a greater than any other it easily succeeds in arriving at—was, I reasoned, in its special, its guarded objectivity. This objectivity, in turn, when achieving its idea, came from the imposed absence of that "going behind," to compass explanations and amplifications, to drag out odds and ends from the "mere" storyteller's great property-shop of aids to illusion: a resource under denial of which it was equally perplexing and delightful, for a change, to proceed. Everything, for that matter, becomes interesting from the moment it has closely to consider, for full effect positively to bestride, the law of its kind. "Kinds" are the very life of literature, and truth and strength come from the complete recognition of them, from abounding to the utmost in their respective senses and sinking deep into their consistency. I myself have scarcely to plead the cause of "going behind," which is right and beautiful and fruitful in its place and order; but as the confusion of kinds is the inelegance of letters and the stultification of values, so to renounce that line utterly and do something quite different instead may become in another connection the true course and the vehicle of effect. (9:xvii)

This seems clear enough, but just why does James renounce "going behind," that is, give up his special line, what he is famous for doing? Why does he attempt to write a novel that is as much as possible like a stage play, or, one might say, is like a report on an imaginary play as seen by a clever spectator? Why does this "form" seem to James especially appropriate for this particular "substance," this "central object," this "situation," this "subject in itself"? The answer, though one hopes this is not the case, may be that no particular consonance between form and substance, in this instance, exists. He just wanted to try something else for a change. The novel could have been written as *The Portrait of a Lady* or *The Golden Bowl* or *The Ambassadors* is written. James just decided to experiment with dramatic or scenic form. Once he had decided to do that, however, an aesthetico-moral obligation not to confuse kinds required that he be strictly consistent.

What primarily happens, on each of these Occasions, is that two, or sometimes three, personages, occasionally a whole group, engage in an intense, witty, highly ironic and indirect give and take of conversation. They, like James in the preface, call it "talk." What do they talk about? They speculate about the sexual misbehavior of those on the periphery of their circle, and they talk about their own situations in relation to Nanda's "coming down," the central "subject" around which they all gather. Each Occasion illuminates some "aspect" of that. It illuminates it by interpreting it in one way or another, whether correctly or not it is sometimes difficult to say, since the reader is given only what the characters say. We can know only their talk, which illuminates one or another "aspect" of the central "situation." Those closest to Nanda do most of the talking—her mother, Mitchy, Vanderbank, Mr. Longdon, Nanda herself. All have in various ways much to hide or to prevaricate about or to be mistaken about.

The Awkward Age's concentration on "talk" makes it somewhat similar to another James work written at more or less the same time, *The Sacred Fount* (1901). In the latter, people spending the weekend together at a country house speculate on the hidden relations of their fellow guests to one another. In *The Sacred Fount*, however, the story is narrated in the first person by one character, perhaps the most deluded of all in his interpretation of the way the illicit sexual relations among his fellow visitors have changed them. In *The Awkward Age*, all the central characters are presented objectively in their acts of interpretation. It will not escape the thoughtful reader that he or she, though less involved, is in just the characters' situation. The reader too must interpret, on the basis of the evidence given, the central situation. Our position as readers is represented by the situation of the "readers" of the social scene inside the novel itself.

The way each "Occasion" is devoted to presenting, often with conspicuous indirection, one or another aspect of the central subject in its manifold relations is obliquely objectified in the way James names each "book" of the ten books in the novel with the name of one or another character. What is strange about these names, to me at least, is the way they sometimes name a character who is clearly central to the chapters in that book, as "Book Tenth" is called "Nanda," but sometimes, as in the case of "Book First," which is called "Lady Julia," name a character who is offstage during those chapters or who may appear peripheral to what happens in that book. Lady Julia is already long dead in "Book First." Tishy Grendon, who gives her name to "Book Eighth," is by no means the center of attention in that book. It centers on an account of Mrs. Brook's deliberate smashup of her circle by putting the finishing touches on the evidence that her daughter Nanda knows everything, knows too much to be marriageable, at least to the man she loves, Vanderbank. The reader is left to puzzle out for himself or herself just why a given book has the title it does. Those titles do, however, make a slow rotation through the names of the chief actors in the drama. They thereby reinforce James's figure of the little circles arranged in a circle around a small central circle. The book titles also reinforce James's claim that his central subject exists in terms of the complex relations among the characters. Each person exists not as himself or herself, in isolation, but as his or her relations to others, his or her exposure to the others. These relations divide the characters from one another as much as they join them. The personages remain other to one another, less than ever joined in a verifiable mutual understanding. James provides a striking formulation for this estrangement of the characters from one another near the end of the novel. There he defines the relation between Mr. Longdon and Nanda, complex enough in truth, the reader knows by this time: "Thus they sat together while their trouble both conjoined and divided them" (9:540). I shall return to this scene and to this formulation.

Going Behind (or Not)

A candid and perceptive reader will note that James is not absolutely faithful to his decision not to "go behind." *The Awkward Age* is punctuated by moments when the narrator tells the reader something a character was thinking, something no mere observer could have known. Here are two examples. The first two chapters of the novel are full of notations of what was going on in Vanderbank's mind as he was first making Mr. Longdon's acquaintance, when the latter was a visitor to his apartment late one night:

> [A]t the end of a few moments more Vanderbank became conscious of having proposed his own rooms as a wind-up to their drive. Wouldn't that be a better finish of the evening than just separating in the wet? He liked his new acquaintance. . . . Vanderbank, for that matter, had the kind of imagination that likes to *place* an object, even to the point of losing sight of it in the conditions; he already saw the nice old nook it must have taken to keep

> a man of intelligence so fresh while suffering him to remain so fine. . . .
> Vanderbank was more and more aware that the kind of amusement he ex-
> cited would never in the least be a bar to affection. . . . Vanderbank won-
> dered a moment what things in particular these might be; he found himself
> wanting to get at everything his visitor represented, to enter into his con-
> sciousness and feel, as it were, on his side. . . . Vanderbank was conscious
> of a deep desire to draw from him whatever might come. (9:4, 6, 7, 8, 19)

Vanderbank is presented in all these opening pages as a typical Jamesian
"center of consciousness." He is a perspective from which the consciousnesses of others can, perhaps, be entered and known. Vanderbank wants
to enter into Longdon's consciousness and feel, as it were, on his side.
James's narrator here enters into Vanderbank's consciousness and makes
it possible for the reader to feel, as it were, on *his* side.

Nevertheless, James's inclusion in the preface to *The Princess Casamassima* of Vanderbank in a list of centers of consciousness in his novels is
extremely odd and misleading. After having cited Densher, Strether,
Prince Amerigo, and Maggie as such centers, James says he could list fifty
others in his work, "intense *perceivers*, all, of their respective predica-
ments," "even to the divided Vanderbank of 'The Awkward Age,' the extreme pinch of whose romance is the vivacity in him, to his positive sorrow
and loss, of the state of being aware" (5:xvi). James as author may know
this. Even the narrator of *The Awkward Age* may know it. They give away
what they know, however, only with scrupulous indirection. They keep
Vanderbank's secrets. The reader can, for the most part, only infer Vanderbank's "being aware" from what he says and how he looks. Vanderbank
is, with a few early exceptions, not presented from the inside as a center
of consciousness at all. What he thinks and feels becomes, as the novel
proceeds, an impenetrable secret for the reader, except as that reader, like
an invisible spectator, can infer his interiority from what people, including
Vanderbank, say or do.[21]

It might be argued that the early moments when the narrator "goes
behind" Vanderbank indicate no more than that James took awhile to get
the hang of what he was trying to do. Since the novel was published in
weekly parts, it was too late, it might be argued, to go back and make the
opening consistent with the whole. Such narrator's intrusions do become
less and less frequent as the novel continues. Vanderbank, for example, is,
perhaps for important strategic reasons, systematically thereafter presented from the outside, with little or no further "going inside." Nevertheless, cases of "going behind" by no means vanish as the novel

progresses. A borderline example is what the narrator says about Vanderbank's reaction to something Nanda says to him. She says, "I always think of you with fear." He answers, "How awfully curious—if it be true!" to which she replies, "Oh Mr. Van, I'm 'true'!" The narrator then intervenes with an odd claim to ignorance matching Vanderbank's ignorance. He can know whatever Vanderbank knows (certainly a claim that he can "go behind"), but in this case Vanderbank did not know, and in any case the narrator will just present what any observer might have seen: "As Mr. Van himself couldn't have expressed at any subsequent time to any interested friend the particular effect upon him of the tone of these words his chronicler takes advantage of the fact not to pretend to a greater intelligence—to limit himself to the simple statement that they produced in Mr. Van's cheek a flush just discernible" (9:212).

This is a wonderfully ironic moment. The narrator knows that Vanderbank did not know, so he, she, or it does, after all "go behind." Since going behind, however, in this case draws a blank (a word used for Vanderbank elsewhere in the novel), the narrator has nothing to say. The chronicler can only chronicle what there is to chronicle. To go beyond that would be to "pretend," to claim a knowledge not possessed. The reader, however, is indirectly made aware of the presence of James behind the narrator. James is the author who has made it all up. He can ascribe to Vanderbank any degree of self-understanding he likes, and report it or not report it. He has chosen in this case to say Vanderbank could not have said at any subsequent time what was the effect on him of "those words."

The reader of the preface will also know, however, that limiting himself to notation of what any attentive spectator would have seen, in this case Vanderbank's just discernible flush, is the strict law of narration in this novel. That law is here enunciated in so many words, in what is, strictly speaking, a parabasis. It is a breaking of the representational illusion in a coming forward to comment on the procedures whereby that illusion is generated. The illusion is generated by what James, in another of the references to the magician's art that punctuate the preface, calls "the conjuror I profess to be" (9:xxii). He is here, however, with great daring, attempting to create illusion while foregoing "to drag out odds and ends from the 'mere' storyteller's great property-shop of aids to illusion" (9:xvii). The narrator refuses to "pretend to a greater intelligence" and limits himself, on the contrary, to objective description of what any spectator would have seen and heard.

The reader sometimes gets notations like the following description of Mr. Longdon's reaction to something Mrs. Brook says. The reader will remember that Longdon had been deeply in love with Mrs. Brook's mother, Lady Julia, now dead, and had been rejected. It was the determining experience of his life: "Mr. Longdon's face reflected for a minute something, he could scarcely have supposed her acute enough to make out, the struggle between his real mistrust of her, founded on the unconscious violence offered by her nature to his every memory of her mother, and his sense on the other hand of the high propriety of his liking her" (9:187). Even here, however, the narrator gives only a peep behind the veil. The report is, after all, a description of what was "reflected" in Mr. Longdon's face. It was therefore evident, "exposed" for any spectator acute enough to read it.

Another example is a two-page sequence beginning "The child herself [little Aggie], the spectator of the incident [Mr. Longdon] was sure enough, understood nothing; but the understandings that surrounded her, filling all the air, made it a heavier compound to breathe than any Mr. Longdon had yet tasted," and so on (9:245–46). The reader is definitely placed by these sentences within Longdon's consciousness.

Much more common, however, so common as to be a leitmotif in the novel, is the appeal to what any sensitive spectator would have seen and thereby inferred. Once more I give a cascade of examples, to demonstrate their frequency and the way they exemplify the narrator's exquisitely careful notation of appearances as clues to intersubjective exchanges:

Just a shade, at this, might have appeared to drop over his [Mr. Longdon's] face, but who was there to know if the girl [Nanda] observed it? (9:148)

[H]er [Mrs. Brook's] method of approach would have interested an observer aware of the unhappy conviction she had just privately expressed [that Mr. Longdon detests her]. (9:186)

Another person present might have felt rather taxed either to determine the degree of provocation represented by Vanderbank's considerate smile, or to say if there was an appreciable interval before he rang out: "I think, you know, you oughtn't to do anything of the sort." (9:269)

A person who knew him [Mr. Longdon] well would, if present at the scene, have found occasion in it to be freshly aware that he was in his quiet way master of two distinct kinds of urbanity, the kind that added to distance and the kind that diminished it. Such an analyst would furthermore have noted, in respect to the aunt and the niece [the Duchess and little Aggie], of which kind each had the benefit, and might even have gone so far as to detect in him some absolute betrayal of the impression produced on him by his actual companion, some irradiation of his certitude that, from the point of view under which she had been formed, she was a remarkable, a rare success. (9:238)

As the reflection of her tone might have been caught by an observer in Vanderbank's face it was in all probability caught by his interlocutress [Nanda], who superficially, however, need have recognized there—what was all she showed—but the right manner of waiting for dinner. (9:389)

What he had already paid, a spectator would easily have gathered from the long, the suppressed wriggle that had ended in his falling back, with some sacrifice of his habit of not privately depreciating those to whom he was publicly civil. (9:400)

"Oh fiendish!" his interlocutor [Vanderbank] said with a short smothered laugh that might have represented for a spectator a sudden start at such a flash of analysis from such a quarter. (9:424)

No spectator worth his salt could have seen them [Mr. and Mrs. Brookenham] more than a little together without feeling how everything that, under his eyes or not, she either did or omitted, rested on a profound acquaintance with his ways. (9:449)

There would have been for a continuous spectator of these episodes an odd resemblance between the manner and all the movements that had followed his [Mitchy's] entrance and those that had accompanied the installation of his predecessor [Vanderbank]. (9:514)

[S]he [Nanda] might on this have been taken as giving him [Mr. Longdon] up with a movement of obedience and a strange soft sigh. The smothered sound might even have represented to a listener at all initiated a consenting retreat before an effort greater than her reckoning—a retreat that was like the snap of a sharp tension. (9:535–36; here the "spectator" becomes a "listener")

Any reader worth his or her salt will notice that in the guise of just naming what was there to be seen or heard the narrative voice often tells the reader how to interpret appearances. It is an effaced form of "going behind," but it is a going behind nevertheless.

What is the effect of the slight lapses in consistency? These lapses occur most overtly at the opening of the novel, but they are present in one way or another throughout. They make the effect of reading *The Awkward Age* quite different from the effect of reading a play's script. They indicate the presence of an all-powerful narrating consciousness or power of speech, the consciousness of the one who is writing down or uttering the words we are reading. He, she, or it could go behind if it liked, but the telepathic narrative voice has to some degree effaced itself for obscure reasons of its own. The narrative voice tells the reader primarily only what can be seen and heard in this fictive reality, with only a few occasional "goings behind." Nevertheless, what can be seen and heard is constantly, in thousands of small comments, interpreted for the reader by the narrator, as in the passage cited above about the reflection in Vanderbank's face of the "tone" with which Nanda says "what's so awfully unutterable is just what we [young unmarried girls] most notice" (9:389). The reader is by no means left alone as if he or she were no more than an invisible spectator.

A Community of Survivors

The mode of narration in *The Awkward Age* now seems clear enough, though it is by no means simple. One big question remains, however. It is a question James never answers in the preface. Why was this particular form, the almost complete forgoing of "going behind," especially appropriate for this particular "situation," this particular "central object"? Or *was* it especially appropriate? Was James's motive perhaps no more than a detached interest in experimenting with a perplexing, challenging, and delightful form, a form quite different from the one he usually adopts?

Only a more penetrating reading of the novel itself can hope to answer these questions. My investigation must be guided by James's own assertion that in a successful literary work substance and form are one. His "picture of Nanda Brookenham's situation," James says, "though perhaps seeming to a careless eye so to wander and sprawl, yet presents itself on absolutely scenic lines, and . . . each of these scenes in itself, and each as related to each and all of its companions, abides without a moment's deflection by the principle of the stage play" (9:xxi). This formal consistency, James goes on to say, "helps us ever so happily to see the grave distinction between substance and form in a really wrought work of art signally break down" (9:xxi). What does it mean, in this case, to say that substance and form are no longer distinct or distinguishable? James is enunciating here a principle that some decades later became one of the most important elements of the New Criticism's credo. Can we really accept this principle at face value? Why cannot the same "substance" be expressed in different "forms"? In the specific case of *The Awkward Age*, just what is the substance that demands this particular form?

James has told the reader that the germ of the novel is the coming downstairs of an adolescent girl to join adults and hear adult talk. The preface, as I have shown, has much to say about how the problems arising from that come from the unfortunate English habit of compromise. The preface, however, says little or nothing about the actual story that James devised to dramatize the complexities of this situation. In the novel itself, he invents a character, Mr. Longdon, who is an older bachelor of great intelligence and sensitivity. He comes up to London after years of seclusion in his country house. He once wooed Mrs. Brook's now dead mother, Lady Julia, and was rejected. Vanderbank's mother also rejected him. Mr. Longdon's life has been determined by two performatives that were infelicitous. He proposed, at different times, to the mother or grandmother, now both dead, of two main characters, and was refused. Both women said "No!" The woman who says "I won't" rather than "I will" in a marriage ceremony is, the reader will remember, one of Austin's examples of an infelicitous performative. It wrecks the marriage event.

Mr. Longdon is so unused to the free talk and free behavior he finds in Lady Julia's daughter's "set" that he is constantly puzzled or shocked. He serves to a considerable degree as the reader's surrogate for the latter's initiation into the people and events of the story. He is an example of a traditional narrative personage, the innocent outsider, the man from the country or from another country, a Chinaman in England or an Englishman in China. Both Mr. Longdon and Vanderbank have lost sisters. Their strikingly warm friendship, which begins in the opening sections of the novel, is posited on the way they share in the experience of death, the deaths of four beloved women. Those deaths hover over all the characters as an implicit definition of their mode of existence. They live as survivors. It is a special case of the way a community rests on the abyssal foundation of the other's or others' death. This motif was by no means intrinsic to the bare germ of the novel.

Nor is it foreseeable, from anything James says in the preface, that he would have Mr. Longdon strongly attracted, in pity and love, to the eighteen-year-old Nanda, Lady Julia's grand-daughter. He comes to love her, as an old man can love a young girl, without concupiscence. He loves her because she is, as he tells Vanderbank, in face, body, gesture, though not in mind, an uncanny repetition of Lady Julia. He loves Nanda by way of his love for the dead Lady Julia. The latter, dead though she is, nevertheless gives her name to the first book of the novel. Longdon's first meeting with Nanda makes him weep with emotion: " 'It's the most extraordinary thing in the world. I'm too absurd to be so upset'—Mr. Longdon smiled through his tears—'but if you had known Lady Julia you'd understand. It's *she* again, as I first knew her, to the life; and not only in feature, in stature, in color, in movement, but in every bodily mark and sign, in every look of the eyes above all—oh to a degree!—and in the sound, in the charm of the voice'" (9:144).

This complex interpersonal situation, involving Mr. Longdon and Nanda, but also Vanderbank, as well as all those dead women, is the true donnée, or presupposition, or foundation, of *The Awkward Age*. It is an odd triangle: Nanda, Longdon, Vanderbank. It hovers, in its interchanges, or, rather, its failure of interchange, over the deaths of others. These dead others exist, not only in the memories of the characters, but in several other ways. They exist, for example, as a component of the photographs of the dead and living that Mr. Longdon encounters in the opening scene. The photographs are hung on the walls of Vanderbank's apartment (9:7–11). Photographs and the telegraph are two modern technologies of communication and preservation that appear in *The Awkward Age*:

> Mr. Longdon had paused. "I'm an old boy who remembers the mothers," he at last replied.
> "Yes, you told me how well you remember Mrs. Brookenham's." [That is Lady Julia, whom Mr. Longdon loved and lost.]
> "Oh, oh!"—and he arrived at a new subject. "That must be your sister Mary,"
> "Yes; it's very bad, but as she's dead—."
> "Dead? Dear, dear!"
> "Oh long ago"—Vanderbank eased him off. (9:11)

The pathos of photographs, we know, is that, when they are of people, they are always of the dead. They record a moment that is gone forever with the click of the shutter. The same thing may be said of the past tense employed by the narrator, as, for example, in the citation just made. The discrete past tenses in "replied," "arrived," and "eased" push the event back into an indefinitely distant past. It becomes something as dead as Lady Julia, though it may be resurrected by our act of reading the words on the page. Realist representation in fiction and photographs are alike in this, whereas everything in a stage play is in the present, however much the characters may be obsessed with the past—as Oedipus, for example, is. The "illustration" of the New York Edition of James's work with photographs taken by Charles Coburn is more than a simple acceptance of publishing convention. These images put all James's work back into a long-dead historical moment, the moment Coburn took those pictures. The reprint of the New York Edition seriously falsifies by omitting the photo-graphs. Coburn's photographs, according to James's stipulations, scrupu-lously leave out people. They are, James says in the preface to *The Golden Bowl*, meant to be "images always confessing themselves mere optical sym-bols or echoes, expressions of no particular thing in the text, but only of the type or idea of this or that thing. They were to remain at the most small pictures of our 'set' stage with the actors left out" (23:xi). A good example of this procedure is the photograph of an empty bench used on the cover of this book. In James's novels and tales, benches often serve as meeting places where crucial speech acts are exchanged or withheld—as in Lord Warburton's proposal to Isabel in *The Portrait of a Lady*, or a crucial discussion between Vanderbank and Nanda in *The Awkward Age*, or the last decisive confrontation between Maggie and Charlotte in *The Golden Bowl*. It is as though Coburn had, as James says, photographed the empty stage set, in this case an outdoor bench, before, or after, some determining meeting between two characters takes place, or has taken place, there. James's penultimate story is called "The Bench of Desola-tion" (1909–10). This is a good name for the bench in Coburn's photo-graph, though it actually illustrates "Saltram's Seat" in an earlier story, "The Coxon Fund" (1894). Frank Saltram, the protagonist of that story, is loosely modeled on Samuel Taylor Coleridge, but it is a Coleridge passed, as James says in the preface, through the alembic of James's autho-rial imagination (15:xvi–xviii). The dead Coleridge haunted James's imagi-nation, just as events that have taken place or will take place seem to haunt Coburn's empty bench.

The figure of resurrection, as of ghosts raised from the dead, appears in another way in an odd interchange between Mrs. Brook and Van. This interchange gives the reader another figure for the way the dead haunt the living. The topic is plans or intentions that have never been carried out. Mrs. Brookenham speaks wittily of these:

> Oh Edward's [her husband's] dead thoughts are indeed a cheerful company and worthy of the perpetual mourning we seem to go about in. They're worse than the relations we're always losing without seeming to have any fewer, and I expect every day to hear that the *Morning Post* regrets to have to announce in that line too [the line of dead thoughts] some new bereave-ment. The apparitions following the deaths of so many thoughts *are* partic-ularly awful in the twilight, so that at this season, while the day drags and drags, I'm glad to have any one with me who may keep them at a distance. (9:282)

This passage is a good example of the speculative freedom and ironic hyperbole that characterizes Mrs. Brookenham's talk, and that of the other members of their "set." This community is strangely joined and disjoined in their joint inability ever fully to understand one another and in mourning for the dead. The passage is also a good example of the subtle relevance of apparently irrelevant remarks.

Exposure to What?

Just what is it that these two innocents, Mr. Longdon from his vantage point of the previous generation and Nanda from her vantage point of virginal ignorance, are exposed to when they hear the free talk in Mrs. Brook's drawing room? The answer to this question will help me along toward an answer to the overall question posed at the beginning of this chapter. Does *The Awkward Age* represent a viable community that endorses and guarantees the felicity of speech acts? This has been constantly, though perhaps somewhat covertly, the guiding thread that has conducted me through the labyrinth of topics a responsible reading of the novel must take up.

Sigmund Freud, in *Jokes and Their Relation to the Unconscious*, asserts that when men are left to talk together, without the presence of women, they talk "smut," that is, they tell one another dirty stories.[22] That is just the case with Mrs. Brook's "circle," though both men and women are present in this case. Their talk consists chiefly in ironic, indirect speculation about the possible sexual misbehavior of their circle's members and, especially, of those at its periphery. One thing is certain about this "community." Few, if any, of its members are able to keep their marriage vows, at least so it seems, since the reader's evidence is always indirect. The conventions of fiction in that day prevented James from showing his characters *in flagrante delicto*, as a modern novelist would do and as film or TV versions of James's novels do. Examples are the way the film versions put the lovemaking of Densher and Kate in *The Wings of the Dove* or of Prince Amerigo and Charlotte in *The Golden Bowl* before the viewers' eyes, whereas they are definitely offstage in the novels themselves.

A fundamental feature of James's novels is that the sex act, especially the illicit sex act, must be spoken of indirectly, hinted at, presented by innuendo, known by guesswork and through covert signs, even to the reader. The sex act is the unspeakable, the unpresentable. This means that any signs for it or words for it are catachreses, words for the wordless and unwordable. Mr. Cashmore, it seems, is betraying his wife, Lady Fanny, through a liaison with Carrie Donner, whose husband is no better than she is. In a striking scene, the two women, lawful wife and mistress, embrace and kiss in Mrs. Brook's drawing room. Lady Fanny remains poised throughout the novel, at least so Mrs. Brook's circle thinks, on the verge of running off with another man. A long passage describes their pleasure in wondering about that: "She's the ornament of our circle," says Mrs. Brookenham. "She will, she won't—she won't, she will! It's the excitement, every day, of plucking the daisy over" (9:178). Though the Duchess is exquisitely careful to keep her niece, little Aggie, in total ignorance of the facts of sex, and even more ignorant of sexual misdemeanors performed by the adults around her, nevertheless the Duchess is, so it seems, carrying on an affair with Lord Petherton. When the Duchess is successful in marrying Aggie to the immensely rich son of a shoemaker, Mitchy, the marriage is only a few months old before Aggie, now sexually initiated, is, as I mentioned earlier, betraying her husband in flirtations with Lord Petherton. She is now fair game for him. It seems that, in this set, women marry just so they can be free to betray their husbands.

Even more darkly hinted at, even more covert, is the possibility of the love that dare not speak its name. James, who, recent biographers have persuasively argued, was covertly gay, did everything he could to keep his own sexual proclivities secret. Nevertheless, it can be plausibly argued that this is the secret at the center of James's "subject" in *The Awkward Age*. The hidden truth that can only be represented by way of its "aspects," that can only be indirectly illuminated by the scenes that encircle it, according to James's model in the preface, is the diversion from heterosexual desire by homosexual desire. Possibly. I shall say more about this later. Overt homosociality abounds, in any case, in *The Awkward Age*. Petherton is "living off" Mitchy's money, and they are intimate friends. The scenes between Mr. Longdon and Vanderbank or between Vanderbank and Mitchy have a warmth lacking in the presentations of the wary give and take in face to face encounters between a man and a woman in the novel. An example is the scenes in which Nanda and Vanderbank are alone together. What a set! Even today so much adultery would disable more or less any community. A community depends, at least in our normal sense of it, on maintaining more or less intact institutions like marriage. Community depends on the possibility of making marriage promises and in keeping those promises, on pain of severe sanctions.

Dirty French Novels

I have said that these deplorable goings-on are the chief subject of the free
talk among the members of Mrs. Brook's circle, and that they are discussed
by innuendo or by indirection. They are presented to the reader in the
same way. One of the means of this indirect presentation is reference to
works of fiction about adultery and sexual misbehavior. Lady Fanny,
poised as she is to run off with a lover, is, in one place, in a tête-à-tête
between Mrs. Brook and Vanderbank, overtly compared to Anna Karenina
or, rather, to "Anna Karénine": "She'll go, she'll go!" says Mrs. Brook.
"Go where?" asks Vanderbank. "Well to the place her companion will
propose. Probably—like Anna Karénine—to one of the smaller Italian
towns." Van answers, "Anna Karénine? She isn't a bit like Anna" (9:280).
That James uses the French version of Anna's surname indicates that they
both (and James too) have read Tolstoy's great novel about adultery in
French. It is one of a string of references to "dirty French novels" that
punctuates *The Awkward Age*. Early in the novel Mrs. Brook complains
about novels Mitchy has loaned to her: "Mitchy dear, those two books you
were so good as to send me and which—really this time, you extraordinary
man! . . . One has taken one's dose and one isn't such a fool as to be
deaf to some true note if it happens to turn up. But for absolute horrid
unredeemed vileness from beginning to end—" (9:79–80). Much later in
the novel, another obscene French novel, this one with Vanderbank's
name in it in Nanda's hand, plays an important role in the climax of the
novel. It triggers the ultimate demonstration of Nanda's exposure, just as
a notorious French "yellow book" plays a role in Wilde's *The Picture of
Dorian Gray*. The French novel with Vanderbank's name in it has apparently circulated throughout Mrs. Brook's set. It has been read by most of
them, including Nanda, who confesses to having done so at the climax of
one chapter. This French book figures in the scandalous scene in which
the now-married Aggie hides the book from Petherton by sitting on it.
She is pulled off the book by Petherton, in a covertly obscene miming of
their liaison by way of the book.

Could it be possible that these deplorable French books are by "the
ingenious and inexhaustible, the charming philosophic 'Gyp'"? Gyp was,
we know, James's confessed model in the preface. James does not say that
the novel in his novel is by Gyp, nor does he say in the preface anything
about what Gyp's novels actually were about. Nor does he, by the way,
observe that she was a violent political reactionary, an anti-Semite and
anti-Dreyfusard, a proto-fascist. He speaks only of his imitation of her

novels' formal properties. This is not the place for anything like a full discussion of Gyp's writings. The titles alone of some of them, however (there are lots), will indicate that their themes are just the scandalous ones James ascribes to the French novels that have such importance in *The Awkward Age*. Here are some examples: *Autour du divorce*, *Bijou*, *Ce que femme veut . . .?*, *Ceux qui s'en f*—(there is an overt obscenity in the title of this one; it means "Those who say, 'Fuck it'") , *La Chasse de Blanche*, *Le Mariage de Chiffon*, *Cloclo*, *Le Coeur de Pierrette*, *Le Cricri*, *Doudou*, *Le Friquet* (a *friquet* is a *moineau*, a brown bird striped in black, so called because it looks like a monk, though figuratively the word is used as a name for a disagreeable or despicable person.), *Joies d'amour*. You get the idea. It is a wonderful litany of provocative book titles. Such books would not have been appropriate reading for an adolescent girl in England in the 1890s, however much their inexhaustible "philosophical" insight may have been appreciated by those two confirmed bachelors, Henry James and Friedrich Nietzsche. It is no wonder that James speaks in the preface of the "Gyp taint," which no one recognized. He says that though his "private inspiration" had been "the Gyp plan," this model was "artfully dissimulated, for dear life, and applied with the very subtlest consistency, but none the less kept in secret view" (9:xiv).

At some point it may occur to the knowing reader that he or she is at that moment reading a novel not all that different from Gyp's works or from the one that provides the final evidence of Nanda's thorough initiation. It may be that reading *The Awkward Age* will have the same sinister effect on me as reading that "nasty" French novel did on Nanda. Henceforth, I shall know too much, more than it is good for me to know, though in my own case it is too late for this knowledge to disqualify me for marriage. Only women, luckily for me, were so disqualified.

What's the Problem?

Well, if what Mrs. Brook's set talk about and read about is in one way or another *les joies d'amour*, what is the big problem? Why should Nanda or Aggie not know about these matters before they are married? It would not be a problem in most "sets" in the Western world today, where premarital knowledge and act are commonplace. Premarital sexual education is generally thought to be a good thing.

A major act of the historical imagination is necessary in order to grasp just what it was that made the period in England James writes about in

The Awkward Age so much of an awkward age for the middle and upper classes. Why was Nanda's coming down or out such an event? It was because unmarried young women were supposed to know nothing about sex, or about the sexual misdoings of their elders. Adultery, however, according to James's representation at least, seems to have been the primary topic of conversation in a "circle" such as that around Mrs. Brookenham in *The Awkward Age*. Has Lady Fanny betrayed her husband or not? Her name is an oxymoron, combining the gentility of "Lady" with the oblique obscenity of "Fanny." This parallels the name *Fanny Assingham* in *The Golden Bowl*. "Fanny Assingham" contains three terms for "backside," just in case you miss the point. Has Carrie Dormer slept with Mr. Cashmore? Will Mr. Vanderbank ever marry at all? If not, why not?

Here is an example of the kind of "talk" that makes up much of *The Awkward Age*. Mrs. Brookenham and Vanderbank are discussing the way the latter's conversations with Nanda have made him feel "so innocent and good" (9:177):

> "She [Nanda] asks *me* nothing."
> "Nothing?" Vanderbank echoed.
> "Nothing."
> He paused again; after which, "It's very disgusting!" he declared. Then while she took it up as he had taken her word of a moment before, "It's very preposterous," he continued.
> Mrs. Brook appeared at a loss. "Do you mean her helping him [Mr. Cashmore]?"
> "It's not of Nanda I'm speaking—it's of him." Vanderbank spoke with a certain impatience. "His being with her in any sort of direct relation at all. His mixing her up with his other beastly affairs."
> Mrs. Brook looked intelligent and wan about it, but also perfectly good-humored. "My dear man, he and his affairs *are* such twaddle!" (9:177)

This is the sort of talk adolescent girls were not supposed to hear, since the absurd myth in that society was that young women were supposed to go to their marriage beds totally ignorant of the facts of sex. Little Aggie in *The Awkward Age* is the improbable incarnation of that ignorance, while Mrs. Brookenham's daughter Nanda is spoiled for marriage, made unmarriageable, by being "brought down" too early, exposed too soon to adult conversation, and by being allowed to have a young unhappily married woman, Tishy Grendon, as an intimate friend. Tishy is presumably unhappy because her husband abuses or neglects or betrays her by having "affairs."

The problem, James says in the preface, is the unfortunate English habit of compromise. The Duchess, English widow of an Italian nobleman, speaks to this point early in the novel: "I must recognize," she says to Mrs. Brookenham about her need to protect her niece, "the predicament I'm placed in by the more and more extraordinary development of English manners. Many things have altered, goodness knows, since I was Aggie's age, but nothing's so different as what you all do with your girls. It's all a muddle, a compromise, a monstrosity, like everything else you produce; there's nothing in it that goes on all-fours" (9:55). Here again is the motif of the monstrous. The social arrangements would have worked well enough if either the American or the continental tradition had been followed. In the United States sexual matters are never discussed at all, with or without the presence of adolescent girls. On the continent young girls are scrupulously protected, sequestered, until the moment of marriage. England has the sexual talk without the sequestration, while still holding to the tradition requiring innocence and purity for unmarried women. It is an unworkable compromise, cause of much confusion and suffering, as *The Awkward Age* demonstrates.

The title has a double reference. It names the awkward adolescent years when a young woman is neither in nor out. It names also the nineties in England, the fin de siècle. That decade was an awkward age of transition from Victorian approximate silence about sexual misdoings in literature to a new century that would see the publication of such things as Molly Bloom's soliloquy in Joyce's *Ulysses*. I say "approximate silence" because of course adultery and fornication are already central topics in Victorian literature, not to speak of Victorian newspapers. George Eliot refers, in one of her letters, to the London *Times*'s report of a court case in which a married couple sued someone who had defamed the wife's character by accusing her of having had sex before marriage, and then lost the case because cross-examination revealed that what has been said about her was true: "I hope you were as glad as I was at the ending of the Tichborne case [another scandalous court case]. And now there is something quite as odious, but happily briefer. Certainly the Times is not 'family reading.' "[23] The editor's footnote gives the facts: "Sir Travers and Lady Twiss prosecuted Alexander Chaffers for libel in imputing immorality to Lady Twiss before her marriage. After one day of cross-examination Lady Twiss fled from London, and the case collapsed 14 March [1872]" (ibid.).

Lady Twiss's catastrophe was not unlike a much more notorious case, this one happening just a few years before *The Awkward Age*. Oscar Wilde made the suicidal mistake of suing for criminal libel the Marquess of

Queensberry, the father of what today we would call his partner, Lord Alfred Douglas. When the homosexual relations between them were proved through cross-examination, Wilde was arrested, tried, and convicted in 1895, under the law against homosexuality even between consenting adults. He was sentenced to two years at hard labor in Reading Gaol. That case received a lot of journalistic attention, like the one George Eliot deplored.

Perhaps young unmarried women were not allowed to read the newspapers. Newspapers are mentioned by the Duchess at one point in *The Awkward Age* as one of the causes of the contamination of young girls:

> "Unfortunate indeed," cried the Duchess, "precisely *because* they're unmarried, and unmarried, if you don't mind my saying so, a good deal because they're unmarriageable. Men, after all, the nice ones—by which I mean the possible ones—are not on the lookout for little brides whose usual associates are so up to snuff. It's not their idea that the girls they marry shall already have been pitchforked—by talk and contacts and visits and newspapers, and the way the poor creatures rush about and all the extraordinary things they do—quite into *everything*." (9:57)

Popular novels, including many now canonical ones, were, however, just as bad. George Eliot's *Adam Bede* (1849), her first great success, is about a young woman who bears an illegitimate child and then kills it by abandoning it in the woods. The heroine of Dickens's *Bleak House* (1850) is the illegitimate daughter of Lady Dedlock. In a celebrated scene in *Oliver Twist*, the housebreaker Sikes murders Nancy, his paramour and a prostitute. Trollope's *Can You Forgive Her?* (1864–65) focuses, in one of its plots, on Lady Glencora's near elopement with Burgo Fitzgerald. Another Trollope novel, *The Vicar of Bullhampton* (1870), has a "fallen woman," Carrie Brattle, as a central character. Trollope apologizes for her in his preface to the book edition:

> There arises, of course, the question whether a novelist, who professes to write for the amusement of the young of both sexes, should allow himself to bring upon his stage such a character as that of Carry Brattle? It is not long since,—it is well within the memory of the author,—that the very existence of such a condition of life, as was hers, was supposed to be unknown to our sisters and daughters, and was, in truth, unknown to many of them. Whether that ignorance was good may be questioned; but that it exists no longer is beyond question. Then arises a further question,—how far the condition of such unfortunates should be made a matter of concern to the sweet young hearts of those whose delicacy and cleanliness of

thought is a matter of pride to so many of us. Cannot women, who are
good, pity the sufferings of the vicious, and do something perhaps to mitigate and shorten them, without contamination from the vice?[24]

The Victorian reading public, including the young women who read
novels, could hardly have remained in ignorance, even if they had not read
Gyp. *The Awkward Age* presupposes a general atmosphere of illicit sex,
performed or contemplated, in the group that makes up the novel's "community." Nevertheless, the presumption of *The Awkward Age*, or at least
of the Duchess, spokeswoman for the proprieties among the members of
Mrs. Brookenham's "set," is that "sweet young hearts" should know nothing whatsoever about such matters. Though the Duchess herself is as bad
as the rest in her own behavior, she is bringing up her niece, Little Aggie,
on the principles she enunciates. Mrs. Brookenham, on the contrary, has
allowed her daughter, Nanda, to learn prematurely about sexual matters,
with disastrous results.

The irony is that little Aggie, as soon as she is married, becomes as bad
as the rest. Nanda, on the contrary, remains of an admirable moral rectitude. She and Mr. Longdon are the only two characters in the whole novel
whose morals are impeccable, or, to put it more strongly, who are in every
way thoroughly admirable. That is in no small part what is so moving, to
me at least, about Nanda and her fate. Nanda simply and directly wants
the best for all those around her. Talking to her even does good to poor
immoral Mr. Cashmore.

Nanda's goodness may have as one of its manifestations her complete
lack of irony. She has no gift for figurative language, nor does she possess
a sense of humor. She is absolutely literal in what she says to the others.
She rarely smiles or laughs, whereas the others are consistently ironic,
figurative, and indirect in what they say, like James himself or like the sly,
evasive narrator who hovers over the whole discourse, making little ironic
comments and concocting outrageous figurative expressions. One of
Vanderbank's most characteristic gestures, the mark of him as a man, is
his laughter, and Mitchy often laughs too. That is a bad sign for both of
them, as is their gift for irony. Irony is immoral, this would imply, a nasty
vice. It does not say what is the case, straightforwardly, but says it is some
other thing, as does figurative language.

Though sexual mores had undoubtedly become looser by the 1890s,
and though the scandal (as it was then thought) of homosexual behavior
had risen nearer the surface of common knowledge, and though talk in
respectable drawing rooms had, if James's testimony can be believed, be-

come freer, the universal assumption was still that a young woman should go to her marriage bed not only a virgin but also entirely ignorant of the facts of sex. I doubt if this was ever really the case, however carefully young girls were protected, but that was the ideological presumption. It followed that if a young woman so much as knew about sex she had figuratively lost her virginity. She was therefore rendered unmarriageable, by a cruel but inexorable logic. By allowing Nanda to enter the circle of adult conversation and to circulate freely in other London drawing rooms or in country houses—for example, in the home of her young, unhappily married friend, Tishy Grendon—her mother has made it inevitable, since Nanda is nothing if not an intelligent listener and observer, that she has come to know "everything."

That this should make Nanda unmarriageable will seem to most people today absurd. A weird patriarchal logic nevertheless lies behind this historical ideologeme. The bridegroom takes possession of his bride by way of the marriage ceremony. This taking over from the father requires in one way or another a considerable outlay of money on his part. This expense is only partly compensated for by whatever dowry his bride may bring. The dowry, if looked at crassly, is payment by the father of the bride to the bridegroom to take his daughter off his hands. Henceforth she is her husband's problem and his possession. Naturally, the bridegroom wants to be sure that he is getting his money's worth, something fresh and new, not already used, as in "used car." This means getting a bride who is a virgin and whose mind is virginal, the proverbial "pious fraud" of a "classic identity with a sheet of white paper" mentioned at one point by Mitchy (9:312). The prospective bridegroom wants to be as sure as possible that his wife will not betray him. Knowing in this case is seen as a kind of doing. The girl who already knows all about sex and about the sexual misbehavior of the adults around her has in a manner of speaking, already betrayed her prospective husband by imagining the sex act, about which she is supposed to know nothing until her husband initiates her.

This strange and unjust but socially effective logic may be expressed as a variant of the incompatibility in speech act theory, at least in Paul de Man's speech act theory or in mine, between knowing and doing things with words. De Man says that performative utterances do something, all right, but that we can never know just what they are going to do or have done. Nanda's fate is an example of the patriarchal logic I am spelling out. She is deprived in the eyes of such a person as the Duchess of the capacity to enunciate felicitous marriage vows. She knows too much to be able to say "I do" and to make it stick. Knowing in this case forbids a successful doing of things with words. Only a girl who is not only physically a virgin but whose mind is also a virgin sheet of white paper is qualified to say "I do." To utter an efficacious marriage vow she must not know what she is doing or saying at the moment of utterance. It may be Nanda's understanding of this, made specific in her knowledge that Vanderbank, whom she loves, will not marry her, that makes her several times in the novel say she will never marry. "I'm one of the people who don't," she says at one point to Mr. Longdon. "I shall be at the end . . . one of those who haven't" (9:232). To her mother, later in the novel, she says, "Oh, . . . I shall never marry" (9:329). These are not just constative statements. They are also speech acts—promises or declarations.

The Duchess enunciates in so many words the implacable social law that makes a girl who knows too much unmarriageable when she persuades Mr. Longdon to join with her in seeing that Nanda is married before it is too late. Marriage hardly leads to happiness in James's fiction, any more than does the failure to marry. The reader may at this point, however, reflect that this society, and maybe even James himself, assumed that all women should marry. Failing to marry was assumed to be a major catastrophe for a woman. A woman's destiny was to marry and bear children. That by no means goes without saying today. For Victorian culture it did. It might also be seen as a remnant of patriarchy that James assumes it is a good thing that Nanda should be, at the end of the novel, adopted and "protected" by Mr. Longdon. That still keeps the semi-emancipated Nanda in a dependent state.

"But we must move fast," says the Duchess to Mr. Longdon. She goes on to explain that if they don't get Nanda married soon, it will be too late: "If Nanda doesn't get a husband early in the business—. . . . Why she won't get one late—she won't get one at all. One, I mean, of the kind she'll take. She'll have been in it over-long for *their* taste." When Mr. Longdon, in his innocence, asks, "Been in what?" she answers "Why in the air they themselves have infected for her!" (9:258).

Nanda's Double Bind

One sees the perfidious double or triple standard here, and the aporia to which it leads. It is all right for men to know all these things and to behave in any way they like. It is all right for married women or women beyond a certain age to know all these things and even, by the 1890s, to behave more or less in any way they like, if they are prepared to take the consequences. Even in the high Victorian period Marian Evans (George Eliot) made such a decision when she lived openly with the already-married George Henry Lewes. An unmarried young woman, however, in that society, may neither know nor act, even though it is the adults themselves that make it impossible for her not to know. They infect the air for her. The result is an impossible impasse or double bind for Nanda, who deeply loves Vanderbank. As the Duchess tells Mr. Longdon, Nanda is secretly "as sick as a little cat—with her passion" for Vanderbank (9:252).

The double bind is the following: Mitchy loves Nanda and is willing to marry her, whatever she knows. He does not care that she has figuratively lost her virginity. Nanda finds marriage with Mitchy impossible just because he does not care what she knows. She can love only someone, like Vanderbank, who does care, but since he does care, he will not marry her. This is expressed most overtly in an interchange in which Nanda persuades Mitchy to promise to propose to little Aggie. Nanda's motive is to "save" them both, to save Aggie from her immoral aunt, the Duchess, and to save Mitchy from an undefined badness that has as least one of its components his too close friendship with Lord Petherton, who "preys" upon him (9:361). A small hint is given that Mitchy is gay, or at least bisexual. At one point the Duchess speaks of him as "living with Petherton" (9:109), though this may mean no more than that they spend a lot of time together. He and Vanderbank seem to have a deep understanding of one another, for example, in the long midnight face to face discussion of their situations that takes place at Mr. Longdon's house. James, you will remember, singles out this interview in the preface for special notice. He speaks of it, in a text already cited, as the "nocturnal passage, under Mr. Longdon's roof, between Vanderbank and Mitchy, where the conduct of so much fine meaning, so many flares of the exhibitory torch through the labyrinth of more immediate appearances, mere familiar allusions, is successfully and safely effected" (9:xxiii). Safe from what? James does not say. He must mean safe from breaking the law he has set for himself against direct expression of his meaning. Why would it be unsafe to express his meaning directly?

In the Occasion just before this one, Nanda tells Mitchy that he has every kind of delicacy except "*the* kind" (9:358), that is, the kind that would make Nanda's full knowledge distasteful. That knowledge has turned her into "a sort of a little drain-pipe with everything flowing through" (9:358). This lacuna, they agree, is enough, as Mitchy says, "to have made me impossible for you because the only man you could, as they say, have 'respected' would be a man who *would* have minded? . . . The man with '*the* kind,' as you call it, happens to be just the type you *can* love? But what's the use . . . in loving a person with the prejudice—hereditary or other—to which you're precisely obnoxious? Do you positively *like* to love in vain?" To which she gives, with her simplicity, candor, and literalness, a "responsible answer": "Yes" (9:358–59). Everyone's recognition of this impasse is the apparent peripeteia or turning point in James's dramatization of his central "subject" in this novel.

Mr. Longdon, who at first loves Nanda because she reincarnates for him her grandmother and then gradually comes to love her for herself, is so anxious to see Nanda married before it is too late that he has solemnly proposed to Vanderbank a "contract" in which he will settle a large sum of money on Nanda (whose parents have nothing, nor does Vanderbank), if Vanderbank will marry her. In the denouement, Vanderbank delays and delays, though Mrs. Brook knows, correctly, from the beginning, as she tells Van when he tells her of Mr. Longdon's offer, "You won't do it."

Nothing is left at the end but for Mr. Longdon to rescue Nanda from the infected air of London and take her to his house in the country. There she will live, forever unmarried, as his beloved companion. Their relation is nothing if not sexually pure, though there are touching kisses and caresses between them. It is a classic James ending: a definitive act of renunciation, with nothing much but increased knowledge and a sense of personal integrity as reward.

Why Does Vanderbank Say No?

Is this, however, quite the whole story in *The Awkward Age*? Just why does Vanderbank refuse Mr. Longdon's generous offer? Is it really just because he finds Nanda an impossible bride, since she knows too much? Is it, as Mrs. Brook predicts, that he is too proud to be "bribed" by Mr. Longdon to marry Nanda? In a Victorian novel, if a pair love one another, the windfall of a fortune for the bride is often just part of the happy ending. Why is it that Mrs. Brook can be so sure that Van won't do it, or, as she says to Mitchy much earlier in the novel, when he tells her that her daughter Nanda loves Vanderbank, "Poor little darling dear! . . . he'll never come to the scratch. And to feel that as *I* do . . . can only be, don't you also see? to want to save her" (9:91). How does Mrs. Brookenham know this? She is hardly disinterested, but her prediction is nevertheless correct.

The obvious way for James to have answered this question for the reader would have been to "go behind" with Vanderbank and to have shown just what he feels and thinks, as is done with the protagonists in James's more famous, and more characteristic, novels. Though a few examples of "going behind" Vanderbank's surface and presenting his interiority occur in the early pages of the novel, as I have shown, quite soon Vanderbank is consistently presented from the outside. We are told what he said, what his expressions and gestures were, but nothing more. This is in strict conformity to the Gyp form and in obedience to the law of kinds.

I conclude that because of this almost complete renunciation of going behind, the reader must decide for herself, on the basis of the evidence that any "spectator worth his salt" (9:449) would have noticed, if that spectator had been an unseen presence in Mrs. Brookenham's drawing room. Why did James do that, and why did Vanderbank refuse Nanda?

I suggest several answers to this final question, all of which may be supported by citations from the text. The text is, after all, all the evidence we have, plus the preface, an entry or two in the *Notebooks*, and comments in the letters. The latter three may or may not be misleading, deliberately or otherwise. In a letter to Mrs. Humphrey Ward, James tells her, "I 'go behind' right and left in 'The Princess Casamassima,' 'The Bostonians,' 'The Tragic Muse,' . . . just as I do it consistently *never at all* (save for a false and limited *appearance*, here and there, of doing it a *little*, which I haven't time to explain) in 'The Awkward Age.'"[25] Well, what does the evidence show?

One may begin by saying that if Vanderbank had married Nanda, as Chiffon is to marry Uncle Marc, it would have gone against the almost universal law of James's fiction. This law says that renunciation is the final act in all his novels. His novels and stories end with a giving up, a giving up most often, though not always, of ordinary marriage or heterosexual relations. Strether refuses Maria Gostrey's offer of herself at the end of *The Ambassadors*. He says: "That, you see, is my only logic. Not, out of the whole affair, to have got anything for myself" (22:326). The unnamed narrator of "The Aspern Papers" refuses to marry Miss Tina, though that is the only way he can get the papers. Isabel refuses Caspar Goodwood's offer to free her from her bad marriage to the perfidious Gilbert Osmond if she will run away with him. Kate Croy refuses to marry Merton Densher in *The Wings of the Dove*, though she has earlier sworn that she gives herself to him forever. Densher is so much "in love with her [Milly's] memory" (20:404), as Kate says, that he will not take Milly's money and then marry Kate, which is the condition Kate sets. The adept reader of James's fiction expects that somehow or other Nanda's passion for Vanderbank will remain unsatisfied. The astute reader will have noted that *renunciation* and *sacrifice* are the words James uses in the preface to define his decision not, in this case, to "Go behind." Novelistic form, for James, is always a matter of sacrifice, a matter of cutting out, of renunciation, in order to avoid sprawl. Form, for James, is mirrored by theme. Each is the allegory of the other.

Well, what is the textual evidence on the basis of which the reader must try to decide why Vanderbank refuses to marry Nanda?

At a certain point in the novel, all the members of Mrs. Brook's circle agree with Mitchy's formulation that Vanderbank arouses a "sacred terror" in all who behold him. He is said to be extremely handsome, but that is hardly enough to explain the fear he inspires. Might it not be that he arouses sacred terror because they understand he cannot feel the heterosexual desire that drives most of them? He is, like a god, "sacred," above or outside the perpetual round of infidelities that keep Mrs. Brook's circle going. Vanderbank can neither make marriage promises nor break them. At least the others are capable of doing that. If Nanda's knowing too much makes her unmarriageable, Vanderbank's homosexuality, if he *is* gay, makes *him* unmarriageable, too. Like Henry James himself, he is not the marrying sort.

It may be that the unnamed and unnameable center of James's subject, the center around which all the scenes hover, the covert point they all illuminate from different aspects, as "Occasions" distributed around in a ring, is the secret of the hidden homosexual component in the London society James describes or imagines. A few faint touches here and there, as evanescent as wisps of smoke, suggest this may be the case. When the Duchess asks Mrs. Brookenham, "What's Mr. Vanderbank looking for?," meaning looking for as a wife, Mrs. Brook answers, "Oh, *he*, I'm afraid, poor dear—for nothing at all!" (9:62). When Mr. Longdon and Vanderbank are discussing the former's offer of a fortune to Nanda if Vanderbank marries her, Vanderbank at one point says, "Well then, we're worthy of each other. When Greek meets Greek—!" (9:265). Well, when Greek meets Greek they know one another instinctively, and quarrel, as the old adage avers, but "Greek love" was also a code name in those days for homosexual love. In another place, already cited, Mitchy and Petherton are spoken of as "living together." That's an odd way to speak of an innocent friendship. In another place Mitchy asks Vanderbank, "Ah aren't we very much the same—simple lovers of life? That is of that finer essence of it which appeals to the consciousness—! . . . Well, enlarged and improved" (9:374). This can be taken as a covert allusion to the famous "Conclusion" to Walter Pater's *The Renaissance*. Pater, notoriously, there counsels the search for "a quickened, multiplied consciousness."[26] The motif of the "sacred terror" Vanderbank inspires is, however, the most overt clue to his possible homosexuality. It picks up what Nanda says to him in their private conversation at Mertle, the country house Mitchy has rented. She says he arouses her fear. She is "horribly—hideously" afraid of him. When he asks "Fear of what?" she says, "I don't know. Fear is fear" (9:211–12). It's the sacred terror.

The *"Unavowable" Community*

I conclude this chapter by formulating an answer to two questions that I asked earlier and left dangling, hanging in the air.

The "form" of *The Awkward Age*, James claims, matches its "substance." Form and substance are indistinguishable. This may be because the "subject" or substance of this novel is something that, for James's reading public, could only be spoken of indirectly. The hidden gay community could only be referred to in the innuendoes of a work chiefly limited to dialogue, without authorial commentary and without much "going behind."

My primary question, however, the big one that has guided all my investigation, is whether or not the "set" James describes in this novel is a community and, if it is, whether or not it is the sort of community that makes felicitous speech acts possible. The answer, I believe, must be that, if it is a community at all, it is what Nancy calls an "unworked community." It is a community whose members are bound together by their ties to the dead and by their ultimate inability to know one another fully. That inability to know, it may be, finds its covert figure in the otherness of homosexual desire for someone who is "straight," or vice versa. In such a community, speech acts are almost always infelicitous. Marriage vows are betrayed as soon as they are made, as happens with little Aggie's marriage to Mitchy. In the case of the contract Mr. Longdon offers, the compact is never even concluded. Vanderbank never signs on the dotted line. He just promises to think it over. Fidelity, promises made and kept, are only possible for those who, like Nanda and Mr. Longdon, exit altogether from the Brookenham circle. As Nanda tells Vanderbank at one point, "My set's Mr. Longdon. . . . He's all of it now" (9:210).

If Mrs. Brook's circle is an "unworked" and unworkable community, the secret community of those who do not feel heterosexual desire is what Maurice Blanchot called a *communauté inavouable*, an "unavowable community." That community is prohibited by society's ban from uttering publicly, in an institutionally sanctioned way, the vows that would seal their loves. They are also even prohibited from avowing in public the liaisons that could be the basis, for them, of sincere promissory speech acts. The continuing of those prohibitions is why the legal sanction of same sex marriages has such social importance these days in the United States and also why it is still so controversial. In James's work that community, if it exists, remained unavowed and unavowable.

That is a wonderfully satisfying conclusion. It puts something definite in that blank center around which all the separate scenes that make up the novel are arranged in a circle, each reflecting one aspect of the unspecified center. James calls this center, evasively, his "subject" or "substance." Moreover, this conclusion is reassuring in that it explains a James novel by way of his biography, in this case his putative homosexuality. Even better, it has the advantage of being fashionable these days. It makes James's work, not just another example of literature written by a dead white canonical male, but something that may be included in "queer studies."

Once More, Matters Are Not So Simple

Only one problem exists with this "satisfying conclusion." This projected unavowable community is so much in the closet that my hypothesis about its covert presence in *The Awkward Age* must remain unproved and unprovable. No conclusive, overt evidence exists supporting my conjecture, only highly indirect hints and suggestions. James says nothing at all in so many words that confirms a conclusion that Vanderbank refuses to marry Nanda because he is not the marrying type.

If the reader looks a little more carefully at the scene in which the phrase "the sacred terror" is introduced, a quite different meaning for it from the one I have hypothesized so far seems enforced by the text. Vanderbank, against his explicit promise to Mr. Longdon, has straightway revealed to Mrs. Brook that Mr. Longdon has proposed to him that if he (Vanderbank) marries Nanda, he (Longdon) will settle a large sum of money on her. Mrs. Brook immediately tells Mitchy when he enters the room. In an apparently frank discussion of this among the three of them, Mitchy, who loves Nanda himself, ruefully and ironically asserts that his extreme moral goodness prevents women—Nanda, for instance—from falling in love with him: "Why, my moral beauty, my dear woman," says Mitchy to Mrs. Brook, ". . . is precisely my curse. What on earth is left for a man just rotten with goodness! It renders necessary the kind of liking that renders unnecessary anything else" (9:308). For this "cheap paradox," Mitchy is fined five pounds, according to the strict rules governing Mrs. Brook's set. The oblique target of this rule against paradoxes is probably Oscar Wilde's celebrated aphoristic paradoxes, the staple of talk in his plays and in his real conversation. Paradoxes were therefore associated with sexual "perversion." Mitchy goes on to explain that what he means is that he doesn't "give out the great thing" (9:308). The great thing is, the context makes clear, a sexual radiance that attracts women's desire. Mitchy then turns to Vanderbank and tells him, "The great thing's the sacred terror. It's you who give *that* out" (9:308). This seems to confirm clearly enough that "sacred terror" refers to Vanderbank's heterosexual charm, not to his covert homosexuality. That charm has inspired Nanda's abysmal love, unless, of course, the phrase is transposed and used with a different sense, when Mrs. Brook employs it later, to name, it may be, his covert homosexuality, his unavailability to women.

This interchange, in any case, is followed by the joint development by the three interlocutors of a curious moral law. This law demonstrates the way these personages are exposed to one another, in Nancy's sense of the word. They are determined as what they are by that exposure. Mrs. Brook explains that the Duchess can carry on her affair with Petherton with impunity because little Aggie is her morality outside herself, whereas she, Mrs. Brook, has her morality within, so that her daughter, Nanda, in a chiasmic reversal, is her external immorality: "Aggie, don't you see? is the Duchess's morality, her virtue; which, by having it that way outside of you, as one may say, you can make a much better thing of. . . . A woman like me has to be *herself*, poor thing, her virtue and her morality. What will you have? It's our lumbering English plan" (9:310–11). That is a slap at the Duchess's "continental" moral plan. Mitchy responds by saying, "So that her daughter . . . can only, by the arrangement, hope to become her immorality and her vice?" (9:311). Talk about paradox! The whole group should have been fined five pounds each for that one.

This conversational sequence, in any case, hardly gives solid support to the hypothesis that Vanderbank is gay. Nor does the sole entry, of any length, about the novel in James's *Notebooks*, a note of March 4, 1895, indicate that any such thing was in James's mind when he first thought of the story: "A young man who likes her—wants to take her out of it—feeling how she's exposed, etc. . . . The young man hesitates, because he thinks she already knows too much; but all the while he hesitates she knows, she learns, more and more. He finds out somehow how much she *does* know, and, terrified at it, drops her: all her ignorance, to his sense, is gone."[27] The "sacred terror" in this note is on Vanderbank's side. He is "terrified" of a young unmarried woman who "knows." Of course James may have changed his mind when he came to write the novel, or he may not have known what he was doing.

Much stronger textual evidence exists, moreover, to support an argument that Mr. Longdon's scheme backfires because Vanderbank is, as Mrs. Brook says, too proud to be bribed to marry Nanda. Or, better, to support the idea that he is terrified of her because she knows too much, has lost her virginal innocence. Or it may be that though he is heterosexual enough, he simply does not love her as she loves him. A plausible case can be made for any one of these four explanations, any one of these four ways of filling in the blank at the center of the ring of little circles. Not enough evidence exists for a conclusive reading.

My hypotheses repeat the kind of speculative hypotheses about one another and about others outside their circle that Mrs. Brook's "set" habitually perform. It is as though what happens inside the novel is contagious. It is "caught" by the reader. The reader performs again something analogous to what the characters perform, though with no more ability to verify speculations than they have, and with the same tinge of performative effect. Talk tends to bring about the thing it projects, as happens for James's imaginary personages. A hypothesis about a given literary work, however arbitrary or not fully supported by the text, tends to generate a plausible critical reading that may come to be widely accepted, or even "canonical," in a circle of readers.

Undecidability Again

Such an object of interpretation is what we call undecidable. *The Awkward Age* is like the famous Gestaltist duck/rabbit. It can be seen (read) in two chief ways, though those ways are logically incompatible. Each reading can be supported by persuasive textual citations, such as I have made. The reader cannot, however, logically affirm both readings at once. They cannot be made to jibe. *Il faut choisir*, but you cannot, on the basis of the evidence, responsibly choose. No solid grounds exist on which to base a choice of one reading over the others. The reader oscillates between two different and irreconcilable ways of reading the novel, each a cover for the other or its shadow, with neither able to take precedence. According to one reading, the decisive (non)event in *The Awkward Age*, Vanderbank's refraining from proposing marriage to Nanda, arises from his covert homosexuality. According to the other reading, Vanderbank's refraining is brought about by his conventional and old-fashioned distaste for girls who know too much and by his unwillingness to be bribed into marrying such a damaged piece of goods. The narrator never "goes behind" to show what Vanderbank's feelings and motives for refusal were. They remain secret. I claim a right reading of *The Awkward Age* reaches this indecision as its endpoint. In such a situation, rather than affirm an unverifiable choice, it is prudent to keep silence, which I shall now proceed to do.

Or, rather, I shall fall silent as soon as I have asked and answered two final questions. What about speech acts in the unworked community of *The Awkward Age*? It is easy to see that Mrs. Brookenham's set provides no solid grounds for felicitous speech acts of the traditional kind. The members of her set habitually break their marriage vows, lie or prevaricate to one another, keep their actual motives and feelings hidden behind a pretence of complete candor and openness, borrow money without repaying it, and so on. They are singularities "other" to one another. They are, moreover, engaged in an implacable battle of wills. In this battle they attempt to coerce the others to act in the ways they want, using language as their chief weapon. What a set! This disabling of speech acts is a primary reason that Mr. Longdon, the man of old-fashioned rectitude from the country, is so scandalized by Mrs. Brookenham's circle. Most conspicuously, the destructive exposure of young unmarried women to premature sexual knowledge makes it impossible for them ever to get a chance to utter marriage vows. This exposure makes it impossible for a man like Vanderbank, secretly conventional, it may be, in requiring virginity of mind as well as body in any prospective wife, to propose marriage to a girl like Nanda. By the time she was of marriageable age, it was, as Mitchy says, "Too late. She was spoiled for him" (9:485). This means that he cannot accept the contract Mr. Longdon offers him.

The two major speech acts in the novel, Mr. Longdon's offer and the marriage of Vanderbank to Nanda that would have ensued, are infelicitous, "misfires," as Austin calls them. They never come off. The worst thing of all is that Nanda's mother seems, out of jealousy, to have deliberately made Nanda unmarriageable by exposing her too soon to sexual knowledge. This knowledge prohibits the particular doing things with words Nanda most wants to perform, that is, to say "I do" to Vanderbank. Though Mrs. Brookenham wants Vanderbank for herself, he ultimately comes to despise her for what she has done, so she too loses in the end.

One might put the effects of this disabling of ordinary speech acts in the following general terms. Most Victorian novels end with the happy marriage of the "vague slip of a daughter." The anxious focus of all the community, including the community of readers, in such novels, is on the question of whether the unmarried young woman will marry well, thereby renewing the community. The marriage of Grace Crawley to Major Grantly is the example of that in Trollope's *The Last Chronicle of Barset*. Esther Summerson's marriage to Allan Woodcourt in Dickens's *Bleak House* plays this role in that novel. Molly Gibson's marriage to Roger Hamley provides the happy ending of Elizabeth Gaskell's *Wives and Daughters*, or was to have done so had Gaskell lived to write the last few pages. Elizabeth Bennett's marriage to Darcy is the happy ending of Jane Austen's *Pride and Prejudice*. Innumerable examples could be adduced from among the sixty thousand or so Victorian novels. As long as a young woman was unmarried, she was seen in Victorian society as a threat to community stability, since it was impossible to predict just whom she would marry. Social convention permitted the young woman to say "No" to a marriage proposal. Novels played an indispensable ideological role by reassuring their readers that a happy resolution of this situation was possible, even quite likely. The happy marriage at the end redistributes property and rank, as I have said, as well as ensuring the continuation of the community in the children to be born of the new couple.

The awkwardness of the new social order James calls "the awkward age" is that this renewal and continuation of the community, keeping it always different and yet always the same, is blocked. Nanda remains unmarried. The community is not renewed through her marriage and motherhood. The community is "unworked," rather than workable, in this awkward age.

A concomitant dismantling, or deconstruction, or "unworking," of the form of Victorian fiction is enacted by *The Awkward Age*, as I shall specify. This dissolution matches the ruination of the assumed Victorian community.

This consonance allows me to answer the questions posed near the beginning of this chapter: Why did James adopt the radical form he used for this novel? Why did he abstain from going behind? Form and substance are indeed one, as James claimed they were. In this new form of fiction, an all-powerful author, in sovereign control of what he writes, is no longer possible. Rather, the novelist's work takes unforeseen and incalculable directions. It escapes the author's control, as James ruefully observes about *The Awkward Age*. The omniscient or telepathic narrator is also no longer

possible. *The Awkward Age* lacks a narrator who knows everything about
the characters, who can penetrate their most hidden intimacies, and who
can then pass those on to the readers, along with wise generalizing analytical comments, as happens in George Eliot's *Middlemarch*. The characters
of *The Awkward Age*, moreover, are not knowable, stable, unified individualities. They are, rather, singularities. In their secrecy they are wholly
other not only to one another but also to the narrator. Mrs. Brookenham
more than once observes that Nanda is a mystery to her. Nanda keeps her
own counsel. She hides herself. Nanda is given to secrecy. So are the other
main characters.

These formal features mean that the traditional novel reader, who, with
the narrator's help, can fully understand the people and their story, is also
no longer possible. *The Awkward Age* is punctuated by numerous confessions of ignorance on the part of the narrator. He or "it" cannot or will
not penetrate the characters' interiors. The narrator cannot or will not
"go behind." This new, "unworked" novel has become, in a manner of
speaking, superficial. It is forced to remain on the surface, limited to the
notation of appearances.

The traditional tacit compact with the reader, to tell all, is broken in
The Awkward Age. It is replaced by a new, more tentative, promissory
compact: "Understand me if you can, and I promise this will be of great
value to you if you do." Whether this promise is kept or not is up to each
reader to decide for himself or herself. The ending in a "they lived happily
ever after" of most Victorian novels is replaced by an uncertain and indefinite future, beyond the last words of the novel. That James worried
about the open-endedness of his novels is indicated by what he says in the
preface to *The Portrait of a Lady*. He feels the need to justify, on formal
grounds, the reader's ignorance of what happens beyond the end of the
novel, when Isabel has returned to Rome and to her bad husband. *The
Awkward Age* is similarly oriented toward an uncertain future. The last
word of *The Awkward Age* is "to-morrow," but the reader cannot be sure
and can never know what the performative Nanda has uttered will bring.
She says, "I'll come if you'll take me as I am," in response to Mr. Longdon's "That puts it then that you *will* come" (9:538). The novel lacks the
neat tying up of all loose ends characteristic, in somewhat different ways,
of Trollope's novels, of George Eliot's, or of Dickens's.

Anomalous but Felicitous Performatives

Three felicitous compacts, however, compacts appropriate for an "unworked community," are enacted in *The Awkward Age*. These occur at its

end, when Nanda has decided to leave her mother's house for good. She makes a free and autonomous decision to leave, one not grounded on community rules or values, though it determines the dénouement. Such ungrounded decisions—usually, as in this case, an act of renunciation—are characteristic of James's fiction.

In *The Awkward Age*, Nanda's definitive decision to detach herself for good from her mother's set gives her a power to utter felicitous performatives, but performatives of an anomalous kind. They are anomalous in that they are not based on a viable community, or guaranteed in their efficacy by such a community, a community with effective institutions, laws, and customs in place. Nanda sees Vanderbank, Mitchy, and Mr. Longdon alone in her private room in her mother's house, one after the other, in that order.

She first successfully exhorts Vanderbank not to abandon her mother, and he promises to resume his visits to her.

Nanda then affirms to poor cuckolded Mitchy that she will "keep my promise" "not to abandon you" (9:530).

Nanda then, in the final scene of all, the last "interview," irrevocably accepts Mr. Longdon's offer to join him permanently in his country house. "You understand clearly, I take it," he says, "that this time it's never to again to leave me—or to *be* left." "I understand," she says. "Never again. That . . . is why I asked you for these days" (9:541–42). Mr. Longdon "adopts" Nanda, but only on condition that she agree to leave her family and her mother's set permanently behind. This condition she accepts, after doing her best for Vanderbank, for her mother, and for Mitchy. Whether or not the promises she extorts from them will be kept, the reader never knows.

The final interview between Mr. Longdon and Nanda needs to be followed in detail by the knowing reader, step by step, since it is made up of a stichomythic give and take, and of looks exchanged in a ceaselessly renewed "interview." Every detail counts, as in the final dialogue between Kate and Densher that ends *The Wings of the Dove*. The whole weight of the almost innumerable small touches that precede this scene rests on everything that is said between Nanda and Mr. Longdon. Everything that has come before is presupposed, for example: Vanderbank's betrayal of Mr. Longdon's confidence in him and his refusal of Longdon's offered compact; Nanda's abysmal love for Vanderbank; Mitchy's unrequited love for Nanda and his disastrous marriage to Aggie because Nanda has asked him to do so; Nanda's mother's deliberate contamination of her daughter so that she becomes unmarriageable, and so on.

All this is in the air in the final give and take. Its salient moments are the following. After saying she will come if he will take her as she is, Nanda says she needs to be sure that he understands just what she is, what she means when she says "as I am." She defends against Mr. Longdon's outrage Vanderbank's using her as an emissary of the latter's apology to Mr. Longdon for not proposing to her, for not responding to his offer. "You don't know what I would have done for him. You don't know, you don't know!" (9:541), says Mr. Longdon. The relation between Mr. Longdon and Nanda is constructed like a bridge over the abyss of their relation-without-relation to Vanderbank. Vanderbank has betrayed the love both bear for him, in a parallel with the situation in James's short story "The Altar of the Dead," where both Stransom and his lady friend have been betrayed by the now-dead Acton Hague.

The reader at this point may remember that the novel opens with a scene that lays out the beginning of the strong affinity, the instant intimate friendship, between Mr. Longdon and Vanderbank. Now at the end, Mr. Longdon says to Nanda: "It would be good for me—by which I mean it would be easier for me—if you didn't quite so immensely care for him. . . . It would be easier for me . . . if you didn't, my poor child, so wonderfully love him," to which she answers "Ah but I don't—please believe me when I assure you I *don't!*," upon which she bursts into "a torrent of tears." These tears are answered by Mr. Longdon's own tears. These tears hover over her lie. Their tears, the narrator says, "both conjoined and divided them" (9:539–40). That final phrase is a wonderful formulation of the exposure to one another of two singularities who remain, however close they are to one another, however much exposed to one another, nevertheless still irremediably other to one another, distant from one another.

Nanda goes on after this to defend Vanderbank's refusal by making clear what his reasons are, as she understands them (whether correctly or incorrectly, who knows?), and to make absolutely sure that Mr. Longdon understands that she is what justifies his reasons: "it's I who am the horrible impossible and who have covered everything else with my own impossibility" (9:541). "I *am* like that," she says. And in answer to Mr. Longdon's "Like what?" she says, "Like what he thinks" (9:543). What she is, the novel has made clear, is an unmarried young woman who knows too much and therefore cannot utter traditional marriage vows. Her knowledge disables her performative power, except for those performatives that are uttered within a now unworked community. Upon this, Mr. Longdon and Nanda seal their compact with kisses that I find infinitely touching. Mr. Longdon "kiss[es] her solemnly on the forehead," and she responds "by doing for him in the pressure of her lips to his cheek what he had just done for herself" (9:543).

Nanda then goes on to generalize about the noncommunity, or un-worked community, or community of "extraordinaries" James calls "the awkward age": "We're many of us, we're most of us—as you long ago saw and showed you felt—extraordinary now. We can't help it. It isn't really our fault. There's so much else that's extraordinary that if we're in it all so much *we* must naturally be" (9:544). And then she pronounces her final judgment, as well as perhaps James's own, on the awkward age: "Every-thing's different from what it used to be" (9:544).

On this basis Nanda exonerates Vanderbank. She sits "enthroned in high justice," passing judgment on Mr. Longdon's willingness to take her in as opposed to Vanderbank's refusal: "Oh he's more old-fashioned than you. . . . He tried . . .—he did his best. But he couldn't. And he's so right—for himself" (9:544). "Justice" is here tacitly opposed to ordinary law, right, or morality, such as determines Vanderbank's behavior and de-cisions. Justice is superior to all that, "enthroned," sovereign, imperial. It must be said, in justice, that this final chapter gives little aid and comfort to the hypothesis that Vanderbank will not marry Nanda because he is gay, unless the reader is to guess that Nanda may be mistaken about Vand-erbank. Nanda takes the whole responsibility on herself. She really is as Vanderbank thinks she is, that is, someone who *knows*, and on the terms of his "old-fashioned" ideology, he is right to reject her. The "moral" of the story seems to be that such catastrophes will continue to happen as long as this feature of patriarchal ideology remains in force.

Nanda's felicitous performative, her saying "yes" in response to Mr. Longdon's kiss that signals his willingness to take her "as she is," provides the bittersweet ending of renunciation. It can be seen in two contradictory ways, as a return to the old-fashioned stable community that secures felici-tous speech acts, out there in Mr. Longdon's country house, or, as I think more plausibly, as the establishment of a new community of two, outside any social circle or set, detached from the awkward age. Such a tiny com-munity is proleptic, it may be, of communities to come, beyond the irrevo-cable dissolution of the old communities. Those old communities were dramatized in high Victorian novels that end in happy marriage. This new community of two is like the one Matthew Arnold, in "Dover Beach," exhorts his beloved to help him establish. "Ah, love, let us be true / To one another! for the world . . . / Hath really neither joy, nor love, nor light."[28] It may be that so much frantic effort, these days—for example, in election rhetoric in the United States—goes into trying to maintain a now vanished community stability just because it *has* vanished and people are unwilling to face that sad truth. They would rather believe the politicians' lies.

Nanda in the end takes matters into her own hands. She gains the upper hand over all the others, including the mother who has harmed her so much. She wins out in the implacable, subterranean, covert battle of wills, beneath all the superficial friendship and openness, that characterizes London society in James's representation of it. In this, Nanda is like many other Jamesian heroines. Such characters seem weak vessels, dependent victims. In the end, however, they triumph over those around them to whom they seem subservient, men and women alike. Examples, each quite different from all the others, but sharing this trait of ultimate triumph, are: Isabel Archer, in *The Portrait of a Lady*; Maisie, in *What Maisie Knew*; Catherine Sloper, in *Washington Square*; Kate Croy, in *The Wings of the Dove*; Maggie Verver, in *The Golden Bowl*.

A final question remains, one I posed earlier in this chapter and promised to answer. I certainly want to keep my promise. Is it a good thing for me to read *The Awkward Age*? Should I let it enact on me its undeniable performative effect by yielding to the imaginary unworked community the words on the page evoke? It is not altogether easy to answer that question. It could be argued that, like other fin-de-siècle works in English literature, this one is immoral and has the effect of spreading immorality. I would argue the reverse. If Jean-Luc Nancy is right to say that we know we live now (and have always lived, whether we knew it or not) only in unworked communities, then *The Awkward Age* is a wonderfully subtle exhibition of what *une communauté désoeuvrée* is like. It also shows, in the compact between Nanda and Mr. Longdon that forms the dénouement of the novel, how a justice beyond what is morally "right" is still possible. It is possible as a horizon of what is still to come in the "community of those who have nothing in common."[29] Having said that, I shall now really fall silent, at least until the next chapter.

CHAPTER 4

Lying against Death:
The Wings of the Dove

Reality was that sort of residue of experience. {*La réalité était cette
espèce de déchet de l'expérience.*}

—MARCEL PROUST, *À la recherche du temps perdu*

Literature as Speech Act

To what reality does *The Wings of the Dove* refer? All language has an
ineluctable referential function. It refers to something that the activity of
referring makes us presume to be real, extralinguistic. It ought to be possible to identify in a given case how that referential function works. The
reader should be able to discover what substantial, nonlinguistic entities a
given piece of language names, describes, or refers to, as a road sign indicates something that really exists but just happens to be at a distance, over
there.

It may be easier to answer this apparently straightforward question by
focusing on a specific passage in *The Wings of the Dove*. This is a synec-
dochic piece of its language, part standing for whole, if it is a whole, a
snippet of the entire texture. Take the opening sentence: "She waited,
Kate Croy, for her father to come in, but he kept her unconscionably, and
there were moments at which she showed herself, in the glass over the
mantel, a face positively pale with the irritation that had brought her to
the point of going away without sight of him" (19:3). What can one say
about the referent of this citation? What reality does it name?

The sentence opens the novel: "She waited, Kate Croy, for her father
to come in. . . ." This is the first thing the reader encounters of the novel

proper, after the title page and other front matter. In the edition I am using, that front matter includes the first page of all, which tells the reader this is "Volume XIX" of the "Scribner Reprint Edition" of the "New York Edition" of "The Novels and Tales of Henry James." Then comes James's preface, and then pages that say "The Wings of the Dove / Volume I" and "Book First." All this preliminary matter tells the adept reader she is about to read a work of fiction, though it is always possible that it might be a real report disguised as a novel. The possibilities of deception with written or printed language are limitless. Such language does not, with certainty, answer our interrogation: "Are you a real report or a work of fiction?" The words just go on imperturbably saying what they say. This is what Plato, or, rather, Socrates, in Plato's *Phaedrus*, objected to about written language in general.[1] The reader has to take it on faith that pieces of language say the truth in those places where they label themselves: "I am a novel," or "I am a biography." These labels are not cognitively verifiable. They are examples of that species of speech act called an attestation: "Believe me. I swear to you that I am really a novel."

Without the external signs that this is a novel, no way, it seems, would exist to distinguish the language of *The Wings of the Dove*'s first sentence from language that is verifiably referential. By "verifiably referential" I mean apparently identifiable as true or false by its correspondence or lack of correspondence to some extralinguistic reality. Examples of the latter would be history, biography, or, it might appear, the testimony of a person in the witness box giving a deposition on oath. The Greeks called the latter a "diegesis," meaning a "statement": "She waited, Kate, Croy, for her father to come in," with an implicit addendum, "I swear to you this is the truth, the whole truth, and nothing but the truth; I saw it with my own eyes," fits the paradigm of a courtroom "statement." The "implicit addendum" makes the act of bearing witness to that degree a speech act, not a straightforward constative statement. The witness may be lying or may be honestly mistaken. She may have thought she saw something that was not there. "No one bears witness for the witness [Niemand / zeugt für den / Zeugen]," as Paul Celan says.[2] The witness is the sole authority for a given particular act of witnessing. This is why the jury in a murder trial must decide unanimously, "beyond reasonable doubt." All the evidence, however empirical, is in the end just credible or not credible, never definitive proof, however contrary to commonsense assumptions this distressing fact may be.

A novel is like a statement, legal deposition, or diegesis. No identifiable marks distinguish for certain a fictional statement from a real one. This makes lies possible, as well as perjury, irony, jokes, wordplay, and other features of everyday spoken as well as written language. It also makes literature possible, as a specific, historically situated, institution or cultural form in the West. Literature as we think of it today did not always exist, even in the Occident. It arose in the Renaissance, or, as some argue, in the Enlightenment. Greek tragedy is not literature in the modern sense of the word, or it becomes literature only in modern times. It had a ritual function lacking in what we call literature in modern times. Non-Western cultures do not have literature in quite the way we mean that word. Literature could cease to exist for us. That would not be the end of the civilized world, though it would change things quite a bit. It may even be that literature is in the process of ceasing to exist, of being replaced by other cultural forms: radio, film, video, television, computer games.

Literature as we know it is, as Derrida has argued, inextricably associated with democracy. It depends on freedom of speech, that is, the freedom to say or to write anything and everything and not be punished for it. (This freedom is never completely realized, of course.) Literature is also concomitant with industrialization prior to the electronic revolution, with the age of the printed book, an age now perhaps coming to an end, according to some people, and with Cartesian and post-Cartesian conceptions of selfhood, along with associated notions of representation and of "reality." All these are intertwined and mutually sustaining factors. Literature as a distinctive way to use language arises, not from any special way of speaking or writing, but from the possibility of taking any piece of language whatsoever as either fictional or, by contrast, as possibly truth telling, as referential in the ordinary sense.[3] No internal way exists to distinguish a fictitious telephone book from a real one. The two would look exactly the same. The difference would be revealed only when someone started dialing the numbers in the fictitious book. The numbers, needless to say, would not work. They would reach no one, or at best a series of wrong numbers.

In a similar fashion, no way exists to tell for sure, from purely internal evidence, that *The Wings of the Dove* is not a historical narration disguised as a novel. This may be exemplified by the sentence "She waited, Kate Croy, for her father to come in." Only if the reader tried to verify its truth or falsity by reference to the real world would she discover that Kate Croy, her father, and all the other characters in the book may, at least so it seems, be encountered only in the pages of *The Wings of the Dove*, nowhere else. Nevertheless, the language of that first sentence does not differ from language that might have been used if Kate Croy were a real, historical personage. And who knows? We may just have failed so far to find the "original" of Kate Croy and of that shabby apartment in "Chirk Street." This is so counter-intuitive, even so scandalous, that it is instinctively resisted. Immense efforts are made, by scholars as well as by ordinary readers, to suppress this self-evident fact and to find referents for a novel's language. After all, such readers assert, many verifiably real places are named in this novel: Chelsea, Lancaster Gate, Kensington Gardens, the Brompton Oratory, Venice, and so on. The novel, it may be, accurately represents the mores and behavior of British and American middle- and upper-class people of the time. The first sentence is followed by a circumstantial description of Kate's father's dreary quarters in what James calls "Chirk Street," though no Chirk Street exists in London, not, at least, as now listed in the authoritative street guide *London A to Z:* "changing her place, moving from the shabby sofa to the armchair upholstered in a glazed cloth that gave at once—she had tried it—the sense of the slippery and of the sticky" (19:3), and so on for another page, including a description of the view from the balcony of "the vulgar little street" that matches so well "the vulgar little room" (ibid.). This accumulation of detail makes it sound like the narrator is describing a real room, or, to put this another way, it seems as if James has the narrator describe a real room that he— James, that is—has really seen. This would allow a reader to measure the novel by its truth telling. Were rooms in rented quarters in the part of London James has in mind really like this at the time the novel is supposed to have taken place?

This piling up of detail, even thematically irrelevant detail, creates what Roland Barthes called *l'effet du réel.*[4] This superabundance, even if it has no thematic or symbolic function, operates, as Barthes said, to tell the reader she is reading a "realistic novel," a novel, that is, that undertakes to obey certain conventions of verisimilitude, just as certain other conventions in other works alert an adept reader that she is reading a work of science fiction or a romance.

James, moreover, obeys another convention of the genre "realistic novel" when he has the vulgar little room looking out on its vulgar little street stand metonymically for the failure and dishonor of Kate's father's life: "she tasted the faint flat emanation of things, the failure of fortune and of honor" (19:4). In realistic novels, things stand for and give the reader indirect access to the interior lives of those who live surrounded by those things. Other examples later in the novel include the correspondence between Kate's Aunt Lowder and her expensive home in Lancaster Gate. Densher "takes in the message of her massive florid furniture, the immense expression of her signs and symbols . . . so almost abnormally affirmative, so aggressively erect, were the huge heavy objects that syllabled his hostess's story" (19:76). Milly's personality, to give other examples, is expressed in the grand palazzo she rents in Venice. Kate Croy is not at all like her sister's dreary house in Chelsea, whereas Densher, so he thinks to himself, would be more likely to feel at home there, while it fits Kate's sister well enough. This echo of person and milieu is a powerful convention in realistic fiction, though it would be dangerous to follow it in real life, to believe it is always "true." A person may or may not correspond to his or her surroundings.

To shift to another register of reference, *The Wings of the Dove* appears, in addition, as scholars have told us, to reflect Henry James's feelings about his cousin Minny Temple, who died of tuberculosis at twenty-four, just as Milly Theale dies in the novel of some unnamed malady (not tuberculosis; the reader is told Milly's lungs are sound). This correspondence may or may not be true, but most readers grasp at it as an explanation. They thereby may feel, with a great sense of relief, that it is unnecessary to read the novel except according to that key, that is, that it is unnecessary, really, to read the novel at all.[5]

Surely, the reader feels, it is legitimate to measure the novel by its relation to these indubitable realities, either social realities of the times and places represented in the novel or realities, truths, about the author's life. Identifications of social or biographical references make up two main penchants, along with formalistic analysis as a third penchant, not just of James criticism but of literary studies generally as they have been and are institutionalized in Europe and America. So-called "cultural studies" are just the latest version of these first two penchants. The real nature of literature is so threatening, it may be, that both ordinary readers and specialists in literary studies, for the most part, do everything they can to avoid confronting this reality. How can language be made to hang in an apparent void like that? Does it refer to nothing at all? One thing seems to be sure, however: Kate Croy and her father can be met nowhere but in the pages of *The Wings of the Dove*. Novels, to alter Marianne Moore's formulation, can be described as real gardens with imaginary toads in them. The opening words of the novel, "She waited, Kate Croy, for her father to come in," refer to nothing but a virtual reality that the words both invent and discover, according to a double law I shall identify. I shall also identify the meaning that must be given in this context to the phrase "virtual reality." That's a promise.

The first sentence, in its invocation of Kate Croy in a particular situation at a particular moment of her life, establishes a contract. It makes the reader an implicit promise. Whatever follows in all the hundreds of pages that make up the novel will in one way or another be consistent with this first sentence, will be continuous with it, will conform to its law. This by no means prescribes some strict obligation of conformity. Laws of genre are established in order to be broken. Every new work to some degree breaks generic laws or establishes a new genre and new modes of consistency of which it may be the only example. All sorts of hiatuses and anacoluthons, or failures in following, are possible. The adept reader will expect them. They will be defined as hiatuses or anacoluthons, however, in the case of *The Wings of the Dove*, by their relation to this first sentence.

The first sentence of this or of any novel is truly inaugural. It is a special kind of performative speech act. It is as though James had waved a magic wand and said, "Let there be Kate Croy waiting in exasperation for her father in his shabby quarters." This speech act is also an implicit promise. It is a pledge to tell the rest of Kate's story and a guarantee that the rest will in one way or another fit with this first sentence. The reader knows that much will follow these words, printed on all those pages in the volume the reader holds in her hands. The reader also knows that she has been plunged in medias res and that what she needs to know of what has preceded will probably be revealed in good time. The first sentence exposes a little of the novel's virtual reality, as it unfolds word by word, but it also leaves many unanswered questions. "She waited, Kate Croy. . . ." "She"? Who is she? Then she is named: "Kate Croy." But who is Kate Croy? The reader then learns that her father is living and that he is late for an appointment with her, to her great irritation. Why he is late, however, the reader never learns. The reader also learns that Kate is in a room with a mantel and with a looking glass over the mantel, but where and when she is in that room is not yet revealed. Nevertheless, the reader assumes that whatever comes after will follow from this first sentence. The first sentence establishes rules and laws for this virtual reality. It is an inaugural first step from which the whole novel grows, just as all United States history follows from the Declaration of Independence. The first sentence of *The Wings of the Dove* functions as a qualified declaration of independence from historical reality. It promises that the text will look like a real account but be a fictional one, an imaginary telephone book. Since Kate Croy and all the other characters are imaginary, not real, the first sentence initiates what I have called a virtual reality into which all the realistic details, with all their verifiable verisimilitude, are transposed, translated, displaced.

Those details are borrowed, given new valences, by the words of the novel. To what then do those words now refer? The reader would like to know.

The Clear Matter of the Tale

A surprising and to some degree scandalous answer to this question is suggested by what James says in the preface to another novel, *The Golden Bowl*, and by what he says in the preface to *The Wings of the Dove* itself. In the preface to *The Golden Bowl*, in a brilliant and difficult passage on which I have commented elsewhere,[6] James asserts that re-reading his novel is like matching the words of the novel against an ideal novel to which the words more or less accurately correspond. The ideal novel, something that exists independently of the actual words on the page, is spoken of as the "clear matter" of the tale. In this strange locution, the word *matter* names a peculiar form of nonmaterial materiality. It also names "matter" in the sense one speaks of "the heart of the matter," that is, the essential subject matter. In this case the word *matter* names the total circumstances of some event, as James in this preface calls his narrator the "historian of the matter" (23:xiii). "Matter" also, more broadly, names the stuff of a multitude of possible stories, as scholars speak of "the matter of Arthur" or "the matter of Troy." These phrases label the whole cycle of Arthurian or Trojan legends. These "matters" make possible innumerable stories. They exist, however, independently of them all. They do not rely on any particular stories for their existence, as anyone knows who has tried to unsnarl the tangle of Arthurian legends and poems from medieval times down to Malory or Tennyson.

That "clear matter," in the case of *The Golden Bowl*, is, says James, in one of his characteristically extravagant metaphors, like a shining, trackless field of snow. This figure is more a catachresis than a metaphor, since the figure does not substitute for any literal way to say what James wants to say. James gives alternative formulations (a silhouette, a dance), but these are figures of speech, too. If the matter of the tale is an untrodden snowfield, the words of the novel are one set of tracks through that field. James expresses his satisfaction on re-reading *The Golden Bowl* by asserting that he finds he would take the same track through the snowfield today. He expresses his dissatisfaction at reading his earlier work by saying he would now take a different path through the snow. His present footsteps sometimes match and sometimes fail to match his old footsteps. The snowfield that is the matter of a given work exceeds them both. It would have continued to exist as the possibility of being turned into words even if he had never written a word of the novel, or of the preface. The latter registers, not only an act of re-reading, but also an act of revisiting the clear matter of the tale, that is, the field of snow. Here is the way James puts this:

> To re-read in their order my final things, all of comparatively recent date, has been to become aware of my putting the process through, for the latter end of my series (as well as, throughout, for most of its later constituents) quite in the same terms as the apparent and actual, the contemporary terms; to become aware in other words that the march of my present attention coincides sufficiently with the march of my original expression; that my apprehension fits, more concretely stated, without an effort or struggle, certainly without bewilderment or anguish, into the innumerable places prepared for it. As the historian of the matter sees and speaks, so my intelligence of it, as a reader, meets him halfway, passive, receptive, appreciative, often even grateful; unconscious, quite blissfully, of any bar to intercourse, any disparity of sense between us. Into his very footsteps the responsive, the imaginative steps of the docile reader that I consentingly become for him all comfortably sink; his vision, superimposed on my own as an image in cut paper is applied to a sharp shadow on a wall, matches, at every point, without excess or deficiency. This truth throws into relief for me the very different dance that the taking in hand of my earlier productions was to lead me; the quite other kind of consciousness proceeding from *that* return. Nothing in my whole renewal of attention to these things, to almost any instance of my work previous to some dozen years ago, was more evident than that no such active, appreciative process could take place on the mere palpable lines of expression—thanks to the so frequent lapse of harmony between my present mode of motion and that to which the existing footprints were due. It was, all sensibly, as if the clear matter being still there, even as a shining expanse of snow spread over a plain, my exploring tread, for application to it, had quite unlearned the old pace and found itself naturally falling into another, which might sometimes indeed more or less agree with the old tracks, but might most often, or very nearly, break the surface in other places. What was thus predominantly interesting to note, at all events, was the high spontaneity of these deviations and differences, which became thus things not of choice, but of immediate and perfect necessity: the necessity to the end of dealing with the quantities in question at all. (23:xiii–xiv)

What is extraordinary about this testimony, and radically contrary to commonsense assumptions, is the way it presupposes that the "matters" of James's various works exist not only outside the words of the novels but also outside James's creating or concocting consciousness. James measures the actual words on the page by their degree of fit to his present apprehension of the matter of the novel. He speaks as though that matter did not depend on his consciousness or on his words for its existence. The "historian of the matter," that is, the narrator of this or that novel, does not invent that matter. He simply "puts the process through" in one way or another, which I take it means he tells it as well as he can. He is a "historian," not a free maker of fictions. He makes one set of tracks out of words among innumerable possible tracks across the trackless snow. James, now as re-reader of his own work, measures that work not against his own ideal of satisfactory form but against his new apprehension of a "matter" that has gone on having a separate existence not only independent of the words on the page but also independent of James's thinking of it or not.

James stresses the spontaneity and necessity of his present apprehension of the matter. It is not a matter of free invention, but a revelation dictated to him by the matter itself. The snow shines and glistens with the force of an illumination, an exposing, a showing forth, an uncovering. It is "clear" in the sense of "transparent," open to comprehension. The clear matter is still there and would still be there even if every copy of *The Golden Bowl* were destroyed and even if James's consciousness were to vanish. Indeed it now has vanished, definitively, though reading James's work may be a kind of resurrection or raising of the dead by way of the words as invocation. The novel invents the story not in the modern sense of making it up but in the older sense of *inventio* as discovery of something hitherto hidden that has nevertheless always been there, waiting to be brought out into the light. Since the reader, unlike James, does not have direct access to the "matter," only the words of *The Golden Bowl* can give the reader access to it.

It is to this separately existing matter that the words of the novel refer. The novel makes transferred use of all the words that apparently refer to historically real places and things in order to refer by catechresis to features of the clear matter of the story. I say "catechresis" because that word names a "forced and abusive transfer" of words naming real entities to make them name more occult entities that have no proper names of their own and therefore can be named only in this indirect way. This is expressed allegorically by James as the relation between the tracks in snow and the shining expanse of trackless snow that was there before anyone walked across it. What actually gets written is always a figurative substitute for what can never be expressed or referred to directly. It can be named only in figures like that of the snowfield, or, for that matter, like that of the novel itself as a vast integument of invented words bringing into existence imaginary personages or consciousnesses in interaction. These give the reader mediated access to the "matter of the tale," but only in one possible version of it.

The Testimony of the Preface

James claims this paradigm is applicable to all his works. Is there any evidence that *The Wings of the Dove* exemplifies it in a specific way? The preface to *Wings* precedes that to *The Golden Bowl* in the New York Edition and was presumably written earlier. It contains one curious feature that confirms in anticipation the strange doctrine of reference in the preface to *The Golden Bowl*. *The Wings of the Dove*, James says in its preface, is, like so many of his works, at once too long and too short. It is too long because the whole first half exceeds its predetermined bounds and leaves James not enough space for the second half.[7] This makes *Wings* a salient example of what James calls in this preface "the inveterate displacement of his general centre" (19:xviii). Elsewhere, in the preface to *The Tragic Muse*, he speaks of the way "again and again, perversely, incurably, the center of my structure would insist on placing itself *not*, so to speak, in the middle" (7:xi). Later in the preface to *Wings*, he says that "the whole actual center of the work" "rest[s] on a misplaced pivot" (19:xxii). The result is that the second half of the novel "is false and deformed." The figure of the misplaced pivot also suggests that it is unbalanced, likely to fall over, or fail to turn evenly. "This whole corner of the picture," says James, "bristles with 'dodges'" because the author had to "produce the illusion of mass without the illusion of extent" (19:xviii, xix). A good reader or critic, he asserts, ought "to recognize and denounce" these shabby expedients "for disguising the reduced scale of the exhibition, for foreshortening at any cost, for imparting to patches the value of presences, for dressing objects in an *air* as of the dimensions they can't possibly have" (ibid.). The second half is just too short to be able to represent adequately what it has to say.

To what is the obligation expressed in my phrase "has to say" a response? The answer is suggested in the examples James gives of something that is inadequately or incompletely expressed. The careful reader of the novel will note that any direct representation of Milly Theale's consciousness vanishes toward the end of the novel, though what she was thinking and feeling may be just what the reader is most curious to know. Milly's consciousness disappears from representation at just the point when she presumably finds that Densher has, tacitly at least, lied to her. He has, falsely, though without ever quite saying so, allowed her to believe that Kate does not love him in return and that he is beginning to care for Milly instead. The reader never learns what Milly thinks and feels in the last days of her life, when she gives up her fight against death and "turn[s] her face to the wall" (20:270, 274). Her inner life at that stage remains an impenetrable secret, just as the reader never encounters the fuller representation of Kate's father and his deplorable life that James originally planned, just as neither the characters nor the reader ever learn what was in Milly's deathbed letter to Densher, and just as the reader never learns of what disease Milly died. We have to believe the narrator's attestation, to take it on faith, that all this that remains secret does exist and could have been represented: "One's poor word of honor," says James, "has *had* to pass muster for the show" (19:xiv, James's italics). "I swear to you that all this does exist and could be represented," James in effect describes himself as saying, or as saying through his surrogate, the narrator.

The opposition is between promising that you could bring something to light and actually doing that, actually "showing" it. The former has to "pass muster" for the latter, as one soldier might stand in for another in a military muster or assembly. The word *muster* comes from Latin *monstrare*, "to show." The author's or narrator's word of honor is a substitute showing for a real showing forth or muster that does not occur. The relation between the author and the part of the matter of his tale that does not get written is not a cognitive one. It is, once more, an example of that particular form of speech act called bearing witness: "I give you my word of honor I saw this." Of the direct representation of Milly's consciousness or of "Kate's relation with Densher and Densher's with Kate" after a certain moment in the novel, James says, "It is as if, for these aspects, the impersonal plate [he presumably means the narrator or author as neutral reflecting surface]—in other words the poor author's comparatively cold affirmation or thin guarantee—had felt itself a figure of attestation at once too gross and too bloodless, likely to affect us as an abuse of privilege when not as an abuse of knowledge" (19:xvii–iii). The things left out would be indecent to talk about by the relatively detached and objective author/narrator, though he could do so if he would.

For the narrator to have represented Milly's consciousness directly, or Kate's, or Densher's, by way of free indirect discourse, that is, to have made good his "comparatively cold affirmation or thin guarantee" of his power to enter into their minds and feelings, would have been an abuse of privilege if not an abuse of knowledge. He has the privilege and the knowledge. To use them, however, would be abusive, as when a doctor, a lawyer, or a clergyman betrays secrets his or her clients have revealed. The narrator knows, but he will not, must not, tell. He will only, discreetly, show these things indirectly, through the registering "plates" of other characters, according to the author's "striking, charming and curious" "instinct everywhere for the *indirect* presentation of his main image" (19:xxii, James's italics). The "main image," in this case, as the preface underlines, is Milly's fight against death. The implication is that these things exist in a place that is independent of the author's words, though not of his knowledge. It would be too terrible to present directly the intimate process of her dying, even from a spectator's perspective, much less her own: "Heaven forbid," says James in the preface, "we say to ourselves during almost the whole Venetian climax, heaven forbid we should 'know' anything more of our ravaged sister than what Densher darkly pieces together, or than what Kate Croy pays, heroically, it must be owned, at the hour of her visit alone to Densher's lodging, for her superior handling and her dire profanation of" (19:xviii). This sentence, it may be noted, is extremely strange, when you think of it. Knowing of Milly's death by what Densher darkly pieces together is one thing, but knowing it by way of Kate's "payment," which is her coming to Densher's apartment to fulfill her promise to sleep with him, is another, particularly when the reader remembers that Kate's "coming" is no more directly represented in the novel than is Milly's death. We know one thing that is too awful to present directly by way of another that is too indecent to present directly, though it is an act of life as against an act of dying.

The novel, it follows, refers to an entire world to which James alone has access, but which he has not invented, except in the sense of discovering it. The evidence for this is the way he says he fails to bring all of it to light. Or, to put this more precisely, it is impossible to know whether James has invented or discovered that world, since all he says in the preface may be a ruse or a false lead, and since no criteria exist for distinguishing between one and the other. The evidence, that is, the words on the page, would be exactly the same in either case. This is another striking example of the disjunction between the cognitive and performative dimensions of language. This disjunction obtains whether it is a question of the speech acts that bring works of literature into being, or of everyday speech acts in the real world, like promises and acts of attestation, or of such promises as those represented within stories told in works of fiction. The writing of *The Wings of the Dove* was, after all, a speech act in the real world. Henry James, on such and such days, dictated the novel, sentence by sentence, to his amanuensis and thereby, performatively, gave the reader at least partial access to a virtual reality only he knew directly. Whether he had invented that reality out of thin air or had only "discovered" it cannot be known, because no certain means of cognitive verification exist.

In an earlier passage in the preface to *The Wings of the Dove*, James's failure to say all he had intended to say and the independent existence of the clear matter of the tale to which this failure, strangely enough, testifies is expressed in one of James's characteristically extravagant, extended, and exfoliating figures. He begins by defining the separate sections or "books" of *Wings*, each usually commanded by a single center of consciousness represented in free indirect discourse by the narrator, as, he hopes, "sufficiently solid *blocks* of wrought material, squared to the sharp edge, as to have weight and mass and carrying power" (19:xii). The novel, this architectural figure implies, is constructed of solid, self-enclosed units with spaces between. These are then set side by side to make a structure. The spaces between might be identified as the gaps created when James shifts abruptly from one reflecting plate or center of consciousness, represented in the narrator's inveterate free indirect discourse, to another one. An example is the shift from Kate's consciousness to Densher's across the blank page between the end of Book First and the beginning of Book Second. At the end of one the reader is still placed within Kate's mind. In the opening pages of Book Second, the reader gradually enters into Densher's mind, from which perspective Kate's mind, so recently presented with intimacy and interiority, is now to a considerable degree alien and other, secret. Much more remains to be said of this law of rotation, but that must be deferred for now. What architectural fabric the novel's building blocks construct, the further development of the figure makes explicit. It is a bridge. This structure carries the reader from here to there over a stream.

It is a bridge, however, of an extremely odd sort. The plan was one thing, namely, an intention to represent fully and adequately the subject or "matter." What James actually succeeded in writing is quite another thing. What he sees on re-reading the novel is not a solid narrative texture or architecture but a torn fabric full of gaps, hiatuses, absences, voids, places where what should have been represented is not represented or only represented inadequately, though it remains there, waiting to be justly said. James measures his failure by the still almost palpable presence of all that part of the matter that did not get said. His account is punctuated by the "alas" of regret and compunction:

> to retrace the way at present is, alas, more than anything else, but to mark
> the gaps and the lapses, to miss, one by one, the intentions that, with the

best will in the world, were not to fructify. I have just said that the process
of the general attempt is described from the moment the "blocks" are numbered, and that would be a true enough picture of my plan. Yet one's plan,
alas, is one thing and one's result another; so that I am perhaps nearer the
point in saying that this last strikes me at present as most characterized by
the happy features that *were*, under my first and most blest illusion, to have
contributed to it. I meet them all, as I renew acquaintance, I mourn for
them all as I remount the stream, the absent values, the palpable voids, the
missing links, the mocking shadows, that reflect, taken together, the early
bloom of one's good faith. (19:xiii)

What is most strange about this failed effort of representation is that it
works. A bridge gets built and bears weight, after all. It carries the reader
over the stream. James enunciates, on the basis of this act of re-reading,
an unforeseen law (unforeseen by me, at least) whereby the failure in
representation is the prerequisite of its success. This is "the 'law' of the
degree in which the artist's energy fairly depends on his fallibility"
(19:xiii). The author must be the "dupe" of "his prime object," or "illusion," the object of his "good faith," that is, his beguiled confidence in the
possibility of adequately rendering or bringing to light what I have been
calling, following James, the "matter" of the story. This belief in an illusion is necessary if he is to be "at all measurably a master, that of his actual
substitute for it" (ibid.). The novelist is a master not of the matter but of
the substitute words he has written that refer to that matter. The actual
novel is not the initially intended work, the ideal representation of the
matter. That remains an impalpable illusion, like a ghost in broad daylight.
What he has produced is a relatively poor substitute for what he initially
planned.

The odd thing, however, is that the substitute is usable. It bears weight.
The reader can get from here to there across it. It is as though the bridge
builder had put down solid piers to hold up his bridge, but had then built
the actual bridge in another place, where it hangs in the air, without solid
foundations or abutments. Nevertheless, this foundationless bridge serves
its purpose. This happens "by the oddest chance in the world" (19: xiii).
It is an odd chance because there is no way to predict it, and it seems
entirely implausible. Nevertheless, there it is:

> He places, after an earnest survey, the piers of his bridge—he has at least
> sounded deep enough, heaven knows, for their brave position; yet the
> bridge spans the stream, after the fact, in apparently complete indepen-
> dence of these properties, the principal grace of the original design. *They*

were an illusion, for their necessary hour; but the span itself, whether of a single arch or of many, seems by the oddest chance in the world to be a reality; since, actually, the rueful builder, passing under it [this continues the figure of retrospective rereading and remembering as "remounting the stream"; now the stream is spanned by the bridge that James imagines himself beneath], sees figures and hears sounds above; he makes out, with his heart in his throat, that it bears and is positively being used. (19:xiii–xiv, James's italics)

The ideal novel that James never wrote exists, even though it never achieved the material existence of words on the page. It would be a mistake to say this ideal novel existed in James's mind, ready to be copied from there. As anyone knows who has done any writing, whether of fiction or of nonfiction prose, such as I am writing now, you do not really know what you are going to write until you write it. It is as though it is waiting there somewhere to be written down. As you write, the words seem to be dictated to you by a voice that is not your own and that comes from somewhere else. The words are a gift, like these words right here that I am now writing. At least that is my experience of invention. I hereby bear witness to that experience. In addition, however, I can also bear witness to the way the critical essay that actually gets written about one of James's great novels bears the same relation to the ideal essay the critic (I at least) has had in mind as James's novel has to the ideal novel that he never succeeded in writing. So much that the critic glimpses in the act of reading never makes it into the essay he or she ultimately writes. There are so many gaps, omissions, and mocking shadows. The critic's only comfort is that he or she is at least no worse off than James himself in this respect, though also under the same kind of implacable obligation and as little capable of fulfilling that obligation. It may be, however, that for the critic, too, his or her failure is the condition of whatever virtues the essay or chapter that does get written may ultimately have. It, too, may bear weight, though lacking the solid foundations the critic originally, as dupe of his or her own illusions, analogous to those of the author, imagined for it. It bears weight just because of those misplaced foundations, which never get registered in the words of the final essay. The critic's energy too, it may be, depends on his or her fallibility.

Just as the ideal triangle, in Husserl's geometry, does not depend for its existence on any actual triangles inscribed on paper, so the matter of *The Wings of the Dove* does not depend on the actual novel James wrote. That novel is a replacement, one might even say an allegory, for the novel that did not get written, that could not, it may be, possibly be written. Just as the triangle does not depend on any triangles drawn on paper, so the matter of *The Wings of the Dove* would exist even if no word of the novel had been written. Those parts that were left out continue to exist, in their unattainable secrecy, like Milly's letter, which no one reads.[8] I call what does get written down a "virtual reality" in a double sense. It is virtual in the way a fictional telephone book is like a real one. The novel mimes the way real people in the real, material, and social world exist. At the same time, the novel is a virtual reality in the sense that it is a replacement or substitute for the true reality to which it refers, the shining matter of the story that James had the illusory good faith to believe he could represent directly. The novel is virtual in its reference to that reality.

The Narrator as Telepath

I have gone the first step over James's swinging bridge, in an attempt to account for that first sentence: "She waited, Kate Croy, for her father to come in, but he kept her unconscionably." I am, however, not quite finished with that sentence. The sentence contains the testimony of the narrator's privilege of knowing the other. These features of the first sentence's language, it must be said, betray the fact that we are most likely reading a work of fiction and not a real deposition, unless, of course, fictional conventions have been cunningly borrowed for a biography of Kate Croy, by this unlikely hypothesis a real historical person. I have indicated already the way Kate is shown as tasting the stale, flat emanation coming from her father's failure of fortune and of honor. She does this tasting by way of his surroundings—the apartment, its furniture, the vulgar street. She understands her father by way of his milieu.

The narrator, however, has an even greater power. This power is so commonplace and so conventional in nineteenth- and twentieth-century novels that readers take it for granted. They do not even notice how strange it is and how contrary to what is possible in the "real world." The narrator can place himself (or itself, since it is an impersonal power) directly, without intermediary, within the consciousness, the feelings, the very body of a character and speak for that character's most intimate experience. The instrument of this "speaking for" is what is called free indirect discourse, the miming of the character's first person present tense language in the third person past tense. Free indirect discourse, like the narrator's telepathic power,[9] is so extraordinary a gift of language that it remains to some degree unfathomable, however ordinary and even ubiquitous it is in novels, for example, those by James. *The Wings of the Dove* especially depends on free indirect discourse, whereas the more or less contemporary *The Golden Bowl* makes much more use of stichomythic dialogue with a minimum of the narrator's commentary, as does a slightly earlier novel, *The Awkward Age*, in both cases in a hyperbolic way.

Free indirect discourse is unfathomable, in part because it is impossible to tell for sure, in a given case, whether the language is the character's or whether it is ascribed to the character by the narrator. No way, in many cases, exists to test the alternatives, since the character exists, for the reader, only in the narrator's language for her or him. In either case, the language the reader reads would be the same. In the novel's first sentence, is "unconscionably" Kate's word or the narrator's? It is impossible to tell for sure. It may be the narrator's word as a comment on Kate's father's behavior, or, alternatively, that part of the sentence may be the narrator's translation, in free indirect discourse, of what Kate was saying to herself. "He is keeping me unconscionably" has in that case become "He kept her unconscionably."

The preface to *The Wings of the Dove* uses the figure of the various characters as reflecting plates, "registers or 'reflectors'" that "work . . . in arranged alternation" (19:xvii). The same figure appears unostentatiously, disguised as a realistic detail, in the first sentence of the novel proper, but it has a different function there. It serves as an indirect expression of the narrator's relation to Kate: "there were moments at which she showed herself, in the glass over the mantel, a face positively pale with the irritation that had brought her to the point of going away without sight of him." Kate sees herself in the mirror and registers her inner irritation by way of her pale face. She sees that irritation "outered" where any spectator might also see it. She also understands that irritation as almost leading to a decision to leave without seeing her father. The narrator puts himself or itself within Kate and matches with total intimacy all these movements of reflection in both senses of the word, reflection as literal mirror image confronted and reflection as inner thoughts. The narrator not only sees Kate's mirrored image, pale with irritation, but also sees that mirrored image with Kate's eyes and with Kate's feelings. He (or it) sees Kate seeing and feels her feeling.

The narrator makes the same claim for penetrating knowledge of Kate and a concomitant ability to represent her in words that James makes in the preface for his ability to concoct at least a substitute, that is, a deferred and figurative representation, of the subject or matter in question. The novel as a whole in relation to its "matter" is homologous with the narrator's language in relation to the characters' inner speech and feelings.

The reader, in turn, has access to Kate's vision and Kate's reflections by way of the narrative language and only by that way. A moment's reflection, however, will remind the reader that Kate Croy exists, for the reader at least, only in that language. The reader cannot verify or measure Kate Croy by reference to any other source of information. The reader has only the narrator's testimony or word for it. The reader must believe that testimony or not. This is evidence that bearing witness is a performative utterance, with the characteristic cognitive uncertainty of all performatives. For the reader, it is a question of belief, not of knowledge.

For James himself, however, as the preface testifies, the linguistic recording of Kate at this moment is to be measured against his ideal conception of her as a feature of his invention (in both senses of the word, as a making up and as a discovery) of the novel's whole matter. It is to that matter that the first sentence of *The Wings of the Dove* and all the other sentences, too, refer. This "matter" is an exceedingly peculiar kind of referent. It is neither exterior nor interior, neither objective nor subjective, neither material nor textual, neither real nor imaginary. It hovers somewhere between all these oppositions, in an impossible combination. This impossibility is not so much an undecidable either/or as the neither/nor of the neutral, the "ne-uter," according to the etymological origin of the word *neutral*. Whichever choice you make in each set of pairings, in a gesture of refraining, refusing, the other, makes the twin you have refrained from seem more likely. Nevertheless, this referent indubitably exists.

The Wings of the Dove, as we have seen, refers to this strange realm indirectly, as a substitute for the perfect rendering or act of reference that never gets written and that can never be written, This relation of substitution and replacement is mimed, emblematized, or allegorized not only in the relation of Kate's mirrored reflection to Kate herself but also in what that mirroring emblematizes, namely, the relation between Kate and the narrator's registering of her in the narrative language. That relation, in turn, is an emblem of the relation of the whole novel to its referent, the ideal existence of the novel's matter.

So much for *The Wings of the Dove*'s first sentence. I claim through my investigation of it to have shown how apparently cognitive assertions in a work of fiction ("She waited, Kate Croy"), assertions that have none of the distinguishing marks of felicitous speech acts as J. L. Austin has attempted to identify them,[10] nevertheless are in a peculiar, complex, and anomalous way performative utterances. Each works as an "Open Sesame!" to give the reader access to an ideal world by way of words on the page that are its indirect replacement. This world can, for the reader at least, be reached in no other way. The world seems to be created by the words of the novel and therefore to be James's invention. After we have entered it, however, this virtual reality seems to refer or correspond at a distance to a realm that has always been there already, waiting to be revealed, dis-covered, uncovered, by the novelist's words. Within that virtual reality the reader, after the first sentence, can now dwell through all the time it takes to read to the end of the novel's last page and last sentence, Kate Croy's "We shall never be again as we were!" (20:405). Beyond that last word the rest is silence, though the reader, after she has finished the novel, has the feeling that the realm it uncovered is always waiting there to be re-entered through a new act of reading any copy of the novel.

Densher's Lie

I turn now to a second sample of the novel's language in order to begin investigating more comprehensively the whole novel. With this turn, I move within the novel and begin to account for what happens within its virtual reality. In doing so I succumb, as most readers do, to what Walter Pater, speaking of the taking literally of mythological personifications, calls yielding to a "real illusion."[11] In novel reading, it is the illusion that the characters in, say, *The Wings of the Dove* are real people in a real world, not phantoms invoked by the words on the page. This leads to speaking of them as such. So powerful is the effect of such imaginary realities as novels are and so capable are readers of being haunted by the characters in them that most critics talk about the characters in novels as if they were real people. I shall not be exempt from this hallucination. The reader will note that it is a convention of such yielding that the critic transposes the novel's past tense to the present tense. The narrator says, "She waited, Kate Croy." The critic says, "Kate Croy waits for her father." It is an odd convention, but a powerful one. It shifts the language from what the narrator says happened once upon a time in the past to what the critic says happens in the eternal now of the illusion generated by words on the page.

Just what is *The Wings of the Dove*'s "matter," the subject that never gets expressed satisfactorily and for which what we read is a substitute?

What are the distinctive features of the imaginary reality the reader enters by way of that first sentence?

My second sample passage comes near the end of the novel, on a Christmas morning. The hero, Merton Densher, has, the night before, that is, on Christmas eve, received a letter from Milly Theale, written from Venice just before she died. The association of Milly's death with Christmas hints at a parallel between Christ's sacrificial death and Milly's. Though neither Densher nor anyone else, including the reader of the novel, ever reads this letter, since Kate Croy burns it unopened, in it Milly presumably tells Densher that she is leaving most of her huge fortune to him. Who knows what she actually wrote?

On that Christmas morning Densher visits Mrs. Lowder, aunt of Kate Croy. Densher is secretly engaged to Kate. Densher calls to find out if Milly has died. It turns out she has. Mrs. Lowder asks Densher, whom she presumes to be devastated by Milly's death, "And now—I dare say—you'll go to church?" (20:360). Densher has had no intention of going to church. He intends, rather, to visit Kate Croy in her father's house, to confront her and to say they must marry now and that he must refuse Milly's bequest. Nevertheless, he tells a gratuitous lie to Mrs. Lowder: "Why yes—I think I will" (ibid.). On his way to Kate, however, "it suddenly [comes] over him that he [has] just lied to Mrs. Lowder—a term it perversely ease[s] him to keep using—even more than [is] necessary" (20:361). (The reader will note the awkward changes I must make to move from the narrator's past tense to the critic's present tense.) Densher has by this time told a lot of lies, compared to which this one is pretty trivial. For some reason, yet to be identified, he decides to go to church after all. He attends a splendid Christmas morning service at the Brompton Oratory, located still today just on the way from Lancaster Gate, north of Hyde Park, where Mrs. Lowder lives in a splendid house, to Chelsea, where Kate's father lives in sordid quarters. As the narrator says, "the desire queerly stirred in him not to have wasted his word" (ibid.). Wasted his word? What does it mean to "waste one's word"? Why does this desire "queerly stir" in him? I shall return to these questions.

In my discussion of the novel's first sentence, I have identified the strange way that sentence is partly performative, partly constative. What James writes is not a free act of invention. His speech act in response to the necessity imposed on him is both inaugural and not inaugural. It is not inaugural since the realm that it names is not made up. At the same time the sentence is initiatory, since only this language gives the reader access to the world of the novel. The language gives that world material existence in the words on the page, making it available to others. The novel, as James himself says, is an act of testimony. It is as though he says: "I have seen this. I feel myself to be under an obligation to describe it for you, to turn it into narrative language."

If this is the relation between the novel and that to which it refers, is anything like this to be found within the novel itself? What is the role of speech acts within the virtual reality of *The Wings of the Dove*? Any work of fiction is almost certain to contain fictional speech acts: promises, pledges, contracts, lies, excuses, bets, declarations, bequests, and the like. J. L. Austin denies efficacy or "felicity" to fictional speech acts. I must not, according to Austin, be acting on the stage, writing a poem, or speaking in soliloquy if my speech act is to be felicitous. This seems commonsensical enough, until, that is, you begin thinking hard about it. Austin's own discourse contains many speech acts of the fictional kind, but they are nevertheless clearly efficacious. They make something happen and are essential to his argument. They are a way of doing things with words.[12]

For Jacques Derrida, on the other hand, performative language and literature are intimately related. The possibility of using words to make something happen as opposed to merely naming, describing, or referring to something makes literature possible, and vice versa. Because there can be literature there can be speech acts. Because there are speech acts there can be literature. In the context of this complex disagreement between Austin and Derrida, what can be said of speech acts in *The Wings of the Dove*?

First, the small and apparently trivial example I have cited is certainly a speech act. It exemplifies a classic and paradigmatic performative utterance, namely, a promise. Densher promises Mrs. Lowder that he will go to church that Christmas morning. This promise is peculiar in two ways, however. First, it is a lying promise. Densher has no intention of going to church. He promises while intending not to keep his promise. This is the example that Kant uses in *The Foundation of the Metaphysics of Morals* to demonstrate the impossibility of ever justifying doing it. The whole moral fabric of society, according to Kant, depends on not making lying promises, even when they seem most ethically justified, for example, to save someone's life, or even if they are no more than what are called "white lies," harmless prevarications made for politeness' sake.[13] Densher here commits that unforgivable crime.

Second, even though what Densher says is a lying promise or perhaps just because it is a lying promise, it seems to have a magic, coercive effect on him. It makes him do something against his will, something he had no intention of doing. This happens, apparently, just because he said he would do it. He goes to church in order not to waste his word. A wasted word is a performative word that does not make anything happen. It is like a marriage ceremony performed on the stage, or like the writing of a poem, or like a promise made in soliloquy. In Austin's view these are "etiolated" speech acts. Lies are mentioned in *How To Do Things With Words* as contrary-to-fact constative statements that are parallel to promises made with the intention not to keep them.[14] The two kinds of utterance are parallel in their apparent lack of purchase on the world, but Austin does not deny them possible infelicitous felicity.

Austin both needs and at the same time must not have the conviction that intention forms part of a felicitous performative. On the one hand, he needs intention because his conception of speech acts is tied to traditional notions of the self-conscious ego in possession of its wits and its intentions, as when the bride and bridegroom say "I will" in the marriage ceremony. If either is drugged, drunk, coerced, or crazy, the ceremony is not valid. On the other hand, Austin must not tie the efficacy of speech acts to conscious intention. To do so would allow "low" people, like welshers on bets, to claim that their lips said one thing while their hearts said something else. They uttered the words but they did not really mean them. That, they might claim, frees them from obligation. Some way to avoid this possible out must be found, if moral law and order are to be kept. It is Austin's prime intention to make that keeping possible. His book is a work of policing. It ought to be the case, says Austin, that "our word is our bond." If I have said something, I am bound by it, whatever my intention.[15] Such a position, however, as the reader can see, in a disquieting way detaches speech acts from consciousness and its intentions. This is disquieting because it gives an autonomous power to language. Words seem to act on their own whether I want them to act or not. They have a dangerous independent power. I promise to go to church, and, even though I do not intend to keep the promise, I magically find myself in church.

A lying promise, such as the one Densher makes to Mrs. Lowder, raises problems about intention in an acute and salient form. In the case of a lying promise, the contrary-to-fact constative element that makes it a lie is the lack of correspondence to the internal intention that ordinarily accompanies a promise. With a lying promise, however, it is not simply the case that the conscious intention is missing. A contrary intention is also consciously present. Densher does not intend to go to church. He intends to go to Kate Croy. In spite of that, he goes to church. It seems as if the

words he utters have a strange power to coerce their utterer to bring about
what they promise whether he wishes it or not. The moral of this strange
fatality might be: "Don't tell lies. Especially don't utter lying performatives. They have a distressing way of coming true." They do this by generating a "queer desire" in the one who has told the lie not to have wasted
his word. He is led to desire to carry out the order that is implicit in the
sentence he has uttered: "Why yes—I think I will." The desire is "queer"
because it seems a desire inherent in the words, not in the feelings of the
one who has uttered the words. The lying promise alienates desire from
the desirer. Of course I do not mean "queer" here as a synonym for "homosexual," nor did James, though it might be hypothesized that gay desire
is "queer" because it is desire that is diverted from what is thought to be
its normal object, that is, someone of the "opposite sex." By all accounts,
Henry James, like Densher, was subject to "queer desires."

Does anything like Densher's fulfillment of his lying promise occur to
bring about more important events in *The Wings of the Dove?* Certainly
there are a great many performative utterances in *The Wings of the Dove.*
The crucial moments of the novel, the moments that constitute dramatic
turning points in its action, are usually brought about by speech acts of
one sort or another. Of course, each sentence of the novel has a performative aspect, if I am right in what I have said about the first sentence. Each
additional sentence after that first one also has its own inaugural performative force, however purely constative it may seem. Each sentence brings a
little more of the novel's imaginary reality, substitute for the unsayable
prime matter, into the open for the reader.

The novel is in this like those computer graphics that are downloaded
from a website, pixel by pixel and line by line until they are all there on
the screen, just as that first sentence begins by telling the reader there is a
"she," then gives that she a proper name, *Kate Croy,* then gives her a location, then an irresponsible father, and so on. Those facts, it seems, were
waiting somewhere to be revealed to the reader by being put into words
by the narrator. The computer with its browser and other software creates
the picture on the screen, but it does so in response to a complex integument of millions of zeroes and ones that already exists somewhere else,
waiting to be downloaded, just as James's full never-to-be-written novel
exists somewhere waiting to be written. Now, however, I am more interested in overt speech acts that appear within the virtual reality that the
novel's words generate. Before investigating those, however, I must identify the social field of forces within which these speech acts take place and
are felicitous or infelicitous.

The Novel as a Field of Forces

I want now to establish what might be called the phenomenological laws of the imaginary reality the novel's words create. The novel's multitudinous speech acts take place not in the real world but in a substitute world. The novel's virtual reality has its own specific laws, limitations, and assumptions. These are by no means necessarily identical with those of the real social world within which Henry James, for example, lived, even though the novel's reality is made of elements transposed from that real world. Nor is it by any means identical with the laws of other novels by other novelists, or even other novels by James himself. Performative utterances will be felicitous or infelicitous within this virtual reality in ways that are determined by that reality's special laws and assumptions, just as speech acts in the "real world" depend on laws and conventions within a particular society at a particular historical moment. Just what are the laws of James's virtual reality in *The Wings of the Dove?*

The first (and last) thing to remember is that this imaginary reality is constructed of words. Remembering this at all times is just as important, and just as difficult, as obeying Fredric Jameson's command "Always historicize." Just as paintings are made of paint on some surface, and just as statues are made of marble or bronze, so novels are made of letters printed on paper. That is their embodiment, one might even say their "incarnation," their mode of entry into the real world of other physical objects and of human beings who can, some of them, read the language in which the novel is written. The virtual reality this language constitutes remains there embodied in volumes nineteen and twenty of the New York Edition, sitting on the shelf waiting to be entered by anyone who takes down a volume and begins to read. It has no other accessible existence except other printed or digitized versions. The film version may be "based on" the novel, but it is so different in so many ways that it does not allow access to the same imaginary reality the reader enters when she reads the novel.

When a reader reads *The Wings of the Dove*, she encounters a narrative voice recording in the past tense what these fictive characters said, thought, and did. Just as everything the reader has access to in "The Aspern Papers" is filtered through the first person narration of the unnamed protagonist, so everything the reader has access to in *The Wings of the Dove* is filtered through the anonymous narrator's language. It would be a big mistake to identify that language with the voice of Henry James, as registered, for example, in his letters, in his notebooks, in his autobiographical writings, or in his prefaces, in spite of the almost irresistible temptation to do so. James in the preface speaks of *The Wings of the Dove* as a novel he has written down, of its failure to represent all he had at first planned, of his negotiations to have the novel printed and published, of the long germination of the novel, and so on. The narrator knows nothing of all that. He (she? it? we?) speaks of the characters as if they had been real people, and never for a moment breaks that illusion, although there are a few rare moments when the narrator speaks of strategies and diffi-culties of narration, as when he, we, or it observes that it is best to present Milly indirectly: "She worked," says the narrator, "—and seemingly quite without design—upon the sympathy, the curiosity, the fancy of her associ-ates, and we shall really ourselves scarce otherwise come closer to her than by feeling their impression and sharing, if need be, their confusion" (19:116).

The narrator of *The Wings of the Dove* has no personality in the ordinary sense, no history, no location in either time or space in the real world. We have no way of knowing what the time lapse is between the now of the events and the now of the narration. The narrator is nothing but a neutral, equable, cool, slightly ironic power of narration. This narrative voice has an admirable gift for making up powerful figures of speech to represent the characters in their interaction. It has lots of leisure to pay attention to minute details in the intercourse of the characters. The neutrality and lack of personality would justify calling the narrative voice an "it" rather than a "he" or a "she." It, the narrative voice, is without gender, class, race, or historical placement, even though the critical reader might be justified in saying that the possibility of such a narrating voice, quite different from the more or less personalized narrators of *Tom Jones*, *Vanity Fair*, *Middle-march*, or *He Knew He Was Right*, belongs to a certain historical moment in the development (or degeneration) of English and United States literature. Such a critical reader might also be justified in saying that the possibility of such a sovereign narrating voice suggests that it is male, white, and of the educated class, but that would be only an inference, not something founded on anything said directly anywhere in the narration.

This narrating voice, this "it," has one power that neither Henry James nor the characters in the novel nor real people in the real world have, namely, what I have called, following Nicholas Royle, telepathic clairvoy-ance. This telepathic power has, however, in *The Wings of the Dove*, one peculiar limitation. It can only be exercised with one character at a time. If the narrative voice is within Kate's consciousness, it cannot at the same time be within Densher's consciousness, but must see Densher from Kate's limited perspective. *The Wings of the Dove*, as James says in the preface, is made up of large rotational blocks of narration in which the narrator enters for a more or less extended time one character's mind, reporting that in free indirect discourse, then shifts to another, then to another, and so on.

James sticks for the most part in this novel to his inveterate strategy of what he calls "scenic" presentation. That is to say, he advances the story through a series of discrete "scenes" in which several characters, usually just two, confront one another at a particular time and place. In this scene, they engage in the give and take of dialogue. In *The Wings of the Dove*, however, these scenes are presented as they appeared from within the consciousness of just one of the participants. Any spectator or participant could have heard what the characters say, but the narrator reports only one character's inner, often secret, responses to these, according to a strict law of self-limitation. It is not that the narrative voice could not, if it chose, go back and tell such and such a scene from the perspective of another character, from a placement inside a different character's mind, feelings, and body. It just does not choose to do so. What the narrative voice cannot do, so it seems, is be in the minds of two of the characters at once.

Nor are the large temporal gaps ever filled in, for example, the gap between Milly's decision to leave for Venice and our finding her already there, domiciled in the Palazzo Leporelli, as the reader turns the page from the end of chapter 2 of Book Seventh and begins reading chapter 3. Far from being constructed of solid blocks fitted tightly together to make a substantial bridge, *The Wings of the Dove* is made up of separate narrative units, each quite limited in what it can reveal, and each separated from the others by more or less wide empty places, hiding secrets that will never be revealed, now that James is dead. James's phrases in the preface about "the absent values, the palpable voids, the missing links, the mocking shadows" well describe these never-to-be-filled emptinesses and gaps. Into these gaps the reader can only project her unverifiable imagination of what may have happened.

Nor are these missing events trivial. They include happenings crucial to the lives, and deaths, of the main characters. Among these are the actual events of Kate's coming to Densher's apartment in Venice, Lord Mark's visit to disabuse Milly of her illusion, Densher's last visit to Milly, and Milly's death. Kate's coming happens in the blank pages between the end of Book Eighth and the beginning of Book Ninth, while Densher's final encounter with Milly happens in the blank between the end of Book Ninth and the beginning of Book Tenth. Densher knows of Lord Mark's visit at first only by inference, when he is denied entrance to Milly's palace. Milly's death occurs while all the main characters but Sir Luke are back in London. No doubt direct literary representation of copulation was against the decorum of James's time, but deathbed scenes abounded. No social or novelistic prohibition prevented James from presenting Lord Mark's visit or Densher's last interview if James had wanted to do so.

If James had not told the reader that *The Wings of the Dove* is full of gaps and hiatuses that are failures in fulfilling his initial plan, the reader might have thought that these signal omissions were deliberate. They might have seemed a strategy of indirection intended to increase dramatic intensity and stimulate the reader's imagination. Whatever the explanation, James's strategy of presentation in *Wings*, as in most of his other works, is to omit some of the most important events. An example from another novel is the omission from direct presentation of the three most important events in *The Princess Casamassima*: Hyacinth's promise to the radical group to commit a terrorist act, his weekend with the Princess, and his suicide. Sex, death, and the decisive speech acts of life—these seem to resist direct presentation within James's virtual realities, though no reader can doubt that they do occur in the ideal realms for which the virtual verbal realities are a substitute that provides indirect and incomplete access.

The Laws of This Virtual Reality

Within the field established by the narrative voice's incomplete and intermittent access to the characters minds, feelings, words, and milieu, further laws, proprieties, and conventions define the limits of what the reader is given to read. Let me name these first and then exemplify them as succinctly as possible through citation and closer analysis.

1. If the narrator can be fully in the minds of the characters but only in one at once, the characters are even more severely limited in their access to the minds of others. Though each character feels the pressure of the consciousness and will of the other and can guess what is going on in the other mind from what the other character says, from his or her face, gesture, and behavior, no certainty is possible. Big mistakes are often made, for example, Milly's mistake in believing Kate's assertion that she does not love Densher. Knowledge of the other is a matter of belief, that is, it is a performative act rather than a cognitive certainty. That belief is in response to a speech act by the other that always in one way or another, explicitly or implicitly, says: "Believe me. I swear I am telling the truth."

2. The free indirect discourse that is the narrator's main tool of story-telling, along with the direct transcription of what the characters said to one another, is characterized by an extraordinary gift for figurative presentation of the nuances of consciousness. Consciousness is in itself impalpable, immaterial, to some degree unworded. There are few adequate names for its specific features in a given person at a given moment. It can only be named in terminology drawn from the material world, the world that is, at least apparently, open to the senses and to literal naming. James's narrator excels in such presentation, both in presenting the dramas of interacting consciousnesses by way of faces, gestures, clothes, rooms, windows, doors, and so on, and in the use of figurative language in catachresis for what has no literal terms. This gift for figures is the way James exemplifies Aristotle's dictum that a command of metaphor is the mark of genius in a poet. The peculiarity of these metaphors for minds is that, according to the fundamental uncertainty in free indirect discourse generally, it is not always possible to tell whether a given figure was actually a feature of the character's thought or whether it is projected there by the narrator as the best way to dramatize the facts of consciousness. The uncertainty derives from the convention that no other access to the minds of the characters but through the narrator's report is possible.

3. The intersubjective field represented by the narrator within the severe limitations I have named is characterized by an implacable battle of social wills for domination. If you do not dominate others, you will be dominated by them.

4. Key terms in James's presentation are *will, idea, belief, lie, there, face,* and *oh,* a strange mixture of conceptual and apparently trivial words. These words occur again and again in a multitude of different contexts, almost like Wagnerian leitmotifs, each one echoing before and after, for the astute reader, all the other uses of the same word. The text is organized (or disorganized) by these repetitions.

The Incalculably Other

One place where the powers and limitations of each character's access to the mind of another person are overtly asserted is the narrator's notation of the way Kate seems "other" to Milly, ultimately wholly impenetrable. Kate seems most other to Milly when she thinks that Kate has looked at Densher, among thousands of other faces, and been looked at by him in return:

just the odd result of the thought was to intensify for the girl that side of
her friend which she had doubtless already been more prepared than she
quite knew to think of as the 'other,' the not wholly calculable. It was fan-
tastic, and Milly was aware of this; but the other side was what had, of a
sudden, been turned straight toward her by the show of Mr. Densher's
propinquity. . . . What happened was that afterwards, on separation, she
wondered if the matter hadn't mainly been that she herself was so 'other,'
so taken up with the unspoken; the strangest thing of all being, subsequently, that when she asked herself how Kate could have failed to feel it
she became conscious of being here on the edge of a great darkness. She
should never know how Kate truly felt about anything such a one as Milly
Theale should give her to feel. Kate would never—and not from ill will or
duplicity, but from a sort of failure of common terms—reduce it to such a
one's comprehension or put it within her convenience. (19:190–91)

In this admirable passage the reference of "other" reverses. Milly's inability ever to understand what Kate may be thinking becomes Milly's sense
of her own otherness, her feeling that she is out of the social loop, so to
speak, that gives the London characters, at least apparently, more access
to one another's minds. Beneath all this is the everyday use of the word
other to name a rival for one's affections, as in the phrase "significant
other."

Another example of the way one person is a great darkness to another
person, in spite of partial and intermittent insights, is an interchange during Milly's evening party in her Venetian palace. In this episode Densher
and Kate, under the cover of the music and the general conversation, ne-
gotiate their dark bargain. I take this example out of almost innumerable
others. Much of the novel is made up of the confrontation of two persons,
as each tries to fathom, more or less unsuccessfully, what the other is
thinking and to dominate that other. The narrator reports what the characters say to one another, while reporting in indirect discourse what goes
on in the mind of one of the interlocutors. Here that "reflector" is Densher. If Densher will promise on his honor to pretend to make love to
Milly, she, Kate, will sleep with him. That is the dark bargain.

Their interchange begins with a remarkable formulation that seems to
support the idea that the characters have clairvoyant knowledge of one
another. Each character, so this passage says, is likely to feel the pressure
of the other's will and idea, even if these are not spoken: "It was constantly
Densher's view that, as between himself and Kate, things were understood
without saying, so that he could catch in her, as she but too freely could
in him, innumerable signs of it, the whole soft breath of consciousness

meeting and promoting consciousness" (20:179). "The whole soft breath of consciousness meeting and promoting consciousness"—that is a marvelous phrase for a reciprocity in which one mind is not only aware of what the other mind is thinking but by an implicit rejoinder and reciprocity "promotes," puts into further motion, that other person's thinking and feeling. What is the referent of "it" in the phrase "signs of it"? Presumably "it" is the power to be conscious of the consciousness of the other. This is the power Charles du Bos, in an admirable phrase, called, apropos of Robert Browning, "l'introspection d'autrui," the introspection of the other.[16] This admirable reciprocity, however, is not a pure spirituality, thought transference, or telepathy. It works through "innumerable signs" that testify to it and promote it, as the evanescent embodiment in the phrase "soft breath" attests. Just what are these signs? They are, for James, gesture, dress, ways of walking, a shrug of the shoulders, a lift of the hand, but most of all the complex signs made by the face—by smiles, frowns, pursings of the lips, blushes, blinks, all that James in one admirable phrase calls the "conscious face." Consciousness is outered in the face and made, though always somewhat ambiguously, visible there. One good example of this is all that is said about Sir Luke Strett's impassive and inscrutable face in the encounters between him and Densher, when Sir Luke comes to minister to the dying Milly in Venice. Another example is Densher's blush when, in a much later scene, he realizes Kate is saying she will marry him now if he assures her that he believes Milly is leaving him her money: "The point she made was clear, as clear as that the blood, while he recognized it, mantled in his face" (20:349).

A moment after the formulation about consciousness meeting and promoting consciousness in the scene of Kate's bargain with Densher, Densher supposes that Kate has not understood the deep reservation with which he has lukewarmly invited Milly to have tea in his apartment. This supposition confirms my assertion of the necessary incompleteness of clairvoyance between even the most intimately connected persons. He thinks she has not understood, but he is not quite sure. James seems clearly to indicate here that the coincidence of consciousnesses is never total and never verifiable: "It gave him on the spot, her failure of perception, almost a beginning of the advantage he had been planning for—that is at least if she too were not darkly dishonest" (20:179). He does not know whether or not she too is darkly dishonest, that is, whether or not she has guessed why he has taken a private apartment and is acting disingenuously by pretending not to know. She may be or she may not be doing that. He does not know. He cannot know for sure.

Densher's consciousness of her consciousness is therefore incomplete, as is characteristically the case in such interchanges throughout the novel. The narrator, however, knows all, though by no means always tells all, as in this case. He (we, it) remains within Densher's puzzling mind and does not tell us just what Kate is thinking, only what she says and how she looks to Densher:

> It wound him up a turn or two further, none the less, to impute to her now a weakness of vision by which he could feel himself the stronger. Whatever apprehension of his motive in shifting his abode might have brushed her with its wings [like the wings of a dove], she at all events certainly didn't guess that he was giving their friend a hollow promise. That was what she had herself imposed on him; there had been in prospect from the first a definite particular point at which hollowness, to call it by its least compromising name, would have to begin. Therefore its hour had now charmingly sounded. (2:179–80)

The most, as opposed to "least," compromising name would be to call it outright a lying promise. Kate has promised (truthfully) to sleep with Densher if he will lie to Milly by leading her to believe that Kate has refused his love and that he is beginning to love Milly instead.

The efficacy of speech acts in *The Wings of the Dove* and also in the "real," historical world, the reader can see from this passage, depends, somewhat paradoxically, on the uncertainty and incompleteness of one consciousness's consciousness of another. I say "somewhat paradoxically," because speech acts would seem to depend for their felicity only on agreed-upon social rules that are transparent to those who accept them.

Here is another evidence, however, that, as Jacques Derrida has seen, the possibility of infelicity is an intrinsic necessity for felicitous speech acts. A promise works as a promise, strangely enough, only because it is possible to make a lying promise. The possibility of infelicity is not adventitious. It is an intrinsic part of felicity's chance. In a social world of complete clairvoyance, performatives would never be needed, only the exercise of thought's telepathic omniscience. The evidence of that in *The Wings of the Dove* is the way the characters' incomplete understanding of one another not only leaves Densher in doubt as to how far Kate understands him but also has made it possible for him to make a "hollow promise" to Milly in fulfillment of his promise to Kate to pretend to court Milly. Whenever promises are possible, hollow promises are also possible. This means, to pick up James's play on "promise" and "compromise," that the possibility of making lying promises, to give Densher's invitation to Milly its most compromising name, makes true promises possible. Densher promises Milly to invite her to go to his rooms, but has no intention of doing any such thing. This is the beginning, as the passage attests, of the long series of lies, implicit and explicit, he tells Milly.

One of the turning points in Densher's relation to Milly, however, is the moment when suddenly his resistance to having Milly enter his rooms, rooms that have been consecrated to the memory that Kate "came to him" there, breaks down completely, and he says, using the very word that has named, with its erotic overtone, his liaison with Kate: "You can come . . . when you like" (20:247). Here is another case where a lying promise magically fulfils itself, against the wishes of the one who had been so unwary as to make it. I shall return to the significance of that remarkable recurring event in this novel.[17]

A Command of Metaphor

A second feature of the virtual reality constituted by the words on the pages of *The Wings of the Dove* is the narrator's extraordinary gift for metaphor. Let me identify more exactly this gift's function. Many examples could be adduced. Here are several: Mrs. Lowder obtrudes into Kate's and Densher's secret courtship: "And she came in, always, while they sat together rather helplessly watching her, as in a coach-and-four; she drove round their prospect as the principal lady at the circus drives round the ring, and she stopped the coach in the middle to alight with majesty" (19:62). Kate's impatient "injunction" to Densher in one of their clandestine meetings early in the novel, "Ah do what you like!" is "like the crack of a great whip in the blue air" (19:74–75). Susan Stringham's feeling about Milly is expressed in the figure of a great passenger steamer: "It was her [Milly's] nature, once for all—a nature that reminded Mrs. Stringham of the term always used in the newspapers about the great new steamers, the inordinate number of 'feet of water' they drew; so that if, in your little boat, you had chosen to hover and approach, you had but yourself to thank, when once the motion was started, for the way the draught pulled you. Milly drew the feet of water" (19:113). Mrs. Stringham's power to introduce Milly to London society makes her "a fairy godmother" who "had only to wave a neat little wand for the fairy-tale to begin at once" (19:145). Mrs. Stringham's sense of Milly's success in London is expressed in another extravagant figure: "Their immediate lesson accordingly was that they just had been caught up by the incalculable strength of a wave that was actually holding them aloft and that would naturally dash them wherever it liked" (19:167). Whose figures are these, the characters' or the narrator's? The first is explicitly ascribed to Mrs. Stringham, but what about the others?

Even more elaborate examples come near the end of the novel. In the two months between the Christmas day when Kate burns unopened Densher's last letter from Milly and his receipt from the New York lawyers of the formal notification of Milly's bequest, Densher is obsessed with something that is "only a thought, but a thought precisely of such freshness and such delicacy as made the precious, of whatever sort, most subject to the hunger of time" (20:395). This thought is of what he has lost forever by not reading Milly's letter: "he should never, never know what had been in Milly's letter" (20:396). The narrator expresses Densher's "thought" in a rapid sequence of three not wholly compatible figures. When he comes home, says the narrator, "Then he took it [the thought] out of its sacred corner and its soft wrappings; he undid them one by one, handling them," handling *it*, as a father, baffled and tender, might handle a maimed child" (20:396). Densher's imagination of the various possibilities in "the turn she would have given her act" "made of them [the possibilities] a revelation the loss of which was like the sight of a precious pearl cast before his eyes—his pledge given not to save it—into the fathomless sea, or rather even it was like the sacrifice of something sentient and throbbing, something that, for the spiritual ear, might have been audible as a faint far wail" (ibid.). A maimed child, a priceless pearl cast in the sea, a sentient creature sacrificed—these are hyperbolic catachreses for Densher's otherwise inexpressible thought. Here it seems likely, though the reader cannot be sure, that the figures are the narrator's own, proffered as the best way to express Densher's feelings and thoughts, as though these could be adequately conveyed to the reader in no other way. Nevertheless, it is impossible to be sure that the narrator is not reporting Densher's figurative thoughts.

Two other passages are slightly different. One is the scene in which Milly wanders off alone in the Alps and is discovered by an anxious Susan Stringham perched on a rock looking out at the great view below. This is seen by Susan as parallel to the episode of Christ's temptation by Satan, in the Bible or in Milton's *Paradise Regained*: "This was the impression that if the girl was deeply and recklessly meditating there she wasn't meditating a jump; she was on the contrary, as she sat, much more in a state of uplifted and unlimited possession that had nothing to gain from violence. She was looking down on the kingdoms of the earth, and though indeed that of itself might well go to the brain, it wouldn't be with a view of renouncing them. Was she choosing among them or did she want them all?" (19:124). The other such scene is the admirable episode when Milly confronts, at Lord Mark's country house, the Bronzino portrait that looks strikingly like Milly herself. This gives Milly her first definite conviction that she is marked by death: "The lady in question, at all events, with her slightly Michael-angelesque squareness, her eyes of other days, her full lips, her long neck, her recorded jewels, her brocaded and wasted reds, was a very great personage—only unaccompanied by a joy. And she was dead, dead, dead" (19:221). Much later in the novel Milly remembers her tears when she looked at the portrait, as if in a mirror, as "the sign of her consciously rounding her protective promontory, quitting the blue gulf of comparative ignorance and reaching her view of the troubled sea" (20:144). I shall return ultimately to what is implied by the fact that both of these passages have to do with death.

These last two examples differ, however, it can be said now, from those cited earlier in that the Alpine view and the Bronzino painting are things in the novel's first level of reality, while the ships, fairy godmother, coach, whip, maimed child, pearls, and sacrificed animal of those figures first cited have only a verbal existence in the narrator's or character's language. Nevertheless, in both kinds of figures something that can be named is transferred to name in catachresis something that has no proper name, that is, an impalpable and imponderable state of mind or quality of consciousness. In both kinds of figures, moreover, it is often (though not always, as in the case of Susan Stringham's figure of the great steamship) impossible to tell for sure whether the figure is the character's own, as reported by the narrator's indirect discourse speaking for what the character thought, or whether the figure is invented by the narrator as the best way to register the character's consciousness at that moment, even though the character did not embody it in that particular figure. It is impossible to tell, for one thing, because, as it is all too easy to forget, the reader has absolutely no access to these imaginary realities except through the figures. The figures are their primary and sole form of existence for the reader. The characters' minds exist, at these moments, as these figures. The reader has nothing to which to compare them, even though for James or for the narrator they may correspond to features of the ideal reality that it is the business of the narrative voice to put into words so the reader may have access to it. The reader, however, has no alternative route to that ideal reality. He has only the simulacrum or phantasm bit by bit invented for him, that is, simultaneously invented and revealed, by the words on the page.

A good example by means of which to understand this figurative procedure better is a moment in Book Sixth in which the reader is put within
Densher's mind as he sits as a guest at Aunt Maud's dinner party and
watches Kate enter the dining room and put on her act for Aunt Maud.
The narrative voice does not drop for one moment the assumption that
Densher has a real existence and that he (we, it) is (are) just reporting what
went on in his mind at some earlier moment, as though it were all stored
up somewhere waiting to be registered in narration. The "voice" of this
narration is the *voix narrative* of which Blanchot speaks,[18] neutral, impersonal, speaking from who knows where or when, able to report things only
as they were seen at some indeterminate earlier time by one or another of
the characters. What exists now, what remains, in the ideal realm that the
narrator reports is not the solid objects, the material bodies of the characters and their surroundings, but the subjective experience that the characters had. The narrator has access to all these, but can present them only
one at a time, so to speak, in the blocks of narration of which the preface
speaks. "It," the narrative voice, does not have a superior view. No superior view exists. The narrative voice is absolutely dependent on the characters' experience in order to have anything to say at all. It can, however,
embroider as it wishes on that data. It is as though only this residue or
debris remains of a world that was once solid and substantial.

    In the passage in question Densher sees Kate enter Aunt Maud's dining
room as a grand actress, with Maud as her manageress, and Densher "relegated to mere spectatorship, a paying place in front, and one of the most
expensive" (20:35). This ornate figure is extended through a long paragraph. It is ascribed to Densher, but elaborated on, verbalized, by the
narrative voice speaking in free indirect discourse. In the midst of the
paragraph comes that rare thing in James, a parabasis in which the narrative voice comments on its own procedures. Calling this a parabasis or
suspension of the dramatic illusion must not be misunderstood. The narrative voice does not break the convention that presumes these were real
people with an existence independent of the narrative notation of them:
"Such impressions as we thus note for Densher come and go, it must be
granted, in very much less time than notation demands; but we may none
the less make the point that there was, still further, time among them for
him to feel almost too scared to take part in the ovation" (ibid.). The
reader will note the momentary shift to the present tense: "such impressions as we thus note for Densher come and go." It is in the present because the narrative voice is talking about such impressions in general, the

kind that Densher's particular impressions exemplify. At any time or place for any person such impressions would be like these.

The narrative voice is answering an imagined rebuke. A reader might object, "Surely you don't mean to tell me that all these words went through Densher's mind in those few seconds it took for Kate to make her grand entrance into the dining room?" The narrative voice answers this imaginary challenge by admitting that this must be granted, but then shifts focus as a kind of diversion from the main question about the noncongruence of the two times, the time of impression and the time of notation, to the assertion that Densher felt scared. The impression was Densher's and it really happened, exterior to and other than the narrative voice. The notation, the narrative voice implies, however, is its own, or "our" own, since it speaks in the first person plural. It speaks, or "we" speak, for Densher, giving words to his more or less wordless impression: "but we may none the less make the point that there was, still further time among them [his impressions] for him to feel almost too scared to take part in the ovation. . . . It was as if the drama—it thus came to him, for the fact of a drama there was no blinking—was between *them* [Kate and Mrs. Lowder, that is], them quite preponderantly; with Merton Densher relegated to mere spectatorship, a paying place in front, and one of the most expensive" (20:35).

Social Relations as Economic Agon

The third characteristic of the field of forces generated by the interacting subjectivities in *The Wings of the Dove*, as the narrator reports and creates these for the reader, is the way those interactions are a field of battle. The novel reports a struggle for domination named by a set of recurring stylistic features. These features, it must always be remembered, do not represent or refer to something other than themselves against which their accuracy may be measured. They name ways intersubjectivity in the novel exists. Nothing other than they exists to which they may be compared for their adequacy. That is why sharp attention to them is necessary. No other way exists by which to understand the novel.

The most explicit testimony to the way London society is an implacable battle for domination comes in an early scene in which Kate tries to explain to the more or less innocent Milly what good she and Lord Mark are to Aunt Maud, and she to them. The narrator reports (in that narrative voice's characteristic free indirect discourse, the reader will note) Kate to

have told Milly, "And he [Lord Mark] wasn't meanwhile himself indifferent—indifferent to himself—for he was working Lancaster Gate [that is,
Aunt Maud and her grandly vulgar house] for all it was worth: just as it
was, no doubt, working *him*, and just as the working and the worked were
in London, as one might explain, the parties to every relation" (19: 178).
This figure of the working and the worked as the parties to *every* relation
is followed by an explicitly economic figuration, one of many in the novel,
that mingles the terminology of giving and taking with the terminology of
bargaining:

> Kate did explain, for her listening friend; every one who had anything to
> give—it was true they were the fewest—made the sharpest possible bargain
> for it, got at least its value in return. The strangest thing furthermore was
> that this might be in cases a happy understanding. The worker in one con-
> nection was the worked in another; it was as broad as it was long—with the
> wheels of the system, as might be seen, wonderfully oiled. (19:179)

These characterizations, it may be noted, are made not by the narrator
as an independent witness but by the somewhat cynical and worldly Kate,
who knows that she is being "worked" by Aunt Maud. To work others is
to coerce them, often against their will and perhaps even against their
knowledge, by deceit, to act in a way that will be beneficial to the worker.
The worker, however, is worked in turn, in a constant reciprocity that
Kate calls a well-oiled system of giving and taking. This system is created
by a sharp making of bargains in which the aim is to get as much as possible and to give as little as possible in return. Of Kate's view of Milly's own
place in this system of exchange, the narrator says, "She declined to treat
any question of Milly's own 'paying' power as discussble; that Milly would
pay a hundred per cent—and even to the end, doubtless, through the
nose—was just the beautiful basis on which they found themselves"
(19:180). Since Milly is unfathomably rich, she is fair game. She loses
nothing by paying through the nose.

Kate is disastrously (for her) wrong about Milly, but just why and how
that is the case must be discussed later. Kate's analysis of the London she
knows might be seen as a cold anthropological delineation of the kinship
system, the totems, and the system of exchange of women and worldly
goods, giving and receiving, investing and drawing interest, that characterizes this particular society. Or it might be seen as showing how the economic system of Western bourgeois capitalism has permeated every corner
of personal life at this historical moment. Capitalism defines courtship and
marriage as much as it does the stock market and the behavior of industrial

magnates or imperialistic entrepreneurs. The rich bourgeois widow Maud Lowder has seen in her beautiful but impoverished niece Kate an opportunity to raise her own social standing by marrying that niece to an aristocrat, Lord Mark. Lord Mark has the rank but not the money, but hopes to get some of Mrs. Lowder's money if he marries Kate. Kate's beauty and manners are also a social asset, a gift she has to give the person she marries. The fathomlessly rich American heiress Milly is prey for all these workers, in a form of imperialistic colonizing of the new world by the old that is one of James's chief themes. That theme is present here in the repeated insistence that Milly is to be seen as a characteristic "American girl" (20:254). "The national character was firm in her" (20:255), whereas Kate is a somewhat anomalous "English girl" (20:89).

No careful reader can doubt that nationalist, class, imperialist, political, and economic themes are obliquely dramatized in the domestic drama of *The Wings of the Dove.* It would be possible to assert without too much apparent distortion that what *The Wings of the Dove* is really about is the marriage market in its relation to class, gender, economic, and national determinations at a certain place and time. That is the moment of late capitalist imperialism at the end of the nineteenth century and the beginning of the twentieth century in England and the United States. Like so many novels before it, *The Wings of the Dove*, it might be said, centers on the question of whom Kate or Milly will marry, if anyone, just as Jane Austin's *Emma* centers on the question of whom Emma will marry, and *Middlemarch* on the question of the marriages of the various marriageable women in the novel, especially Dorothea, but also Mary Garth, Rosamond Vincy, and Dorothea's sister Celia. The problem with such a formulation is that it would not wholly justify James's excessively subtle, rarefied, and detailed attention to nuances of interaction among people investing in the marriage market. A more adequate formulation would say that James is interested in the subtleties of intersubjective relations among people in the context of such class, gender, economic, and nationalist determinations.

Do others or be done by them, work or be worked, work others but inevitably be worked by them—this struggle for domination, within the given conditions of capitalism as they were embodied at the novel's moment in England and America, is dramatized, given a local habitation and readable names, in the recurrent terms so important in the novel: *idea, will, belief, lie, there, face,* and *oh.* The terms are inextricably intertwined with one another, in James's use of them, as I shall show.

Idea

Idea names the preconception or desire that is private to the character. Such an idea remains secret unless it is "outered," materialized in some way. In itself an "idea" is immaterial, powerless. It is a disembodied fact of consciousness. It has no purchase on the material world or on other people until it is expressed in words or other signs, that is, given a material existence. Aunt Maud's idea is to break up the relation between Kate and Densher so she can marry Kate to Lord Mark. Densher's desire to persuade Kate to sleep with him remains an "idea" until he figures out a way to "master" her and get her to come to his rooms. Kate's idea is to get Densher to make love to Milly so he will inherit her money, thereby making it possible for Kate and Densher to have their cake and eat it too, to marry and also be rich. Milly's idea is to get Densher for herself, as Densher realizes when he begins visiting Milly in her Venetian palazzo: "he was not *there*, not just as he was in so doing it, through Kate and Kate's idea, but through Milly and Milly's own, and through himself and *his* own, unmistakeably—as well as through the little facts, whatever they had amounted to, of his time in New York" (20:186). Here Densher begins to be dimly aware that, to use Kate's words for it, he is beginning to be in love with Milly. "You *are* in love with her, you know," says Kate to him, with her implacable lucidity (20:195). Each character is defined at a given moment or through a long temporal sequence as inhabited by a more or less secret idea. This idea/project defines what that character most is. The idea is the focus of the vitality that Densher calls, in Kate's case, "her pure talent for life" (20:176). Even Sir Luke, when he is ministering to the dying Milly, presents himself at Densher's door in Venice armed with an "idea" (20:302). This is the idea that Densher can save Milly by giving her, in her love for him, something to live for, and also, though the novel never quite says this explicitly, by giving her sexual experience.

Two passages, both involving interchanges between Kate and Densher, will show how *idea* becomes a charged word in the novel. In the first, the two argue about who is responsible for the decision to defraud Milly. This attempt has failed, now that Lord Mark has told Milly the pair are secretly engaged. "It isn't a question," says Densher, "for us of apportioning shares or distinguishing invidiously among such impressions as it was our idea to give." Kate replies that "It wasn't *your* idea to give impressions," to which Densher says in return, "Don't go into that!" The narrator then picks up the word: "It was perhaps not as going into it that she had another idea—an idea born, she showed, of the vision he had just evoked" (20:322). Her new idea is that Densher might even yet save the day by an outright lie to Milly denying that he and Kate are engaged.

The other passage comes after Milly has died. Densher has gone to Kate proposing that they marry immediately, to which Kate replies that she will do what he wants if he can assure her that he has an "idea" that Milly has left him a big part of her immense fortune. Their interchange plays again on the word *idea*. It also offers an example of the way one character responds to another by repeating almost the same words with a different valence or tone. There would be much to say about this, but I defer that saying to the chapter on *The Golden Bowl*, in which the procedure is even more salient:

> "I know nothing whatever."
> "You've not an idea?"
> "I've not an idea."
> "I'd consent," she said—"I'd announce it tomorrow, today, I'd go home this moment and announce it to Aunt Maud, for an idea: I mean an idea straight *from* you, I mean as your own, given me in good faith." (20:349–50)

Once more the narrator picks up the word and plays with it, highlights it for the reader's meditation: "She made it all out, bent upon her—the idea he didn't have, and the idea he had, and his failure of insistence when it brought up *that* challenge, and his sense of her personal presence, and his horror, almost, of her lucidity. They made in him a mixture that might have been rage, but that was turning quickly to mere cold thought, thought which led to something else and was like a new dim dawn" (20:350). "Thought" here is almost a synonym of "idea," in this case the dim dawn of an idea that his unwillingness to go on with their game, or to take Milly's bequest if she makes one, may in the end separate him forever from Kate.

Will

Will names the impetus within an embodied consciousness to make idea real. James's characters are measured by the strengths of their wills. These wills, as in the case of Milly's legal will, can persist and be efficacious even beyond death if those wills have been embodied in efficacious speech acts, for example, in a bequest. Aunt Maud has an implacable will to make her ideas for Kate become real. As Kate tells Milly, in a passage to be discussed later, she has a way of making her willed ideas come true. "She'll get rid of it [our relation]," Kate tells Densher of Aunt Maud, "as she believes, by ignoring it and sinking it—if she only does so hard enough. Therefore *she*, in her manner, 'denies' it if you will" (20:27). The "circle of petticoats" (20:209) with which Densher is surrounded makes him, as he is uncomfortably aware, subject to the contradictory wills of all these women. Kate in particular has an extraordinary way of making Densher do as she wills, as Densher is ruefully aware: "His question, as we have called it, was the interesting question of whether he had really no will left. . . . [W]hereas he had done absolutely everything that Kate had wanted, she had done nothing whatever that he had" (20:177). His successful attempt to persuade her to come to his rooms in Venice is presented as only a partial conquest of his will against hers: "there were plenty of things left in which he must feel her will. They only told him, these indications, how much she was, in such close quarters, feeling his" (20:216). Earlier he had been somewhat ruefully aware of what he thinks of, or what the narrator thinks of, as "the whole present play of her charming strong will" (20:19).

The most extraordinary act of will in the novel, however, is Milly's will to go on living in the face of death, as Sir Luke Strett has told her she can do: "If I want to live," Milly tells Densher, "I *can*" (20:246). She makes use here of what she calls to herself, much earlier in the novel, "the famous 'will-power' she had heard about, read about, and which was what her medical adviser had mainly thrown her back on" (19:258). I shall return later to this most important and problematic act of willing in *The Wings of the Dove*. Its context is late nineteenth-century pseudo-scientific vitalist ideas about will power as successful defiance even of death. Traces of this vitalism may be found in Nietzsche, Bergson, Freud, in Henry's brother William, and in many other writers. "Will-power" was in the air.

Belief

Belief names the response of a character to the performative speech acts, outer expressions of an idea powered by will, even lying speech acts, of another. An example is Densher's response to Milly's question about what he thinks of her health, "You suppose me so awfully bad?" by saying, "I'll believe whatever you tell me" (20:245). Aunt Maud tells Susan Stringham that if they can just get everyone to believe the lie that Kate does not love Densher, their love will really come to an end: "*You* don't know it—,"

Aunt Maud says to Susan, "that must be your line. Or rather your line must be that you deny it utterly" (20:115). Later Kate explains to Densher that Aunt Maud "believes" Milly won't die if Densher stays in Venice, and "what she believes is the principal thing for us" (20:228). Lord Mark, when he proposes to Milly, entreats her "To believe in me. To believe in me" (20:157). Kate exhorts Densher to do what she wants: "Dear man, . . . only believe in me, and it will be beautiful" (20:19). Much later in the novel, after Milly has heard from Lord Mark the truth about the secret engagement of Kate and Densher, Susan tells Densher that she will believe him if he denies it, even though she knows it is true: "What I believe will inevitably depend more or less on your action. You can perfectly settle it—if you care. I promise to believe you down to the ground if, to save her life, you consent to a denial" (20:292).

Lie names a contrary-to-fact statement that functions as a speech act to determine the behavior of another if that other believes the lie or even acts as though she or he believes it. *The Wings of the Dove* is full of lies, so many of them that the novel might almost be defined as an exploration of the social efficacy of lies. "We've told too many lies," says Kate to Densher in their great colloquy on the Piazza San Marco, to which he not quite truthfully replies, "I, my dear, have told none!" (20:199). Kate and Aunt Maud lie to Milly about Kate's feelings for Densher. Milly lies over and over about her health. Densher, in spite of his silence, lies to Milly by his mere presence in Venice and in Milly's palazzo after the others have gone. Milly experiments with what it feels like to be a "dove," as Kate has called her, by lying to Mrs. Lowder. She says, when she knows perfectly well from one look at Kate that Densher has returned from America, "I don't *think*, dear lady, he's here" (19:284). To be a dove is, paradoxically, to be adept at lies that will be believed. "I'm not worrying, Milly," says Susan Stringham when she fears Milly is dying. "And poor Susie's face registered the sublimity of her lie" (20:102). "And luckily for *me*, I lie badly," says Mrs. Stringham in a later scene, to which Mrs. Lowder "almost snorted" in reply, "*I* lie well, thank God, . . . when, as sometimes will happen, there's nothing else so good" (20:116). Since a lie has no cognitive value, it may function as a more or less pure performative utterance. Such a performative will be, in a paradoxical sense, felicitous if it is believed, but only so long as it is believed, no longer. As soon as Milly no longer believes that Densher is free she turns her face to the wall. She ceases to will to go on living.

There You Are!

There appears most often in phrases like "There you are," or "There we are." It names the triumphant moment when one character has scored a point against another in the ceaseless battle for domination. It also indicates, however, the extraordinary sense all the characters have that each is at a given moment situated in a certain inexorably empirical social place and time. All the character's life stretches out before and after, but at this moment the character is nowhere else but "there" and must make the best of it: "There you are." An amazing number of such locutions punctuate the novel, like a rhythmically recurring leitmotif. Variants on the phrase are repeated so many times that, though such expressions are colloquial enough, they call attention to themselves and invite a careful reader to speculate on their function and import. Here is an incomplete list: "There it is" (19:74), says Kate to Densher of their need to placate Aunt Maud. "There you are," says Aunt Maud when she tells Densher of her plan to marry Kate to a "great man" (19:83). Milly registers to herself at Maud Lowder's dinner party her sense of her rapid social success in London: "There they were again—yes, certainly" (19:158). "Then there it is," says Milly when Susan Stringham explains to her that Aunt Maud likes Densher but won't think of him as a husband for Kate. "So there we are," says Milly to Kate of her plan not to trouble her friends with her illness. She then goes on to think: "There they were then, since Kate had so to take it; but there, Milly felt, she herself in particular was" (19:229). When the great doctor, Sir Luke Strett, tells Milly, on her first visit to him, that she is "a capital case" because she is American, she replies, "Ah there you are!" His reponse is to say, playing on the phrase and underlining it, in case the reader had not yet noticed its import, "Oh no; there 'we' aren't at all! There I am only—but as much as you like. I've no end of American friends: there *they* are, if you please" (19:242). In a slightly later scene Milly responds to Mrs. Lowder's observation that Kate has not mentioned Densher to Milly by saying, "Ah there we are!" (19:269), and later in the same scene she plays on the phrase by saying that Densher will probably visit her when he comes back, "Then *there* . . . we shall be" (19:271). "Ah there you are!" says Kate to Densher at the dinner party at Mrs. Lowder's Milly misses, "with much gay expression, though what it expressed he failed at the time to make out" (20:40).

"There you are," it can be seen, means something, but sometimes what it means can only be figured out in retrospect, by thinking hard about the possibilities. "There she is," says Kate to Densher of Milly's instant social success in London and of her huge fortune (19:51). "Then there you are!" says Densher when Kate says women cannot tell whether Lord Mark's indubitable power is agreeable or not. "He has somehow an effect without his being in any traceable way a cause" (2:61). The narrator reports Densher as thinking, when he realizes Aunt Maud is offering to help him get Milly to marry him, by telling "the proper lie" for him, "Ah there she was, Aunt Maud!" (20:67). Later Densher imagines Milly as implicitly saying to him, "So there you are; worry about me, spare me, please, as little as you can" (20:78). In the clandestine conversation Kate and Densher have in Milly's rooms in London, they in effect reflect on the nuances of the phrase, "I'm all right with her," says Kate of Milly, "So there you are." To which Densher replies, "You mean *here* I am, . . . it's unmistakeable. If you also mean that her believing in you is all I have to do with you're so far right as that she certainly does believe in you" (20:92). Densher appears to mean that Milly's believing the lies she has been told about Kate's not loving Densher puts him in a particular situation. Milly's belief forces him either to sustain the lie to Milly or to betray Kate by telling Milly the truth. "Ah there you are!" says Milly when she catches Susie assuming Sir Luke takes her case so seriously because he pities her, upon which "Mrs. Stringham colored, for there indeed she was again" (20:123). "There she was," the narrator reports Milly as thinking to herself when she has told Lord Mark, in response to his proposal, that she is mortally ill (20:155). Later in this scene, she tells Lord Mark, "I give and give and give—there you are; stick to me as close as you like and see if I don't" (20:161).

When Susan Stringham makes her appeal to Densher to stay on in Venice to help Milly to will to go on living, variants of the phrase appear in rapid succession. The narrator registers Densher's sense that he is trapped and compromised: "So there he was" (20:208). A moment later Susan rubs it in by saying to him, apropos of her own "whole sacrifice" to Milly, her "princess": "There you are!" (20:209). In one of Kate's and Densher's last painful colloquies, when Densher is trying to find out how Lord Mark learned of their secret engagement, Densher says, "Ah there you are!" when she tells him Lord Mark has proposed to her. "Well," replies Kate, "if I'm 'there,' as you so gracefully call it, by having refused to meet him as he wanted—as he pressed—I plead guilty to being so" (20:379). She means she has not told Lord Mark that she is engaged to Densher. The final play on this expression, in the last words of the novel, now in the past tense, gathers the nuances and subtleties of all the previous ones:

Then he only said: "I'll marry you, mind you, in an hour."
"As we were?"
"As we were."
But she turned to the door, and her headshake was now the end. "We shall never be again as we were!" (20:405)

The characters, who utter most of these quasi-performative, quasi-cognitive assertions, characteristically speak, until the final interchange, in the present tense, "There you are," while the narrator speaks in the past tense, "There they were." It is as though all the events that make up the virtual reality of the novel exist somewhere in a simultaneous happening. They go on happening all the time over and over in the state of having already happened. All are happening at a single interval of closeness and distance from the narrator, though he chooses to tell the events he does tell in chronological sequence, one after the other, as they happened. This simultaneity is registered in the way, as I said earlier, the critic by instinct retranslates the events of the novel back into the eternal present of the words on the page that make the last episode contemporaneous with the first. The critic says: "At the beginning Kate Croy waits for her father," and "At the end Kate tells Densher they never again will be as they were." To the characters, however, "there you are" names a single instant of existence, a now with an already ineluctably determined past and an uncertain future, as well as a close mesh of defining circumstances: Kate's beauty and poverty, Densher's journalistic gifts and the certainty that he will never be rich, Milly's mortal illness, and so on.

Kate's final "We shall never be again as we were!" signals the remorseless passage of time and the impossibility of ever recovering a past "There you are!" Now that Densher's falling in love with Milly's memory has occurred, they can never be again as they were, whereas for the narrator all their times are coexistant in the mode of "There they were," and for the critic all times are in the eternal present of "There they are."

The phrase "There you are" and its variants puts together a deictic, a pronoun shifter, and a present tense version of the verb *to be* to make an exceedingly ambiguous and untranslatable idiom, something like *il y a* in French or *es gibt* in German. Most of all, perhaps, like *Dasein* in Heideger's German.

There you are. Where? Over there, somewhere else, as opposed to here? The phrase "Here you are" would have an entirely different meaning. The "there" in "There you are" indicates a triumph of the speaker over the other to whom he or she utters the phrase. It registers and at the same time effects a movement of the "you" from here to there, which is why it can be called partly cognitive, partly performative.

You. Who? You as the particular person to whom the assertion is addressed, or the universal "you," as in an idiom like "You never know"? The "you" at once names the person addressed and generalizes that you by making him or her subject to a universal and universalizing force: "There you are."

Are? In what sense of isness is that "are" meant: topographical, existential, temporal, historical, interpersonal, or perhaps, rather, all of these at once, that is, the verb *to be* in the present tense as the name for a global, all-encompassing situation, plight, predicament, fix? There you are. To be put there in that particular situation at that particular moment, in part by someone else's act of saying "Ah, there you are!" is to be made subject to the necessity of an implacable and inescapable "isness." As Jean-Luc Nancy, or, rather, his translator, puts this in *Le sens du monde (The Sense of the World)*, this is the situation "where *there* means also *da*, the *there* of *Dasein*, which is 'being-the-there,' that is, the *here* as the right-*here* of this world *here*."[19] What I am is the person who *is* in this particular plight. I may be still free to act, but my action will necessarily be in terms of the "are" that may not be evaded: "There you are."

James has an extraordinary sense of the remorseless pressure of the moment's net of imprisoning circumstances and of the way each new moment constitutes an event that cannot ever later on be made by whatever recuperative efforts not to have happened. Of each "There you are" it can be said that it marks an event that cuts the person put there by it off from what came before. After each, one can say, "We shall never be again as we were!" To this degree, the event marked by each "There you are" is as definitive and irreversible as death, for example, Milly's death in *The Wings of the Dove*. I shall return later to this analogy.

"There you are" names a kind of irreducible being there, an embeddedness in a situation that is both a life situation, that is, a social and familial situation in relation to others, and a material situation. Milly's being there, her *da sein* or, in Heideggerian idiom, her *Dasein*, includes having no family whatsoever, having immense amounts of money, limitless money, and having a mortal illness that dooms her to die young. There she is.

The notation is also a temporal one. When you say "There you are," you name a situation that is present, now, inescapable. Human beings are always in one time or another, never in more than one at once, not in the past that is gone forever and not in the future that is not yet, whatever

Heidegger may say about human temporality as a reaching out toward the future in order to return to my past and decisively appropriate it. We are there in the fleetingness of temporality. To say "There we are," however, is at once to say that we are, here and now, and to characterize this being there as having always built into it a certain distance. We are not here but there. Moreover, being there is never a matter of solitude, not even for Milly. James never, or at least rarely, says, or has his characters say, "There I am." In order to say "There you are," there must be a *Mitsein*, a being together. Uttering it is a violence done to the other, a triumph of the performative will.

Nevertheless, being there is not the same thing as saying it, as saying "There we are." Saying it ratifies it, acknowledges it, in a sense brings it into existence, since, it might be argued, it is distinctively human not only to be able to say "There we are," but to make it come about by saying it. "There we are" has a distinct performative dimension. When Kate at the end says, "We shall never be again as we were!" she testifies to the irrevocable in what has happened to change their being there. Densher is now in love with Milly's memory. That is now his being there. He is now there with Milly rather than here with Kate.

"There you are" does not name any sort of presence, for example, the full presence of a self or consciousness to itself. "There I am," as I have said, rarely appears. The phrase is something one person does to another by saying it. It is a way of doing something to another with words. "There you are" names, rather, displacement, temporalization, what Derrida calls *différance* in one of its senses, the differing and deferring that characterizes each of the characters as they are labeled by another character's "There you are." The phrase names Kate's impossible desire to have Densher and Milly's money too, Densher's impossible desire to have Kate by doing what she wants and at the same time not tell lies to Milly, Milly's desire to live, in the face of death, and her desire to believe that Densher is free to love her.

Face

Face is another of these recurrent motifs. The word names in *The Wings of the Dove* the most conspicuous and subtle way in which consciousness is always, for James, externalized, embodied. Consciousness, for James, is incarnated in material manifestations that may be read as signs. These are, however, ambiguous and never wholly transparent or verifiable signs. In this the face is like the words that face speaks. The novel opens, the reader will remember, with a description of Kate Croy looking at her pale face in the mirror as she waits for her father. The phrase "face to face" recurs frequently to name the absorbed attention each character gives the other's face in those mutual interrogations of the characters two by two that make up most of the novel's scenes (see, e.g., 20:138, 20:327, 20:363, 20:379). When Kate refuses Densher's plea that they marry immediately, he stands there "with his wasted passion . . . in his face" (20:350). Later, when Kate asks whether Milly has left him a bequest, "her face, wondering, pressed it more than her words" (20:368). Later still, Densher "faces" Kate over the letter that he has received from the dying Milly and that Kate will burn before either of them has read it. When Densher, in the last scene of all, tells Kate he has sent her the formal letter from Milly's lawyers unopened as a test, "She was struck—it showed in her face—by his expression" (20:399). A little later, as their rupture looms closer, "It had come to the point really that they showed each other pale faces" (20:401). Finally, at the last moment of the novel, just before he says, "I'll marry you, mind you, in an hour," Densher listens to what Kate says about the way Milly's "memory's your love. You *want* no other": "He heard her out in stillness, watching her face but not moving" (20:404). In one admirable phrase the narrator speaks of the "conscious face" Densher presents to Mrs. Stringham. Consciousness, for James, does not remain wholly secret and sequestered. It embodies itself, often against a person's will, in that person's face, as in all the many blushes that punctuate the novel, usually Densher's blushes (see, e.g., 20:383).

James's characters scrutinize with absorbed and often baffled attention the other's face in order to try to figure out what the other is thinking and feeling. The whole chapter of Densher's final encounters with Sir Luke Strett plays on the inscrutability and impassivity of Sir Luke's face. In one place, the narrator says, Densher "studied his fine closed face as much as ever in vain" (20:306), and when they part at the Venice train station, he thinks, "Sir Luke's face was wonderful" (20:309).

The most important use of "face," however, is in the phrase a despairing Susan Stringham uses to tell Densher Milly has given up her will to live: "She has turned her face to the wall" (20:270). To remain within the circuit of giving, taking, bargaining, promising, and lying, one must be face to face with others. To turn your face to the wall, with its echo of Melville's Bartleby's last act of doing rather than saying, of acting out his "I should prefer not to," is to turn away from all social intercourse and to face the blank wall of one's own end, the death that each man or woman dies alone and can share with no one.

Oh!

About *Oh!* in *The Wings of the Dove* there would be much to say. It is an example of the performative power within the virtual reality of *Wings* of a word that is not really a word, though it can be spelled and written down. It is, rather, an exclamation, an expiration of sounded air devoid of definite semantic content: "Oh!" The exclamation point that almost always accompanies "Oh" in James's transcription indicates its exclamatory character as a little explosion of involuntary sound. "Oh!" has an overdetermined and indeterminable content. It is so rich in meaning and in ambiguous performative force that each "Oh!" might require an interminable commentary. "Oh!" is halfway between articulate language and mere facial expression, at the border between body and word. It is the materialization of language into pure noise, as a kind of dumb expression of body and will in their "thereness," their *Dasein*. It combines suspiration and inspiration in a way that calls attention to the physical side of speaking, the way it depends on indrawn air and expelled breath. The performative efficacy of "Oh!" shows the way the power of speech acts depends on the materiality of language, that is, on its nonsensical side as mere sound. The power of "Oh," or, more usually, "O," has been appropriated as the mark of prosopopoetic apostrophe, as in translations of the vocative in Cicero's address to the absent Catiline: "When, O Catiline, do you mean to cease abusing our patience? [*Quo usque tandem abutere, Catilina, patientia nostra*],"[20] or in W. B. Yeats's many apostrophic "O's," as, for example, "O sages standing in God's holy fire" ("Sailing to Byzantium," l. 17), or "O Presences / That passion, piety, or affection knows" ("Among School Children," ll. 53–54).[21] "Oh!" and "O" are pronounced the same but written differently. One is a perhaps involuntary exclamation, the other the prelude to a deliberate address to some other person or thing. Nevertheless, the shadow of "O" as the personifying invocation of a ghostly presence lurks in all James's "Oh!'s." "Oh!" is always spoken to someone, or supposed to be overheard by someone, even if only by oneself, as one kind or another of invocation of the other, a plea for sympathy or an assertion of mastery.

There are no speech acts without language. Sometimes "Oh!" will do as well as the most elaborate promise or commitment. "Oh!" is a marker of class and of social sensitivity in those who use it and those who hear it. It also signals surprise and a sense of danger or of being in a predicament, of being found out and left with nothing to say but "Oh!," though "Oh!" may also express a sense of wordless mastery.

The narrator calls attention to the power of "Oh!" at one moment in the novel. Kate introduces Lord Mark to Densher at one of Aunt Maud's parties, naming each to each in a formal way. They both would like to marry Kate. Lord Mark does not say, "Pleased to meet you," or "How do you do," but simply, "Oh!" Densher reflects on what is implied in that aristocratic snub. He says nothing in response to Lord Mark's "Oh!" That is perhaps the only move he can make in return for Lord Mark's insolence. Lord Mark is the blocking agent in *The Wings of the Dove*, the figure who stands between Densher and both Kate and Milly. Being an aristocrat, however impecunious, he is qualified within the novel's class and money system to marry either, while Densher, being a hardworking and gifted journalist who will never be rich, is qualified to marry neither. The episode is reported in free indirect discourse from Densher's perspective, which controls this "block" of the narrative:

> "Oh!" said the other party while Densher said nothing—occupied as he mainly was on the spot with weighing the sound in question. He recognized it in a moment as less imponderable than it might have appeared, as having indeed positive claims. It wasn't, that is, he knew, the "Oh!" of the idiot, however great the superficial resemblance: it was that of the clever, the accomplished man; it was the very speciality of the speaker, and a deal of expensive training and experience had gone to producing it. Densher felt somehow that, as a thing of value accidentally picked up, it would retain an interest of curiosity. The three stood for a little together in an awkwardness to which he was conscious of contributing his share. (20:57)

Lord Mark's "Oh!" is "imponderable" as weighing nothing, as being a mere puff of air, no more than a "sound." It is, however, also a "sound in question," that is, a sound whose import may be questioned, "weighed," pondered. When it is pondered it reveals itself to be by no means wholly imponderable. It has weight and force. It expresses the whole of Lord Mark's class power as a clever, expensively educated aristocrat who brings about results without seeming to be a cause. It is also Lord Mark's defining mark. Lord Mark's "Oh!" has the power to render the by no means inarticulate Densher for the moment mute. That initial "Oh!" is repeated a moment later, when he says to Kate, "Oh and Miss Theale I suppose" (20:57). Lord Mark's "Oh!" is repeated as a putdown of Densher much later in the novel, when Lord Mark has comes to visit Milly in Venice in order to propose to her. He encounters Densher just arriving as he leaves, having failed in his mission. Milly names Densher in introduction to Lord Mark: "'Oh!' said Lord Mark—in a manner that, making it resound through the great cool hall, might have carried it even to Densher's ear as a judgment of his identity heard and noted once before" (20:167). This "Oh!" echoes not only the first one, but also an "Oh" of incredulity he has a few moments before uttered on hearing Milly's insistence that she believes Kate has told her the truth in saying she does not love Densher: "'Oh,' said Lord Mark" (20:166).

The astute reader, once alerted, will notice how frequently "Oh!" recurs at crucial moments. Here is a partial list, all from the second volume: 20:108, 145, 164, 166, 167, 207, 225, 247, 249, 250, 273, 274, 283, 290, 293, 297, 319, 328, 332, 333. "Oh!" echoes in irregular rhythm all through the novel, especially the last part. Each "Oh!," whether uttered by Milly, Aunt Maud, Kate, or Densher, would merit its own separate analysis in its context of subtle interaction of one consciousness with another as registered by the narrator through the sensibility of one or another of the characters as they rotate. I shall forgo the pleasure of doing that. Such analysis, however, would reveal one salient and curious fact. Lord Mark's "Oh!," mark of his class superiority, is more and more appropriated by Densher to mark his sense of his predicament, even though it is the "speciality" of Lord Mark. It is as though Densher's shrewd situation, caught as he is in multiple double binds within his circle of petticoats, unable to fulfill simultaneously his obligations to Kate, to Aunt Maud, to Susan Stringham, and to Milly, had, through the increasing complication of his situation as he is acutely conscious of it, earned a sort of pseudo-aristocratic status within the novel. The sign of that status is that he has gained the right and the necessity of saying "Oh!," the "thing of value accidentally picked up" from hearing Lord Mark say it. Aunt Maud says "Oh!" when Susan Stringham tells her Milly won't cry even when she knows she is dying (20:108); Lord Mark says "Oh!" several times during his abortive proposal to Milly (20:151–66); Milly occasionally says "Oh" herself (20:250), as does Mrs. Stringham (20:274); Sir Luke says "Oh!" in response to Densher's assertion that he no longer visits Milly (20:297); and yet I have noted only one "Oh!" uttered by the self-possessed and unsurprisable Kate. She says "Oh!" in response to Densher's assertion that he went to Milly that last time "like another visit" (20:328).

Most instances of "Oh!"—twelve of them by my count after Lord Mark's initial "Oh!," pondered so subtly by Densher—belong, however, to Densher himself. They register his increasing anguish as his predicament worsens and he begins, in spite of himself, to fall in love with Milly, thereby betraying his sworn love for Kate. Here are the most salient. The reader will note that Densher becomes adept at the repeated "Oh!," or, rather, is forced by his anguish to utter it twice or three times in succession, something quite different in nuance from Lord Mark's single, decisive, controlled, and insolent "Oh!" Densher says " 'Oh!' and again 'Oh!' " when he first visits Milly alone in the Palazzo Leporelli (20:145). He "softly murmurs" "Oh, oh, oh" when he first fully understands Kate's plot to have him marry Milly, inherit her money, and then marry Kate when Milly dies (20:225). He brings "out in a groan a doubting 'Oh, oh!' " when Susan Stringham comes to tell him Milly has turned her face to the wall (20:273), and he says "Oh" twice more in that scene, ending it with an "Oh!" "simply moaned into the gloom" (20:293). Densher "murmurs" "Oh!" again when Kate, later on, back in London, tells him Milly died in "the peace of having loved" and "of having *been* loved. . . . That is. Of having . . . realized her passion. She wanted nothing more. She has had *all* she wanted" (20:332). Now, in consequence, Kate argues, they will be free to take her bequest, marry, and live happily ever after.

Densher's last "Oh!," the most poignant of all, is uttered on the novel's last page. Densher says in response to Kate's assertion that he is in love with Milly's memory: "Oh—her memory!" (20:405). That last "Oh," answered by Kate's "Ah," gathers the accumulated power of all the other instances of "Oh" that have preceded.

Speech Acts in Wings: *A Pack of Lies*

One might call these recurrent motifs the lexicon or word horde of the novel. They define the laws, limits, and stylistic regularities of the imaginary reality generated by the words of *The Wings of the Dove*. Taken together, they make an intertwined system of representational proprieties.

Now my question: Within the field delimited by this system, what is the role of speech acts? How do speech acts function in the intersubjective drama, the battle for domination by "wills" armed with "ideas" and "beliefs," that makes up the diachronic sequence of events in the novel? The efficacy or "felicity" of these speech acts is determined by the particular field of forces that makes up the novel's virtual reality. Milly's death also occurs within this context, but of that more later.

No careful reader can fail to notice that a large number and variety of speech acts punctuate *The Wings of the Dove*. Once the reader begins to look for them, she finds a surprising number, especially if that reader has a sharp eye for somewhat anomalous speech acts such as lies, or acts of naming, or affirmations of belief, or valuations that say implicitly, "I declare this has such and such a value." Among the most salient and overt performatives are Kate's pledging of herself to Densher, her naming of Milly a "dove," the lies Aunt Maud Lowder and Kate Croy tell Milly when they persuade her that Kate does not return Densher's love, Lord Mark's proposal to Milly (he asks her, as I have said, "To believe in me. To believe in me"; 20:157), Kate's promise, much later on in the novel, to "come" to Densher's apartment in recompense for his promise to pretend to make love to the dying Milly, Densher's fulfillment of that promise in the lies, tacit and overt, he tells Milly, Milly's lies to various people about how ill she is, her declaration that she *will* live, in defiance of death, and her bequest of her fortune to Densher, followed by Densher's and Kate's ultimate, decisive speech acts in response to that bequest. All of these are indubitable ways of doing things with words. All are in one way or another turning points in the novel. They make something happen that is inaugural or originary in the sense that they give a determining deflection to the course of the events. After each speech act, all the characters, even those who are ignorant of it, could say what Kate says in that last sentence of the novel: "We shall never be again as we were!" (20:405). Though all these utterances are indubitably speech acts, however, each of them in one way or another fails to conform to the ideal paradigm of a felicitous speech act as Austin defines it. (I put aside for the moment the way each is performed in a novel, not in the real world.) Let me show what is lacking in several of these.

Kate's commitment of herself to Densher takes place during one of their clandestine meetings in Kensington Gardens. This place is the site of many events of the sort in Victorian novels, for example, in Trollope's *Ayala's Angel*. What is striking about Kate's speech act is its spontaneity and suddenness. Her utterance is no doubt prepared for by the situation. She is in love with him, and he is about to depart for an extended absence in the United States. He is going there to continue his work as a journalist. Nevertheless, her pledge is not invited or demanded by Densher, nor is it preceded by any similar attestation on his part. Her performative utterance occurs with unpredictable suddenness: "Suddenly she said to him with extraordinary beauty: 'I engage myself to you for ever.' . . . Yet her face had a new light. 'And I pledge you—I call God to witness!—every spark of my faith; I give you every drop of my life'" (19:95). This is a performative utterance if there ever was one. It is expressed in the first person present tense, the grammatical form characteristic of Austin's ideal felicitous performatives: "I engage myself. . . . I pledge you." What she says does not name or describe anything. It cannot, at least so it seems, be tested for its truth value. It is neither true nor false. It makes something happen. It is a way of doing things with words. Kate (and Densher too) will forever after be different. Whatever Kate does thereafter can be measured by whether or not it is faithful to her pledge, her engagement of herself. The pledge is in that sense irrevocable. Even if the engagement is broken later on, as indeed it is, it will be broken in the context of having been made. Kate even invokes a witness, often a requisite for legal performatives, as when one must have a signature on a legal document notarized, that is, guaranteed as to its authenticity by someone who has authority to do that. Here Kate invokes God as witness, just as the witness in the witness box is asked to raise his or her right hand and "swear to tell the truth, the whole truth, and nothing but the truth, so help me God," and just as, so I am told, patriotic United States citizens swear "on the tomb of George Washington." I never heard this myself, nor ever so swore, but I heard an expert on American oaths swear that it happens.

Kate's pledge is ratified by bodily gestures that are a necessary concomitant of the speech acts that pledge two persons to one another as a preparation for marriage or simply for sexual union. Jacques Derrida insists on this feature of such pledges in a marvelous unpublished seminar on the performative force of the locution, *Je t'aime*, "I love you." Even in a letter or a telephone conversation, says Derrida, *Je t'aime* is accompanied by some hint of a caress or a solicitation.[22] This feature of love pledges is striking evidence that performative utterances are not abstract or purely verbal. They are always embodied. They are, necessarily, materialized in the here and now of a once and once only that needs the bodies of those committing themselves for its efficacy. Ghosts, it would follow, cannot pledge or engage themselves because they cannot embrace or be embraced. A performative is always embodied in a specific time, in a specific place, and in particular material circumstances. That explains why it is necessary in many legal documents to specify not only the date but also the place in which the document is signed. Without understanding this necessity of time and place embodiment, it would be difficult to grasp why it matters where I am when I sign a mortgage or a will. If I sign it, what does it matter where or when I am when I do that? It matters because an unlocated signature is no signature. It is the counterfeit, simulacrum, or ghost of a signature.

After Kate speaks, she and Densher retire to a more private spot in Kensington Gardens. There they endorse their compact with appropriate bodily seals:

> They moved by a common instinct to a spot, within sight, that struck them as fairly sequestered, and there, before their time together was spent, they had extorted from concentration every advance it could make them. They had exchanged vows and tokens, sealed their rich compact, solemnized, so far as breathed words and murmured sounds and lighted eyes and clasped hands could do it, their agreement to belong only, and to belong tremendously, to each other. They were to leave the place accordingly an affianced couple, but before they had left it other things still had passed. (19:95)

What is infelicitous about this speech act? It seems to have everything requisite for felicity. The answer is obvious. It is a secret engagement, one not known or sanctioned by the families and friends of the two parties. A secret engagement, even if it calls God to witness, is no real engagement, since it has no witnesses from the human world. A true engagement must be public. It must be sanctioned and approved by the families and friends of the engaged couple. God is no help as witness in fulfilling this requirement. If no human witness is present, nothing keeps the privately engaged couple from silently and privately disengaging themselves. A secret engagement, even one ratified by God as witness, is something like a private game or a private language. These, according to Ludwig Wittgenstein, are impossibilities, because it takes a community to keep the rules of a language or a game stable over time and in different circumstances. A secret engagement is like one of those infelicitous performatives spoken in soliloquy that Austin mentions. How could I be held to a promise that only one other knows about, that I make in secret, speaking only to another who swears to keep my pledging secret? The oath in the witness box, even though it is sworn in God's name, is performed and must be performed before the judge and jury, before the assembled lawyers and before others in the courtroom. Those human spectators are essential to legal testimony's efficacy. In order to be valid, a wedding ceremony requires a human witness as well as an authorized person in charge of the ceremony, a minister or justice of the peace. That witness, even if there is only one, stands for the whole community that sanctions and validates the wedding, even if God's power and sanction, in a religious wedding ceremony, is also invoked: "Whom God hath joined, let no man put asunder." The secret

engagement of Kate and Densher has no such public and community sanction. Therefore it is not a real engagement. Either of the parties could
break it without penalty, as indeed in the end they do.

The infelicity of a secret engagement is indicated, in addition, by the
way it involves a tacit lie to everyone. Specifically, here, it involves a lie to
Aunt Maud Lowder, who has taken Kate as her informal ward. A lie is a
performative speech act. Though its truth value is nil, if I can get you to
believe my lie you will act on that belief, just as a perjuring lie in the
witness box may get a man or woman executed if the jury believes the lie.
A lie can therefore be an efficacious way of doing things with words. This
is exemplified in Kate and Densher's decision to keep their engagement
secret. The "other things still" that pass before Kate and Densher separate
as "an affianced couple" is their plotting of a strategy to deceive Aunt
Maud without telling her outright lies. Densher does not think Aunt Maud
will ask him outright: "She'll let me off. I shan't have to lie to her" (19:98).
Kate, on the contrary, may have to lie directly. She tells her new fiancé
that while he is in the United States she will post her letters to him secretly, a tacit lie, while he will send his to her directly to Aunt Maud's
house. The only "straight" thing would be to tell Aunt Maud as Kate's
guardian immediately that they are now engaged. This they do not do.
This is the first of many decisive lies in this novel, lies that form turning
points in the action.

Kate's engagement to Densher is therefore doubly infelicitous. It does
not obey the laws of a valid engagement, and it necessitates a new speech
act of a malign, deceptive kind, the kind that Kant says no one in any
circumstances, even the most extreme, can ever be justified in enunciating.[23]

All the other speech acts in my list are in one way or another disabled
in somewhat similar ways. Kate, it will be noticed, originates many of these
performatives. This might be seen as corresponding to what Densher finds
most attractive and most mysterious about her, that is, her remarkable
vitality, her life force: "All he had originally felt in her came back to him,
was indeed actually as present as ever—how he had admired and envied
what he called to himself her pure talent for life" (20:176). In another
place Kate has to Densher "the look of a consciousness charged with life
to the brim and wishing not to overflow" (20:315). That so many of the
speech acts are Kate's designates her as the prime manipulator of events
in the novel. She is the one who most often makes things happen as they
do happen, though she is up against a formidable opponent in Aunt Maud,
and though in the end Milly, who speaks with the power of death, wins

out over all the others, Kate included. What Kate says of Aunt Maud might, mutatis mutandis, be said of all the other characters: "The very essence of her, as you surely by this time have made out for yourself, is that when she adopts a view she—well, to her own sense, really brings the thing about, fairly terrorizes with her view any other, any opposite view, and those, not less, who represent that. I've often thought success comes to her . . . by the spirit in her that dares and defies her idea not to prove the right one" (20:188).

Each character in the novel has his or her own "idea." Each works through the use of language and other signs to bring that idea into material existence. The novel might be charted as a life-and-death social game with high stakes in which the decisive moves are made by speech acts. Each of these puts all the players on the board in a different situation, whether they know it or not.

Kate's naming of Milly a dove, to cite another performative in *The Wings of the Dove*, is the eponymous act of the novel. It gives the novel its name. The title names not just Milly's malign, death-dealing beneficence but also the novel itself as repeating that. The novel, like Milly, in spite of its wonderful verbal vitality as a virtual reality's representation, brings death into the reader's world. A christening or naming of the unnamed is a classic performative, like the "I do" of the marriage ceremony, or "I promise," or "I pledge": "I christen thee so and so." Calling Milly a dove is, however, not a real christening. It does not have the normal institutional accompaniments of a christening. It is more like Austin's bad example of the "low fellow" who mischristens the British warship the *Generalissimo Stalin* than like a normal, felicitous christening. Misnamings have their irreversible power, however. To call Milly a dove is a metaphorical naming that identifies, from Kate's perspective, Milly's innocence and purity. It names also her celestial beneficence, the power of her money, which is like a spiritual power. She is like the dove of the Noah's Ark story or like the dove of the Annunciation. Kate's naming Milly a dove is also condescending and a warning to her. It puts Milly in her place: "You poor thing. You are as innocent, helpless, and vulnerable as a dove in this London social world of foxes and serpents. Something bad is bound to happen to you." Milly, however, it turns out, is a dove of a different kind from Kate's idea of her. Like other victimized women in James's novels, like Isabel Archer in *Portrait of a Lady* or Maggie in *The Golden Bowl*, Milly uses her beneficence to bring devastation to the world she enters, here by ultimately separating Kate and Densher forever. Kate's naming, like many other performative acts, comes true, if one can twist that term to apply to a noncognitive utterance. Milly does behave like a dove, by leaving a huge fortune to the perjuring Densher. This fulfillment of the promise implicit in the name occurs, however, in a way radically different from the one Kate intends.

A lie is an exceedingly precarious form of performative speech act, since its efficacy depends on its not being found out, that is, on the faith of the one to whom the lie is uttered. Believe, *belief*, and their compounds are key words in *The Wings of the Dove*, as I have already demonstrated. The words name the credence given to something said or implied by another. When Lord Mark proposes to Milly (another classic speech act), he does not say, "Marry me!" but, as I have noted, "Believe in me," that is, at least in part, believe that I love you. Belief is a response to the performative dimension of something said, as opposed to acquiescence to its cognitive dimension, which is a matter of knowledge or proof. Whether or not Lord Mark loves Milly can never be proved, any more than any other *Je t'aime* can be verified. Every "I love you" is qualified by an implicit appeal: "Please believe me."

Aunt Maud, Susan Stringham, and Kate all want Milly to believe something intrinsically unverifiable one way or the other, namely that Kate does not return Densher's love. Their reasons for wanting this, however, are quite different from one to another. Aunt Maud wants Kate to marry some well-placed Englishman, for example, Lord Mark, not an impecunious journalist. If she can get Milly to believe Densher is free because his love for Kate is hopeless, then Milly may "set her cap" for Densher and may take Densher away from his position as a blocking agent in Aunt Maud's plans. Susan wants Milly to believe Densher is free because then Milly might be able to fulfill Sir Luke Strett's prescription for her cure, that she should do what she wants, meaning by that marry and, to put it crudely, have sex. Only this will cure her, at least so Aunt Maud and Susan have been brought to believe, as is indicated in a wonderfully comic interchange between them. This is one of the few places in James where copulation and its benefits are discussed even so obliquely, as an "it." "The point is will it *cure?*" asks Susan. To which Aunt Maud asks in her turn, "Precisely. Is it absolutely a remedy—*the* specific?" "Well, I should think we might know!" Mrs. Stringham "delicately" responds (20:112). They might know because both have been married, though both are now widows.

Kate, in her turn, wants Milly to believe she (Kate) does not love Densher so that Milly will feel free to respond to Densher's lying advances, leave him her money, then die, so Kate and Densher can marry and be rich, no longer in need of Aunt Maud's patronage. Kate and Aunt Maud both have exceedingly shabby, sinister, and manipulative plots or "ideas," to use, as the reader will remember, another key word in the novel. Susan's idea is born of her affection for Milly, but her idea is not the same as Kate's or Aunt Maud's. The three women are working to some degree at cross-purposes. They are allies up to a point, but deadly enemies beyond that. This exemplifies the economic law of London society that says there are only users and used, those who "work" others and those who are worked. Each of the three women attempts to use the others and to use Milly, as well as to use and manipulate Densher, who meditates at one point on the way all these women want him to do the same thing, make love to Milly, but for different reasons.

One way to see the possible infelicity of the lies about Kate's true feelings that both Kate and Aunt Maud tell is to ask the unanswerable question of whether Milly ever believes the lie. Though she appears to do so, for example, in her behavior toward Densher on the day in London when Densher visits her and she takes him for a ride in her grand carriage, it is impossible to tell for sure on the basis of the evidence the reader is given. This is so, even though knowing the truth about this one way or the other is crucially important in reading the novel. It is a matter of the reader's belief, not of her certain knowledge. The reader is not given consistent access to Milly's thoughts on this crucial point. The narrative voice at one point tells the reader in so many words: " 'Proper' indeed it was, her lie— the very properest possible and the most deeply, richly diplomatic. So Milly was successfully deceived" (20:69). This, however, is the narrative voice reporting in indirect discourse what Densher believed and has worked out for himself on the basis of the evidence. The reader is never given entry to what is in Milly's mind about this. She acts as though she has believed Aunt Maud's "proper lie" (20:68) to her, that is, Maud's assurance through Susan Stringham as well as to Milly herself that "Kate didn't care for him" (20:69). That, however, may be deep deception. It may be part of her determination to live, to do what she wants, as Sir Luke has ordered her to do. Milly is shown to be extraordinarily sensitive to, even clairvoyant about, the relations between Kate and Densher. She knows, for example, just from looking at Kate that Densher has returned from America and that Kate has seen him. She has the extraordinary experience, carefully noted by the narrator, of seeing Kate as *other* because she suddenly sees her as being seen by Densher. She sees Kate as she feels certain she must look to Densher. This is not a matter of seeing oneself being seen, but of seeing another as another sees that other, here with slightly disturbing homoerotic connotations. Such connotations are also present in the narrator's report that to Milly Kate seems sometimes to have "something rather of a breezy boy in the carriage of her arms and the occasional freedom of her slang" (19:172).

Kate is, in a number of ways, "masculine" in her aggressive domination of others. It would be possible for a critic interested in biographical interpretations to read the triangular relation Densher finds himself in as a closet allegory of Henry James's conflict between homosexual desire (here figured in disguise as Densher's love for Kate) and the heterosexual desire he was not quite successfully able to feel for his cousin Minny Temple (here figured in Densher's relation to Milly).

It is just barely possible, in any case, though ultimately implausible when all the evidence is considered, to read Milly's behavior as a deep strategy to pretend to believe Aunt Maud's lies and Kate's in order to get her way in the end and to dominate the others, which indeed she does do. Milly's feelings and knowledge about this remain impenetrably secret, even though they are secrets the narrator could presumably tell if he (it) wanted to do so. The reader is put in the position of a jury member sifting the evidence in a difficult case and obliged ultimately to come up with a verdict "beyond a reasonable doubt," even though that verdict is an act of belief, not an act of certain cognition. The reader has only the narrator's word for it, along with some further evidence in Milly's behavior and speech to others, to support the assumption that she was successfully fooled. We know Milly is adept at prevarication, however, as in her constant assurance to others that she is not ill.

The lies to her are therefore dubious as to their performative efficacy. This is true even though Aunt Maud, in her discussion of strategy with Susan, is shown to be confident that if something is denied often enough and with enough firmness—here, if they deny that Kate "thinks she cares" for Densher—it will come to be the case, or will be believed, which amounts to the same thing (20:115). *The Wings of the Dove* dramatizes not the coercive power of thinking, as Sharon Cameron in her admirable book, one of the best ever written on James, avers,[24] but the power of doing things with words. Even Aunt Maud's "ideas," which Kate so much admires and fears, come about not just because Aunt Maud thinks them but because she sets about using words performatively to manipulate people so as to make her ideas come true. She does this, for example, by telling through Mrs. Stringham her "proper lie" to Milly (that Kate does not love Densher). She does this, as she disingenuously says, in order to give Densher a chance at Milly's money. Aunt Maud also lies directly to Milly when she tells her of Kate's feelings about Densher: "She doesn't care for him" (19:265). Her true motive is to get Kate free from Densher, though she is also shown as being attracted to Densher for herself. *The Wings of the Dove* dramatizes not the omnipotence of thoughts but the (non)omnipotence of words.

In spite of the possibility that Milly knows all along she is being lied to, I believe the reader is meant to believe that he or she believes Aunt Maud's lies and Kate's. The clearest evidence for this is the interchange with Lord Mark in Venice when he proposes. When Lord Mark insinuates that Kate loves Densher, Milly replies categorically, "You're wholly mistaken." She goes on to say that she is "very intimate" with Kate, and though she cannot quite claim that Kate has "taken her oath," she can say, "She has given me her word for it," and, a little later, in response to Lord Mark's continued "catechising": "She left me in no doubt whatever of her being free" (20:164–65). It is hard to believe that Milly is lying at this point, though I suppose it is possible. It is a matter of the reader's belief, on the basis of the evidence.

In the end, the lies all three women have told Milly fail when Lord Mark comes to Venice to tell Milly the cruel truth, that Kate and Densher are secretly engaged. Milly apparently believes what he says and in response "turns her face to the wall." She ceases to will to go on living in the face of death, in defiance of death, as she has told Densher earlier she can do. "I mean," she tells Densher, "that I want so to live—!" She goes on to make the extraordinary assertion, in response to Densher's question "If you want to do it?," meaning "Want to live?" that she can go on living in the face of death if she wants to: "If I want to live. I *can*" (20:246). If she can will successfully to go on living, her death, when she turns her face to the wall, must also be an act of willing. She wills to die, just as she has willed to go on living.

It can be seen from what I have said about several of the performatives in *The Wings of the Dove* that each of them is in one way or another anomalous. Each requires extended analysis to adjudicate its "felicity" or lack of it. A similar analysis of the other speech acts I have mentioned could be made.

Kate's promise, "on her honor," to come to Densher's apartment in return for his promise to pretend to make love to Milly (She says: "I'll come"; 20:231), like their pledge to one another in their secret engagement, is another clandestine promise that does not have community ratification. No one else will know whether such promises are fulfilled or not.

Milly's (apparent) bequest to Densher of most of her huge fortune is, to turn to my final example, a classic performative act. A testamentary will is mentioned by Austin among his initial examples of speech acts.[25] A will is felicitous if it is ratified by the proper legal formalities. Milly does have the money she bequeaths. Her bequest is no doubt properly endorsed by signatures and legal forms. Its infelicity, however, lies in what Densher does with the bequest. He will marry Kate without the money, but with the money he will not. He pledges to give Kate the entire bequest if she will not marry him after he has refused it: "You lose me?" he asks. "Well, you lose nothing else. I make over to you every penny" (20:404). The mystery, the unfathomable secret, unfathomable in part because Kate destroys Milly's last letter to Densher, is whether or not Milly foresaw this outcome. Is her bequest the last act of her benevolent love for Densher, making it possible for him to marry the woman he loves and be enormously rich to boot? Or does she foresee that making this bequest is a certain way to have her revenge on those who have tricked her and to separate Kate and Densher for good? It is impossible to know. It remains as secret as death and the grave.

Lying against Death: Out of the Loop

death does not consummate existence, one would, rather, have to say
that it prevents it from turning into essence.

—JEAN-LUC NANCY, *The Sense of the World*

The Wings of the Dove is in "essence" a novel about death. James in the preface says so, and there is no reason to doubt his word. Or, to put this another way, we must believe or not believe what he says, as the characters within the novel believe one another or do not. Or, rather, it might be even better to say *The Wings of the Dove* is a novel about the relation of speech acts to death. Or, yet again, refining further, it might be best to say that it is a novel about that peculiar kind of speech act called a lie in its relation to death. Let me try to explain how this is so.

Certainly James himself, if the preface is to be believed, thought of *The Wings of the Dove* as having death as its primary theme, to be specific, the death of a young woman who has everything for which to live. As usual, James speaks so eloquently and so forcefully in the preface that it is hard after reading it to see beyond or beneath James's own self-criticism. It is hard to think out what he may have, for more or less secret reasons of his own, omitted saying that the novel itself nevertheless says, however indirectly, or that might by another reader be put differently from the way he puts it in the preface. "The idea," says James, writing, or, rather, dictating, six years after the novel was written, "reduced to its essence, is that of a young person conscious of a great capacity for life, but early stricken and doomed, condemned to die under short respite, while also enamored of the world; aware moreover of the condemnation and passionately desiring to 'put in' before extinction as many of the finer vibrations as possible, and so achieve, however briefly, the sense of having lived" (19:v).

James says four things about this "idea" in the preface. First, he tells the reader that he had the theme of *Wings* in his mind for many years before actually writing the novel. The notebook entries for *The Wings of the Dove* precede by many years the writing of the novel.[26] It seems as though he may have felt some deep resistance toward writing this particular story: "Long had I turned it over, standing off from it, yet coming back to it; convinced of what might be done with it, yet seeing the theme as formidable" (19:v). "It" in this sentence refers to what he has just called the "idea" of the novel. The reader will remember that *idea* is a key word in the novel itself. James goes on a bit later in the preface to speak of the idea or theme as somehow hiding a secret, an impenetrable mystery: "The expression of her state and that of one's intimate relation to it might therefore well need to be discreet and ingenious; a reflection that fortunately grew and grew, however, in proportion as I focused my image— roundabout which, as it persisted, I repeat, the interesting possibilities and the attaching wonderments, not to say the insoluble mysteries, thickened apace" (19:vi). What does he mean by "one's intimate relation" to the heroine's "state"? Is not the heroine an imaginary character? How can one have an intimate relation to a fictitious character? Does "intimate" here mean "secret," "hidden," perhaps shameful or at any rate inexpressible? "Insoluble mysteries"? What could James mean by that? An insoluble mystery is a true secret, if there is such a thing, a secret that can never be found out. What is there about the idea of a young woman doomed to die and fighting death every inch of the way that incorporates an insoluble mystery? I shall return to these questions.

Second, James in the preface recognizes that it is impossible to write a narrative about death, or even about dying, in itself. On the one hand death and dying are too dark as subjects. A work on such a gloomy topic is not likely to be a commercial success. Indeed James was wholly unsuccessful in his attempts to sell *The Wings of the Dove* for serial publication. On the other hand there is not enough to say about death and dying. They resist language. That is what Paul de Man means, in part at least, when he says, in one of his more disturbing or even scandalous pronouncements, "Death is a displaced name for a linguistic predicament."[27] I shall return to this allergy between language and death.

Because of this allergy, James's novel will need to be about his heroine's resistance to death: "the poet essentially *can't* be concerned with the act of dying. Let him deal with the sickest of the sick, it is still by the act of living that they appeal to him, and appeal the more as the conditions plot against them and prescribe the battle" (19:vi). In the case of Milly Theale, the act of living, as James makes clear, takes the form of a passionate resistance to death: "she had been given me from far back as contesting every inch of the road, as catching at every object the grasp of which might make for delay, as clutching these things to the last moment of her strength" (19:vii).

Third, James indicates that even the act of living in defiance of death can only be represented directly up to a certain point. Beyond that point it must be presented indirectly, by way of one or more reflectors of that act of living/dying. After the climactic scene at the end of Book Seventh, when Milly's solitary wandering through the rooms of her great palazzo in Venice is interrupted by Lord Mark, who has come to propose to her, Milly's consciousness is never again directly presented. The presiding consciousness becomes Densher's for the rest of the novel. In a sense Milly is already dead, for the reader at least, since her consciousness has vanished once and for all from intimate representation, however intimate James's own relation to Milly's state may have been. "Milly's situation," says James, "ceases at a given moment to be 'renderable' in terms closer than those supplied by Kate's intelligence, or, in a richer degree, by Densher's, or, for one fond hour, by poor Mrs. Stringham's" (19:xvii). James in the last reference apparently means the scene in which Susan Stringham comes to Densher's Venice apartment to tell him that Milly has "turned her face to the wall" (20:270). The nonpresentation of Milly's thoughts and feelings toward the end of her life is a striking example of what James calls "the author's instinct everywhere for the *indirect* presentation of his main image" (19:xxii, James's emphasis). Some subjects—the act of dying, for example (but it is more than a nominal example)—cannot be presented directly.

Fourth, James tells the reader that this death will wreak havoc among the living, for such a person as Milly Theale, an extremely rich young American woman without any living family, will almost inevitably fall among thieves, so to speak. She will in one way or another be cheated, swindled: "What one had discerned, at all events, from an early stage, was that a young person so devoted and exposed, a creature with her security hanging so by a hair, couldn't but fall somehow into some abysmal trap— this being, dramatically speaking, what such a situation most naturally implied and imposed" (19:ix). By "devoted and exposed," James means devoted to death, as the idiom has it, as a sacrificial animal is devoted, in the sense of "sworn by a sacred oath," to be killed, or as a "votary" is a certain kind of religious devotee. Milly is "exposed," not just in the sense of being vulnerable to fraud, but also in the sense that a scapegoat is exposed, left in isolation, outside social confines of reciprocal obligations, to die. This is one significance of the appellation "dove" Kate invents for Milly. Doves were one kind of sacrificial creature, among the Romans, for example.

Even though Milly is certain to fall into some abysmal trap, as indeed she does, nevertheless she is an extreme danger to all those who have anything to do with her, especially those who try to swindle and exploit her. James uses three striking, and not wholly compatible, figures to name the disaster Milly's death brings others, even though they are bent on "working" her for all she is worth. Milly is like the Lorelei, the Rhine-maiden who lures men to their death. The persons around Milly, those who promote her illusion that she may yet continue to live, are "drawn in as by some pool of a Lorelei—. . . terrified and tempted and charmed; bribed away, it may even be, from more prescribed and natural orbits, inheriting from their connection with her strange difficulties and still stranger opportunities, confronted with rare questions and called upon for new discriminations" (19:viii). It is Densher more than Kate, Aunt Maud, or Susan Stringham who is most drawn out of his orbit, made exorbitant, by his attraction to Milly. Though his prescribed orbit is to remain faithful to the oaths he and Kate have sworn to one another ("prescribed" in the sense of being written down beforehand as commands to follow), he is forced into ethical discriminations, decisions, and responsibilities that he knew nothing of before. Nevertheless, the other characters too have their lives decisively deflected, by no means necessarily for the better, even by selfish measurements, much less ideal ethical ones, through their association with Milly, however much of a dove, in the sense of gentle and innocent, she may seem to be.

A little later in the preface, the figure of the Lorelei is replaced by two overlapping metaphors, one of which (the sinking of a great ship) echoes a trope already used for Milly in the body of the novel. The other picks up the economic imagery in the novel, about which I shall say more later.

"I have named the Rhine-maiden," says James, "but our young friend's existence would create rather, all round her, very much that whirlpool movement of the waters produced by the sinking of a big vessel or the failure of a great business; when we figure to ourselves the strong narrowing eddies, the immense force of suction, the general engulfment that, for any neighboring object, makes immersion inevitable" (19:x). A big ship goes down and everything else in its neighborhood goes down too. A big business fails and all the investors as well as many adjacent businesses may fail too. Having anything to do with Milly is extremely dangerous.

James goes on to say that though he is primarily interested in Milly's own sense of what happens to her through others, nevertheless, her extravagant generosity and mild goodness are, paradoxically, what brings disaster to those around her. James needs to adjudicate carefully here the question of who causes the catastrophe. He even needs to do so to some degree against the implication of his figures, which is that Milly as Lorelei, sinking vessel, or failing business causes the disaster of the others. No, James in effect says, the surrounding figures bring their own doom upon themselves. They do this just by trying to capitalize on Milly's goodness and her fortune, as investors are to blame if they think a certain investment is a "sure thing" and try to make money on it. Nevertheless, Milly's best qualities were themselves "provoking." In that ironic sense they caused the catastrophes to the others. It is almost as if James were saying, "Watch out. Bad things will happen to you if you come too close to someone who is extravagantly generous and good." Or, to put this from Milly's own perspective: "Don't be too generous and good. If you are, you will, by a perverse moral law, cause harm to those around you." Nevertheless, James wants also to exonerate Milly. "I need scarce say, however," he asserts in the sentence after the one just quoted from the preface, "that in spite of these communities of doom [all those taken down by the sinking of the great ship *The Milly*] I saw the main dramatic complication much more prepared *for* my vessel of sensibility than by her—the work of other hands (though with her own imbrued too, after all, in the measure of their never not being, in some direction, generous and extravagant, and thereby provoking)" (19:x).

Why is this? Why is Milly's particular form of generosity destructively provoking? The answer lies in the tangle of relations in the novel between death and lies. Society in *The Wings of the Dove* is a reciprocal system of working and being worked, as I have shown. It is, that is, modeled on venture capitalism. London society is economic through and through. Like the capitalist monetary system of which it is a part, this society works

only so long as the participants go on believing in the distribution of relative values that makes it up. As Milly observes of these London people,
"they appeared all—every one they saw—to think tremendously of
money" (19:195), to which Susie replies, sensibly enough, that Milly has
so much money that she does not need to think about it: "it came, as a
subject of indifference, money did, easier to some people than to others"
(19:196). Money has value just because it is valued. This is the model for
other valuations in the novel. Lord Mark is not really any more valuable
just because he is a nobleman, but if everyone believes in his value, he has
it. Milly's great success in London is a matter of fashion. Nothing more
interesting than Milly happens to be around at the time, and so Milly
becomes an instant success. Milly has an "image" of herself as "being, as
Lord Mark had declared, a success. This depended more or less of course
on his idea of the thing" (19:160). Precisely. Success is a matter of people's, the right people's, "ideas," and of their faith in those ideas. Lord
Mark in this interchange goes on to say of Aunt Maud, who has launched
Milly by taking her up as a protégé, "She'll get back . . . her money. . . .
Nobody here, you know, does anything for nothing" (19:160). The whole
system of relative valuations is based on nothing of substantial worth as
foundation, at least not on any insight into that, nor on an objectively valid
method of measuring value. Another more hyperbolic way to put this is to
say that this social system is based on a set of lies that everyone knows are
lies and yet agrees to pretend to believe. The whole airy fabric of giving
and taking, of exchange, substitution, and appropriation, has no substance
and is suspended over nothing.

Yet another way to express this is to say that the social system is sustained by a complex set of constantly renewed speech acts that declare that
such and such a person, rank, or thing has such and such a value. The
paradigmatic type of such speech acts in the novel is the lie, exemplified
in all those dozens of lies the characters tell one another. A lie, as I have
said, is a pure example of a way to do things with words, since its truth
value is nil, while its effectiveness as a performative utterance depends only
on its being believed in or on someone's pretending to believe it. All
speech acts are in a sense lies, since they bring about the condition they
name, a condition that, as it is being named, does not yet exist as something to which truthful reference can be made. When the minister or justice of the peace says, "I pronounce you man and wife," the couple is not
man and wife until the last syllable of that sentence echoes in the air. The
condition comes into being after the fact, after it has been invoked by the
speech act. It only works if everyone believes in it, just as two people are

legally married only if everyone has confidence in the authority of the one who says, "I pronounce you man and wife."

Speech acts—for example, lies—have a complex relation to death. Lies, as Marlow reflects in Conrad's *Heart of Darkness*, have a flavor of mortality about them.²⁸ They are connected in some obscure and not easily identifiable way with death, with the fact that all human beings will sooner or later die. One way to identify this relation is to see that only creatures that can die can utter speech acts. This is in part because it is a distinctive feature of speech acts that their efficacy is unpredictable. A god cannot utter a performative. A god knows for certain what will happen. Jehovah's "Let there be light" is not a performative, whereas a human being's "I bet the sun will rise tomorrow" is a genuine performative. The person who says the sun will rise has no way of knowing for sure whether that will happen or not, just as the one who makes a promise or engages himself or herself to be married, secretly or publicly, has no way of knowing whether or not he or she will remain faithful to the pledge, for one thing, because he or she may die before fulfilling the promise. All promises have an implicit added clause: "I promise to do so and so if I do not die first."

This more or less obscure and secret connection of speech acts with death surfaces more overtly in three of the most common performatives: wills, bequests, and mortgages. When I sign a mortgage note, as its name implies, I am offering my death as a gage that guarantees I shall pay so much a month until the loan is paid off, even if I die before that happens. Or you could say that a mortgage is a bet, as the syllable *gage* suggests: "I bet I will die before this is paid off." Or perhaps it is the reverse: "If I do not die I promise to pay this off." In any event, the one who signs a mortgage puts his or her death on the line, signs in the name of his or her mortality. A ghost could not sign a mortgage note or be held responsible if it did sign.

A bequest, such as Milly's bequest of her money to Densher, is a way of controlling what happens after the death of the person signing the bequest: "On my death, my estate, or such and such a part of it, goes to so and so as my beneficiary." A will is a way of using words to make my will effective after my death, to make what I will or want to happen happen, even when I am no longer around to make sure it happens. As Marcel Proust well knew, a person is most likely to invoke death as a guarantee when he or she is lying, to say, for example, as Marcel reports Albertine as doing, "I can swear to you by anything you like, the honor of my aunt, the grave of my poor mother [*la tombe de ma pauvre mère*]," when she is most blatantly lying. Or at least so Marcel suspects, though he can never find out for sure.[29] There are no literal mortgages in *The Wings of the Dove*, but in a sense all the speech acts in the novel—pledges, promises, bequests, lies—are mortgages, mort-gages, bets against death or in death's name: "I wish I may die if I am not telling the truth, if I do not fulfill my promise, if I am not faithful to my pledge."

The relation between death and the system of continuously renewed speech acts that keeps society going might be expressed as a paradox. On the one hand, death has to be constantly invoked as the guarantee of a performative's seriousness and felicity, as in the word *mortgage*, or as in "I swear on my mother's grave." On the other hand, death has to be obscured, forgotten, covered over in order for the system to go on working. The social system must go on as if it and all those participating in its round of exchanges and substitutions were immortal. The system depends on remembering and forgetting death at the same time. This forgetting of death, while at the same time remembering it, is made explicit in *The Wings of the Dove* in a reflection Densher makes toward the end of the novel about the way everyone pretends not to know that Milly is dying, while at the same time knowing it perfectly well:

> He hadn't only never been near the facts of her condition—which counted so as a blessing for him; he hadn't only, with all the world, hovered outside an impenetrable ring fence, within which there reigned a kind of expensive vagueness made up of smiles and silences and beautiful fictions and priceless arrangements, all strained to breaking; but he had also, with every one else, as he now felt, actively fostered suppressions which were in the direct interest of every one's good manner, every one's pity, every one's really quite generous idea. It was a conspiracy of silence, as the *cliché* went, to which no one had made an exception, the great smudge of mortality across the picture, the shadow of pain and horror, finding in no quarter a surface of spirit or of speech that consented to reflect it. "The mere aesthetic instinct of mankind—!" our young man had more than once, in the connection, said to himself; letting the rest of the proposition drop, but touching again thus sufficiently on the outrage even to taste involved in one's having to *see*. So then it had been—a general conscious fool's paradise, from which the specified had been chased like a dangerous animal. (20:298–99)

Everyone knows, but everyone pretends, by a "beautiful fiction," not to know, in a conspiracy of silence. That conspiracy assumes that if you do not mention something it does not exist or ceases to exist. You have chased it away, like a dangerous animal. Silence here is a paradoxical speech act, akin to Aunt Maud's assumption that she can make Kate stop thinking she loves Densher by saying nothing about it or by asserting the opposite. Silence can be a species of effective lie, as in Densher's failure to tell Milly outright that Kate loves him and that they are engaged. Beyond that, however, James implies that mortality cannot be a fact of consciousness or a fact of speech within the circuit of polite society. That society is like a mirror that reflects many things but does not consent, either because of some tacit decision or because of an innate disability, to reflect it. "The great smudge of mortality across the picture," says James, in a majestic phrase, "the shadow of pain and horror," namely, just what Milly is suffering and confronting, "find[s] in no quarter a surface of spirit or of speech that consent[s] to reflect it." James himself, or, rather, his narrator, participates in this conspiracy of silence. He (it), as I have said, presents Milly's final pain and horror only indirectly.

Densher is shown reflecting on this silence by calling it "the mere aesthetic instinct of mankind." Mankind generally shares with the artist—for example, James in this novel—an unwillingness to consent to represent the great smudge of mortality across the picture. That smudge destroys the aesthetic. The aesthetic, as a system of representation, as the general system of the fine arts in the West since romanticism—for example, in Hegel's so-called *Ästhetik*—is allergic to death. The aesthetic, as the making of beautiful artworks, depends on ignoring death.

The phrase "the great smudge of mortality across the picture" has, however, another function, namely, its reference back to the great scene early in the novel when Milly confronts at Matcham,[30] Lord Mark's splendid country house, the Bronzino portrait that everyone says closely resembles Milly. The confrontation is Milly's first clear recognition that she is dying. This is figured as her leaving a safe harbor for the dangerous open sea. This episode is Milly's own sinister mirror stage. It also recalls Kate's confrontation of her mirror image in the first sentence of the novel. Milly has her self-recognition of her mortality through seeing herself in the Bronzino. She weeps when she sees this. I cite the passage again:

> Perhaps it was her tears that made it just then so strange and fair—as wonderful as he had said: the face of a young woman, all splendidly drawn, down to the hands, and splendidly dressed; a face almost livid in hue, yet handsome in sadness and crowned with a mass of hair, rolled back and high, that must, before fading with time, have had a family resemblance to her own [Milly has striking red hair]. The lady in question, at all events, with her slightly Michael-angelesque squareness, her eyes of other days, her full lips, her long neck, her recorded jewels, her brocaded and wasted reds, was

a very great personage—only unaccompanied by a joy. And she was dead, dead, dead. (19:220–21)

As in Poe's "The Oval Portrait" or Wilde's *The Picture of Dorian Gray*, with its associated work "The Portrait of Mr. W. H.," so in *The Wings of the Dove* Milly is, in a manner of speaking, killed by a portrait. The picture has a great smudge of mortality across it. The lady is "dead, dead, dead." The portrait, in spite of its aesthetic beauty, brings death into Milly's life. It does this by breaking the conspiracy of silence and making her conscious of death. In an analogous way, James may have felt he was killing his cousin Minny Temple, the supposed "original" of Milly,[31] by finally doing a portrait of her and of his intimate relation to her condition, however indirect and discrete a portrait it was. He had kept her alive until then by remaining in love with her memory, as he says in a letter of 1870 to his brother William, written after her death. Part of the passage is, oddly, addressed to the dead Minny: "The more I think of her the more perfectly satisfied I am to have her translated from this changing realm of fact to the steady realm of thought. . . . She lives as a steady unfaltering luminary in the mind rather than as a flickering wasting earth-stifled lamp. . . . In exchange, for you, dearest Minny, we'll all keep your future. Don't fancy that your task is done. Twenty years hence we shall be living with your love and longing with your eagerness and suffering with your patience."[32]

It seems as if either the portrait or the person may be alive, not both. All portraits, of whatever ladies or gentlemen, are death dealing. This may explain why some people resist having their portraits painted or photographs made of them. Bronzino's great lady "was dead, dead, dead." This mortality tells Milly she is mortal too. If Kate sees her vitality, her "talent for life," when she looks at herself in the mirror above her father's mantlepiece, she also unwittingly confronts her death, her mortality, just as does Milly in the later scene that echoes the first. Kate's talent for life is not the opposite of Milly's devotion to death, but its mirror image. All mirrorings, such as the mirrorings in James's portraits of ladies, are death dealing as well as life preserving.

Just how does Milly destroy the society of working and being worked, sustained by an endless round of lies, into which she enters? All the characters, in one way or another, want to appropriate her for their own purposes. Milly, however, cannot be used in this way. She cannot be incorporated into the economy that says you must "work" others or be yourself "worked." Milly brings the great smudge of mortality into the self-sustaining aesthetic system of London society. Her innocence and her betrothal to death are dovelike weapons that allow her to defeat all the others and bring their projects to shipwreck, including Densher's desire to marry Kate. This is true even though Milly passionately loves Densher, at least so the reader is led to believe. She (apparently) acts on that love to sacrifice her right to retaliation and to leave Densher a huge fortune so he can marry Kate. This, however, as I shall show, is just what separates Kate and Densher forever. In this Milly is like James's other heroines, for example, Isabel Archer or Maggie Verver. Their cruelty lies in their goodness and self-sacrificing generosity. Milly triumphs over all around her by way of her dovelike beneficence and her mortal illness. These are the match for Kate's vitality. Neither Milly's goodness nor her proximity to death can be worked into their calculations. The whole social system, its reciprocal working and being worked, its exchanges and substitutions, depends on lies against death that are believed. These lies depend for their efficacy on forgetting death or on pretending to do so. Milly brings death into this system and thereby ruins it. She ruins the possibility Kate worked for, to have Densher and the money too. Milly's act also makes Kate, after all, after the end of the novel, fulfill Aunt Maud's plans for her and marry Lord Mark. At least James says so in the notes. Whether this really happens is another complete secret we can never know, since the novel itself says nothing explicit about this.

Milly can give but never take or bargain in the sense of entering into the calculated give and take that characterizes London society and that is often named by the narrator in economic metaphors. Milly belongs to a separate realm, where she is fighting a moment-to-moment losing battle against death. As she says, it would kill her if she were to turn away even for a minute from that battle and enter the ordinary social world. This is said in an extraordinary speech she makes to Lord Mark when refusing his proposal:

> "No, I mustn't listen to you—that's just what I mustn't do. The reason is, please, that it simply kills me. I must be as attached to you as you will, since you give that lovely account of yourselves. I give you in return the fullest possible belief of what it would be—" And here she pulled up a little. "I give and give and give—there you are; stick to me as close as you like and see if I don't. Only I can't listen or receive or accept—I can't *agree*. I can't make a bargain. You must believe that from me. It's all I've wanted to say to you, and why should it spoil anything?" (20:160–61)

To make a bargain would be to accept Lord Mark's proposal, to make a promise in response to his proffer of himself, to utter a speech act of acceptance in answer to his speech act of proposal. Milly remains alive, paradoxically, only so long as she stays sequestered from life, just as she survives in Venice by remaining immured like a Maeterlinckian princess in the Palazzo Leporelli.[33] As devoted to death, Milly can enter life only by pretending not to be dying, as she consistently does until the scene when she refuses Lord Mark's proposal and tells him the truth, that she is "very badly ill" (20:155), even though, as Milly feels, "nothing—nothing to make a deadly difference for him—ever *could* happen" (20:159). Milly is the personage who does, in spite of the mere aesthetic instinct of mankind, make a deadly difference for every one of the major characters. She does this by her extravagant generosity, giving and giving and giving, but taking nothing in return. Such a gift, however, is a gift of death, a monstrous donation that puts the one who receives it infinitely and unrepayably in debt.

Gift giving and receiving in the ordinary sense belongs to the everyday economic social round. If I give something to you, that puts you under an obligation to return the gift, and so on, in an endless benign circle of gift giving and receiving in which the balance always comes right or is always on the brink of coming right. Milly's giving is outside that circuit of exchange and recompense. She represents the secret ground of the circuit that destroys the whole system when it is brought into the open. To listen to Lord Mark, to entertain his offer, would, paradoxically, simply kill Milly. It would kill her because she goes on living only by way of her relation to death and her insulation from life on her Maeterlinckian island. She is like one of those tomb artifacts or mummies that remains intact for thousands of years as long as it is sealed, but crumbles to dust the moment it is exposed to the air. For her, belief in what Lord Mark implores her to believe, namely that he and everyone else truly loves her ("We're all in love with you"; 20:160), can only be borne witness to in an incomplete and incompletable sentence that uses once more the key word *belief*: " 'I give you in return the fullest possible belief in what it would be—' And here she pulled up a little." Presumably the sentence would be completed with something like "what it would be like if I were not dying." That, however, is what she cannot say, just as she is placed by her proximity to death beyond the possibility of uttering a felicitous speech act, even though death is the hidden ground of all speech acts.

Milly cannot take, cannot "listen or receive or accept." She can only give. This means that she cannot "agree" or "make a bargain." To agree or enter into a bargain are speech acts in the strictest sense. They are a reciprocal response in which someone says, "Yes, I agree to accept this as a quid pro quo for that," or "I accept the bargain you offer in which I take so and so and give you so and so in return." Milly cannot do that. Milly is out of the loop, but she brings the ground of the loop into the loop, with disastrous results. She can give but not take. That giving makes her a kind of black hole in reverse, not a place that absorbs everything and from which nothing ever returns, but a place from which things are emitted but into which nothing can enter. What is emitted, however, disastrously imposes on those who receive it an infinite obligation.

The devastating effects of Milly's inability to agree or bargain, to utter the most essential of speech acts, "I agree" and "I accept," on the economy of relations among the main characters in the novel, Kate, Densher, Aunt Maud, Susan Stringham, Lord Mark, can best be seen in what happens to Densher. The bargain Kate makes with Densher (she will sleep with him if he will pretend to make love to Milly and so get her money) backfires when Densher's fulfillment of his side of the agreement brings about what it mendaciously asserts. It does come about that Densher falls in love with Milly, against his every wish and intention. Or, rather, as Kate says in the final scene of the novel, he comes to be "in love with her memory" after her death (20:404). To be in love with someone's memory—it is an odd and striking locution. To be in love with someone's memory, that is, more or less, loving him or her after he or she is dead, is radically different from loving that person while he or she is alive.

A love for a living person may be fulfilled or not fulfilled. Pledges, promises made to the living, like Kate's pledge to Densher, may be kept or betrayed, as her pledge to him is in the end not kept. This may happen by an intricate balance of competing obligations that may in a certain sense justify the betrayal. To put this another way, new performative utterances may cancel and annul the old, but only so long as both parties remain alive. An unfulfilled promise made to someone who then dies, however, even if it is a lying promise, imposes an infinite obligation that devastates competing obligations to the living. This is what happens with Densher, Kate, and Milly, as it does in the analogous short story of 1896, "The Way It Came" (reprinted as "The Friends of the Friends").[34] Densher fulfills his part of the bargain by allowing Milly, as much through his silence as through anything he says or does, to believe he is free to love her because Kate does not love him. After Milly's death Densher comes to Kate proposing that he will refuse Milly's bequest and that they should marry immediately. If not, he will make over every penny of Milly's money to Kate, but will not marry her. Kate, with her lucidity and "high grasp," sees these as alternatives between which she must choose: "You'll marry me without the money; you won't marry me with it. If I don't consent *you* don't. . . .—so that I must choose" (20:404). Kate's choice, the ultimate determining event of the novel, takes the form of saying she will choose to marry him if he can give "[his] word of honor that [he's] not in love with her memory" (ibid.). Densher's reply is the climactic "Oh" of the novel. I have earlier discussed the repeated "Oh" and its significance. Densher here says, ""Oh—her memory!,"" neither confirming nor denying her imputation, which means implicitly confirming it, upon which Kate lucidly asserts, "Her memory's your love. You *want* no other." His reply is to say he'll marry her in an hour, to which she replies with another question, "As we were?" His answer is to say, yes, "As we were," upon which she turns to the door to leave him for good with a final headshake: "We shall never be again as we were!," thereby using the last, ironically altered, form of the phrase "There you are" that has echoed through the novel (20:405). They can never again be as they were because Densher's lie to Milly has now become a solemn obligation to repay her love with his own love. You cannot bargain with the dead, but your relation to them may make it impossible for you to keep bargains made with the living.

The lesson of *The Wings of the Dove* might be expressed as the command: "Don't tell lies. They have a way of coming true, of their own accord, through the power of words, through the power of words, that is, in their secret relation to death, against all your wishes and intentions." This, it may be, is that "insoluble mystery" about which James speaks in the preface. Marcel Proust has the narrator of *À la recherche du temps perdu* express elegantly this disastrous law that makes lies truth. He makes his formulation apropos of the lies he has told Albertine: "Time passes, and little by little everything we have spoken in falsehood becomes true [*tout ce qu'on disait par mensonge devient vrai*]."[35] If this is both novels' ironic "lesson," this lesson must not be misunderstood as an ethical command not to lie, since it is perhaps impossible not to lie and certainly impossible to control the effects lies or any other speech acts will have.

This is one reason why it is also impossible to judge whether Densher or Kate acted in ways that are ethically admirable or vicious. It is impossible therefore to draw moral lessons from *The Wings of the Dove*, for example, by saying, in Kantian fashion: "Everyone ought to act as Densher acted. It is possible to establish a universal moral law on the basis of his behavior." The actions of the characters are ultimately determined by forces beyond their control, namely, by the power of death. Milly is the personification of death's power. She is the one who brings death's devastation into the circle of giving and taking within which Densher and Kate have lived.

Moreover, since death is wholly unintelligible, its effects on the living are unintelligible also. *The Wings of the Dove* is a novel about the blank unknowability of death as it disastrously effects the living, including our ability to pass ethical judgment on the acts of the living in response to death. This happens according to those figures of Milly as like the Lorelei or like a sinking ship that draws all around into its dark vortex, including even the reader of the novel. The reader's power to draw moral lessons from the novel is disabled as much as are the projects of the characters.

Milly's lies about her illness are efficacious only up to a point, as is her performative assertion that she "will live." In the end, death wins the game, though only when she, Bartlebylike, turns her face to the wall. She turns away not only from Densher but from all others. She wills not to go on willing to live. Death always wins in the end. It is, in this novel, the one power that is not subject to the performative power of words, since it is the ground of all performatives. You can know nothing about death, nor can you coerce or bind it with performative oaths, even though all speech acts are in one way or another made in death's name, as when one swears on his or her mother's grave. This is the significance of the reader's ignorance of a series of facts that it would be important to know: what it was that Kate's father did that ostracized him from polite society; the precise nature of the illness that kills Milly; the contents of the letter Milly writes Densher on her deathbed, timing its arrival for Christmas eve; the exact amount of her bequest to him; what happens after the last scene and last sentence of the novel. Does Kate take the money and marry Lord Mark, as James's notes of 1894 indicate?[36] The reader can never know any of these secrets. They remain impenetrable enigmas.

These secrets stand figuratively, as what can be called allegorical catachreses, for the relation of the whole novel, as a virtual reality the reader can enter through the words, to the unwritten and unwritable ideal novel for which the actual novel is, as James's preface laments and celebrates, a poor but successful substitute: "the artist's energy fairly depends on his fallibility" (19:xiii). The critic's or reader's access to the hidden and unspeakable motivation for the entire action is, in turn, subject to the same limitations. What he or she can know and say circles around an unknowable and unsayable center for which "death," Milly's particular death as stand-in for all human mortality, the great smudge of mortality across the picture, is a displaced name. The endpoint of the reader's understanding of *The Wings of the Dove*, or, rather, the frontier where nonunderstanding begins, is a recognition of a congruence between the novel itself in its relation to its "origin," what James in the preface to *The Golden Bowl*, the reader will remember, calls the "clear matter" of the tale, on the one hand, and, on the other hand, the characters in their relation to death. Each is so to speak, the allegory of the other. The story told is in this case a figure for James's act of storytelling, as well as for the reader's relation to both.

CHAPTER 5

"Conscious Perjury": Declarations of Ignorance in *The Golden Bowl*

We know nothing on earth.

—FANNY AND BOB ASSINGHAM, in *The Golden Bowl*

I know nothing.

—MAGGIE VERVER, in *The Golden Bowl*

Justice would begin with this perjury. [*La justice commencerait avec ce parjure.*]

—JACQUES DERRIDA

Maggie's Perjury

The turning point or, to give it its austere Greek name, *peripeteia*, of *The Golden Bowl* is a moment of double perjury. The word *perjury* is James's own, or, rather, that of his deputy and delegate, the narrative voice. In a carefully planned private encounter, Charlotte has found Maggie alone and asks her if she has anything to complain of in her (Charlotte's) behavior. Though Maggie knows, or thinks she knows, knows "more and more," that Charlotte, her stepmother, has betrayed her by renewing her old affair with Maggie's husband, Prince Amerigo, she, Maggie, swears that she has nothing to complain of to Charlotte: "I've *not* felt at any time that you've wronged me" (24:249). Charlotte, on her side, swears that she has not knowingly wronged Maggie: "I'm aware of no point whatever at which I may have failed you" (24:248). Both of these assertions are outright lies. Maggie believes she knows Charlotte has been sleeping with her husband, under her nose, so to speak, and Charlotte, the reader is led to think, knows she has "failed" Maggie in the worst way possible: by sleeping with her husband. At least the reader has been made to believe that is the case. We are never told this in so many words or shown a direct representation of the event. The recent television version of *The Golden*

228

Bowl leaves no doubt. It shows Charlotte and the Prince making love at the Gloucester Inn. In the novel itself, the reader has only indirect signs and insinuations. The reader no more has certain knowledge than does Maggie. This means that the novel and the film are fundamentally different in meaning.

Though *lie* is a key word in *The Golden Bowl*, appearing far more often than *perjury*, the narrator calls these particular lies "conscious perjuries": "With which she saw soon enough what more was to come. She saw it in Charlotte's face and felt it make between them, in the air, a chill that completed the coldness of their conscious perjury. 'Will you kiss me on it then?'" (24:251). Strictly speaking, neither a lie nor a perjury are, seen from one aspect at least, performative utterances. They are contrary-to-fact constative statements, that is, statements that the speaker believes to be false. A performative utterance is neither true nor false. A lie or a perjury can, however, as J. L Austin recognizes in *How to Do Things with Words*, have a performative function if it is believed or if those who hear it act as if they believe it. The lie or the perjury is then a way to do things with words.

What justifies the word *perjury* in the narrator's formulation? Or the adjective *conscious*? A lie may be a private matter, perhaps between two people only. It is even possible to "lie to oneself," or at any rate ordinary language permits saying that. Lying to oneself presupposes a doubling of the self into liar and the one lied to. Perjury, on the other hand, is necessarily public. It means bearing false witness before other witnesses. Perjury involves, at least implicitly, the minimum presence of one other person, the third as witness, testifier, *terstis*, potentially able to give testimony that the lie occurred. Unless a third is present, however vicariously or symbolically, an event, in a sense, does not occur for the community, for example, for the legal authorities, since no one can be forced to testify against himself or herself, at least not within United States law. If whatever Charlotte and the Prince have done together remains secret, it has for the community not happened. It has not happened as a social event, that is, as something for which they are answerable to the community. O. J. Simpson may possibly (who knows?) have killed his wife, Othellolike, in a fit of jealous rage, but for the community this did not happen, if it did happen, since a jury decided there was not enough evidence to convict him.

Perjury, moreover, involves, at least implicitly, an act of public and formal swearing or oath taking: "I swear I am telling the truth, the whole truth, and nothing but the truth, so help me God." This formula is carefully phrased. It forbids virtual lying by telling only part of the truth or by telling the truth mixed with some lies, fixing things up a bit, for example, to make a good story out of it, as when Huckleberry Finn, says Mark Twain, has, in *The Adventures of Tom Sawyer*, "told the truth, mainly."[1] That "mainly" is disquieting and ominous. We want the whole truth and nothing but the truth. Perjury is lying under oath, in defiance of a promise to tell the whole truth.

Perjury differs from lying, as the word *perjury* suggests, in being the violation of a prior oath. *Per* functions here as a prefix meaning "away," plus *jure*, meaning "swear." To perjure oneself is to swear away a prior oath or to swear away the truth, whereas I may lie on my own hook without having promised that I would tell the truth. Paradigmatic acts of perjury take place in a courtroom when someone has been served a subpoena and forced to testify under pain (that's what *sub poena* means in Latin) of imprisonment or fine. The whole machinery of law, justice, and the bonds of society are threatened by an act of perjury. That explains why it is taken so seriously and punished so severely.

Though both lies and perjuries are performative utterances, perjury is a speech act crime that is punishable by law, whereas a private lie or even a public political lie is not a crime, even though it may function as an efficacious speech act, as do many of the lies in *The Golden Bowl*. Unless they lie under oath, politicians lie all the time and are not punished for it, as in "Saddam Hussein has weapons of mass destruction." A lie may nevertheless endanger the community, as Kant presumes it does when he asserts that lying is never justified, not even to save someone's life.[2] One might argue, therefore, that all lies are perjuries in the sense that they violate a tacit social commitment never to tell a lie. Even so, a citizen is not jailed for lying as such, only for "lying under oath."

What Charlotte and Maggie say are perjuries as well as lies for two reasons. First, they are presented as secured by an explicit oath. Charlotte says, "I only wanted your denial," to which Maggie answers, "Well then you have it." This is followed by one of those repetitive stichomythias that are so important an ingredient in the grammar of dialogue in *The Golden Bowl*. I shall return to this stylistic feature. Charlotte speaks first and Maggie echoes her, as though they were in a courtroom:

> "Upon your honor?"
> "Upon my honor." (24:251)

The second feature making this a scene of perjury is that the seal and signature of these lying oaths is publicly attested. "The prodigious kiss," a Judas kiss, that Maggie receives from Charlotte is witnessed by Maggie's husband (also Charlotte's stepson and her lover) and her father (also Char-lotte's husband and, presumably, cuckold, in this quasi-incestuous tangle), as well as by their friends the Assinghams: "Her husband and her father were in front, and Charlotte's embrace of her—which wasn't to be distin-guished for them either, she felt, from her embrace of Charlotte—took on with their arrival a high publicity" (24:252).

The word *conscious* in James's formulation "conscious perjury" is odd because it is apparently tautological. All perjuries, it would seem, must be conscious in the sense that they deliberately violate a prior oath that is remembered at the time of the perjury and in the sense not that perjuries necessarily swear what the perjurer knows to be false but that they swear what the perjurer believes to be false. The witness can always be making an honest mistake. Testimony is always an assertion of belief, not of knowledge, even if the witness has seen whatever is sworn to "with his or her own eyes." This makes the whole region of lies, testimony, and perjury partly a matter of belief, not simply of cognition. This region is therefore a domain of speech acts, not simply of constative statements. That is why, as I mentioned in the previous chapter, the jury in a criminal trial is in-structed to decide not on the basis of certain knowledge but "beyond the shadow of a doubt," that is, with strong inner conviction on the basis of the evidence as presented. The jury's decision is a collective act of con-science. Legal proof is always indirect. It is carefully staged by the lawyers within definite rules for what counts as legitimate testimony or evidence. A potential juror is excluded, somewhat paradoxically, if he or she happens to have prior knowledge of the scene of the crime, since he or she is sup-posed to decide only on the basis of what is presented in the courtroom.

An "unconscious perjury" would, it seems, therefore be a contradiction in terms, an oxymoron, like "heavy feathers" or "light lead." You always know you are doing it. The perjurer might, however, and often does, claim, after the fact, that he or she had forgotten and so misspoke in a prior testimony. One way perjury may be identified is by contradictions in a witness's testimony. He or she must in one assertion or the other be lying, therefore committing perjury, since it is a case of lying under oath. The witness, however, can always claim that he or she had not remem-bered right the first time and has now remembered correctly: "Now it all comes back to me. I remembered wrong when I first testified." This way out is not an option in *The Golden Bowl*. All the characters are presented as having total and accurate memories, even excessive, haunted, or hyper-bolic memories, just as James himself did. Or thought he did, since how can we be certain that James's memories, in his autobiographical books, for example, are accurate? James's characters are haunted by ghosts of past moments. They are haunted by a "sense of the past" (to borrow the title of James's last, unfinished novel, read in the last chapter here). This hyperbolic memory goes along with a sense of present possibilities that is immediate and almost material, as a ghost in broad daylight seems almost material.

Memory as Raising Ghosts

The image of memory or imagination as raising specters, revenants, ghosts returned from the dead, is James's own. It is used at crucial moments in *The Golden Bowl* and in its preface. In the preface to the New York Edition, discussing the problematic custom of providing illustrations for novels, that is, representations in a different and competing medium, James speaks of the novelist's power as the ability to raise ghosts, to give the reader hallucinatory visions of the characters and actions he calls forth by force of words: "That one should, as an author, reduce one's reader, 'artistically' inclined, to such a state of hallucination by the images one has evoked as doesn't permit him to rest till he has noted or recorded them, set up some semblance of them in his own other medium, by his own other art— nothing could better consort than *that*, I naturally allow, with the desire or the pretension to cast a literary spell" (23:x). A moment later James says the novelist can so effectively cast this spell that his "figures and scenes" "become more or less visible appearances" (*ibid.*).

In *The Golden Bowl* itself, a figurative strand defining the characters' imaginations as haunted or as raising ghosts, a line of images as evanescent and unnoticeable almost as a wisp of smoke, threads its way through the narration, appearing here and there like faint knots in an intricate embroidery. Maggie's perjuring lie to Charlotte seems to Charlotte to have been as performatively effective as a successful act of exorcism or the laying of ghosts would be: "her stepdaughter's word, wiping out, as she might have said, everything, had restored them to the serenity of a relation without a cloud. It had been in short by this light ideally conclusive, so that no ghost of anything it referred to could ever walk again" (24:279). A little later Maggie, so strong is her imagination of what Charlotte is suffering, thinks of herself as a specter following Charlotte about unseen: "Marvelous the manner in which, under such imaginations, Maggie thus circled and lingered—quite as if she were, materially, following her unseen, counting every step she helplessly wasted, noting every hindrance that brought her to a pause" (24:282–83). Though Maggie has learned only indirectly of the intimate relation between her husband and Charlotte, her projection of figures into the void of her ignorance is spoken of as a raising of spectral presences such as haunt the woods at night:

> There had been through life, as we know, few quarters in which the Princess's fancy could let itself loose; but it shook off restraint when it plunged into the figured void of the detail of that relation. This was a realm it could people with images—again and again with fresh ones; they swarmed there like the strange combinations that lurked in the woods at twilight; they loomed into the definite and faded into the vague, their main present sign for her being however that they were always, that they were duskily, agitated. (24:280)

A few pages further on, Maggie is said to imagine all the main actors in her family drama to be living in a haunted house. They are haunted by what they are thinking about the others but cannot say: "They learned fairly to live in the perfunctory; they remained in it as many hours of the day as might be; it took on finally the likeness of some spacious central chamber in a haunted house, a great overarched and overglazed rotunda where gaiety might reign, but the doors of which opened into sinister circular passages" (24:288). About ghosts in James there would be much more to say, but I reserve that for my last chapter, observing now only that using words to raise ghosts is a speech act par excellence, an act of invocation or conjuration, just as laying ghosts is an act of abjuration, exorcism, or swearing away.

Maggie's "conscious perjury" is such an abjuration. By calling the perjury "conscious" James apparently means that by looking in one another's eyes and swearing falsely, then sealing those falsehoods with a public kiss, both Maggie and Charlotte are "coldly" and lucidly aware that they are perjuring themselves. They are aware also, coldly, that the other is also at that moment committing a respondent blatant act of perjury. Maggie's perjury is at the same time, it might be added, another kind of speech act. It is implicitly an act of renunciation. It is as though she were saying, "I hereby renounce my right as an injured wife to denounce you and my husband and to sue for divorce."

Why does Maggie perjure herself? Why does she renounce her right as the victim of her husband's presumed adultery? Is what she says a felicitous speech act, an efficacious way to do things with words? Does it make anything happen? If so, just what does it make happen? How could it do anything if each perjurer is aware of the other's perjury? Can it, finally, be justified? On what grounds? Does Maggie, as she claims, do the right thing when she perjures herself in this way? What would you have done in her place? Maggie thinks to herself, as reported in indirect discourse by the narrative voice, that she has successfully done something with her words: "The heart of the Princess swelled accordingly even in her abasement; she had kept in tune with the right, and something, certainly, something that might resemble a rare flower snatched from an impossible ledge, would, and possibly soon, come of it for her. The right, the right— yes, it took this extraordinary form of humbugging, as she had called it, to the end. It was only a question of not by a hair's breadth deflecting into the truth" (24:250–51). Is Maggie really "in tune with the right"? Is the right line for her not to deflect a hair's breadth into the truth? Can it ever be just, justified, or right to lie and perjure oneself in this humbugging way? How can this perjury be a felicitous speech act if Charlotte knows, or believes she knows, Maggie is lying, just as Maggie knows, or believes she knows, that Charlotte is lying? These are the central questions for the thoughtful reader of *The Golden Bowl*. I mean the reader who sees reading literature as James in the preface sees writing it, that is, as a particularly exigent and responsible part of "the conduct of life" (23:xxiv).

The Speech Act Field

These questions can only begin to be answered on the basis of a prior understanding of the context within which the double perjury takes place. This context can be thought of as a field that lays down certain laws and rules determining the functioning of any speech act within its dynamic array of forces. The field includes not only assumptions about society that are more or less mimetic of those in James's day: for example, the impossibility of marrying without money, sharp class and gender distinctions, distinct national characteristics that make it hard, perhaps impossible, for Prince Amerigo to understand Anglo-Saxons, as well as hard, perhaps impossible, for them to understand him,[3] a certain stage of imperialism and late capitalism in England and the United States, and so on. The contextual field also includes assumptions about consciousness and language, about the way minds are related to one another, that are specific to this work. Complex formal assumptions are presupposed about the novel as a genre. Finally, within all that, James makes tacit, and to some degree anomalous, assumptions about what makes a speech act felicitous or infelicitous. These laws, rules, and conventions are not laid down in so many words. They are implicit. They are exemplified concretely. The reader is therefore left to figure out for himself or herself the rules the examples obey. These laws are similar to those in other James novels, for example, *The Wings of the Dove*, but they are not identical. Each new work by James to some degree sets up conventions of its own, laws that operate only within that novel or short story.

By the time the careful reader reaches Maggie's "I've *not* felt at any time that you've wronged me," he or she will have internalized the set of assumptions making up what I have called the dynamic field within which any enunciation takes place in the novel. This field may be compared to the vast expanse of untrodden snow that James in the preface proposes as a figure for "the clear matter" of the tale (23:xiii). It is at once bland and unspecified and absolutely compelling, just as James finds that only one way to make the tracks in the snow that constitute the actual telling of the story is the right one, even though the field of snow is featureless, apparently an open space where one is free to walk as one likes. The critic can attempt to make those tacit rules and conventions explicit by a process that combines citation with commentary and generalizing induction, finding out the law implicit in analogous examples.

Happy Speech Acts

Maggie's and Charlotte's perjuries take place toward the end of a long line of speech acts that mark crucial moments in the narrative sequence of *The Golden Bowl*. Or one might say this double reciprocal perjury takes place within an array of other speech acts that remain or should remain at that point in the reader's memory as a context for what Maggie and Charlotte say, what they do by saying. If, as J. L. Austin claims, the "felicity" of a speech act depends on established rules, conventions, and institutions, one might argue that James's work generally, or, better, each particular work in its own incomparable way, establishes through its own rhetoric unique conventions that determine the efficacy of speech acts within that particular imaginary world. The "world" of *The Golden Bowl* no doubt bears some close relation, some family resemblance, to that of other James works, not to speak of its representational resemblance to the "real" historical world of the time of its writing. Nevertheless, each new novel establishes its own to some degree *sui generis* conventions for the way speech acts work. Each new speech act takes place within the discursive field established by all the prior speech acts in the novel as they are reported and evaluated for their effectiveness by the narrative voice, by his (or its) delegates, the perspectival protagonists. The latter are primarily the Prince or Maggie, as represented in free indirect discourse by the narrative voice in the first and second volumes respectively. The speech acts are also evaluated by the behavior and speech proffered by the surrounding community of characters in response to the performatives after they are uttered.

Salient speech acts punctuate *The Golden Bowl* at rhythmic intervals, often forming the climax of chapters or scenes and giving thereby a new impetus to the action. A repertoire of the most important will indicate their diversity, as well as their power to determine what happens. Of course a multitude of small speech acts occur almost from moment to moment in the narration. When one character says to another one, "You're too splendid," and is answered in dialogic echo by "Splendid?" to which the first character responds, "Splendid" (24:303), these utterances are not just constative descriptions. They are declarations that in a special way create the reality they name. They implicitly take the form, "I declare you're splendid." If the one spoken to accepts or believes that and declares that belief by echoing the phrase, then for all practical purposes the person *is*, henceforth, splendid. This might be called the performative power of adjectives. This power is conspicuously used and underlined through repetition by certain characters in *The Golden Bowl*. Being "splendid" is not an intrinsic, verifiable property of a person. It is a property that must be ascribed by another in an utterance that is properly performative. Using adjectives is a power we have over other people.

Another example comes at the very end of the novel, in the last interview between Maggie and her father. Maggie first calls Charlotte "incomparable" (24:363), and then is said, in the narrator's careful notation, to feel the full force of this word: "It took thirty seconds, but she was to feel when these were over that she had pronounced one of the happiest words of her life" (24: 363). The word is happy because it works. It is, in J. L. Austin's sense, "felicitous." Maggie goes on to say, "Father, father— Charlotte's great!," to which Adam Verver answers, "Charlotte's great" (24:364). This echoes an earlier interchange (23:180) in which the same adjective for Charlotte is exchanged between father and daughter when they are discussing the invitation to Charlotte to visit that leads to Adam's marriage to her. It is not an accident that so many of these performative adjectives are applied to Charlotte. She is the character who is in the end most subject to the manipulations of the others, who loses most, who loses everything, and whom, moreover, the reader never, or almost never, sees from the inside or who almost never has her consciousness reported in free indirect discourse by the narrator.

Another form of diffused continuous performative language in *The Golden Bowl* is the narration itself. All the words of the novel taken as a whole, as well as each sentence as they unfold one after the other in series as the reader reads them one by one, have a performative dimension. The words of the narration are a magic speech act. They are an invocation calling forth the characters and all they say, do, think, and feel from some inaccessible place of virtuality, the untrodden field of snow that makes the clear matter of the tale. Only the author and his delegate, the narrator, have access to this source. *The Golden Bowl* has existed eternally somewhere as a possibility. Only the words of the narration make that possibility actual by a speech act that may be compared to the raising of ghosts.

Nevertheless, in spite of this pervasive presence of diverse performative aspects of *The Golden Bowl*'s language, a series of more overt performatives punctuates the novel at crucial moments. These form turning points or reorientations of the action.

The novel opens with the Prince uneasily aware that the marriage contract he (with the help of his lawyers) has signed that day has made an irrevocable change in his life: "What had happened was that shortly before, at three o'clock, his fate had practically been sealed, and that even when one pretended to no quarrel with it the moment had something of the grimness of a crunched key in the strongest lock that could be made. . . . It was already as if he were married, so definitely had the solicitors, at three o'clock, enabled the date to be fixed, and by so few days was that date now distant" (23:5). The reader will note the iterated reference to the exact time of day. It is a convention in this novel, as in the real world, that performatives must not only be signed but also dated and located in order to be felicitous. The "I do" spoken by the bride and groom in the marriage ceremony is one of Austin's prime examples of a felicitous performative. (Austin's posthumous editor, J. O. Urmson, claims that Austin made a mistake. The participants, according to Urmson, do not say "I do," but, as Urmson observes, the example is clear enough.[4]) For Prince Amerigo, the actual moment of his marriage seems not to be the ceremony but his signing of the marriage contract. That is when he burns his bridges. Though the reader is not aware of it yet, he or she soon learns that the Prince's uneasiness arises in part because he loves Charlotte, not Maggie, and has betrayed that allegiance by signing a contract to marry someone else. This signing is in effect a double perjury. He has falsely sworn that there is no impediment to his marriage with Maggie, and he has betrayed whatever obligation he has incurred toward Charlotte through the way she has given herself to him.

This opening performative is followed not many pages later by Charlotte's overt act of giving herself once more to the Prince without demanding anything in return. This happens when they meet privately just before the marriage, ostensibly so that Charlotte can, with Amerigo's help, buy a wedding present for Maggie. The gift of oneself to another is perhaps the greatest gift one can make, and it is often, as in this case, accompanied by an explicit speech act of the form "I give myself to you." Charlotte says:

> I wanted you to understand. I wanted you, that is, to hear. I don't care, I think, whether you understand or not. If I ask nothing of you I don't—I mayn't—ask even so much as that. What you may think of me—that doesn't in the least matter. What I want is that it shall always be with you—so that you'll never be able quite to get rid of it—that I *did*. I won't say that *you* did—you may make as little of that as you like. But that I was here with you where we are and *as* we are—I just saying this. Giving myself, in other words, away—and perfectly willing to do it for nothing. That's all. (23:97–98)

This is a doing by saying, a felicitous performative. It explicitly confers on the Prince a limitless obligation to her, in spite of his spurious sense of relief that "she let him off, definitely let him off. She let him off, it seemed, even from so much as answering" (23:98). Even though Charlotte does not require any response from Amerigo, lets him off in that sense, nevertheless the words will echo within him permanently as a bill rendered and bound to come due sooner or later for payment of some kind. Charlotte's words are a fact, an ineradicable fact, once she has uttered them. They are even a material fact registered in the circumambient material world, even if they were not registered in the Prince's ears. Once uttered, the words cannot ever not have happened, even though the Prince pretends not to have heard them and makes no verbal response whatever: "She paused as if her demonstration was complete—yet for the moment without moving; as if in fact to give it a few minutes to sink in; into the listening air, into the watching space, into the conscious hospitality of nature, so far as nature was, all Londonized, all vulgarized, with them there; or even for that matter into her own open ears rather than into the attention of her passive and prudent friend" (23:98).

Two utterances that are examples of the paradigmatic speech act, the promise, signal determining moments in the novel. They give a decisive deflection to the action. Charlotte's engagement to Adam Verver takes place as a series of speech acts. The proposal itself is described as Adam's decisive burning not of his bridges but of his boats: "He had put the question on which there was no going back and which represented thereby the sacrifice of his vessels" (23:218). Charlotte delays answering, delays putting Adam "right," as he puts it. Finally she promises to be satisfied if Maggie, who is in Paris with the Prince, says she approves:

> "I promise you."
> "Quite for ever?"
> "Quite for ever." (23:237)

Ultimately a telegram comes not from Maggie but from the Prince, a telegram that she reads but that Adam refuses to read. This telegram decides her, even though if Adam had read it, it would "in all probability at once have dished her marriage" (23:291). The reader confirms this when he or she is given a chance to read it later. It alludes obliquely to the prior intimacy of Charlotte and the Prince and even can be read as implicitly promising further intimacy, or at least as alluding to the necessity to fight hard to resist its temptations: "'*À la guerre comme à la guerre, then*'—it had been couched in the French tongue. '*We must lead our lives as we see them; but I am charmed with your courage and almost surprised at my own*'" (23:290). Putting it in French makes it a sort of secret code that Adam might not be able to understand, since he may well be a monolingual American. Finally, Charlotte "puts Adam right," though in fact quite wrong, by saying, "simply," "I'll give you . . . what you ask" (23:239). This loveless giving of herself, spoken of later as a "bargain" (23:264), is strangely echoed by a more sincere, though deeply illicit, promise. This is the climax and last words of the scene at Matcham in which the Prince and Charlotte make plans for their long clandestine afternoon at Gloucester. Charlotte says, "These days, yesterday, last night, this morning, I've wanted everything." The Prince responds: "You shall *have* everything" (23:363). It is a promise the reader has every reason to believe is felicitous in the sense that the Prince carries it out to the letter, thereby exemplifying his conviction that the best way to deal with women in general is to make love to them.

The first half of the novel concludes with another speech act, this one explicitly formulated as such, at the end of the second long midnight colloquy between Fanny Assingham and her husband. Fanny knows she has brought Maggie and the Prince, Charlotte and Maggie's father, together under false pretenses, that is, by keeping secret the prior affair of Amerigo and Charlotte. She suspects, on the basis of the evidence, that Charlotte and Amerigo may be renewing their liaison, as the reader knows they have apparently done in Gloucester on that very day. Fanny knows she bears a heavy responsibility for this, but she wants to avoid the consequences of her act. She wants to disclaim responsibility. Her way of doing this is to decide to be prepared to swear on any occasion that she is completely ignorant. She will swear, in the teeth of evidence to the contrary, that she knows nothing, that "Nothing—in spite of everything—*will* happen. Nothing *has* happened, Nothing *is* happening" (23:400). This decision to lie and to use that lie as what she hopes will be a performatively effective speech act is registered in a solemn oath she takes with her husband, thereby incorporating him into her conspiracy to obstruct justice by lying under oath. The figure is a double one, doubly solemn. It is a like a legal deposition: both sign before witnesses, here, before the narrator as witness. It is also like a soldiers' watchword, a secret code phrase that ensures safe passage amongst enemies. When they meet one another they will whisper, "We know nothing on earth":

> "We know nothing on earth—!" It was an undertaking he must sign.
> So he wrote, as it were, his name. "We know nothing on earth." It was like the soldiers' watchword at night. (23:400)

This lying deposition is compounded when Maggie, somewhat later in the narrative sequence, asks Fanny point-blank what she knows or what she believes about the relation of Amerigo and Charlotte: "What awfulness, in heaven's name, is there between them? What do you believe, what do you *know*?" (24:107). Fanny swears, mendaciously and repeatedly as the scene continues, that she believes and knows nothing, that it is impossible the Prince and Charlotte could be lovers. She swears she has never even "entertained" the idea. Maggie demands that she make this a formal oath: "Pardon my being so horrid. But by all you hold sacred?" Fanny answers, facing her, "Ah my dear, upon my positive word as an honest woman" (24:120). This is not quite the same thing as what Maggie asks, since she is not an honest woman, but rather a woman who is at that moment lying through her teeth. Who knows whether there is anything such a woman holds sacred? In any case, she does *not* swear by all she holds sacred. It is a slight evasion of Maggie's demand. The face-to-face look is important here, as so often in the dialogic encounters of one person with another that make up most of this novel. Each character in these face-to-face exchanges interrogates the face of the other, especially the eyes, but also facial expressions, changes in color, and so on, trying to read them as signs of what the other is thinking, trying to tell whether or not the other is telling the truth. In this case, Maggie professes herself to be satisfied. "But do you

believe it, love?" Fanny asks, to which Maggie replies, "I believe *you*."
Fanny responds to that in turn, "Well, as I've faith in *them* it comes to the
same thing." "I've convinced you it's impossible?" asks Fanny, to which
Maggie answers, "Impossible, impossible." That would seem to indicate
that Fanny's lying speech act has worked. It has made Maggie believe the
lie. It has created an illusory world in which the adultery has not occurred.

The chapter ends unexpectedly, however, with Maggie embracing
Fanny and with both women weeping, with Maggie "pressing, clinging,
sobbing" (24:120). The lying performative, or the lie as performative,
seems to have been felicitous only in the sense that it leads each to swear
to act as if they believed the lie. Maggie's tears are outward signs of an
inner dubiety that belie her words, just as Fanny's "sympathetic" and
"perverse" tears in response belie her claim that she knows and believes
nothing. Their exchange of oaths is more a promise to behave as if they
knew and believed nothing than a truthful report of what they actually
know by believing. This aspect of the episode directly echoes the deposition "signed" and used as a protective watchword by Fanny and her husband: "We know nothing on earth." The true contract, however, it might
be argued, a contract that cancels the lying one, is the spontaneous compact sealed between the two suffering women in their embrace and tears.

The final important explicit speech act prior to Maggie's perjury is the
great climactic, melodramatic scene in which Fanny smashes the golden
bowl. Maggie has bought the bowl as a present for her father. She has
then learned, fortuitously, from the strange little shopkeeper about the
visit Charlotte and the Prince made to the same shop, where they considered buying the bowl. Maggie calls Fanny to her side to tell her in great
anxiety that the bowl is "confirmation" that Charlotte and the Prince were
"intimate," "too intimate" (24:161) before his marriage to her, Maggie.
"That bowl," Maggie says, "is, so strangely—too strangely almost to believe at this time of day—the proof" (24:162). "That cup there has turned
witness" (24:163). The long face-to-face dialogue between Maggie and
Fanny that follows circles around the bowl, which is spoken of as "the
incriminating piece" (24:166), as "her damnatory piece" (24:170), as "representing" the Prince's infidelity (24:166), as "that complicating object on
the chimney" (24:176), as "evidence" (24:180). An object can never,
strictly speaking, be a witness. It becomes a witness offering incriminating
evidence only through the meanings that are imputed to it by acts of language of one sort or another. Symbols are made, not given. In itself the
bowl just sits there, as the narrator stresses, seeing it for us through Fanny's eyes: "Her eyes rested on this odd acquisition and then quitted it,

went back to it and again turned from it: it was inscrutable in its rather stupid elegance, and yet, from the moment one had thus appraised it, vivid and definite in its domination of the scene. . . . The golden bowl put on, under consideration, a sturdy, a conscious perversity; as a 'document,' somehow, it was ugly, though it might have a decorative grace" (24:165).

If the bowl is a "document," it must be read, as Maggie is in this chapter reading for Fanny in no uncertain terms the meaning it has for her and as generations of readers have conferred on it one symbolic meaning or another—associating it, for example, with the biblical passage to which it perhaps alludes: "Or ever the silver chord be loosed, or the golden bowl be broken, or the pitcher be broken at the fountain, or the wheel broken at the cistern" (Ecclesiastes, 12:6). I say "perhaps" because no direct evidence that I know of confirms that James had this text in mind. Moreover, the connection between the biblical passage and *The Golden Bowl* is not, for me at least, all that easy to see. The passage is extremely beautiful and powerful, as is the whole chapter in *Ecclesiastes* from which it is drawn. The syntax of the sentence from which verse six is drawn is not entirely clear, to me at least. I think the antecedent is verse one: "Remember now thy Creator in the days of thy youth, while the evil days come not, nor the years draw nigh, when thou shalt say, I have no pleasure in them." This verse is followed by a litany of disasters, for example, "the grasshopper shall be a burden, and desire shall fail: because man goeth to his long home, and the mourners go about the streets" (12:5). Then comes the verse in question. It follows a colon, so it must be read as somehow part of the long sentence beginning in verse one and bound together, in the King James version, by somewhat enigmatic colons, semicolons, and commas, chosen no doubt by the translators to suggest various ligatures in the meaning: "Or ever [meaning, I take it, "before it happens that"] the silver chord is loosed, or the golden bowl be broken." Verses 1–7 seem to be a warning from the preacher, who says, in verse eight, "Vanity of vanities, . . . all is vanity." We are exhorted to remember God while we are still young, while we still have desire and before old age and then death come, figured metonymically by the plague of grasshoppers, the darkening of the sun, moon, and stars (verse two), and the ultimate breaking of the golden bowl: "Then shall the dust return to the earth as it was: and the spirit shall return unto God who gave it" (12:7). Another, quite contrary, piece of advice is hinted at, however: We should live it up while we can, before desire fails and we head to our long home in the cemetery. The loosening of the silver chain, the breaking of the golden bowl, the fountain's pitcher, and the cistern's wheel figure powerfully the disastrous weakenings of old age. All may be vanity, but the only time when we can enjoy vanities is when we are still young enough to feel desire.

How on earth are these biblical verses relevant to *The Golden Bowl*? I confess that I cannot see a clear connection, though verse twelve may have come home to James, if he happened to know it, as it comes home to me, as I crouch over my books and my computer: "of making many books there is no end; and much study is a weariness of the flesh." Verses one through seven, however, may be taken either to suggest that Charlotte and the Prince were right to commit adultery while they were still young enough to do so, and enjoy it, or, contrariwise, that they should have re-membered God in the days of their youth and not have indulged in illicit sex, since all is vanity. As verse fourteen, which ends the chapter and the whole book of *Ecclesiastes*, roundly asserts, "God shall bring every work into judgment, with every secret thing, whether it be good, or whether it be evil." Fanny's smashing of the golden bowl, with its sinister crack, in James's novel does not make the secret of Charlotte's and the Prince's renewed liaison "cease to exist," as Fanny asserts (24:179). The smashed bowl's three pieces, confronted by the Prince when he enters the room, are, rather, readable signs of the destructive triangle of husband, wife, and husband's lover. They bring the secret out into the open, where all who can read may see.

In the first scene of its appearance, when Charlotte does not buy the bowl, it may be taken to stand for the secret "crack" in the Prince (his previous affair with Charlotte; his lack of "straightness" about this), and for his superstitious fear of such flaws in art objects. The latter is part of his "racial," that is, Italian-Catholic, makeup. Charlotte and the Prince recognize, in the same scene, when the Prince offers to buy Charlotte a present, that no *ricordo* can be bought as a symbolic remembrance of their love. This is because it is as if that love had never occurred. A *ricordo*, bought by the Prince for Charlotte would be "a ricordo of nothing. It has no reference" (23:108). It would not "refer," since the Prince refuses to recognize publicly that he has any obligation to her, or that their liaison ever existed. Charlotte, however, could buy the bowl as a wedding present for the Prince and Maggie, since that will be a publicly attested, licit, event. He refuses to let her buy it, since he can see it has a crack.

The climax of the chapter concerning Maggie's discovery of the bowl and her decision to make it "refer" to her husband's adultery comes when Fanny raises the bowl high over her head and deliberately smashes it on the marble floor so that it breaks into three pieces. This division is expres-sive, perhaps, of the continually alternating triangles of mediated relationships that make up the various stories in the novel: for example, Maggie's relation to the Prince and Charlotte, just as its original crack stands for the "rift within the lute," as the Victorian cliché expressed it, that secretly vitiates the apparent serenity of the relations among the main characters.[5] The bowl, after it is broken, can serve as a symbol, a *sumbolon* in the Greek sense of "thrown together." This bowl, that is, is now something like the broken pieces of a whole, each of which might be possessed by a different person. The pieces would then act as a secret password or scene of recognition when they are matched.

Echoing this figure of a divided whole is a later scene in which Maggie initiates her final private colloquy with Charlotte by bringing her the first volume of a novel Charlotte has mistakenly begun reading in the second volume (or possibly the third, if it is a "three decker," as many nineteenth-century novels were; *The Golden Bowl* appeared in two volumes): "I saw you come out—saw you from my window and couldn't bear to think you should find yourself here without the beginning of your book. *This* is the beginning; you've got the wrong volume and I've brought you the right" (24:311). This gesture can be read as a "symbolic" indication of the way Maggie has taken it upon herself to teach Charlotte how to read her situation and how she must now behave, whether she likes it or not. Maggie teaches Charlotte how to begin with volume one. In a similar way I might in error begin reading volume two of *The Golden Bowl* in the New York Edition before I had read volume one and might then be even more baffled as to what is going on than if I had begun correctly with volume one. My reading is like putting together the parts of a broken *sumbolon*, "throwing them together," in the etymological meaning of the Greek word—for example, fitting or reconciling volume one, seen through the Prince's eyes, to volume two, seen through Maggie's eyes.

The bowl is explicitly given a further meaning in a later scene. During the bridge game episode that leads to Maggie's perjury, the narrator reports that Maggie is aware she could with a few words shatter the apparent "serenities and dignities and decencies" of their family circle into "terrors and shames and ruins, things as ugly as those formless fragments of the golden bowl she was trying so hard to pick up" (24:236). The various meanings that can be ascribed to the bowl that give the novel its name echo and resonate through its pages in overdetermined multiplicity.

Fanny's act of destroying the bowl is accompanied by the words that make what she does not simply a symbolic gesture but also explicitly a magic speech act, an attempt to do something with words. Fanny says, in an incantation I have already cited in part: "Whatever you meant by it—

and I don't want to know *now*—has ceased to exist" (24:179). The magic
lies in the claim that, by destroying what had represented Charlotte's and
the Prince's adultery, she can also destroy what the bowl represented. By
destroying the sign, she destroys what the sign stands for. Does this performative utterance work? In one sense, obviously, it cannot, since what
has happened has happened and cannot "cease to exist." In another sense,
however, since the meaning the bowl had as witness to Amerigo's infidelity
depends for its existence, like everything else in this novel, on the signs
for it and on our belief in the sign, therefore, by destroying the sign she
can destroy also what the sign represents, just as the reader would have no
access whatsoever to the pre-existing "clear matter" of the story if James
had not represented that matter in words. If the characters in the novel go
on to behave as if the adultery had not occurred, as indeed they do, then
it does not, in a sense, exist and has no power to determine what happens.
This would not have been the case if Maggie had spoken her grievance
publicly. As Maggie thinks to herself in a later chapter, the chapter of her
perjury, "if the beauty of appearances had been so consistently preserved,
it was only the golden bowl as Maggie herself knew it that had been broken. The breakage stood not for any wrought discomposure among the
triumphant three [Charlotte, Amerigo, and Adam]—it stood merely for
the dire deformity of her attitude toward them" (24:240). The broken
bowl, however, as I have said, in its brokenness, functions, in spite of Fanny's exorcism, as ineradicable testimony to the Prince's and Charlotte's
infidelity. The broken bowl has its own mute performative efficacy, whatever contrary words are spoken over it.

Maggie's "conscious perjury," toward the end of the novel, the speech
event all my commentary is for the sake of interpreting, does no more, it
could be argued, than to continue and try to ratify Fanny's admirable
speech act that negates what she knows to be so.

In one way or another, I claim, all of these performative utterances are
felicitous. They work. They make something happen. Each, however. is
in one way or another anomalous, cracked, like the golden bowl. Each is
illicit, nonstandard. None would meet Austin's criteria for a happy speech
act. Amerigo signs his marriage contract in bad faith, hiding a prior liaison
that makes him an unfit husband for Maggie, just as Charlotte lies when
she promises to give Adam Verver what he wants, since she marries him,
in part at least, so she can be near her lover, Amerigo. Fanny's oaths are
lies, or at least she believes they are lies. It is not true that she "knows
nothing on earth," nor does it make sense, at least within "common
sense," to say you can make what the sign stands for cease to exist by

destroying the sign. It is, in any case, a striking and problematic claim about signs. That all these speech acts nevertheless are performatives that perform makes their array form a context, a strange set of rules or conventions or conditions for a happy speech act special to this novel. Within that context Maggie's conscious perjury, and Charlotte's, when they take place after all the other prior speech acts I have named, can be measured and understood.

Maggie's Place

Jacques Lacan has, in his commentary on Poe's "The Purloined Letter," forcefully argued that a given person's behavior is not a matter of autonomous choice. Each person acts through an irresistible coercion generated by his or her place in a dynamic field made up of the interaction of various persons with one another. This is the law of the three ostriches. If you are the middle ostrich, you behave willy-nilly as the middle ostrich does.[6] It is not quite so simple as that for *The Golden Bowl*. This complexity is indicated by the image of Maggie deciding to get off the coach that has carried her, her husband, her father, and Charlotte along. It is as if the middle ostrich had decided to move out of the overlapping triangles within which she is seemingly trapped. Nevertheless, Maggie must act, however autonomously and inaugurally, on the basis of her given relation at a given moment to the other three, and even on the basis of her relation to Fanny Assingham.

Maggie is in an extremely shrewd situation at the late point in the novel when she publicly perjures herself by giving her false word of honor and by accepting Charlotte's "prodigious" kiss. That kiss, according to the etymological implications of *prodigious*, is full of omens and ominous prognostications for the future. Maggie is intimately close to her widowed father, so close that it may be said they love one another almost too much, almost to the point of incestuous affection. Even so, in the normal course of things she has married. That she is deeply, fathomlessly, abysmally, helplessly in love with her husband, with a violent sexual attraction, is an immutable given of the novel. In no other of James's works has the physical or sexual side of married love been treated more powerfully than here. A salient example is a scene in which Maggie, with enormous effort, resists her husband's sexual advances. She resists because she knows she will be "lost" in her plan to deal responsibly, "rightly," with his adultery if she yields (24:56–57).

Maggie's father, whom she so inordinately loves, is suggestively named "Adam Verver." Quiet verve he certainly has, though whether he is Adam in the sense of innocence, an "American Adam," Adam before the fall, or, rather, Adam in the sense of "the old Adam," that is, possessed by the original sin and the knowledge of good and evil we all inherit from our first father, is left for the reader to decide. Adam Verver is a fathomlessly rich American who has made his money in some unspecified, ruthlessly conducted business in the American West. Now, like William Randolph Hearst, he has become a connoisseur of art objects. Reversing the rape of the New World by old Europe, he is plundering Europe to endow a museum in his home town of American City. This parallel is made clear by the comparison Verver is shown making between his discovery that he has a gift for art appreciation and Cortez's discovery of the Pacific Ocean as he stood, in Keats's erroneous sonnet (since Balboa, not Cortez, discovered the Pacific), "silent, upon a peak in Darien." Whether James knew Keats had it wrong and meant the further irony that the comparison shows something is amiss with Adam's sense of discovery is not clear. The repetition of the mistake adds, however, a further, slightly ominous dimension to Adam's ecstatic moment of self-recognition:

> He had, like many other persons, in the course of his reading, been struck with Keats's sonnet about stout Cortez in the presence of the Pacific; but it was probable that few persons had so devoutly fitted the poet's grand image to a fact of experience. It consorted so with Mr. Verver's consciousness of the way in which at a given moment he had stared at his Pacific that a couple of perusals of the immortal lines had sufficed to stamp them into his memory. His "peak in Darien" was the sudden hour that had transformed his life, the hour of his perceiving with a mute inward gasp akin to the low moan of apprehensive passion that a world was left him to conquer and that he might conquer it if he tried. (23:141)

American City is located at some unidentified site in the western United States, probably California, which James did not much like, to put it mildly, on his one visit there in 1905. The evidence for putting American City in California is the way Charlotte's ultimate exile in the States away from her lover and with her unloved husband is spoken of, toward the end of the novel, by Fanny Assingham: "I see the long miles of ocean [this is the Atlantic ocean, which Adam and Charlotte will have to cross to reach the United States] and the dreadful great country, State after State—which have never seemed to me so big or so terrible. I see *them* [Charlotte and Adam Verver] at last, day by day and step by step, at the

far end—and I see them never come back. But *never*—simply" (24:304).
The "far end" sounds like California to me, though this is never made
certain in the novel. Exile in California! What a fate.

Adam's idea is to civilize the uncivilized Americans by giving them
great European artworks to enjoy. This is analogous to the way we English
teachers still have as our mission to civilize young citizens of the United
States by passing on to them the beauties and the ethical values embodied
in British literature. Adam burns with a hard, gemlike flame. The allusion
to Pater's notorious Conclusion to *The Renaissance* is explicit enough: "It
was all at bottom in him, the aesthetic principle, planted where it could
burn with a cold still flame" (23:197). A curious and disquieting symmetry
is implied between Adam's brilliant implacable acquistiveness as a specu-
lating businessman and his appreciative acquisition of artworks. Among
the other artworks he has acquired, as a husband for his daughter, is an
impecunious Italian prince who has one of the less moral popes for an
ancestor. The Prince is, suggestively and symbolically, named "Amerigo."
He has as ancestor Amerigo Vespucci, who, if he did not actually discover
America, was early enough on the scene to get the whole continent named
for him. Books about Amerigo's family fill a whole section of the British
Library. Maggie goes to inspect those records just before she gets, as she
thinks, irrefutable proof of her husband's adultery. That means she finds
out "the truth" just at a moment when, in spite of her obsessive doubts,
she has come to "believe" in her husband again: "I believed in him again
as much as ever, and I *felt* how I believed in him" (24:155–56). "Belief"
functions here more or less as it does in *The Wings of the Dove*. It is a name
for faith in things unseen and unprovable. "Believe in me," says Lord
Mark when he proposes to Milly, in *The Wings of the Dove*.

After "buying" Prince Amerigo, Adam acquires Charlotte, who also
seems to ring true to him, as a wife. He marries so as to leave his daughter
Maggie free of the responsibility to protect him from hordes of females
hungry to marry him for his fortune, now that he is left exposed by the
marriage of his daughter. Prince Amerigo and Charlotte Stant are just two
more exquisite artifacts for Adam's collection. Amerigo is spoken of as "a
representative precious object." Adam's evaluation of him is based on his
long experience of appraising such objects:

> Representative precious objects, great ancient pictures and other works of
> art, fine eminent "pieces" in gold, in silver, in enamel, majolica, ivory,
> bronze, had for a number of years so multiplied themselves round him and,
> as a general challenge to acquisition and appreciation, so engaged all the

faculties of his mind, that the instinct, the particular sharpened appetite of the collector, had fairly served as the basis for his acceptance of the Prince's suit.

Over and above the signal fact of the impression made on Maggie herself, the aspirant to his daughter's hand showed somehow the great marks and signs, stood before him with the high authenticities, he had learnt to look for in pieces of the first order. (23:140)

Later in the novel, almost as an aside, the reader is told something a little ominous about Adam's attitude toward his acquisitions. This passing comment can be taken as the key to understanding the whole novel, since it states in a particular case the principle according to which all the six main characters, each in his or her own way, act: "there was henceforth only one ground in all the world, he felt, on which the question of appearance would ever really again count for him. He cared that a work of art of price should 'look like' the master to whom it might perhaps be deceitfully attributed; but he had ceased on the whole to know any matter of the rest of life by its looks" (23:147). For all his connoisseurship, Adam is still a canny businessman. He knows, or thinks he knows, that the worth of anything, including an artwork, is not intrinsic but a matter of its exchange value, of what people can be brought to think it is worth. Value is a matter of belief, or even of pretended belief, like so much else in this novel. It does not matter whether Bernardino Luini really painted a given painting or not, so long as everyone thinks he did. It does not matter whether Amerigo has a hidden crack, namely, his prior affair with Charlotte, so long as no one knows of it or so long as everyone can be made to behave as if they do not know of it. This offhand remark by the narrator about Adam suggests that Adam will go to great lengths to keep up appearances and hide from the world that Amerigo is not the flawless Italian prince he had judged him to be on the basis of his great marks and signs, his high authenticities. Adam will keep it a secret that he has made an unfortunate purchase, just as he would if he found out that the supposed Luini he has bought is not really a Luini. Adam will make the same effort to hide the way Charlotte is not the flawless acquisition he has presumed her to be. In a similar way, Maggie, early in the novel, tells the Prince, at that moment still just her fiancé, that not only has she paid a lot for him, or her father has, but also that she will pay a lot to keep him. Like father, like daughter. Maggie has been telling the prince that he is just one more of the valuable pieces she and her father have collected: "You're at any rate a part of his collection. . . . one of the things that can only be got over here.

You're a rarity, an object of beauty, an object of price. You're not perhaps absolutely unique, but you're so curious and eminent that there are very few others like you—you belong to a class about which everything is known. You're what they call a *morceau de musée"* (23:12). When Amerigo says that he has the great sign of being such an object, that he "cost a lot of money," she replies, snubbing him a little for his vulgarity in referring to the marriage settlements, that she hasn't the least idea what he cost, but she assures him, "I'd pay rather than lose you" (23:12–13). In the light of what happens later, this has a profoundly ironic ring, since Maggie comes to pay dearly for keeping Prince Amerigo. She pays ultimately not with money but with more or less permanent separation by a continent and an ocean from her beloved father. Adam Verver, however, the narrator assures us, "had ceased on the whole to know any matter of the rest of life by its looks." That means, I take it, that in all areas but art he does not assume that things and people are what they seem or, rather, he does not assume that their value is based on what they seem to be. His disastrous mistake is to treat Amerigo as an art object, not as part of "the rest of life," that is, life outside art.

The reader can only assent to what the narrator, with however much or little irony it is hard to gauge, says of Adam's treatment of human beings as acquisitions. "Nothing perhaps might affect us as queerer, had we time to look into it, than this application of the same measure of value to such different pieces of property as old Persian carpets, say, and new human acquisitions" (23:196). The phrase "low moan of apprehensive passion," cited earlier, shows how Adam's acquisitiveness is quasi-erotic, anxious, and prehensile or grasping, all three at once. In James's characteristically ornate figure, Adam is said to taste everything he acquires out of the same glass, "a little glass cut with a fineness of which the art had long since been lost": "As it had served him to satisfy himself, so to speak, both about Amerigo and about the Bernardino Luini he had happened to come to knowledge of at the time he was consenting to the announcement of his daughter's betrothal, so it served him at present to satisfy himself about Charlotte Stant and an extraordinary set of oriental tiles of which he had lately got wind, to which a provoking legend was attached" (23:196–97). If a "provoking legend" is attached to those tiles, so also, though Adam does not know it, a provoking legend is attached to both Amerigo and Charlotte. Their liaison is a secret and effaced legend, a legend that has never been written down or told. (The word *legend* means "readable inscription," from Latin *legere*, to read.) Charlotte and Amerigo's legend is a legend without legend, so to speak, though Fanny Assingham knows of it.

The novel as a whole, it could be said, devotes itself to "looking into" the queer mistake involved in seeing another human being as an object of price that can be bought, acquired, possessed, enjoyed. Beyond the general immorality of treating a person as a thing, a danger derives from the way human beings have wills, feelings, an ability to think and do, of their own. They do not just rest passively in glass cabinets. In this case Adam, who has "never spoken of himself as infallible" but who is confident that "no man in Europe or America . . . [is] for such estimates less capable of vulgar mistakes" (23:140), has made a big mistake. This mistake, among other things, is symbolized by the hidden crack in the golden bowl, actually crystal with gold overlay. That bowl, the reader will remember, the Prince and Charlotte discover in an antique shop and do not buy because the Prince perceives it has a crack. Maggie later, by an extraordinary coincidence, comes upon the bowl in the same shop and buys it as a birthday present for her father.

Though the Prince and Charlotte have had an affair before either of them marries and are deeply in love, they have not married because neither is independently wealthy. This requirement seems absurd to readers in the United States today, since most people work for a living. It is, however, an absolute given in James's fictional world. Amerigo and Charlotte remain in love, or at any rate Charlotte loves Amerigo, after the Prince marries Maggie and then Charlotte marries Maggie's father. Amerigo seems naturally and unashamedly polyandrous, at least until Maggie conquers him. Charlotte and the Prince renew their liaison on a fateful day in Gloucester that makes them late to return home to London, where their respective spouses await them. They justify this adultery to one another by the way Adam has neglected Charlotte for Maggie, while Maggie has neglected the Prince for her father. Their late return and the looks on their faces when they do return clinch Maggie's growing certainty that her husband is betraying her with her stepmother.

What should Maggie do now? What *ought* she to do? How can she act responsibly and effectively, in tune with the right? She is caught between two equal incompatible and infinitely exigent obligations: that to her father, that to her husband. In both cases these are present to her not as abstract responsibilities but as deeply compelling physical attractions engendered in the face-to-face or body-to-body encounter of two incarnated subjectivities. Her affection and loyalty to her father, her intimacy with him, are presented as quite extraordinary in their intensity, just as is

her abject love for her husband. She finds him "heart-breakingly handsome, clever, irresistible." He reduces her, in the narrator's extravagant
phrase, to "passive pulp" (23:165).

The Infinite Unfulfillable Obligation

The demand made on any person by each other person, *The Golden Bowl*
presupposes, is unique and limitless. It exceeds any general moral or social
laws, any universal rules of justice. It is incommensurate with any other
obligation. It leaves no room for any third person, since the presence of a
third person would make the face to face a miniature community subject
to generalizable moral laws and a distributive justice. The demands made
on me by a single other person exceed the bounds of such a justice. They
are beyond justice, in that sense, unjust. Without some third person as
witness to make the isolated duo into a society, my relations to the single
and singular other are lawless, violent, antisocial, as is, for example, the
secret liaison of Charlotte and the Prince. Each of the characters in *The
Golden Bowl* has, a priori, a similarly absolute and unique obligation to
each of the others. This obligation is in each case incompatible and incomparable with any other responsibility. This situation includes the Assinghams in their relations to one another and to each of the four main
participants, in what Fanny Assingham calls a "vicious circle." Fanny expresses the way each one-on-one relation forms a separate "case" incommensurate with all the others. She formulates this case law in a passage
in her first nighttime colloquy with her husband. This happens near the
beginning of the novel, when Charlotte has unexpectedly turned up to
stay with the Assinghams and to be present at the Prince's marriage to
Maggie:

> "Of which case," she asked, "are you speaking?"
> He smoked a minute: then with a groan: "Lord, are there so many?"
> "There's Maggie's and the Prince's, and there's the Prince's and Char-
> lotte's."
> "Oh yes; and then," the Colonel scoffed, "there's Charlotte's and the
> Prince's."
> "There's Maggie's and Charlotte's," she went on—"and there's also
> Maggie's and mine. Yes," she mused, "Charlotte's and mine is certainly a
> case. In short, you see, there are plenty." (23:75)

Fanny's phrase "vicious circle" names the way my fulfillment of my
obligation to one person, in a given case, causes me to neglect and betray

my obligations to all the others. Or, one could say, insofar as each obligation presupposes an explicit or at least tacit promise, an oath to be faithful to that person, then my competing obligation to any person other than that first one leads me, necessarily, to perjure myself whenever I turn to that second person. The marriage ceremony, with its promise to love, honor, and obey until death do us part, is a salient example of an explicit oath of this sort. Any married person will know how a friendship with another person, of either sex, not to speak of a sexual attraction for another person, is experienced as a violation and betrayal, however slight or seemingly benign, of the marriage oath. Analogously, marriage itself is a violation of the command to love and honor one's parents. Sexual obligation, however, is only a symbol, allegory, or synecdoche of a more general obligation each person has to every other, an obligation that is, of course, not necessarily sexual.

The law of the vicious circle has commanded Maggie's behavior as well as that of the other three main characters, with disastrous results. The circle is "vicious" not only because it generates its own endless and fruitless self-compounding circulation but because it leads those caught into it to betray one another, to perjure their oaths of fidelity, to act viciously. They do this just through their efforts to fulfill their equally exigent obligation to the others in the circle. It is vicious also because the effort to act justly causes the others to act viciously. The phrase "vicious circle" comes up in the extraordinary midnight colloquy of Fanny Assingham and her husband that ends Book First of the novel:

> "Maggie has done the most."
> He wondered. "What do you call the most?"
> "Well, she did it originally—she *began* the vicious circle. For that—though you make round eyes at my associating her with 'vice'—is simply what it has been. It's their mutual consideration, all round, that has made it the bottomless gulf; and they're really embroiled but because, in their way, they've been so improbably *good*."
> "In their way—yes!" the Colonel grinned.
> "Which was above all Maggie's way." No flicker of his ribaldry was anything to her now. "Maggie had in the first place to make up to her father for her having suffered herself to become—poor little dear, as she believed—so intensely married. Then she had to make up to her husband for taking so much of the time they might otherwise have spent together to make this reparation to Mr. Verver perfect. And her way to do this, precisely, was by allowing the Prince the use, the enjoyment, whatever you may call it, of Charlotte to cheer his path—by installments, as it were—in

proportion as she herself, making sure her father was all right, might be missed from his side. By so much, at the same time, however," Mrs. Assingham further explained, "by so much as she took her young stepmother, for this purpose, away from Mr. Verver, by just so much did this too strike her as something again to be made up for. It has saddled her, you'll easily see, with a positively new obligation to her father, an obligation created and aggravated by her unfortunate even if quite heroic little sense of justice. She began by wanting to show him that marriage could never, under whatever temptation of her own bliss with the Prince, become for her a pretext for deserting or neglecting *him*. Then that, in its order, entailed her wanting to show the Prince that she recognized how the other desire—this wish to remain, intensely, the same passionate little daughter she had always been—involved in some degree and just for the present, so to speak, her neglecting and deserting *him*. . . . Before she knew it at any rate her little scruples and her little lucidities, which were really so divinely blind—her feverish little sense of justice, as I say—had brought the two others together as her grossest misconduct couldn't have done." (23:394–96}

This is of course only Fanny's lucid and ironic reading of the situation. The reader is left to decide whether or not to accept her analysis, though he or she will suspect that Fanny may speak here vicariously for James's own reading of the situation he has invented. The reader will also see that justice is here defined as the need to make the multiple obligations one has to various people come out right, with a zero balance, so to speak, incomes and payments coming out even, in tune with the right. The reader will also see how the story James tells shows that it is impossible to fulfill this need for an evenly distributed justice. To be just to one person means being unjust to another, perjuring one's promises, tacit or explicit, to that other, which is perhaps one of the things Derrida means by saying that justice begins in perjury. If one had only one other to be faithful to, there would be no problem, or if one lacked a sense of justice and responsibility, there would be no problem. The problem begins, the vicious circle begins turning, when one attempts the impossible task of fulfilling one's limitless obligations to more than one person. Far from making things better by a successive loving kindness to first one and then another, Maggie's feverish and unfortunate little sense of justice has brought about the vice of her husband and stepmother. They renew their liaison with the explicit conviction that they have been neglected by their respective spouses, so that those spouses, father and daughter, can spend endless hours together, leaving Charlotte and the Prince to themselves (see 23:334–35).

Responsibility: Fanny and Bob as Stand-ins for the Reader

Fanny Assingham is a responsible protagonist in the action of *The Golden Bowl*, as well as a passive witness who is the reader's delegate. She first introduced the Ververs to the Prince, even though she knew something of the Prince's prior affair with Charlotte. At the same time she is the reader's vicarious stand-in. She exemplifies in a hyperbolic way the supersubtle hermeneutic acts of figuring out, on the basis of the evidence or signs presented, that James hopes his readers will perform. The Colonel, her husband, represents the ephebe in reading who is being instructed by an adept. Or, one might say, the Colonel represents the reader who is being taught by Fanny's example how to read *The Golden Bowl* for himself or herself. No other work by James has the act of reading, that is, what the reader is at that moment doing, so ostentatiously or so saliently dramatized in the work itself.

Fanny represents an exigent demonstration or lesson in the narrative principle James enunciates, in the preface to *The Golden Bowl*, as having presided over all his work. What he specifies in the preface for this novel is not Fanny Assingham's role as exemplary reader of signs but the way Book First is presented primarily through the Prince's eyes, Book Second through Maggie's. Nevertheless, what James says also defines admirably Fanny's role in the novel:

> Again and again, on review, the shorter things in especial that I have gath-ered into this Series have ranged themselves not as my own impersonal account of the affair in hand, but as my account of somebody's impression of it—the terms of this person's access to it and estimate of it contributing thus by some fine little law to intensification of interest. The somebody is often, among my shorter tales I recognise, but an unnamed, unintroduced and (save by right of instrinsic wit) unwarranted participant, the impersonal author's concrete deputy or delegate, a convenient substitute or apologist for the creative power otherwise so veiled and disembodied. My instinct appears repeatedly to have been that to arrive at the facts retailed and the figures introduced by the given help of some other conscious and confessed agent is essentially to find the whole business—that is, as I say, its effective interest—enriched *by the way*. I have in other words constantly inclined to the idea of the particular attaching case *plus* some near individual view of it; that nearness quite having thus to become an imagined observer's, a projected, charmed painter's or poet's—however avowed the "minor" quality in the latter—close and sensitive contact with it. Anything, in short, I now reflect, must always have seemed to me better—better for the process

and the effect of representation, my irrepressible ideal—than the mere muffled majesty of irresponsible "authorship." Beset constantly with the sense that the painter of the picture or the chanter of the ballad (whatever we may call him) can never be responsible *enough*, and for every inch of his surface and note of his song, I track my uncontrollable footsteps, right and left, after the fact, while they take their quick turn, even on stealthiest tiptoe, toward the point of view that, within the compass, will give me the most instead of least to answer for. (23:v–vi)

Responsibility is a key word here, as it is in the novel itself. Being responsible means having a lot to answer for. Responsibility means an obligation to be just, to do justice. The word *responsibility* names for James not just the burden or guilt that lies on someone for having done something, for example, Fanny's heavy responsibility for introducing the Prince to the Ververs. *Responsibility* names also the way narration, the act of making a coherent story out of an entangled mesh of "cases," also, strangely, makes me responsible for that sense making and its consequences. "Responsibility" names, in addition, as the passage just quoted indicates, the double bind of interpreting someone else's narration. If I do not read carefully, with infinite care, tiptoeing to and fro as I follow the track laid down by the author and his or her surrogates, I am acting irresponsibly, failing to fulfill my ultimately unfulfillable obligation to be a good reader. No one is ever a good enough reader. At the same time, the more successful I am as a reader, the more, in a strange way, I actively intervene by making sense of the data, a sense they do not have in themselves, do not have unless they are read. Reading is intervention. This intervention makes me responsible for what happens in reading. It makes me not just a passive and detached witness but also a protagonist. I become a responsible agent who can be held accountable. James says this when he stresses the way each narrative point of view, figured as painter of the picture or chanter of the ballad, "can never be responsible *enough*, and for every inch of his surface and note of his song." The author, however, with his or her apparent freedom to make up anything he or she likes, to hide, masked and silenced behind the narrators, like Joyce's Godlike writer off somewhere indifferently paring his fingernails, exemplifies "the mere muffled majesty of irresponsible 'authorship'" (23:vi).

The involved, responsive, and responsible spectator-narrator covertly represents that hidden, muffled, authorial (ir)responsibility. As James says, the witness-narrator is "a convenient substitute for the creative power otherwise so veiled and disembodied" (23:v). This substitutive role is signaled by the way the narrator does not just narrate but also actively interprets. He, she, or it reads the evidence and must take responsibility for that act of reading. The most obvious figure for this in the novel is Fanny Assingham, as she tirelessly attempts to figure out the relations among the four main protagonists. She struggles to come to terms with the responsibility she bears for having introduced the Prince to the Ververs, while knowing of his prior affair with Charlotte, though not, she claims how "far it has gone." She then has to accept responsibility for having allowed Adam Verver to marry Charlotte without letting him know of Charlotte's intimacy with the Prince, who is now his daughter's husband. If she were not so imaginative herself, she would bear less responsibility, as she indicates at the end of the third and last of her prolonged interchanges with her husband. She has been talking of the way none of them will ever know how much Adam Verver knows: "we shall never know." That, she says, will be their punishment, even her own punishment. When her husband asks what will be his punishment, Fanny answers, somewhat contradictorily: "Nothing—you're not worthy of any. One's punishment is in what one feels, and what will make ours effective is that we *shall* feel" (24:136–37). The shift from "one" to "ours" and "we" matches the progression from claimed irresponsibility to accepted responsibility on Colonel Bob's part. If we are unimaginative readers, we can escape responsibility, but only by being grossly irresponsible. Either way we have had it, in a painful double bind that might lead one to conclude it would be better not to read *The Golden Bowl* at all.

Knowledge confers responsibility, even knowledge imputed by an imaginative putting together of data. Such putting together is an act that is performative rather than constative. An example of this is presented in the process by which Colonel Bob Assingham begins with an inveterate denial of responsibility. He is then led gradually to join his wife in an oath that is a strange acceptance of responsibility by way of a prevaricating denial of knowledge. Colonel Bob is a moral example for the reader. The reader may think that reading *The Golden Bowl* is an objective matter of understanding. It does not touch him or her personally, certainly not to the extent of conferring any kind of responsibility. Reading, however, is always a not wholly warranted putting of two and two together, a partly performative, not purely cognitive, act. No reading can be entirely justified by appeal to the text. Any interpretation always involves some reading between the lines, however discreet this may be. Insofar as it is performative, reading confers responsibility on the one who reads, just as much as writing, according to James in the preface, is part of the conduct of life.

Writing allows the writer, or even obliges him or her, to say, "Yes, I wrote that. I accept responsibility for what I wrote."

Fanny's husband Bob functions as the straight man and interlocutor. He is the man of down-to-earth, worldly common sense. He is a sounding board for Fanny's baroque or arabesque imaginative readings of the evidence she has about Adam, Maggie, Charlotte, and Amerigo. Bob is a man of the world. He is an old soldier who "knew everything that could be known about life, which he regarded as, for far the greater part, a matter of pecuniary arrangement" (23:67). Fanny's readings lead her both to take responsibility ("'I was really at the bottom of it,' she declared"; 23:388), and to go to extreme lengths to escape or deny that responsibility. Colonel Bob, on the other hand, begins with a stubborn refusal to accept responsibility. He claims to be a disengaged, amused spectator. He is like a reader who reads in a cool, detached manner, who denies that the book involves him or her in any way, or invokes and demands a response. Bob's refusal is expressed in apparently harmless swearing that the narrator assures us is habitual: "He disengaged, he would be damned if he didn't—they were both phrases he repeatedly used—his responsibility" (23:64). To say "I'll be damned if I don't disengage myself from responsibility" is an odd, even perverse, species of speech act. On the one hand, it is a curse, a taking of God's name in vain, here by arrogating God's power. People do not damn themselves. They commit acts that lead God to damn them. What Bob says might be transposed as "May God damn me if I take responsibility." Such curse words are also bets, another sort of speech act. "I am so sure I won't be led to take responsibility that I'm willing to ask God to damn me if I do. I'll bet I don't. I'll be damned if I will be responsible." Of course, Bob's words are not meant seriously, as most curses are not, though it is always risky to play with fire. Someone, perhaps God himself, if he exists, might take you seriously if you swear, even if it is an etiolated or denatured oath. Fanny compares her husband's propensity for harmless swearing to the way a retired general she knew played with toy soldiers, like Uncle Toby in *Tristram Shandy*:

> Her husband's exaggerated emphasis was *his* box of toy soldiers, his military game. It harmlessly gratified in him, for his declining years, the military instinct; bad words, when sufficiently numerous and arrayed in their might, could represent battalions, squadrons, tremendous cannonades and glorious charges of cavalry. It was natural, it was delightful—the romance, and for her as well, of camp life and the perpetual booming of guns. It was fighting to the end, to the death, but no one was ever killed. (23:64)

This might be taken as a perfect definition of literature as fiction. *The Golden Bowl* is a fight to the death in which Charlotte and the Prince are ultimately turned, by the combined efforts of Maggie and her father, into wax images, "sitting as still, to be thus appraised, as a pair of effigies of the contemporary great on one of the platforms of Madame Tussaud" (24:360–61). This is a terrifying denouement, or would be such in real life, but in the novel no one is ever killed. "It's only a story." Like Colonel Bob, we are always free to disengage ourselves without danger by saying the story is only imaginary. It can be historically placed and explained. Therefore it has nothing to do with me, who live in a different place and time. If, as Jacques Derrida repeatedly says, literature is historically associated with freedom of speech and with the right to say anything and disclaim responsibility for it[7] ("Any resemblance to real persons, living or dead, is purely coincidental"), then literature is like Bob Assingham's swearing. It makes nothing happen.

Nevertheless, the drama of Bob's part in *The Golden Bowl* is the way he is gradually inveigled, partly through his love for his wife and sense of responsibility for her anxiety, partly through sheer fascination by the drama unfolding before his eyes, to share in his wife's sense of responsibility and to join her in their strange oath, "We know nothing on earth" (24:400). This joint oath is intended to function as an apotropaic speech act holding off and neutralizing their responsibility for what has happened. I cite the passage again: "It was an undertaking he must sign. So he wrote, as it were, his name. 'We know nothing on earth.' It was like the soldier's watchword at night" (24:400). Whether Bob's acceptance of responsibility constitutes a kind of damnation for a sin, fulfilling the negative possibility in his habitual oath, the reader is left to decide. The further allusion here to the military context, however, indicates that Bob is no longer playing with toy soldiers. He is a participant in a real battle.

Insofar as Bob is the reader's delegate, or the representative, at least, of a certain reader, he dramatizes the way even the most detached reader may gradually become a participant. Such a reader may be led to take responsibility even for something fictional, feigned, something, moreover, that he has not in any case done himself or herself. It is all very well for Colonel Bob to say he'll be damned if he doesn't disengage himself from responsibility. This is a classic double bind. You are damned if you do (take responsibility for reading) and you are damned if you don't (since you are responsible in any case).

Maggie's story, in another version of the drama of responsibility, is presented as a taking of responsibility on her part after she comes to believe her husband is deceiving her. Her taking of responsibility is figured as her deciding to jump off the carriage that is carrying her with her husband, her father, and her stepmother along in such a duplicitous pretence of felicity and openness. It is figured also, at a much later moment in the novel, in her reflection that sooner or later she will need to confess to her local priest (she and the Prince are Catholics) that she has not confessed to what she has done. She will have an obligation to confess that she has not confessed. What she has done is to try her best to keep her father in ignorance and, in order to do that, to lie to Charlotte, in the act of "conscious perjury" whose purport my whole effort in this chapter is focused on understanding.

Adam Verver, finally, the reader guesses, knows very well what is going on, though he remains inscrutably "muffled." He quietly takes responsibility for saving the situation, at the expense of Charlotte's everlasting misery, by separating Charlotte from the Prince, as well as himself from his daughter. He takes Charlotte back to endless exile in American City. There, in a living death, she will tend his museum and serve as the elegant hostess at his dinner parties.

The novel, I conclude, is made of a chain of competing responsibilities, each canceling the ones before.

James's preface, as I have observed in my introduction, is pervaded by a lot of high-minded Emersonian talk about "responsibility" and about the way writing can, if the author acknowledges what he has written, be a part of the "conduct of life" that "consists of things done, which do other things in their turn" (23:xxiv): "to 'put' things is very exactly and responsibly and interminably to do them"; "Not to *be* disconnected, for the tradition of behavior, he has but to feel that he is not; by his lightest touch the whole chain of relation and responsibility is reconstituted. . . . All of which means for him conduct with a vengeance, since it is conduct minutely and publicly attested" (23:xxiv, xxv). What the preface does not say is a salient example of the way the prefaces are as much false leads, the covering of tracks, as trustworthy readings. James does not observe that the acts of responsibility in the novel that represent vicariously, according to James himself, the author's own responsible doing are in every case lies and perjuries: the oath that Fanny and her husband sign when they swear together that they know nothing; Maggie's conscious perjury when she swears she has nothing to complain of in Charlotte; her father's silence to everyone, including the reader (who is never allowed access to his mind at this stage of the action), about his motives for taking Charlotte home to American City. This consitutes a kind of tacit lie.

What, the astute reader might ask, corresponds, in James's own behavior, to the strange law within the novel that says the most responsible thing to do, in certain extreme circumstances, at any rate, is to lie and perjure? Do James's prefaces constitute false and misleading testimony? Do the novels and tales themselves bear full witness to the "clear matters" of the various tales, the données to which only James himself had direct access? The reader may possibly find out the first question through discrepancies between the prefaces and the works themselves, though he or she would need to take responsibility for deductions that are drawn from these discrepancies. Whether the novel bears false witness to the "clear matter of the tale," however, the reader will never know, any more than Marcel, in À la recherche du temps perdu, can ever find out for sure whether or not Albertine is lying to him when she swears she has not had lesbian experiences. The reader is left to make a performative act of belief. This belief can never be based on certain knowledge. Therefore, the reader must be held responsible for it, just as he or she must be held responsible, as Maggie is, for what he or she imagines to have taken place between Charlotte and the Prince on that long afternoon in the inn at Gloucester. The recent BBC television version of the novel, as I have already observed, admirable as it is, fundamentally perjures the novel. It shows Charlotte and the Prince making love in their room in the inn at Gloucester. The novel James wrote depends on keeping whether or not that happened a forever unknowable secret.

The Other's Opacity: Figures for the Void

For James, human life, at least as it is represented in *The Golden Bowl*, takes place as a series of face-to-face encounters with one other person, usually in the absence of anyone else. The novel proceeds, for the most part, through intense, slow-motion tête-à-têtes of two of the characters at a time, the Prince with Fanny, Fanny with her husband or with Maggie, Maggie with her father, the Prince with Charlotte, Maggie with the Prince, Charlotte with Maggie, and so on, in an excruciating rotation, as each "case" is manifested and interrogated in turn. Each encounter is excruciating because each is usually in one way or another painful. Each encounter is a kind of duel to the death. Moreover, each is presented in such detail, rendered with such subtlety of nuance and commentating embroidery, and in such a retarded tempo, that all the reader's patience and hermeneutic skill is required to follow a given scene. The reader must not miss a single detail or fail to interrogate a single figure or phrase, on pain of not being a responsible reader.

James stresses in the preface to the New York Edition, as I have shown, the way he has been true in *The Golden Bowl* to his inveterate habit of indirect presentation. He has eschewed the "mere muffled majesty of irresponsible authorship." He has, instead, presented the action through the consciousness of one or another of the embroiled and responsible characters. The characters' consciousnesses are registered in the narrator's free indirect discourse. These characters are both witnesses and interpreters of the action. They thereby serve as the reader's delegate, or vicar. In *The Golden Bowl*, as I have noted, the first half (books one through three) is presented, for the most part, through the Prince's eyes, the second half (books four to six) primarily through what Maggie sees and knows or thinks she knows. This mode of narration is the predominant one, but it is in contrapuntal conflict with a scenic method that presents the face-to-face dialogues of the characters two by two, often with a minimum of commentary. The latter mode of presentation is a dramatic exemplification of my claim that for James moral life transpires in private encounters of two persons with one another.

The limitation to a single "point of view" in each half of the novel is not total. The Prince is not present, he cannot in principle be present, in the section in which the narrator presents for the first and last time the inner consciousness and nature of Adam Verver, though this happens in the Prince's section, nor is he present at the midnight colloquies of Fanny Assingham and her husband, which are so important as models for the reader's efforts at responsible evaluation and understanding. Nor can the Prince be present when Maggie and her father have the fateful discussion that leads to Adam's marriage to Charlotte. Nor can Maggie be present, in the second half, any more than the Prince can in the first, at the endlessly renewed and iterative colloquies between Fanny and her husband, as they go over and over their understanding of the situation. These colloquies are part of what Maggie does not know, but the reader does.

The formal expression of the rhythmic counterpoint in *The Golden Bowl* between James's two dominant modes of representation, the scenic and the perspectival, is the juxtaposition of presentation by way of more or less uninterpreted dialogue and presentation in free indirect discourse. More specifically, it is the juxtaposition of passages adorned by some of James's most baroque extended metaphors for consciousness, or for how things seemed to a consciousness, with stichomythic passages in which the action goes forward, if it does go forward, by way of the exact repetition by one character of what the other character has just said. These modes are not opposites but complementary ways to represent the "clear matter" of the story. Both are authorized, and yet not authorized, by that "matter." They are authorized in the sense that they are valid modes of representation. They are unauthorized in the sense that the matter does not, apparently, legislate just these figures or just these dialogical interchanges. Each mode is an odd form of catachresis—the arbitrary, performative representation of something for which no literal representation exists. Let me exemplify and interrogate the way these two methods of representation work.

One of the most extravagant exploitations of the scenic method in *The Golden Bowl* recalls the starkness of unadorned dialogue in *The Awkward Age*. It comes near the end of the novel, in the last intimate colloquy between Fanny and Maggie. I give only the last part of the interchange, the part that ends the chapter, but I must cite enough to show the odd effect of the repetitions and the complete lack of the other major representational resource in the novel, presentation in free indirect discourse of the interior of a character's consciousness. What is given is only what any detached spectator might have seen and heard. The narrative voice, for inscrutable purposes of its own, almost completely abrogates its ability and right to "go behind":

> And Mrs. Assingham, emboldened, smiled. "So he knows—?"
> But Maggie hung back. "Amerigo—?" After which, however, she blushed—to her companion's recognition.
> "Your father. He knows what *you* know? I mean," Fanny faltered— "well, how much does he know?" Maggie's silence and Maggie's eyes had in fact arrested the push of the question—which for a decent consistency she couldn't yet quite abandon. "What I should rather say is does he know how much?" She found it still awkward. "How much, I mean, they did. How far"—she touched it up—"they went."
> Maggie had waited, but only with a question. "Do you think he does?"
> "Know at least something? Oh about *him* I can't think. He's beyond me," said Fanny Assingham.
> "Then do yourself know?"
> "How much—?"
> "How much."
> "How far—?"
> "How far."
> Fanny had appeared to wish to make sure, but there was something she remembered—remembered in time and even with a smile. "I've told you before that I know absolutely nothing."

"Well—that's what *I* know," said the Princess.

Her friend again hesitated. "Then nobody knows—? I mean," Mrs. Assingham explained, "how much your father does."

Oh Maggie showed she understood. "Nobody."

"Not—a little—Charlotte?"

"A little?" the Princess echoed. "To know anything would be, for her, to know enough."

"And she doesn't know anything?"

"If she did," Maggie answered, "Amerigo would."

"And that's just it—that he doesn't?"

"That's just it," said the Princess profoundly.

On which Mrs. Assingham reflected. "Then how is Charlotte so held?"

"Just *by* that."

"By her ignorance?"

"By her ignorance."

Fanny wondered. "A torment—?"

"A torment," said Maggie with tears in her eyes.

Her companion a moment watched them. "But the Prince then—?"

"How *he's* held?" Maggie asked.

"How *he's* held."

"Oh I can't tell you that!" And the Princess again broke off. (24:334–36)

She can't tell Fanny that, presumably, because it has to do with the intimacy between her and Amerigo. Maggie has vanquished Charlotte by bringing him to replace his sexual tie to Charlotte with his sexual tie to her, so that at the very end of the novel he says to Maggie, in response to her asking whether he sees how Charlotte's being "splendid" is their help, "I see nothing but *you*" (24:367). I have already quoted this, but must cite it again here, in this new context. The reader will see (and feel) the odd effect of the repetitions and the absence of "going behind" in the long passage quoted above. Here, as in so many other cases in this novel, one character repeats exactly or almost exactly what his or her interlocutor has said. This isolates the words for the reader's inspection, as though they were free for a moment from any context or referential vector and allowed to function with a naked verbal force. The words, like the adjectives the characters apply to one another, are, by this procedure of repetition and reduction to the simplest syntactic expression, given a performative as opposed to constative function. They posit the terms in which the imaginary people and events of the novel are to be understood. The passage I have cited sounds somewhat like one of the language games in Wittgenstein's *Philosophical Investigations*. These games invent an artificial language that consists in only a handful of words and permissible locutions such as "Bring me a slab."[8] A word is highlighted by being repeated. In another dialogue, for example, the final one between Maggie and Charlotte, Charlotte says, "I'm tired—!" and Maggie answers, " 'Tired'—?" (24:313). The repetition almost empties the word of meaning. It becomes a word in the dictionary, a dead word. This word might be used in any number of different ways, but is not used verifiably in any one single way here. Nevertheless, the word has a power of resurrection. It resurrects the people who use it or to whom it is applied as different from what they were before the word was used. In this scene, Maggie is aware that she has "done it all." She has, that is, brought her father, without ever saying anything explicit about her grievance, to take Charlotte back for good to American City. She has done it all by using words, interrogative intonations, and gestures in ways that coerce the others to behave in the way she wants. In the case of the longer passage quoted above, the key word is *know*. The whole interchange focuses on the question of how much each of the main characters, including Fanny, knows or is willing to say he or she knows about "how far" the Prince and Charlotte have gone. *Know* is a crucial word throughout *The Golden Bowl*. By exploring various ways in which the word can be used, this dialogue singles out the way saying "I know absolutely nothing" can be an effective speech act, the way knowing is deprived of force if the one who knows can get away with denying that he or she knows. In a sense, the passage is a reflection on the performative rhetoric of the novel itself. The novel has raised ghosts through the naked power of language and has made the reader believe in people and actions that have absolutely no reality outside that conferred on them by the narrative voice. In a similar way, the characters can, more or less, make something vanish by denying knowledge of it.

A distinctive feature of the other chief mode of presentation, free indirect discourse, is the exuberant and extravagant use of tropes to aid the representation of an individual inner consciousness in its transactions with other consciousnesses. The consciousness of the other is, for James, in principle at least, opaque, never to be known directly, only to be inferred from external audible, visible, or even tangible signs. Some of the peculiarities of this mode of presentation have already been identified in the chapter on *The Wings of the Dove*, but their configurations, functions, and ways of working are somewhat different in *The Golden Bowl*. In both cases an extravagant and somewhat obscure figure gives its title to the novel. No real dove is to be found in *Wings*, however, whereas the golden bowl is a substantial object with a complex role to play on the first mimetic level of

The Golden Bowl. In neither novel do the strings of tropes make a pattern, a discernible subtext that has its own coherence. In both novels the figures go all the way from a brief phrase to an amply extended trope. Those in *The Golden Bowl* seem, if anything, more extended and baroque in their ornamentation than those in *The Wings of the Dove*. They stick in the mind as precious clues to what is going on.

In both novels many, but not all, of the tropes indicate a basic undecidability in free indirect discourse. It is often, but not always, impossible to tell whether the figure is invented by the character as a trope for his or her state of mind or whether it is attributed to the character's wordless state of mind by the narrative voice. This would be a way of getting something wordless worded and so communicable to another, here, the reader. A brief example of this uncertainty is a figure given for Maggie's sense of obligation to Amerigo for not having interfered in her close intimacy with her father, not, at least, until Charlotte came into the picture: "What she had gone on owing him for this mounted up again to her eyes like a column of figures—or call it even if one would a house of cards; it was her father's wonderful act that had tipped the house down and made the sum wrong" (24:81). It is not clear whether these are Maggie's tropes or the narrator's, though they are most probably the latter's. In either case, these tropes earn the right to be called catachreses. They do not substitute for some "literal" name for the state of mind in question, but are the only way that state of mind can be, or at any rate is, named by the narrative voice. The reader does not have access to any other language that might be used to "interpret" the trope. The trope is all we are given at that particular moment in the narration. That means that the tropes are performative as well as catachrestic. They are performative catachreses. They bring into existence the states of mind they name. They wave a magic wand and import the wordless, infinitely private and isolated elements of consciousness into a public realm of socially interchanged language where those elements can now be read by others, for example, by other characters, if they learn them, but most of all by the reader. These catachreses are primary data in the novel, not secondary adornments. They are the way the elements they name exist.

Some of these figures, such as the reference to Poe's *A. Gordon Pym*, discussed below, are explicitly reported by the narrative voice as used by the character himself or herself to express a certain state of mind. In the case of the reference to Poe, this is Prince Amerigo's anxiety at not being able to understand the Anglo-Saxons on whom his prosperity and happiness depend. Some figures are explicitly proffered by one character as a way of explaining his or her feelings to another character. When Amerigo asks his bride-to-be whether "You do believe I'm not a hypocrite? You recognize that I don't lie nor dissemble nor deceive? Is *that* water-tight?" (23:15), he is blatantly lying or, rather, blatantly asking Maggie to believe a lie. Maggie, in her innocence, asserts that she believes he doesn't lie or dissemble or deceive. She says this by picking up Amerigo's word *water-tight*. She makes out of the word a hyperbolic metaphor from her repertoire of "images . . . that were drawn from steamers and trains, from a familiarity with 'lines,' a command of 'own' cars, from an experience of continents and seas, that he was unable yet to emulate" (23:15). She says, "Water-tight—the biggest compartment of all? Why it's the best cabin and the main deck and the engine-room and the steward's pantry! It's the ship itself—it's the whole line. It's the captain's table and all one's luggage—one's reading for the trip" (23:15). In view of what happened to the supposedly unsinkable *Titanic* a few years later, this figure has a retrospectively ominous aspect, prophesying the doom of Maggie's misplaced confidence in her fiancé's probity.

A good bit later in the novel, the way the Prince, now Maggie's husband, is slowly learning to understand the English and Americans is expressed in a figure that is explicitly attributed to Fanny Assingham: "she [Maggie] was able to live more or less in the light of the fact expressed so lucidly by their common comforter [Fanny as comforter of both Maggie and Amerigo]—the fact that the Prince was saving up, for some very mysterious but very fine eventual purpose, all the wisdom, all the answers to his questions, all the impressions and generalizations he gathered; putting them away and packing them down because he wanted his great gun to be loaded to the brim the day he should decide to fire it off" (24:163).

An extended figure toward the end of the first volume expresses Bob Assingham's rescue of his wife by listening to her and sympathizing with her in the second of their midnight discussions. It is impossible, I believe, to be sure whether this is Bob's figure or one projected by the narrative voice. Bob is beginning to share in his wife's sense of responsibility and her sense of how complex the situation of the four main characters is, her "consciousness of deep waters" (23:366). That phrase is elaborately developed in the paragraph that follows. The trope may be Bob's own, but it looks to me more likely to be a figure elaborated by the narrative voice. The reader cannot tell for certain, in a striking confirmation of the principle that free indirect discourse is intrinsically undecidable, if an explicit assignation of the language's source is not given:

His present position, clearly, was that of seeing her in the center of her sheet of dark water, and of wondering if her actual mute gaze at him didn't perhaps mean that her planks *were* now parting. He held himself so ready that it was quite as if the inward man had pulled off coat and waistcoat. Before he had plunged, however—that is before he had uttered a question—he saw, not without relief, that she was making for land. He watched her steadily paddle, always a little nearer, and at last he felt her boat bump. The bump was distinct, and in fact she stepped ashore. "We were all wrong. There's nothing."

"Nothing—?" It was like giving her his hand up the bank. (23:366)

The effect of this passage is a little weird. Surely no real boat is present, nor is Fanny in one, nor does her husband help her ashore, but the complex and subtle transaction between Fanny and Bob exists only in this figurative notation of it by the narrative voice.

The second volume opens with what is probably the most extravagant and powerful of such figures, if we except the imputation of symbolic or displaced meaning to things that exist on the first level of the narration, such as the golden bowl or the bridge game that Fanny, Charlotte, Adam, and Bob Assingham play on one memorable evening at Matcham. The bridge game is clearly a figure for the complex relations among the characters at that point, for the way they are playing an elaborate social game by rules and conventions, but are nevertheless pitted against one another. Maggie, as nonplaying spectator of the game, realizes that she can, by a word, a word telling the truth of her suspicions about Amerigo and Charlotte, destroy the ordered serenity of the game and of the social conventions that have kept their family life apparently serene.

The extended figure that opens the novel's second volume, however, is the narrative voice's elaborate way of expressing the way Maggie has come to suspect that something secret and very wrong is going on between her husband and her stepmother. The passage goes on for several pages. It is too long to quote here. It comes just before Maggie confronts her husband when he returns so late from his presumed assignation with Charlotte. It figures the relation she now has to her husband, her father, and her stepmother. Here the narrator for once and quite exceptionally speaks of himself (itself) as an "I" and takes personal responsibility for the figures: "might I so far multiply my metaphors" (24:7). Among a cascade of incoherent figures proffered by the narrative voice, figures of a spaniel shaking water off after a plunge, of "the frightened but clinging young mother of an unlawful child" (24:7), of a timid crouching tigress, the narrator describes Maggie as feeling as if she were outside a "Mahometan mosque" or a "pagoda in her blooming garden" (24:4, 5). This pagoda has no doors or windows. It is entirely encased in shining porcelain tiles. The first tiny evidence Maggie has of the truth is expressed in a figure apparently invented by the narrative voice, not by Maggie, though it is impossible to be sure. The figure imagines her as knocking on the pagoda's tiles and getting a response from within: "She had knocked in short—though she could scarce have said whether for admission or for what; she had applied her hand to a cool smooth spot and had waited to see what would happen. Something *had* happened; it was as if a sound, at her touch, after a little, had come back to her from within; a sound sufficiently suggesting that her approach had been noted" (24:4).

The reader will "note" that all these figures express, not the isolated relation of a consciousness to itself in self-consciousness, but one character's sense of his or her relation to other consciousnesses, as it is expressed either by the character or by the narrative voice. A final example, already mentioned, will need to be discussed later. I mention it again here for its saliency and importance, also for the way it exemplifies the law that makes these catachreses figures not for an isolated subjectivity but for intersubjectivity. The passage also exemplifies the degree to which the right understanding of these tropes—some brief, some extended—that punctuate the verbal texture of the novel is crucial to any responsible reading of it. Maggie figures to herself the way she is suddenly detaching herself from the game they are all collectively playing as her decision to jump off the coach they have all been riding on together. She has a moment before been figured as one of the coach's wheels. The figure has a dreamlike, hallucinatory quality, as consciousness often does for itself at moments of great stress or crisis: "She had seen herself at last, in the picture she was studying, suddenly jump from the coach; whereupon, frankly, with the wonder of the sight, her eyes opened wider and her heart stood still for a moment. She looked at the person so acting as if this person were somebody else, waiting with intensity to see what would follow" (24:24).

The "omniscient" narrator is the presiding consciousness that makes plausible the breaks in the consistency of James's formal limitation in the first part to what the Prince can know, in the second part to what the Princess can know or think she knows. In these interludes the narrator leaves Amerigo or Maggie to enter Adam's mind or to report dialogue between the Assinghams that neither primary consciousness was present to hear. I put "omniscient" in quotation marks because the narrator's omniscience is curiously limited. He, she, or "it," since the narrator is remarkably unindividualized, what James in the preface calls a "creative power. . . . so veiled and disembodied" (23:v), can in principle enter into the minds of all of the characters at any time, but in practice can know them only one at a time. This, as I have shown, is also the case in *The Wings of the Dove*. It is better, given the narrative voice's limitations, to follow Nicholas Royle and call it a telepathic power rather than a godlike omniscience.[9] It is an absolute principle, in *The Golden Bowl*, that each person has no direct access to the mind of another person. It is a radical and irremediable ignorance. This nonknowledge is given an early dramatic expression near the beginning of the novel. There the narrative voice, speaking in free indirect discourse for the Prince, tells us that he has been made extremely uneasy by his inability to fathom the motives of the Americans who have just, so to speak, bought him as another object of price for their collection. This uneasiness at an inveterate ignorance is expressed in a figure drawn from Poe's *The Narrative of Arthur Gordon Pym*, which Amerigo, somewhat implausibly, is said to have read. The figure universalizes Amerigo's nonknowledge. Another person is, for the characters in *The Golden Bowl*, wholly other, wholly impenetrable. One can only read the signs, for example the words and facial expressions of the other. One can then guess on that basis, and then believe one has it right, in a blind speech act, implicit or explicit, such as the tacit "I believe you" that may be uttered when the other says "I love you":

> These things [the Prince thinks to himself], the motives of such people were obscure—a little alarmingly so; they contributed to that element of the impenetrable which alone slightly qualified his sense of his good fortune. He remembered to have read as a boy a wonderful tale by Allan Poe, his prospective wife's countryman—which was a thing to show, by the way, what imagination Americans *could* have: the story of the shipwrecked Gordon Pym, who, drifting in a small boat further toward the North Pole—or was it the South?—than any one had ever done, found at a given moment before him a thickness of white air that was like a dazzling curtain of light, concealing as darkness conceals, yet of the color of milk or of snow. There were some moments when he felt his own boat move upon some such mystery. The state of mind of his new friends, including Mrs. Assingham herself, had resemblances to a great white curtain. He had never known curtains but as purple even to blackness—but as producing where they hung a darkness intended and ominous. When they were so disposed as to shelter surprises the surprises were apt to be shocks. (23:22–23)

The reader will remember that the climax of Pym's experience is the confrontation of a giant human figure in the dazzling curtain of white

light. Ignorance gives rise to an inveterate prosopopoeia, the projection of
a human shape on the white veil, just as Prince Amerigo must assume that
human personalities somehow like his own are hidden behind the enigmatic appearances of his "new friends." The vision of the white figure
coincides with Pym's approach to the immense vortex of waterfall that
will, perhaps, sweep him to his doom: "And now we rushed into the embrace of the cataract, where a chasm threw itself open to receive us. But
there arose in our pathway a shrouded human figure, very far larger in its
proportions than any dweller among men. And the hue of the skin of the
figure was of the perfect whiteness of the snow."[10] Will the white figure
save them from the cataract or hurry them to their death? Since Poe's
novel stops just there, what happens next can never be known. James's
novel, however, shows just what doom awaits Prince Amerigo, a doom
that he so presciently, obscurely, and anxiously foresees.

The narrator, by the terms of James's apparently arbitrary but implaca-
bly binding conventions of narration, is forced to share Amerigo's ignorance. Whenever "it," the narrative voice and power, enters into the mind
and feelings of a given character, it must endure and report that character's
limitations and lack of insight. The rule is that the narrator can only be
within one character at a time. When the narrator is within the Prince, all
the other characters are opaque not only to the Prince but also to the
narrative voice. Only in this way can the narration do justice to the
Prince's situation or to that of any of the other characters who become
from time to time the perspective center. This justifies and demands what
I have just called a somewhat arbitrary convention and shows its necessity.

The reader, in an odd way, is subject to similar limitations. The narrative voice, as I have said, is clairvoyant, telepathic. It can enter, if it wishes,
into the minds and feelings of any of the characters at any time, though
only one at a time. He or it, however, does not choose to give a complete
repertoire of what all the characters were thinking and feeling at all times
of the major action. The reader is forced to share the Prince's ignorance
in the first half, Maggie's ignorance in the second half. The reader too is
forced to read, as the Prince or Maggie do, the signs of behavior, gesture,
and speech in those who are other to whatever perspective is at a given
moment dominant. The reader too must take responsibility, as Fanny and
ultimately even the Colonel do, for the interpretations he or she formulates.

Oddest of all, however, is the reader's ignorance of what James calls, in
the preface, the "clear matter of the tale," the broad expanse of untrodden
snow, in his figure, that pre-exists the words of the novel. The latter are

imaged as tracks across the snow. This snowfield remains still there after the novel is written. James refers to it for validation of his work when he re-reads or, as he puts it, re-visions, his novel in order to write the preface. James, and presumably his delegate, the narrative voice, can refer to that clear matter, the snowfield, to compare it to the finished novel and measure the adequacy of the latter. The reader, as I observed earlier, is unable ever to do that. He or she is forced to take the narrator's word for it, and James's word in the preface. For the reader it is a matter or belief, not of knowledge, since he or she can never know, whereas the narrator, the reader believes, knows.

The reader is condemned to an invincible ignorance that is like that of the characters in their inability to have other than an indirect and never verifiable access to the minds and feelings of others. They too must believe rather than know. Maggie has only indirect knowledge of her husband's infidelity. Fanny's elaborate hermeneutical exegeses are so many castles in the air built of her readings of the data she is given, just as the reader has nothing to go on but the words James wrote, plus the extremely dubious evidence of James's reading of his own work in the preface. I say extremely dubious because James is by no means an innocent and uninvolved witness. He may have hidden reasons to put the reader on a false scent. It would be a naïve reader, to say the least, who would blithely take James's say-so as the last word about the novel.

I have said that the ethical life, for James, is made up of solitary confrontations of one person with one other person. The uniqueness and limitless responsibility of this face to face is signaled by the absence of any third person. A third person or witness would stand for the whole community or society, with its requirement that what I decide or do be generalizable in words and able to be made public. One might for convenience call the solitary confrontation "ethical," the responsibility to others within a community "moral."

A curious and, when you think of it, disquieting breaking of this law is, however, universal in *The Golden Bowl*. However alone Maggie and her father are when they "slope," that is, sneak away from their guests to have a private conversation on a secluded bench in the grounds of Fawns, Adam's palatial country house, there *is* a third "person" present as witness and judge: the narrator. By way of the narrator, the reader is also made present to each private pas de deux of the characters. The reader is thereby given the responsibility to see, to understand, and to judge in her or his turn. This makes it possible for me to ask and, at my peril, to answer, my questions: "Did Maggie do right? Did she act justly? Was her perjury an efficacious speech act? Was it 'felicitous'?"

This ghostly, unseen narrative presence may be thought of in either of two ways. On the one hand, since the narrative voice speaks in the past tense, it can be thought of as raising the ghosts, by magic, conjuring speech acts, of persons and events that have already occurred at some indeterminate time in the past. They are still going on happening interminably, over and over, in some place of otherness and virtuality. They remain there, ready to be invoked again by the narrative voice or by any reader of the novel. James figures this ghostly virtuality in the preface as the untrodden snow that is the eternally pre-existing "matter of the tale." This matter is something not dependent on the author for its existence, though it is very much dependent on him for getting represented in words and thereby made publicly available to all who slow down to read. As an advocate of slow reading, I put it this way to vary the old saying: "all who run may read."

The temporal and spatial placement of the narrative voice is unidentifiable. It speaks from a "now" and "here" that are everywhere and nowhere, every when and no when. That place without place and time without time become actualized anew in the here and now of the reading, whenever the novel is picked up by someone and read again, from the first sentence ("The Prince had always liked his London, when it had come to him"; 23:3) to the last three, with their naming of the emotions Aristotle said were appropriate for tragedy: " ' "See"? I see nothing but *you*.' And the truth of it had with this force after a moment so strangely lighted his eyes that as for pity and dread of them she buried her own in his breast" (24:369). The characters are revenants that the narrative voice has called up by the magic performatives of narrating language: "Let Prince Amerigo and the rest rise up and appear before the reader's eyes through the power of my words."

On the other hand, if you think of the narrating presence from the perspective of the characters, it is as if each of them were haunted by a ghostly, invisible presence. They are wholly unaware of this spectator. This clairvoyant consciousness and power of articulation steals their most secret thoughts and feelings. It is present at their most private conversations. It makes those privacies public by turning them into language where anyone who reads may see, know, and judge them. From the perspective of whichever dimension is taken to be real, the other is a ghost.

The effect of this witnessing is dramatized or allegorized in the novel in the one case in which a third person is literally present to overhear a private conversation. The shopkeeper in the curiosity shop where Charlotte and the Prince discover the golden bowl is present while the latter discuss, speaking in Italian so they will not be understood, whether either can give a gift to the other. The Prince refuses the bowl as a wedding gift from Charlotte because he can see it has a hidden flaw, "a crack" (23:119). Charlotte, as I remarked earlier, refuses the gift or *ricordo* the Prince offers to buy her because, as she says, since their liaison has been secret, unacknowledged by the world, illicit, recorded in no transmissible legend, it would be a sign without referent, a remembrance of nothing: "A ricordo from you—from you to me—," she says, "is a ricordo of nothing. It has no reference" (23:108). A moment later she says: "You don't refer. . . . *I* refer" (23:109). She presumably means by this that since he refuses to acknowledge the obligation to her that results from the way she has given herself to him, nothing he can say or do, for example, by giving her a *ricordo* of their time together, will refer to anything real, whereas she is prepared to acknowledge her relation to him and refer to it. She does that in their first talk alone together, just a few days before his marriage to Maggie, in a passage already cited. She tells Amerigo that she just wants him to hear her speak, not even necessarily to understand what she says. Her words will remain as material evidence, as they echo against the trees in the park as well as in the ears of both Charlotte and the Prince, even though he gives no sign of having heard. Her words are a permanent *ricordo*. They are testimony to the way she has given herself to him and has asked nothing in return. They refer to that in the most provoking way.

All this transaction, this uneven giving and taking not just of external signs, *ricordos*, but of the whole substance of the self, takes place, so Charlotte and the Prince think, in private and without witnesses. It is, however, of course overheard by the ghostly narrating presence. Their conversation in the shop when they consider buying the golden bowl is also, it turns out, overheard by the shopkeeper. He, unexpectedly, understands and speaks Italian perfectly. This literal witness, as opposed to the spectral, virtual one of the narrator, brings it about later, when Maggie buys the bowl for her father, that she gets, as she thinks, the first indubitable, material evidence of her husband's infidelity. That bearing witness is initiated by the photographs of Charlotte and the Prince the shopkeeper sees and recognizes in Maggie's house. What are photographs but specters, revenants from the past, congealed, frozen in a permanent resurrection? Of course, in itself the bowl is not evidence of anything. It has to be endowed by a human performative act with symbolic or semiotic value in order to become a sign, mute testimony of Charlotte and the Prince's intimacy.

What seems to Maggie her indubitable knowledge precipitates her actions, including her perjury. That perjury brings about the denouement of the novel. As Colonel Assingham, Fanny's husband, says, "Murder will out," to which Fanny answers, "Murder will—but this isn't murder. Quite the contrary perhaps!" (24:134), meaning, I suppose that it is the act that may give birth to new life. This novel, like so many of James's works, presupposes a prior illicit sexual relation that has occurred before the novel begins. This past event is the fundamental precondition of everything that happens during the part of the story that the novel *does* narrate. All the characters are haunted by the ghost of a prior illicit conjugation or copulation. The law of this situation might be expressed by saying "Adultery (or fornication) will out." Always some witness or evidence exists. Sooner or later the witness, the evidence, will come forth. The ghosts will return. A ghost never dies, just as the "clear matter" of James's novel remains somewhere, in what Maurice Blanchot calls "literary space," ready to be revisited when James compares what he has written with that "matter."

It is within the context of this unalterable set of givens that Maggie must make her decision about what to do when she comes to believe she knows her husband and her stepmother are committing adultery. In order to understand the purport and force of what she does, however, it will first be necessary to understand better the conditions of ignorance, accompanied, paradoxically, by responsibility, under which all the characters in *The Golden Bowl* live.

Knowledge and Belief: What Maggie Knew

A tense conversation, like a duel in dialogue, between Maggie and Fanny Assingham is initiated when Maggie suddenly asks Fanny, one afternoon when they are alone in Maggie's house, "What awfulness, in heaven's name, is there between them? What do you believe, what do you *know*?" (24:107). *Believe* and *know*, with their cognates, are key words in *The Golden Bowl*. They appear again and again in different forms. The reader will see the distinction. An assertion of knowledge is constative. It is based on verifiable evidence. It is provably right or wrong. An assertion of belief is performative. Belief is faith in things unseen, therefore not verifiable one way or the other. Maggie asks Fanny whether she believes Charlotte and Amerigo are lovers, then changes that in the next moment to a radically different question, "What do you *know* of their relation?"

In *The Golden Bowl*, the characters have no direct knowledge of what others are thinking and feeling. They can only make inferences on the basis of signs, that is, on the basis of what the others say, what their words, eyes, faces, and gestures reveal, or appear to reveal. In consequence, knowledge is impossible in the area where knowledge is most necessary and desired. The entire drama of the novel's action follows from this unhappy limitation, from the opacity of the other's heart. This means that the statements "I know nothing" and "We know nothing on earth," said by Maggie and by Fanny and her husband (cited as epigraphs to this chapter), have a curious status as utterances. In one sense they are perfectly true, since Fanny and Bob can say truthfully that they have not seen Amerigo's and Charlotte's adultery with their own eyes, any more than the narrative voice has told us of it in so many words. Maggie can say truthfully that she does not know how much her father knows of the double infidelity of Amerigo and Charlotte. The heart of another is a dark forest, a forest that no other person can enter.

This impenetrable darkness behind a white curtain is one justification for the Prince's sinister aphorism, said to Maggie toward the end of the novel. Maggie says, apropos of Charlotte's suffering, "I see it's *always* terrible for women," to which the Prince replies, "Everything's terrible, cara—in the heart of man" (24:349). This is another example of the repetition that highlights a word. Maggie says "terrible" and the Prince answers "terrible." Their two sentences, however, by no means say the same thing. Maggie's "I see it's *always* terrible for women" is an outcry against invidious gender roles in the society James depicts in *The Golden Bowl*. These have left Charlotte to live as a poor gentlewoman helpless to avoid her fate either of no marriage at all or a loveless marriage for money and social status. The same gender placement has left Maggie with the responsibility to act with great cruelty to Charlotte if she is to save her marriage. It is terrible for both of them. The Prince's response, "Everything's terrible, cara—in the heart of man," with its ironic address to the wife he has betrayed as "cara [dear]," generalizes beyond Maggie's feminist outcry to say that all humankind, men and women alike, live lives of quiet, or not so quiet, desperation. All secretly suffer from some irremediable lack that transcends gender, class, and national distinctions. In effect Amerigo is saying, "I am suffering too, as much as Charlotte or you. So is Adam Verver suffering."

Taking either of these two forceful aphorisms as the key to the novel, like taking Hamlet's "Readiness is all" (5.2. 224) or Edgar's "Ripeness is all," in *King Lear* (5.2.11), as keys to their plays, produces two strikingly

different novels, depending on which one you take to be salient. It is impossible to be sure which one the narrative voice endorses. The novel as a
whole would support either reading. The reader is left to see the novel as
hovering between these two possibilities, however unsatisfactory it is not
to be able to decide between them without taking responsibility oneself,
as reader, for the choice. I lean, myself, toward the feminist reading. The
novel focuses more narrowly on the plights of Maggie and Charlotte as
women in a patriarchal society. I will remember longest the inward projection toward the end of the novel of Charlotte's "shriek of a soul in pain"
(24:292), "the voice . . . of a creature in anguish" (24:294). It is as though
she were in purgatory, like the ghost of Hamlet's father. Charlotte's suffering is said to remind Maggie of two noble tragic precursors: "There
came to her confusedly some echo of an ancient fable—some vision of Io
goaded by the gadfly or of Ariadne roaming the lone sea-strand" (24:307).
I shall also remember longest Maggie's corresponding pain through all
her part of the novel, the second half, as well as her extreme stratagems to
take possession of her life, to make her declaration of independence, using
the limited freedom her surrounding society permits her. The remembrance of these two pains, testifying that it's always terrible for women,
remains with me longer than the corresponding suffering of Amerigo and
Adam. All these pains, like haunting ghosts, stay safely enclosed, I hope,
within the covers of the various copies of *The Golden Bowl* on my shelves.

If Charlotte's silent shriek, her cry as of a soul in pain, recalls the ghost
of Hamlet's father and, behind that, Dante's *Inferno* or *Purgatorio*, why Io,
why Ariadne? Why does James resurrect at just these moments these two
heroines from Greek myth, calling them, so to speak, back from the dead?
Io was a nymph raped by Zeus in the form of a cloud. "Tenuitque fugam,
rapuitque pudorem," says Ovid (*Metamorphoses*, 1:600). The Latin is much
more rapid, economical, and powerfully laconic than Mary M. Innes's
translation: "Then he halted the maiden's flight, and robbed her of her
maidenhood."[11] Io was then transformed by jealous Hera into a heifer. As
if that were not enough, she was then tormented and driven from place to
place by a gadfly sent from Hera. In a similar way jealous Maggie (though
she refuses that adjective) torments Charlotte by keeping her ignorant and
by exiling her from the Prince. Ovid, whom I have cited, tells Io's story in
the *Metamorphoses*, 1:582–750. Aeschylus earlier, in another tongue, had,
as Gerard Manley Hopkins observes, made repeated references to Io and
the gadfly as a figurative underthought, counterpoint, or echo of the main
action in his *The Supplants*.[12] Earlier, in Aeschylus's *Prometheus Bound*

(561–887), Io, pursued by the gadfly, comes to Prometheus chained to his rock. Prometheus tells her story in retrospect and in prophecy.

Ovid tells Ariadne's story too, though briefly (*Metamorphoses*, 8:169–81). Just as Prince Amerigo has abandoned Charlotte, so Theseus abandoned Ariadne on the island of Naxos, though she had helped him kill the monster, half man, half bull, offspring of Pasiphae's unnatural love, hidden in the Daedalean labyrinth. Bacchus rescued Ariadne as she lamented on the lone seastrand. "Desertae, et multa querenti, / Amplexus et opem Liber tulit" (8:176–77), as Ovid puts it with characteristic brevity, using a Latin name (Liber) for Dionysus or Bacchus: "Deserted and lamenting bitterly, Bacchus brought her an embrace and help." No such rescue is likely for Charlotte, who seems doomed to lament interminably and in vain on the lone seastrand of the Pacific coast, where I am at this moment writing these words.

James's allusions to Io and Ariadne make *The Golden Bowl* a repetition with a difference, a "confused echo" of these myths, to borrow Gerard Manley Hopkins's phrase describing Io's presence in Aeschylus's *The Suppliants*. It is as though Io and Ariadne had been waiting somewhere to be conjured into a spectral presence as the "underthought" of this modern novel about European and American imperialism, about the plight of women under bourgeois capitalism, and about the power of lying speech acts to make something happen. Charlotte is a repetition of Io and of Ariadne, just as the myths of Io and Ariadne echo one another, though with many differences. What Hopkins called "aftering," "over and overing," that is, repetition with a difference, is, he said, necessary to detach an "inscape," some underlying structural principle, whether of art or nature, and make it perceptible.[13]

Such repetition, which is always a resurrection of the dead as dead, necessarily depends on some technical or technological means of copying, storage, and retrieval. From cuneiform scratched on baked clay tablets, through various forms of writing on papyrus, parchment, or paper, up to printing, photography, telegraph. telephone, gramophone, magnetic tape recordings, down to our present day CDs, videotapes, floppies, Zip cartridges, and hard disks, some mechanical means of storage and retrieval is necessary. These devices store the dead as dead, but allow them to be resurrected interminably every time a book is read, a CD played, a file called back from hard disk storage, just as James has here recalled Io and Ariadne from wherever it is that they tarry, and just as we bring back the spectral presences of Maggie, Charlotte, Amerigo, Adam, Fanny, and Bob whenever we read *The Golden Bowl*. The section of Joyce's *Ulysses* about the newspaper office and the printing press is called "Aeolus." It is preceded by "Hades," in which Bloom's remembrance of the dead is implicitly parallel to Joyce's recording in *Ulysses*, where all who read may resurrect them, of all those events of Bloomsday (June 16, 1904). That day is now (February 13, 1999), as I write this, receding moment by moment toward being a century in the past, but *Ulysses*, so far, remains. Derrida's wonderful book about Joyce is called *Ulysse Gramophone*, taking its cue from the passage in which Bloom thinks of the gramophone as a way to raise the dead: "Besides how could you remember everybody? Eyes, walk, voice. Well, the voice, yes: gramophone. Have a gramophone in every grave or keep it in the house. After dinner on a Sunday. Put on poor old greatgrandfather Kraahraark! Hellohellohello amawfullyglad kraark awfullygladaseeragain hellohello amarawf kopthsth. Remind you of the voice like the photograph reminds you of the face. Otherwise you couldn't remember the face after fifteen years, say."[14]

The figures in literary works, like everything else that can be stored in print, or on gramophone records, or today in some digital form, must first die, literally or figuratively, before they can become ghosts and enter the house of the dead, from which they can interminably be conjured forth again when the stored file is retrieved. One commodious room of that house is what Blanchot calls *l'espace littéraire*. That space swarms with literary apparitions. Ghosts never die, since they are already dead. As Derrida says in *Specters of Marx*, "un fantôme ne meurt jamais, il reste toujours à venir et à revenir."[15] Peggy Kamuf's translation raises the ghost again, this time in another language. What is translation but a double act, both exorcising ghosts and conjuring them? Kamuf translates Derrida's French as: "a ghost never dies, it remains always to come and to come-back."[16] The phantoms that inhabit all the books on all shelves can always be called up, conjured into the strange presence without presence they have for the living reader, as, for example, Charlotte, Maggie, and the others live without living as spectral "presences" when you or I read *The Golden Bowl*. They will remain as virtual revenants ready to be invoked again as long as a single copy of the novel or online version remains. Their possibility or virtuality does not even depend on the existence of any copies at all. All the novels and stories James did not live to write still remain somewhere as possibilities waiting to be born, just as do all the novels Dostoevsky endlessly projected in his extraordinarily creative imagination, and just as remain somewhere all the intervening chapters of *The Trial* Kafka did not write that would have been inserted between where he stopped and the last chapter he did write, and just as a ghost does not vanish entirely when it is exorcised, but waits somewhere to be raised again by the appropriate invocation.

Maggie's suffering, and Charlotte's too, derive in part from the impossibility of knowing for sure, the impossibility of entering into the solitary "terrible" at the heart of the other. Any system of justice depends not on knowledge but on belief ("beyond the shadow of a doubt"). Perhaps because of that uncertainty, any justice system works to punish some guilty ones and exonerate others. For all practical purposes, Fanny can tell from the evidence she has that Amerigo and Charlotte have, beyond the shadow of a doubt, renewed their liaison. The reader knows too, beyond the shadow of a doubt, just as Maggie knows of her husband's infidelity, partly from the damning mute testimony of the golden bowl, partly from Amerigo's momentary betraying expression when he returns from his tryst with Charlotte at Gloucester, and partly from the verbal testimony of the shopman who recognizes Amerigo's and Charlotte's photographs in Maggie's house and tells her of their visit to his shop just days before Amerigo's marriage to Maggie. Maggie knows also that her father must know, even though he has not given the slightest sign that he does. He apparently wants to keep intact the value of his investments in Amerigo and Charlotte, by far the most expensive art objects he has bought.

Much of the action of the second volume of the novel, Maggie's part, centers on the attempts of the various characters to find out for sure how much the others know, or think they know, in the teeth of their protestations of ignorance. Both the Prince and Charlotte are, it seems, kept in ignorance of how much Adam Verver knows. That is their torment, not knowing whether if he knows he will take revenge and just what form that revenge might take. Maggie thinks of Charlotte at Fawns "having gropingly to go on, always not knowing, and not knowing!" (24:202). At the end of the novel, just before Adam and Charlotte go back for good to American City, Amerigo proposes to Maggie that he should disabuse Charlotte. "I shall tell her I lied to her" (24:355), he says. He means he has mendaciously assured Charlotte that neither Maggie nor Adam knows of their affair. Maggie imperiously forbids him to say a word. Charlotte's proper punishment is not to know, not ever to know. Earlier, when Amerigo tries to find out from Maggie whether her father knows, in which case his marriage may be dished and he may be back in abject poverty again, Maggie taunts him. In response to his asking whether her father knows, assuring her that "I know nothing but what you tell me," she says, "Find out for yourself!" (24:203).

The fact that many of the characters, Fanny and Maggie at least, do, for all practical purposes, know, or believe firmly, however secretly, that they do know, means that when they say "I know nothing" or "We know nothing on earth," they are lying. They really do know, or think they know, just as Amerigo, if not Charlotte, comes to know, or firmly to believe that he knows, that they know. Their assertions are perjuries, like Maggie's assurance to Charlotte that she has nothing to complain of in her behavior, in response to Charlotte's assurance that she is not aware of having failed in her obligation in the slightest degree, or like Fanny and Bob's mutual oath, "We know nothing on earth," or like the perjury Maggie imagines the Prince to have committed by lying to Charlotte in the face of "her appeal to his honor" by assuring her Maggie and her father know nothing: "He'll simply, he'll insistently have lied" (24:218).

These mendacious perjuries, however, even if they are not believed, function as felicitous speech acts. They are utterances that make something happen, since other people are brought to act as if they believe them. They then establish a fictitious social game that can have real effects. This is the triumph achieved by Maggie's conscious perjury. It is a perjury of which the others are also conscious. Her lies are not vitiated in their effect by the knowledge the others have, or believe they have, that she is committing perjury. This triumph follows what might be called Maggie's declaration of independence. To that I turn now for an answer to the questions with which this chapter began. Did Maggie act justly, in tune with the right, by not deviating a hair's breadth into the truth? Just how is it that her speech act, so anomalous in every way, can nevertheless be described as, in J. L. Austin's sense of the word, felicitous?

Maggie's Declaration of Independence

Maggie has been trying to have her cake and eat it too, that is, she has been trying to retain her intimate relation to her father, developed during the long years since her mother died, while being "intensely married" to the Prince her father has bought for her. As I have said, the fixed intensity of her attachment to both is a given in the novel. It might even be argued that *The Golden Bowl* has a banal, or at any rate highly traditional, moral, the moral of the Grimm fairy tale "All-Kinds-of-Fur" or of the Book of Ruth in the Hebrew Bible. In order to grow up and be worthy to carry on the line of generations, young women must replace their fathers with their husbands and be willing to give up everything, even citizenship, associated with their childhood homes. They must be willing to say to their husbands, as Ruth the Moabite does to her Judaic mother-in-law, Naomi: "whither thou goest, I will go; and where thou lodgest, I will lodge, thy people shall be my people, and thy God my God" (Ruth 1:16). That Maggie already happens to be Catholic, because her mother was, is a convenient detail that solves a problem James might have had in making Maggie's marriage to Amerigo without "conversion" probable. Little is made of Maggie's change of citizenship or national allegiance. Nevertheless, Maggie, as the mother of Amerigo's son, the Principino, is at the end of the novel ready to fulfill her destiny as the wife of an Italian prince. She will be the means by which his family line is continued, just as Ruth the Moabite continued Boaz's Judaic line and thereby became the ancestress of David and, ultimately, of Jesus. The Principino is, in a manner of speaking, "the last of the Vespuccis," to alter the title of a James short story that also deals with an American girl's marriage to an Italian: "The Last of the Valerii."

It might seem that Maggie's responsibility is to accept passively her place as an object of exchange. She should play as best she can the new role assigned to her. Matters are not so simple, however. Just as Ruth the Moabite intervenes actively to bring about her marriage to Boaz of Bethlehem-Judah, so Maggie, at a certain moment, takes stock of her situation and acts decisively. Her situation is to know, or think she knows, that Amerigo is betraying her. He is "lying and dissembling and deceiving," as he asked her before their marriage to believe he has not and would not do. Her decisive act is figured not only in her knocking on the porcelain outer tiles of the great windowless, doorless pagoda and hearing a faint response from within, but also, more dramatically, in a passage already cited, as Maggie seeing herself in a hallucinatory vision jump suddenly from the coach that carries herself and her father, while being drawn by Charlotte and Amerigo. A moment before in her vision, the four were the four wheels of the coach, but the vision changes, as dreams do. Maggie divides herself into the one who acts and the one who self-consciously and reflectively watches that acting self act. Maggie wonders, the reader will remember, just what her other self will do. What she actually does is to dress up in her best new frock and wait for her husband to come home for dinner after his escapade with Charlotte. She does this rather than, as everyone has expected, wait with her father at her father's house for Charlotte and Amerigo to show up. She does this to elicit a sign from Amerigo, to see if he allows some evidence, however faint, of his guilt to escape. This is her knocking gently on the porcelain tiles. Her instigation works. Just for a moment, when Amerigo first enters the drawing room and finds her alone in her own house, Amerigo is *"visibly* uncertain—this was written in the face he for the first minute showed her" (24:15). That is sign enough, for Maggie: "while it lasted it had been written large" (ibid.). Amerigo's visible uncertainty is a sign to be read, like all the signs emitted by the others that each character must read.

Maggie's strategy thereafter is to behave so as to elicit more signs from Charlotte and Amerigo. At the same time she acts so as not by one iota to make a sign to her father that will testify to him that she knows, or that will force him to acknowledge that he knows and knows she knows. She also acts and speaks to Fanny Assingham in such a way as to get Fanny to lie and to go on lying for her. "We shall have," says Fanny to her husband, "to lie for her—to lie till we're black in the face" (24:122). Maggie's strategy culminates first in the scene of the discovery and destruction of the golden bowl (the latter a dramatic fulfillment of Fanny's tacit promise to lie and lie again, interminably, for Maggie), and then in the scene of Charlotte's and Maggie's conscious perjury to one another. The whole second volume of the novel is an ever so delicate notation, from chapter to chapter, of the way the six main characters (if the Assinghams are included, as they should be) try to read the signs proffered by the others, while each of them is in his or her own way trying to lie effectively. To lie effectively is not to get the others to believe the lie, but, by affirming mendaciously that he or she knows nothing on earth, to make the others behave *as if* they believe this perjury.

In its close focus on the way a reading of signs can generate a global interpretation of the situation that has performative efficacy if others can be got to believe in it or to act as if they believed, *The Golden Bowl* echoes in a different register an earlier, more overtly experimental James novel, *The Sacred Fount.* That novel turns on the way the signs exhibited by a social group, in this case a group of guests at an English country house, can be read in more than one way by involved spectators, though no participant can verify beyond the shadow of a doubt his or her reading of the data. The difference is that *The Sacred Fount* is told in the first person. The reader has no access to a more objective grounding. The perspectives of the Prince, Maggie, and the others, in *The Golden Bowl,* are grounded to some degree and at least ironized by the overarching presence of the telepathic narrator. I say "to some degree," because the narrative voice in *The Golden Bowl* by no means tells the reader everything he or she would like to know. The reader would like to know, for example, what Adam Verver is thinking during all the later time of the action, or whether Char-

lotte and Amerigo did actually commit adultery on that afternoon in
Gloucester. We are not all that much better off than Maggie or than the
narrator-participant of *The Sacred Fount*, except that we are permitted by
the narrative voice to juxtapose several different perspectives. We have
several different acts of reading the signs elaborately presented to us, most
notably Fanny's and Maggie's. *The Sacred Fount*, however, focuses primarily on what is problematic and dismayingly unverifiable about the passive/
active event of reading signs, making a global interpretation of a presented
social scene, and then establishing a law of interpersonal exchange on that
basis. *The Golden Bowl* focuses more on the way a reading of social signs
can be performatively felicitous if others can be got to believe it or to act
as if they believe it.

   The Golden Bowl ratchets *The Sacred Fount* up another notch in complexity and subtlety. Both novels, however, figure, in the protagonist's acts of
creating an imaginary world by the displaying and reading of signs, the
novelist's act of creating the novel out of words in response to the demand
made on him by the "donnée," the "clear matter" of the story. This analogy is made explicit in *The Golden Bowl* in the great scene of the bridge
game at Matcham. In that scene Maggie, watching the others play bridge,
thinks to herself, or the narrative voice thinks for her, positing a metaphor
she may or may not have created, that "they might have been figures re-
hearsing some play of which she herself was the author" (24:235). The
protagonist as creative reader is also a trope for the activity in which James
was engaged when he was writing the novel. The reader of the novel is at
that moment engaged in an analogous activity.

   Sharon Cameron, in the best and most brilliant essay so far written on
The Golden Bowl, asserts, erroneously in my view, that James, in this novel
and in *The Wings of the Dove* especially, characteristically assumes that a
given character can by the sheer power of thinking, by a kind of telepathic
thought projection, coerce another into behaving in a desired way, even
against the other's will. *The Sacred Fount* would seem to support this view
of James. That novel dramatizes the way a given couple, married or in
sexual liaison, may magically affect one another, the younger becoming
older, the older younger, the dumb one smart, the smart one dumb, as
though there were a single "sacred fount" of such qualities, with only so
much youth and so much intelligence to go around. What is given to one
person must be taken from some other. This supposition that James had a
magical view of human relations provides a beguiling way of reading *The
Golden Bowl* or *The Wings of the Dove*. It has the merit of recognizing that
these novels are exceedingly peculiar, that something strange is going on

in them. Cameron is to be commended, moreover, for having had the courage to say that *The Golden Bowl* is "unintelligible."[17] I agree that it is "unintelligible" when read with her phenomenological presuppositions. I claim, however, that the novel becomes, if not intelligible, since speech acts are never "intelligible," because they are foreign to cognition, at least explicable or capable of being accounted for if the reader changes the focus from consciousness, that is the power of thinking, to language, or, more broadly, to the proffering and reading of signs. The novel becomes quasi-intelligible if the reader shifts his or her attention to the speech acts in the novel.

Cameron is right to note that *The Golden Bowl* puts great stress on each character's independent and solitary, ever so isolated, power of thinking. The most salient and overt evidence of this is passages in which Fanny Assingham asserts her recognition that Maggie is "deep," that a lot of hidden thinking is going on under her quiet surface. Later Fanny tells Maggie that she thinks too much. In the first such passage, Fanny says: "I'm bound to confess I've never been so awfully sure of what I may call knowing you. Here you are indeed, as you say—such a deep little person! . . . What I've always been conscious of is of your having concealed about you somewhere no small amount of character; quite as much in fact . . . as one could suppose a person of your size able to carry" (24:110, 112). Much later, in a more extended interchange between Fanny and Maggie about the latter's thinking, Fanny tells Maggie that "It's your nature to think too much," to which Maggie replies that she needed to think because Amerigo and Charlotte "on their side thought of everything *but* that. They thought of everything but that I might think" (24:332). A little later in the interchange Fanny uses, speaking of Maggie and her father, another of the key words in the novel, *saved*, which sometimes appears as *safe*. These words recur in connection with *knowledge* and *belief*. A given character thinks of himself or herself as "safe" if he or she can get the others to believe or to act as if they believe in the way the first character wants. "You think, both of you, so abysmally and yet so quietly," says Fanny. "But it's what will have saved you," to which Maggie answers that it is rather what will have saved Charlotte and the Prince, while making her and her father lost, since their actions on the basis of their thinking will cause them to lose one another for good when Adam returns alone to American City with Charlotte (24:333).

Nevertheless, in spite of all the emphasis on the power of thinking in this novel, as in James's other works, solitary, private thinking in itself is powerless. This is as true in *The Golden Bowl* as in *The Wings of the Dove*.

Thinking does not, pace Cameron, have some spooky, telepathic effect, not even in *The Sacred Fount*. Thinking for James exerts influence over other people only when it has been "outered" in one way or another in words or other signs, for example, in Maggie's putting on her best new dress and waiting for her husband in her drawing room, or in her saying to Charlotte, "I've *not* felt at any time that you've wronged me" (24:249).

Just how does this work? The "felicity" of a normal or standard speech act, in Austin's view, depends on being grounded in a previously established set of conventions and rules. It also depends on being enunciated at the correct place and time by someone who has the right to perform that particular performative. I cannot, according to Austin, just casually walk up and christen a new British warship *The Joseph Stalin*, nor can I marry someone to a monkey, nor can I be writing poetry, or uttering a soliloquy, or acting on the stage—not if I want my speech acts to work, that is. A felicitous performative also depends (though Austin waffles on this point and is self-contradictory) on my good faith and sincere intentions. I must mean what I say, not be lying or perjuring myself. Maggie's speech acts or "sign acts," culminating in her resounding conscious perjury to Charlotte, disobey all these conditions for a felicitous performative. Nevertheless, they work, they do something, they do what Maggie wants. They are felicitous, though the word certainly has an ironic ring in this case, since the felicity of Maggie's speech acts inflicts "torment" on Charlotte and takes effective revenge on Amerigo by depriving him of his mistress.

How can Maggie's speech acts work if they have no precedent that grounds them, if they obey no pre-established rules? They are based, rather, on Maggie's own private, unsponsored, unauthorized decision to act. They are accomplished through lies and perjuries. Her lies, moreover, are not believed. They happen, to boot, in a work of literature, where, if Austin is right, nothing serious is ever supposed to be brought about by words. Literature, according to Austin, is frivolous, nonserious. It lacks purchase on the "real world." Nevertheless Maggie's "sign acts" work. What Maggie does by saying or "signing" works to bring about the denouement of the action. It works also to change the life of the reader, if he or she is a responsible reader, responsible to the demand made by the work. How can this be?

A parallel with the American Declaration of Independence may be useful here. As Jacques Derrida in a brilliant short article, as well as, more recently, David Arndt, in a superb section of a dissertation chapter, have shown,[18] the Declaration of Independence is a peculiar document. Its peculiarity is characteristic of such foundational political acts. In spite of its appeals to precedent and to divine sanction as well as to "self-evident" truths, the Declaration of Independence both is groundless and at the same time creates its own grounds. It does this in a metaleptic speech act gesture that brings into existence as an immediate future, just after or in the same moment as the speech act, in speaking or by speaking, what it needed to have already in place in order to be efficacious. The "good people of these colonies" are brought into existence as a national community by the Declaration. The Declaration also brings into existence the right of Jefferson and the other signers to represent the states that are created as the United States by the document they sign. To say "We hold these truths to be self-evident," Arndt argues, is to say two different, incompatible things at once. It appeals constatively to the self-evidence of the "truths" that justify, or are claimed, or are believed, to justify the act of revolution. At the same time, performatively, the words "declare," or say "we hold," that these truths are self-evident. To say "we hold" is a speech act. The words bring about the thing they name.

Maggie's speech acts or sign acts are of the same nature. In their small way, in their small arena, they are truly revolutionary, truly inaugural. They institute a radical change in the configuration of relations among the main characters. As Fanny says, "She'll take it [the responsibility] all herself" (23:380). For this reason it is proper to speak of what Maggie does as a "declaration of independence." It is a declaration whose independence is signaled in James's trope figuring her as getting off the coach that is bearing the four main characters irresistibly, it might seem, along.

Maggie's declaration of independence is felicitous only because she chooses not to exert her privilege as an injured wife and not to make public her grievance. If she had "gone public," she would have been "lost." She saves herself, however, only to be lost in another way, by losing her beloved father. Her choice is to pretend not to know, to be willing, like Fanny, to perjure herself by swearing that she knows nothing, and then to manipulate carefully how she behaves and what she says to her husband, to Charlotte, and to her father in such a way that they are coerced into acting the way she wants. This works because they do not know for sure how much she knows or believes she knows. They do not know what she may do next. She creates a precarious and delicate pretense among them all that nothing has happened. This keeps alive and functional the fiction that all is well. This fiction then becomes the basis on which all the others must act. In one of her late face-to-face dialogues with Fanny, she tells Fanny that "Everything that has come up for them has come up, in an extraordinary way, without my having by a sound or a sign given myself away. . . . And that's how I make them do what I like!" In reply to this, Fanny tells her, "My dear child, you're amazing. . . . You're terrible" (24:115). This gives another, proleptic, meaning to Maggie's later claim that it is always terrible for women. Maggie inflicts terror as well as passively suffering it. Maggie makes the others do what she likes not by the solitary power of thinking but by what she says and does, by signs that she puts forth for them to see and to try to read. These tokens are the lying signs that she knows nothing.

Later, in the scene in which Maggie brings Charlotte the right volume of her novel, Charlotte tells Maggie she is "tired" and is going back to American City with her husband, Adam. "I place my husband first," says Charlotte (24:314). She tells Maggie that in order to keep her husband (Maggie's beloved father) for herself she must separate him from his daughter. Maggie asks, "You want to take my father *from* me?" (24:316), and ends by saying, "I've failed!" (24:318), meaning "I've failed to keep my father for myself." She says this, but she secretly thinks to herself that she has succeeded magnificently in getting Charlotte to do just what she wants: "Yes, she had done all" (24:318). This is an example of what I mean by saying that Maggie's thinking is always outered, in however negative or mendacious a way, in speech or other signs. That is how she gets the others to act as she wishes.

Maggie has "done it all" in order to get Amerigo to herself. She has even been willing to lose her father in order to secure that. The novel ends with a long suspense as Adam and Charlotte say good-bye to Maggie and the Prince, just before the former two leave for America. This suspense is figured as Maggie's waiting to be "paid" for what she has done and wondering just what the figure of her recompense will be. Her reward is to get the Prince for herself. The last two pages make this clear in formulations about "the measure of her course and the full face of her act," her "terror that, when there has been suspense, always precedes, on the part of the creature to be paid, the certification of the amount. Amerigo knew it, the amount; he still held it. . . . She had thrown the dice, but his hand was over her cast. . . . [T]hen with her sight of him renewed to intensity she seemed to have a view of the number. His presence alone, as he paused to look at her, somehow made it the highest, and even before he had spoken she had begun to be paid in full" (24:367–68).

The reader will note that word *terror* again. It is echoed once more by a synonym in the Aristotelian formulation in the last sentence of the novel. In that last sentence, Maggie, "for pity and dread" of what she sees in Amerigo's eyes, hides her own eyes in his breast. Maggie is being paid for not having made a fuss and divorced him, for not having put him back in penury, for not ever having forced him to make a "confession" (24:368). In this bridge game Maggie has made a grand slam, precisely by getting off the coach, by not playing the game, to mix two of the salient figures the narrative voice provides. Her "act," which has been a speech act through and through, is recompensed at the very end by Amerigo's act: "close to her, her face kept before him, his hands holding her shoulders, his whole act enclosing her, he presently echoed: 'See? I see nothing but *you*'" (24:369).

One final question remains. This question circles back to the beginning of this chapter. Has Maggie acted in justice, in tune with the right? Can what she has done be justified? No unequivocal answer to that can be made, any more than an unequivocal answer can be given to the question of whether the colonists were justified in declaring independence from England. In one sense the colonists were totally unjustified, since they had defied and disobeyed the laws and the sovereignty under which they lived. If the revolution had not come off, if the Continental Army had been defeated, all those who signed the Declaration of Independence would probably have been hanged. This would have been a just imposition of judgment according to the laws of England. Those who instigate a revolution are risking their necks. Since the revolution worked, since it was secured by a military victory, the Declaration of Independence was justified in the event, as they say. It was a felicitous performative of the anomalous sort that is truly inaugural. It was a decisive break in history. Groundless in itself, it created its own ground and validation in a speech act that at the same time established a ground and did something on the basis of that ground. Maggie's act is like that. It is without precedent or justification, but it creates by the act itself the grounds that justify it. Maggie takes the responsibility on herself. She does indeed have a heavy burden on her conscience, something to confess to her priest that she has not confessed. The reader is told that she makes that confession.

Maggie finds herself in a location within her immediate social or intersubjective field in which only she can act to resolve the situation. The resolution inflicts torment on Charlotte, but it gets Maggie undivided possession of Amerigo. That is the purchase she told him she would pay to keep. It also preserves intact the apparently successful acquisition of Amerigo and Charlotte that is so important to her father. It makes efficacious the public lie that these false works of art are genuine. In the last, chilling exchange between Adam and Maggie, Adam says, "*Le compte y est.* [The amount is there.] You've got some good things," and she answers, as they both look at Charlotte and Amerigo taking tea in Maggie's drawing room, sitting like "things," like wax figures "on one of the platforms of Madame Tussaud": "Ah don't they look well?" (24:360. 361). In their last exchange of all, Maggie says, "It's success, father," to which he answers, "It's success" (24:366).

This "success" could be defined as the triumph of the American ethical sense, its implicit assumption that each ethical act is autonomous, initiatory, an act of unjustified power, like the American Revolution. This ethics wins out over the morality or immorality of old Europe. In acting as she does, Maggie is acting in the spirit of the Declaration of Independence. She also acts as her father's daughter, that is, she acts in the spirit of his ruthless business dealings and his unscrupulous acquisition of European artworks. Such an act is both justified and not justified. It is both in tune with the right and at the same time an unjustified act, a lawless taking of power, just as the Declaration of Independence was both justified and not justified by its precedent. That precedent was the English "Glorious Revolution" of 1688, which brought a new dynasty to the English throne and gave new power to Parliament and the people. Analogously, Maggie is both justified and not justified by the example of her father.

In a similar way, I claim, my reading of *The Golden Bowl* is justified by the text, while, if it is a responsible reading, if it is responsive to the demand the text makes, it is also to some degree interventionist, originating, and in that sense unjustified. Nothing justifies, in the sense of prescribing it, the analogy between Maggie's perjury and the Declaration of Independence I have drawn. I draw the analogy on my own hook. I hold, nevertheless, that the analogy is a self-evident truth.

The reader is, in the end, in a situation like Maggie's. The reader must act on his or her own, on the basis of a reading that has no fully prescribed basis, though that reading must try to follow as closely as possible the tracks James has made in the snow. The reader-critic must then take responsibility for what results from the act of retracing that is, for example, the chapter you have just been reading.

CHAPTER 6

The "Quasi-Turn-of-Screw Effect,"
or How to Raise a Ghost with Words:
The Sense of the Past

Jacques Derrida as a Reader of English Literature

I begin with an apparent detour, an account of Jacques Derrida as a critic of English literature and of my admiration for that criticism. This is in acknowledgment of Derrida's influence on my own work. Sometimes, however, the longest way round is the shortest way home. Derrida and literature in English! It is a fathomless subject. I adduce three reasons for that abyss. Each is another turn of a screw that goes down and down into unplumbed depths.

For one thing, Derrida has written or given seminars on a surprising number of literary works in English—works by Shakespeare, Defoe, Shelley, Poe, Hopkins, Melville, Henry James, Joyce, and no doubt others I have forgotten or about which I do not know. He began his pedagogical career as a teacher of English in a children's school in Algiers. This was his required military service during the Algerian War (1957–59). Since Derrida was one of the great readers of literature and one of the greatest literary critics of our time (as well as one of the greatest literary theorists), his essays and seminars on literature tend to be so novel and so penetrating that they give at least one more turn of the screw to all previous readings. Examples are: his essay on aphorism in *Romeo and Juliet*; or his reading of

the ghost scene in *Hamlet*, in *Specters of Marx*; or his overturning of Lacan's reading of Poe's "The Purloined Letter," in "Le facteur de la vé-
rité"; or his admirable comments in a seminar on the last sentence of
Melville's "Bartleby the Scrivener," with its allusion to Job, "He's with
kings and counselors now." Derrida saw that Bartleby's strange nay-saying
("I would prefer not to"), like Job's challenges to God's justice, made him
sovereign, above the law, like kings and counselors. A king, Job, and Bartleby are analogous, different examples of sovereign otherness. Other examples of Derrida's gifts as a reader of literature were his wonderfully
funny observations, in the midst of a seminar on the secret, about what
Martin Heidegger might be imagined to have thought about James's "The
Aspern Papers," if he had ever happened to read it. Derrida speculated
especially about what Heidegger might have thought about Miss Tina's
denunciation, in that story, of the first person narrator as a "publishing
scoundrel." More recent examples are his extended reading of *Robinson
Crusoe* in his last ten seminars, entitled "The Beast and the Sovereign"
(second year), and a long discussion, in one of his last papers, of the phrase
"The just man justices," in a poem by Gerard Manley Hopkins.[1]

In a second turn of the screw, Derrida's readings of literary works tend
to be embedded in theoretical or philosophical investigations. He is, after
all, a great theorist of literature as well as a great literary critic. These
are, to some degree, two different things. Sometimes, as in "Aphorism
Countertime," the essay on *Romeo and Juliet*,[2] Derrida's readings are in-
separable from investigations of literary theory, in this case, the question
of aphorism as a genre. Sometimes, however, perhaps most often, the
readings of literary works arise in the context of philosophical investigations that have nothing to do, at least prima facie, with literature or with
literary theory as such. Examples are the remarks on Melville or on "The
Aspern Papers" already mentioned, or the wonderful essay on Kafka's parable "Before the Law."[3] The latter was originally part of a seminar on
Kant's second Critique, *The Critique of Practical Reason*. Another example
is the reading of "The Purloined Letter," which was in aid of a put down
of Jacques Lacan.[4] The penetrating readings of literature burst suddenly,
explosively, and to some degree intrusively into the midst of discourses
that are ostensibly devoted to some properly philosophical question about
the secret, or about hospitality, or about Kant's ethical theory, or about
sovereignty, or some such topic.

The relation between philosophical discourse and literary criticism in
Derrida's work is not all that easy to define. It is not that the readings
simply "illustrate" the ideas. Nor are the philosophical reflections

straightforwardly consonant with the readings of particular literary works. The readings are somewhat aside or askew. They exceed their contexts, exorbitantly. At the same time, they are essential to the philosophical thinking. It seems as if Derrida cannot carry on his investigations of even such apparently nonliterary topics as political sovereignty, or capital punishment, or hospitality without sooner or later bringing in literature, sometimes works of English literature. It seems as though, for Derrida, these general political, ethical, or philosophical questions could not, in the end, be kept detached from literature. Literature or the literary somehow contaminates them, like a parasite or ghost that has entered the house of philosophy. A good example of this is the way speech acts, in Derrida's speech act theory, are always "acts of literature." In "The Time of a Thesis, Punctuations," Derrida says, "For I have to remind you, somewhat bluntly and simply, that my most constant interest, coming even before my philosophical interest I should say, if this is possible, has been directed towards literature, towards that writing which is called literary."[5] This statement is a little misleading. It suggests that our commonsense assumption is correct: literature and philosophy are two different things. No doubt that is true enough. It nevertheless seems to be the case that, for Derrida, the philosophical is inhabited by the literary. To "do philosophy," for him, is always sooner or later to come back to literature.

One consequence of this is that a mere literary critic, like me, finds three somewhat different sources of inspiration in Derrida's work. First is the wonderful example he gives of how to do literary criticism, though I would have to add, "Try to imitate him if you can! Good luck!" Second, Derrida has made major contributions to literary theory, as opposed to doing readings, if the distinction holds, which in the end it does not. These theoretical insights may be helpful to someone doing literary criticism. Finally, works by Derrida that apparently have nothing whatsoever overtly to do with literature, and are not "illustrated" by readings of literature performed by Derrida himself, nevertheless may have admirable power to redirect the work of literary criticism at the most practical level of particular works' readings. An example of this is Nicholas Royle's recent appropriation of Derrida's reflections on telepathy to redefine the "omniscient narrator" in fiction. Royle then uses that recognition of the telepathy effect in the relation between narrator and character to read specific novels.[6] Someone interested in "Derrida and English literature" will find himself or herself provoked or inspired by parts of Derrida's writing that have nothing explicitly to do with English literature.

I began by saying that there are three turns of the screw leading the question of Derrida and English literature into a deep hole. I have identified two. The third is the most difficult to state, since it has to do with the unsaid and unsayable in Derrida's work. A silence or secret inhabits that work, including the readings of works in English literature. In Derrida's more recent work, that unspeakable silence often takes the name of *le tout autre*, the "wholly other." In a quite recent book, *Voyous (Rogues)*, Derrida says, in a passage already cited as an epigraph to chapter 3, "The unavowable in community is also a sovereignty that cannot but posit itself and impose itself in silence, in the unsaid."[7] This might be transposed to say that what is unavowable in Derrida's work, that is, unsayable in the form of a vow or any sort of confessional speech act, is a sovereignty that cannot help positing itself and imposing itself in silence, in the unsaid. This unsaid, it might be argued, is the most important thing about Derrida's work. The authority or sovereignty of that work, including the authority of his readings of literary works in English, comes from that unreachable source. Though all Derrida's work is devoted to circling around the unsaid, trying to say it, as matter swirls around a black hole, that center remains, in the end, wholly other, silent, unsaid. Try to say it if you can!

I want now to exemplify what I have said about the way Derrida's work, not necessarily or even primarily work about literature, can be provocative in the effort to read works of literature in English. I have in mind five motifs in Derrida's work: the theory of telepathy in "Télépathie"; his "hauntology" as developed especially in *Specters of Marx*; his notion of the "ideality of the literary work" as expressed in "Le temps d'un these: ponctuations" ("The Time of a Thesis: Punctuations"); his preoccupation with thresholds, enclosures, crypts, inside/outside oppositions, hospitality to strangers, archives, and so on, as in "*Fors*" and in the seminars on hospitality; and his revisionist version of speech act theory in *Limited Inc* and in many other places in recent works.[8] I cannot, in this chapter, investigate the intricacies of these works. I must assume that my reader has read them, or will read them straightway.[9] It is important to note that all five of these motifs, as could be shown in detail, describe might be called "textual effects," not purely phenomenal or perceptual experiences. Language, especially versions of performative language, intervenes decisively in all five. All five, moreover, involve the encounter, by way of language or other signs, with the strange, the uncanny, that is, "the wholly other," *le tout autre*. I want to keep these five Derridean motifs in mind as a sort of spectral penumbra hovering in the background as I look at my example.

Why The Sense of the Past *Is Unfinished*

That example is a work that Derrida probably never read. Though one never knows, and now I shall presumably never know. He took that secret, along with others, to the grave. My example is one of Henry James's strangest novels, the unfinished *The Sense of the Past*. James began work on this novel in 1900, soon after finishing *The Turn of the Screw*. He then abandoned it, after writing the two first books and part of the third. Other work interrupted it, including the writing of his three great late masterpieces: *The Ambassadors*, *The Wings of the Dove*, and *The Golden Bowl*. James began work on the novel again in 1914, in the first winter of World War I, when he felt he could not continue work on the novel of contemporary life, *The Ivory Tower*, he was then writing. The latter was also left unfinished at his death in February 1916. James needed to get in imagination out of the present and back in time by way of his "sense of the past." In 1914 he dictated a long series of notes that work out the course the rest of the novel would take. He then revised all he had so far written, finished Book Three, and wrote another 171 pages (in the printed version in the New York Edition), of Book Four. Death then supervened. The manuscript stops in the middle of a characteristically Jamesian sentence, of which I give only the interrupted part, after a dash: "—so odd it was that the sense of her understanding wouldn't be abated, which even a particular lapse, he could see" (26:287). He could see what? What he (Ralph Pendrel, the hero and center of consciousness or of "focalization" in *The Sense of the Past*) saw remains an impenetrable secret. This secret James carried with him to the grave. I shall return to the word *see*. It is a key word in James's "Notes for *The Sense of the Past*."

The first three books total only 115 pages, while the incomplete Book Four totals 171 pages. This suggests that something was going wrong, as it often did, with James's attempt to keep his work within predetermined bounds. Perhaps *The Sense of the Past* was for some reason intrinsically impossible to finish. One can imagine a series of the segments James called "books," each geometrically longer than the previous one, until quite rapidly James might have found himself writing a novel of virtually infinite length. An author's inability to finish a work, after putting it aside unfinished and then picking it up again much later, as James did in this case, is always more than merely contingent, particularly for so abundant a writer as James. An inability or unwillingness to finish is always a symptom of something or other. It may be, however, difficult or impossible to tell of what it may be a symptom, since the reluctance to finish may be an unconscious attempt to hide what the finished work would have "given away." Who knows? How would you tell? So what was the problem?

In the case of *The Sense of the Past*, a small clue may be given as to what may have inhibited James from finishing in what he says, in the last three sentences of "Notes for *The Sense of the Past*," about his intention to have the novel end "happily" with the marriage of the hero to the woman he loved and left behind in New York. He left her when he went abroad to London to take possession of the old house he had inherited there. Or, rather, the novel was to end with the *prefiguring* of that marriage in a final scene between Ralph and the American Ambassador to the Court of St. James, Ralph's confidant earlier (modeled, provocatively enough, on James Russell Lowell, James's friend):

> The present and conclusive scene in the Square [between Ralph and the Ambassador] all sufficiently brings her [Aurora, Ralph's lady-love from New York] on, all sufficiently prefigures Ralph's reunion, not to say union, with her, and in short acquits me of everything. A far more ingenious stroke, surely, and to be made more ministrant to effect and to the kind of note of the strange that I want than the comparatively platitudinous direct *duo* between the parties! He has only to give us in advance all that the duo must and will consist of in order to leave us just where, or at least just *as*, we want! (26:358)

"Acquits me of everything"? What an odd phrase! Of what crime or responsibility did James think himself in need of being acquitted? What obligation could he fulfill, what debt pay off, by way of this scene between Ralph and the Ambassador? I suppose he means he had an obligation to round the novel off somehow. Nevertheless, he could not bring himself to show directly the hero and heroine singing, as it were, a love duo such as ends an opera. He thought he could get away with, acquit himself by, anticipating that duo, proleptically, in a dialogue between two men. Since that would be stranger, that is, the merely spectral presence of the love duo, it would therefore be more in keeping with the general tone of strangeness James wanted to keep up, as in his avowed model for this last novel, *The Turn of the Screw*.

Kafka's inability to finish *The Trial* can be imputed to his understandable desire to postpone death, the death of his protagonist, which would allegorize his own death. A happy ending in a heterosexual embrace, it might be argued, seems to have played a similar role in James's imagination. The heroine's name, *Aurora*, is more than a little ominous for a reader who remembers Greek mythology or Tennyson's "Tithonus." In the latter, Tithonus, granted by Aurora, Goddess of the Dawn, endless life but not eternal youth, dwells for an eternity in her embrace, longing for the release of death. Aurora no longer has any charms for him:

> The woods decay, the woods decay and fall,
> The vapours weep their burthen to the ground,
> Man comes and tills the field and lies beneath,
> And after many a summer dies the swan,
> Me only cruel immortality
> Consumes: I wither slowly in thine arms. (ll. 1–6)

After a lifetime of writing novels and short stories that, for the most part, precisely do not end in happy "unions" between hero and heroine, James was at last, at least in what he says he intended to do, to have reached that felicitous borne, but death intervened. Maggie Verver's straightforward sexual passion for her husband is relatively unusual in James's works, though the Prince, it may be, does not feel quite the same way about her, even at the end of the novel. Death interrupted and postponed forever getting an answer to the question of whether James could ever have brought himself to write the planned happy ending of *The Sense of the Past*. The indications are not propitious. Not only did James interrupt writing the novel and take it up again only when he was already mortally ill, but what he did write in his last days kept, as I have said, getting longer and longer in a way that suggests the novel may have been going to be of inordinate length.

This macro-form, an accelerating expansion of the original germ, may be mirrored in the micro-form of the novel's style. *The Sense of the Past* is written in super-Jamesian circumlocutions. This is particularly true of the unfinished fourth book, written in 1914–15. Reading the novel, I continually find myself bogged down just trying to follow the syntactical sense of its long, complicated sentences. Often even when I figure out their sense, it is not clear to me just how they further the action. The whole fourth book takes place in excruciatingly extreme slow motion, like some ominous dream. James employs an almost Blanchotian or Kafkesque stylistic refinement, as he makes notations of what goes on from micro-second to micro-second in Ralph's mind while he confronts those he encounters in his strange trip back into the past. The stylistic texture is of a weirdly detailed intersubjective exchange, all presented through his subjectivity. In one hallucinatory event, Molly Midmore comes across the room to embrace Ralph in response to his attempts to soothe her fears. He literally goes to sleep in her arms. He awakes to find that Molly's mother and brother have, in the indefinitely prolonged interval of their miniature "love-death," left the room. Their embrace is "like a resistance to something unseen," whatever *that* might be. During the embrace's duration it is "as if they had been wholly and incalculably absent: so absent, and for so long, that on his reckoning again with the conditions about him they struck him at once as different and as somehow mastered. Had he literally and in so extraordinary a manner slept in his mistress's arms?" (26:268). This sounds like something out of *The Trial* or *The Castle* or *Death Sentence*, not much like the usual, slightly ironic, realist narrative tone in most of James's fiction. Here is just one more example out of almost innumerable ones:

> There was a singular space of time during which, while the consideration on the part of the two women so approved him, approved him verily as against himself, approved him almost as if their soft hands had stroked him for their pleasure, there hovered before him the wonder of what they would have done had he been ugly, what they would in fact do should he become so, in any manner or form—this idea of his full free range suddenly indulging in a glance at that mode of reaction. (26:180)

Could it be that James was, at this limit of his life, just a little mad? After all, on his deathbed, after his stroke, he imagined himself to be Napoleon Bonaparte. The question of the protagonist's possible madness, in any case, comes up repeatedly in *The Sense of the Past*. The narrator's goal is to put the reader within the mind and feelings of a possibly mad protagonist, mad, for example, in the way he has an amazing gift for always saying the wrong thing in the painful give and take with Molly and the other Midmores; demented, in the Ambassador's judgment, for thinking he has met his double from 1820 and has agreed to change places with him.

James seems to have been aware of the exaggerated *lento* tempo of the narration. He reported his sense of how slow his progress was, even though he spent his accustomed two or three hours a day at the work. He was, he said, pushing the novel "uphill at the rate of about an inch a day." His work "was very slow, very difficult, very delayed."[10] James's extreme refinements of style, his desire to break down the instant of Ralph's experience into its multitudinous components so as to leave the reader hovering interminably over that instant and James's tangled expressions of it, work, it can be argued, to put off making progress. They work to put off indefinitely ever reaching the end that James apparently so desired and at the same time so feared. Even in his imagination of the end, James, as I have noted, substitutes a scene between two men, Ralph and the Ambassador, for the "platitudinous" "*duo*" of Ralph and Aurora singing together their fulfilled love. That duo was never to have been written, even if James had finished the novel. It was only to have been "prefigured" as occurring beyond the last words of the text, just as Isabel Archer's reunion with her perfidious husband, Gilbert Osmond, in *The Portrait of a Lady*, takes place, if it can be said ever really to "take place," beyond the end of the novel.

What Is a Ghost Story?

I do not, myself, believe in ghosts. I do not think Henry James believed in them either. Nevertheless, *The Sense of the Past* is a ghost story, James's strangest. I believe in *The Sense of the Past*, though just what it means to "believe in" a work of fiction might be hard to determine. I mean, among other things, that the characters in their settings more or less come alive for me in my imagination, as if they were real people.

James wrote a whole series, about ten, of what are, strictly speaking, ghost stories, as well as many other quasi-ghost stories or stories in which the ghostly is used as a figurative resource. An example of the latter is the way Maggie imagines herself a ghost haunting Charlotte in the climactic parts of *The Golden Bowl*. James's ghost stories proper are stories in which apparitions appear, or at least appear to appear, to one or more of the characters. Usually it is one character, the reader's surrogate, who sees ghosts. The most celebrated of James's ghost stories, the most subject to extended commentary, are *The Turn of the Screw* and "The Jolly Corner." An immense secondary literature exists for *The Turn of the Screw*. That novella has been turned this way and that, screwed down and then un-screwed, by a long series of distinguished critics, from Edmund Wilson down to relatively recent essays by Shoshana Felman and others.[11]

My double hypothesis about James's ghost stories: (1) All James's stories and novels are ghost stories; (2) The ghost stories "proper" are really, obliquely, about the act of literature. They bring into the open the way all works of fiction that are "believed in" by the reader work their magic by using language to "raise the ghosts" of the characters. These characters then have a spectral existence in the mind, feelings, and imagination of the reader. They go on permanently dwelling there, obscurely haunting the reader's mind. They abide there permanently, ready to be brought for-ward again if the reader thinks of the story, or, especially, re-reads it. All those works of fiction on my shelves are inhabited by specters, waiting to be re-invoked by reading, though I conjure up Dorothea Brooke, in

George Eliot's *Middlemarch*, or Isabel Archer, in James's *The Portrait of a Lady*, just by thinking of them. James's ghost stories "proper" are about this primary act of literature, its inaugural performative effect. These stories bring into the open the mechanism whereby the raising of ghosts works in fictions that are not, in the traditional sense, ghost stories at all.

James's remarks about *The Turn of the Screw* in the preface to volume twelve of the New York Edition are his most explicit account of what in the "Notes for *The Sense of the Past*" he calls the "quasi-Turn-of-Screw-effect." That is his phrase for what he says he wants *The Sense of the Past* to bring about. What is the "Turn-of-Screw-effect"? What would a "quasi" one be? The effect of *The Turn of the Screw*, James tells the reader, is produced by a mechanical, contrived, and concocted set of words that is so screwed down, so airtight, that so consistently maintains an unbroken "tone," that it forces the reader to read the presence of ghosts into it. *The Turn of the Screw*, James says, "is a piece of ingenuity pure and simple, of cold artistic calculation, an *amusette* to catch those not easily caught (the 'fun' of the capture of the merely witless being ever but small), the jaded, the disillusioned, the fastidious. Otherwise expressed, the study is of a conceived 'tone,' the tone of suspected and felt trouble, of an inordinate and incalculable sort—the tone of tragic, yet of exquisite, mystification" (9:xviii). Felman has commented perceptively on these sentences and on the way psychoanalytic critics, for all their cleverness, have consistently been caught in the story's trap, just as James said he wanted to bring about.[12]

Friedrich Schlegel, in a central passage about irony in his "Critical Fragments," says that the person most trapped by irony is the one who thinks he understands it. Irony is a case of *Unverständlichkeit*, "nonunderstandability."[13] James is saying something of the same sort about *The Turn of the Screw* and, implicitly, about all his ghost stories. His special victims, he says, will be the jaded, the disillusioned, the fastidious, those who not only do not believe in ghosts, as I have said is my own case, but who also think they can understand and resist anything a literary work tries to put over on them, my own case once more. Most literary study, including both that using formalist methods and that based on "cultural studies" procedures, is carried out in order to resist mystification by literature, at all costs. We critics do not want to be taken in by literature. James is saying it is just such readers who will be most mystified by *The Turn of the Screw*, in spite of themselves. Why? Partly because the aesthetic surface of the work is so perfect, so consistent, so much made up of a single tone. "For," says James, "it has the small strength—if I shouldn't say rather the unattackable ease—of a perfect homogeneity, of being, to the very last grain of its virtue, all of a kind; the very kind, as happens, least apt to be baited by earnest criticism, the only sort of criticism of which account need be taken" (9: xiv). The work has such a uniformity of surface, such homogeneity of content, that criticism cannot catch it with any sort of bait, nor torment it either, as a bear is tied to a stake and "baited." A second reason the novella is unattackable is the way it has always been there ahead of the critic. It already contains within itself all the moves the critic might make, as Shoshana Felman has brilliantly shown. This is one meaning (there are several possible ones) of the enigmatic title. Each of the narrative moves or scenes is another turn of the screw tightening the trap the work has set for the reader.

Perhaps the most important feature of this "finish" is the impossibility, in the terms given by the story, of deciding whether or not the ghosts are "real." This is so even though that is the thing the reader would most like to decide about. It is also the thing critics have tended to be most decisive about and most in contradiction with one another. "The ghosts are real." "No, the ghosts are a figment of the governess's fevered imagination." If you make the second choice, on the basis of the fact that only the governess sees the ghosts, then you may remember that, though Mrs. Grose, the grossly unimaginative housekeeper, does not see the ghosts, she confirms from the circumstantial detail the governess gives of what the two ghosts (which the latter alone has seen) look like that these are indeed Peter Quint and Miss Jessel. The story is like a Gestaltist duck-rabbit or like an Escher drawing. It does not make rational sense. Either way you move, the text tells you you must be wrong. It therefore imperturbably resists the critic's baiting, like the fencing bear in Heinrich von Kleist's "The Marionette Theater."

This means that whatever meaning is ascribed to this "*amusette* to catch those not easily caught" is an interpretation the reader has imposed on the text, imported into the words. It is not something verifiably and unequivocally found there. The words have acted performatively to force the reader to do that importing. James begins his remarks about *The Turn of the Screw* by calling it "this perfectly independent and irresponsible little fiction" (9: xiv). It is irresponsible and independent, unattached, because it does not give any definite answers to the urgent questions the critic puts to it. Like a stern literary critic, Hamlet interrogates his father's ghost in the opening scene of *Hamlet*. Jacques Derrida reads this scene with much penetration at the beginning of *Specters of Marx*. One can imagine a teacher saying to the story, "Tell me. 'Fess up. Stand and unfold. Are the ghosts real or not?

I need urgently to know, since I must teach the story tomorrow." "Find out if you can," says the story. "I am not going to tell you." To say that *The Turn of the Screw* is "irresponsible" is to say that the reader must take responsibility for whatever meanings he or she reads into it. Doing that is the way he or she inevitably falls into the trap. This is said quite explicitly and even defiantly at the end of James's remarks on this novella in the Preface:

> Only make the reader's general vision of evil intense enough, I said to myself—and that already is a charming job—and his own experience, his own imagination, his own sympathy (with the children) and horror (of their false friends) will supply him quite sufficiently with all the particulars. Make him *think* the evil, make him think it for himself, and you are released from weak specifications. . . . There is not only from beginning to end of the matter not an inch of expatiation [i.e., any developing in detail the evil done by the ghosts to the children, expatiating on it], but my values are positively all blanks save so far as an excited horror, a promoted pity, a created expertness—on which punctual effects of strong causes no writer can ever fail to plume himself—proceed to read into them more or less fantastic figures. (9:xxii).

Sentences of an admirable specificity! They echo the description of the way Maggie, in *The Golden Bowl*, peoples the "figured void" with images of her husband and her father's wife Charlotte in sexual congress. James's words here about *The Turn of the Screw* defiantly boast that he will turn the reader into another Maggie. The words on the page will work infallibly as speech acts forcing the reader, even, or especially, the jaded, the disillusioned, the fastidious reader, against his or her will, to "read into" the words meanings that are not there. The reader will fill in the blanks out of his or her imagination and so be responsible for whatever evil thoughts he or she may have. An example would be the imagination (I give myself away) that the ghosts, when alive, have sexually molested the children, taken away their innocence, given them a precocious practical knowledge of "the facts of life." I suppose, though without any specific evidence at all, that this is what James wants his readers to put in the blanks where no explicit "values," either in the economic sense or in the painterly sense, are to be found. This is an example of what I mean by speaking of literature's performative power to use words to raise ghosts.

The Sense of the Past *as Ghost Story*

Does this proposed reading of the preface to *The Turn of the Screw* at all help to understand what James meant when he said, in "Notes for *The*

Sense of the Past," that he wanted to achieve a "quasi-Turn-of-Screw effect" in the latter novel? *The Sense of the Past* certainly takes some explaining.

Nor is it much help to note that James's last novel picks up motifs from one of his earliest short stories, "A Passionate Pilgrim."[14] The latter was first published in *Atlantic Monthly*, March–April 1871. That story has the motif of the man who returns to England to take possession of a house he has a claim to there. "A Passionate Pilgrim" also has the figures of the daughter of the English family, whom the hero courts, though thwarted by her blocking-agent brother. The hero of "A Passionate Pilgrim" even sees a ghost at a crucial turning point in the action. The story could therefore be counted as one of James's ghost stories.[15] "A Passionate Pilgrim" also adumbrates Ralph Pendrel's return to the past, in *The Sense of the Past*, as a ghost haunting long-dead persons. Clement Searle, the hero of "A Passionate Pilgrim," identifies himself with an eighteenth-century Clement Searle, whose life ended tragically: "He had already taken a fancy to confound his identity with that of the earlier Clement Searle; he now began to speak almost wholly as from the imagined consciousness of his old-time kinsman."[16] Clement Searle anticipates his encounter with the ghost of the girl the earlier Clement Searle had cruelly wronged by defining himself as a ghost, just as Ralph Pendrel, in *The Sense of the Past*, is a ghost haunting the Midmore family of 1820. "But I should be hugely tickled," says the modern Clement Searle, "if this poor ghost should be deceived by my resemblance and mistake me for her cruel lover. She's welcome to the comfort of it. What one can do in the case I shall be glad to do. But can a ghost haunt a ghost? I *am* a ghost."[17] "A Passionate Pilgrim" also anticipates *The Sense of the Past* in its use of a hyperbolic and slightly hallucinatory style, as though the narrator were recounting a dream. *The Sense of the Past*, no reader of both texts can doubt, is constructed out of permutations of the elements of a story that James had published forty-five years before he died, leaving the later novel unfinished. This echoing is evidence that some part of James's mind or imagination remained haunted by this story and by a need to tell it right. Just why he was so haunted is more difficult to ascertain.

A sketch of the plot of *The Sense of the Past* makes it sound so absurd that the critic may say, "No wonder James had so much trouble finishing this quite implausible story." It differs from the rest of James's ghost stories in two ways. For one thing, it is, or was meant to be, a full-length novel, not a short story or a novella. For another thing, the story is told from the point of view of the ghost. This is something pretty unusual in

ghost stories, I should think. The usual goal is to generate the frisson of
fear in the reader by way of his or her sympathy with someone who sees a
ghost, whereas Ralph Pendrel, the hero of *The Sense of the Past, is* a ghost.
Imagine Hamlet told from the perspective of Hamlet's father's ghost!

The Sense of the Past begins with the hero's, Ralph Pendrel's, rejection
by Aurora Coyne, his beloved in New York. She says she will only marry
someone who is an adventurer, not a supersensitive, meditative dreamer
like Ralph (and like Henry James himself). He cares more, she says, for
travel to decadent old Europe than for wholesome American marriage to
her. This again echoes James's life, here his long expatriation and, perhaps,
his abandonment of his cousin Minnie, who apparently loved him. She
died young, while James was abroad. Ralph then discovers that he has
inherited an old house in London from a distant relative who has admired
Ralph's slender little Paterian book, significantly named *An Essay in Aid of
the Reading of History* (26:42). (Clement Searle, by the way, in "A Passionate Pilgrim," has published "a little volume of verses," which "sing[s] the
charms of love and idleness" and "reads like the poetry of fifty years ago,"
that is, of Percy Bysshe Shelley's time.[18]) Ralph takes possession of the
house. There he meets his early-nineteenth-century double. The double
steps down from a portrait. Ralph changes places with his double, who
wants to journey to the "present" of 1910, that is, into the future, while
Ralph wants to indulge his "sense of the past" by journeying back to 1820:
"If his idea in fine was to recover the lost moment, to feel the stopped
pulse, it was to do so as experience, in order to be again consciously the
creature that *had* been, to breathe as he had breathed and feel the pressure
that he had felt" (26:48). This describes obliquely most novelists' goal, as
is attested to by the use of the past tense in most novels and stories. Most
fiction fictively recovers a fictive past. The writer of fiction, however,
wants to be in imagination an imaginary personage who lived in an imaginary past, not, like Ralph or like some historians, to re-enter the life of
some real historical personage. *The Sense of the Past* recalls H. G. Wells's
The Time Machine (1895). Ralph's "time machine" is the house itself, with
its odd portrait of his double, painted with his back to the viewer.

James's ghost stories characteristically involve houses in one way or another. Houses for James are always "haunted," in ways that are analogous
to Derrida's sense that houses involve aporias about thresholds, inside/
outside oppositions, inheritances, ghosts/guests, invasion by strangers or
hospitality offered to strangers. "In him outside of him," says Derrida in
Specters of Marx, "this is the place outside of place of ghosts wherever they
may feign to take up their abode."[19] Derrida's houses too, like Ralph's

London house, are always occupied by ghostly crypts, as is worked out brilliantly in "*Fors*."

The topic of haunted houses comes up explicitly in an odd passage in *The Sense of the Past*. Ralph, now back in 1820, accuses his new beloved there of misspelling *ghost* in a letter to him: "Your guilty secret is that of the 'goast' at some haunted house where you had paid a visit—unless it was but a case of a plural gone wrong and a house really haunted with goats!" (26:189). Ralph is at that point a ghost haunting the house, perhaps compulsively confessing indirectly to that by bringing up the topic, as he does more than once, just as James may be slyly telling his readers that they may be the "goats" of a joke, an *amusette*. They are goats if they are taken in by this mechanical linguistic foolery and submit to the "quasi-Turn-of-Screw effect" generated by the words on the page. Readers are likely to be "screwed" by James's ghost stories, in vulgar parlance. The word refers both to the sex act (perhaps forced) and to economic fraud, as in: "Investors in Enron were all screwed by the company executives." A "thumb-screw" is an instrument of torture. I shall return to this sense of *screw*, as in "screw down tight."

Ralph goes into the past, back to 1820, by entering into his own inherited house. There he takes on the role of his double, proposes to Molly Midmore, and then was to discover that he has made love to the wrong sister, that he is much more attracted to Molly's younger sister, Nan. (The same thing happens, by the way, to Nostromo at the end of Conrad's novel of that name.) Ralph is the ghost from the future haunting the Midmore family of 1820, but he is also inhabited by the ghost of his early-nineteenth-century double, just as Marx, in Derrida's reading of him, was inhabited by ghosts from the past of old imperial Europe. Gradually the Midmores come to be made uneasy by Ralph. They suffer what James in the "Notes" repeatedly calls "malaise," just as Ralph himself suffers increasing "malaise" at his false position, his "suspicion of being suspected" (26:346). The novel may also produce more "malaise" than fear in the reader. Its central action was to have been the gradual production of that double fear. James speaks in the "Notes" of "The slow growth on the part of the others of their fear of Ralph, even in the midst of their making much of him, as abnormal, as uncanny, as not *like* those they know of their own kind etc., etc.; and his fear just *of* theirs, with his double consciousness, alas, his being *almost* as right as possible for the 'period,' and yet so intimately and secretly wrong; with his desire to mitigate so far as he can the malaise that he feels himself, do what he will, more and more produce" (26:295).

Ralph produces that malaise in the others in two ways. One way is by
not quite knowing enough, by not knowing things that he ought to know,
most notably the existence of Molly's sister, Nan. The other way is by his
uncanny knowledge of too much, for example, his telepathic insight into
what Molly's brother Perry knows and is trying to hide from the others,
namely, that Molly's sister Nan has smashed a beautiful old vase in their
country house. Ralph sees by way of what the others see or have seen,
knows what they know, just as the narrator, the reader might reflect, can
see, know, and feel only what Ralph sees, knows, and feels, as James more
than once asserts in the "Notes," most strongly in the following passage:
"I of course, under penalty of the last infamy, stick here still, as everywhere, to our knowing these things but through Ralph's knowing them"
(26:350). It would be "infamous" on James's part if he broke the aesthetic
law of sticking to a single "focalization." Just why it would be infamous
James does not say. Presumably because it would muddy up the presentation and open the door to turning his novel into what James reproached
eighteenth- and nineteenth-century English novels for being, "a large
loose baggy monster." It is remarkable how consistently James uses stern
ethical terms to define the aesthetic obligations of the novelist. The reader
must, on pain of infamy, only know what Ralph knows, through the narrator's telepathic insight into Ralph's mind and feelings. Ralph, in turn,
however, has uneasy-making telepathic insight into those around him.
This insight or "second sight" produces the kind of spooky fear in the
others that one would feel in the presence of a penetratingly prescient
specter, as in the following example:

> Wasn't he seeing something that Perry himself had seen, or learning at
> least something that Perry knew, just by this compulsion of feeding, as it
> were, on his young kinsman's terror—for it had frankly to be taken for
> nothing less—and drawing to himself the sense of it? "Sweet Nan, poor
> sweet Nan!" he next found himself exclaiming, for what had happened was
> that he had with the strangest celerity read a particular knowledge into
> Perry's expression, and read into it as well the consciousness that he was
> giving it up, though to one's self only [that is, to the narrator, Ralph Pen-
> drel], not to the others, and that nothing so strange had in all his life be-
> fallen the hapless youth [Perry] as to feel thus under the pressure of such
> an intelligence, which did definitely at last show the man betraying it for
> different, quite dreadfully different, from other men. (26:248–49)

Perry here recognizes that he must be in the presence of a spirit endowed with mind-reading powers. So horrified, so anxious, so given over

to a reciprocal malaise is Ralph made by his discovery that he possesses such powers and that they have a frightening effect on others that he straightway denies that he has those powers. His denial, however, gives the truth a proper definition by denegation: "I am not a prophet or a soothsayer, and still less a charlatan, and don't pretend to the gift of second sight—I only confess to have cultivated my imagination, as one has to in a country where there is nothing to take that trouble off one's hands. Therefore perhaps it is that things glimmer upon me at moments from a distance, so that I find myself in the act of catching them. . . . I'm *not* mad" (26:251). Here is one place where the question of Ralph's madness comes up explicitly, in Ralph's somewhat mad denial that he is mad. "Getting a glimmer of things at a distance": that is a good definition of telepathy.

Why the Slow Motion?

The quite extraordinary slow-motion stylistic texture of *The Sense of the Past*, already noted, is overdetermined. It has several causes, functions, or rationales. In this last work, it might be argued, James is giving an amazingly subtle representation of what he feels does actually go on from moment to moment in intersubjective encounters. We are not, as it might seem, wholly enclosed in our own egos. We are not windowless monads. We have, rather, a quite uncanny, imperfect, but nevertheless distinct ability to guess what the other person is thinking and feeling. Edmund Husserl spilled much ink in his last years trying to work out the form of exposure one ego has to others. This was a big problem for him: how to avoid the solipsism his phenomenological presuppositions seemed to imply. Husserl, in the *Cartesian Meditations*, called our knowledge of others' hidden interiorities "analogical apperception,"[20] as Derrida in his seminars more than once noted.

The whole long tradition of the realist novel has occupied itself incessantly with just this issue and with the concomitant problem of representing plausible forms of intersubjectivity in imaginary fictions. A good bit of variation in conventions about this issue has existed. This variation is visible, for example, in the contrast between Jane Austen or George Eliot (who tend to assume that other people are more or less opaque, even for intelligent and sensitive protagonists like Elizabeth Bennett in *Pride and Prejudice* or Dorothea Brooke in *Middlemarch*) and Anthony Trollope (who grants his characters a considerable power to know what other people are thinking). James in most of his works is more like Austen and Eliot than like Trollope, but *The Sense of the Past* is different. It permits a high degree of clairvoyance on Ralph's part.

In James's work, as in the work of other novelists, though with perhaps an unusual insistence, intersubjectivity is represented in a drama of looks. This especially appears as the mutual exchange of looks by two people who gaze directly into each other's eyes and as the contrary drama of the look averted. An example of the latter in *The Sense of the Past* is a scene in which Molly's mother will not, at first, look Ralph in the eye. When she does so, she betrays her growing fear of him: "holding up her head, drawing in her lips, meeting his eyes and after an instant letting him see, as he thought, something in them like the strange long look, the questioning fear, that he had just been dealing with in her son" (26:259). Another case, also involving Ralph and Mrs. Midmore, is anticipated in the "Notes," though of course never actually written as such. Rather than discuss openly Molly's breaking of her engagement to Ralph, "the question is really had out between them without either of them so speaking, and only by his looking her very hard in the eye, and her so looking at him, and his keeping it up on this and her keeping it up on that" (26:321).

James was a novelist exceptionally gifted with the ability to be, in his phrase for what a writer of fiction most needs, "one of the people on whom nothing is lost."[21] He was prone to read much into something so fleeting as a momentary look. This, it might be imagined, made him a somewhat formidable companion for friends or on social occasions. He may, one might guess, have been somewhat embarrassed by his gift of insight and anxious to hide it from others, as Ralph does. It is even possible, though we shall never know, that James associated this difference from others with his latent homosexuality, if indeed he was gay. He may have felt himself obliged to make delicate maneuvers in social interchanges to keep in the closet, so to speak, to keep from giving himself away. This precarious situation may be obliquely dramatized in the way Ralph must maneuver to keep secret the fact that he is a ghost from the future for whom Molly and all her family and friends have been dead for almost a century. If Ralph is a ghost, he has by returning to the past raised them as ghosts, which is just what his "sense of the past" most wants to do. The narrator speaks of Ralph as "ridden . . . by the wish to lose nothing that he could on any terms whatever grasp" (26:232), grasp, that is, by way of his extraordinary journey back into the past: "he had come out for the whole, the finest integrity of the thing—the insistence of which now flashed upon him with the hard cold light of a flourished steel blade" (26:233).

The general theme, central to the whole tradition of realist fiction, of one character's consciousness of the consciousness of others, is in *The Sense of the Past* given hyperbolic dramatization. It is presented in the situation of an impostor, a revenant, a spook, a specter, someone who has taken on, but not wholly, the personality of another person from the quite distant past. Ralph's situation is extremely precarious. If he does not know enough, he gives himself away, as in his not knowing at first about Molly's sister Nan. If he knows too much, he gives himself away, as in his knowing by telepathic insight something about Nan that only Perry, among those present in the room, knows. If he deviates a hair's breadth in either direction, toward too much or too little, he is lost. He is lost by the way his strangeness or uncanniness inspires "malaise" in the others, the malaise of those who have seen a ghost in broad daylight. He most fears their fear.

Fear is a key word in the "Notes." The word appears again and again as essential to the "malaise" that is the "Turn-of-Screw effect." In spite of all his efforts, Ralph constantly betrays himself, sometimes, it appears, almost intentionally, by the kind of deliberate/inadvertent revelation that leads someone to confess to a crime no one has any way of knowing he has committed. The result is that his perceived uncanny "difference" makes the others more and more fearful. It is as if they had seen a ghost, which indeed they have.

When Ralph enters his house in London and steps back into the past, he is endowed by his double, the "other man," with an almost complete memory of what that other man would have remembered in 1820. Almost complete, but not quite. As James makes clear in the "Notes," Ralph was to be shown as having "everything *en double* regulated and exhibited: he is doing over what the other fellow has done (although it acts for the other persons in it as if it were the first time)" (26:342). The difficulty begins, as I shall show, when he "deflects" (26:341) from the pre-established script. This is a feature of time travel narratives that James does not make explicit. If I return to the past, if I enter the personage of one of my ancestors, and then marry a woman my ancestor did not marry, that would presumably extinguish my present-day self like a snuffed candle, and so for every other "deflection" I import into the past. To change the past is to change the present.

Ralph's artificial or transfused memory, the memory his double has and shares with him, is not present all at once, as my memory of my past life appears to me to be. Ralph's memories come to him out of the blue, when he needs them, in "visitations" from the double that haunts him, as he haunts the others. These visitations come via a species of inadvertent telepathy. An example is Ralph's sudden memory that he has in his coat pocket a miniature portrait of Molly, or, later on, his knowledge that he has in another pocket a small fortune in coins. There they are when he needs them. He pulls them out and flourishes them over his head in his fist, in another scene whose hallucinatory dreamlike character anticipates Kafka: "And he chinked and chinked. . . . And he so liked his clutch that he drew it forth and held it high, shaking it in the air and laughing. 'Guess what this alone comes to'" (26:275–76). That's really weird! "Ralph *did,*" the narrator tells the reader, "as we know, grow many of his perceptions and possibilities from moment to moment and as they were wanted" (26:235). His "memory," however, seems to exceed what his double would have known. It becomes clairvoyant insight into what the others secretly know, as in his telepathic penetration into Perry's mind. Ralph's strange powers are like something out of a science fiction novel or out of a strangely reversed ghost story. Those imputed powers are calculated to aid what James called his "generally intended production of the 'new' frisson, as artfully as can be managed" (26:325).

Ralph's situation, strange as it is, may, however, be no more than a hyperbolic version of a feeling anyone may sometimes have when in the company of other people. This is the sense of not quite fitting in, of being "other" to these people. They seem to have no trouble going on solidly being themselves, while I feel like a ghostly intruding revenant, a species of "charlatan." This may especially be so when I am a visitor to another culture, an American, for example, being introduced to English society. This was the situation of James's "passionate pilgrim," Clement Searle, of Ralph Pendrel, and of James himself at one point, however adept he gradually became at understanding English middle- and upper-class behavior.

The Sense of the Past is a work of undoubted, though extremely peculiar, genius. That genius lies in its ability to represent the uncanny strangeness of the ordinary human consciousness of other people. One primary instrument of this representation is the excruciatingly slow motion I have identified. That *lento* seems to break down each second into component parts and to find fit words for each part by way of the advances, hesitations, qualifications, and subordinations of James's super-Jamesian style. This microscopic method, it may be, serves as an allegory of James's own experience of "inventing" the characters and their story as he dictates it, sentence by sentence. I mean inventing in the archaic sense of discovering. "Find it find it," he says at one point in the "Notes"; "get it right and it will be the making of the story" (26:311). Just as Ralph's "memory" comes to him from moment to moment, as he needs it, so the quite amazing

"Notes" show James from moment to moment getting clearer and clearer glimpses of the story he has not yet written. I shall say more about this later.

A splendid example of James's micro-narration in *The Sense of the Past* is a sequence beginning at the bottom of page 209 in the New York Edition. This passage is a good example not only because it is typical but also because it gives the reader terms and figures to understand just what James's stylistic procedures are up to. The sequence has to do with Ralph's admission to Molly that he has, back in New York, loved a woman who has refused him. This is, of course, a memory of Aurora Coyne. This memory suddenly comes to him from his other, 1910 life. This he more or less completely forgets as soon as he becomes the "other man" of 1820, though he gradually re-remembers more and more of it. He gradually becomes more and more again the man of 1910, but now that man trapped in 1820. Ralph's memory of Aurora is spoken of as a "visitation," as in "ghostly visitation." It is a term Derrida analyzes and plays with in *Specters of Marx*. It is also the term James uses in the "Notes" to name the return of Ralph's double or "alter ego" (26:312). That double reproaches Ralph for not playing his part, just as the ghost of Hamlet's father reproaches Hamlet. "He had," says the narrator, "visitations, had been having them uninterruptedly and with a vengeance—looking for them, invoking them [as one invokes a ghost or conjures it up], enjoying them as they came; but there was one that took him by surprise and that in the oddest way sinned by excess" (26:209–10). This is the memory of Aurora. When Ralph tells Molly that he "seem[s] to have let" the lady know he loved her, Molly taunts him by saying that if he only "seems to have" that makes her a pale ghost. She says, "even if her ghost does hover I shan't be afraid of so very thin a shade," to which Ralph replies: "Yes, it's a thin shade—and melts away hiding its face, even while I look back at it" (26:210). Ralph goes on to try to explain to Molly, to her mother, and to her brother just the way his knowledge works. This is a big mistake. It arouses amazement, fear, and incomprehension in the others, as he, so to speak, "blows his cover." Ralph has, the narrator says, a "wonder at himself which had on occasion, as appeared, a sharper play than any inspired by his friends" (26:211). Ralph goes on to say that, "I had to learn—that was my point—about sweet Nan; but now that I have, but now that I know it's as if I had known always, or have at any rate lived down my surprise" (26:211).

What Ralph says here violates the order of nature. Usually one has a memory stored away somewhere in one's mind and calls it up, perhaps in a conquering of forgetfulness. Ralph, however, gets the knowledge in the present. It then becomes, unnaturally, a memory, "as if he had known it always." The effect of this on his hearers is that his "fine ingenuity" back-fires: "to judge by something in their faces, [they] couldn't sufficiently admire [that ingenuity] in him or couldn't sufficiently follow [it]" (26:211). Ralph goes on to make matters worse by developing an elaborate domicili-ary metaphor that is literally true. His words are interspersed with elabo-rate accounts by the narrator of his moment-to-moment state of mind. "The case is," says Ralph, "that when once I *am* in the room it takes on quite the look of nature—at the end of almost no time" (26:211). This produces, as well it might, "a certain hush" in his auditors "beyond any of the several he had already had occasion to note his bringing about" (26:211). It is the hush of amazement and incomprehension, like suddenly seeing a ghost. Rather than changing the subject, as he would have been wise to do, Ralph "plunged deeper rather than shook himself free, dived to pick up, as who should say, just the right pearl of cheer" (26:211–12). So we might imagine James himself trying to explain one of his notorious tropological circumlocutions by adding yet another extravagant tropologi-cal circumlocution, as the figure of the pearl-diver here has been added to the more or less innocent quasi-figure in "dived." If James talked in com-pany at all as he represents Ralph as having talked, and apparently he did do so, he too must often have received blank stares of somewhat alarmed incomprehension in response to some elaborate Jamesian circumlocution. One remembers the famous story of James asking road directions from an uncomprehending English countryman when he was out driving with Edith Wharton. Ralph plunges deeper, to the growing consternation and bewilderment of his friends, by trying to explain that he has been speaking figuratively: "I mean a kind of idea of a room; so that catching the idea is what I call crossing the threshold. The thing is that when I catch it I really hold it, don't you see?" (26:212). His auditors don't see at all. Though Ralph says it is a figure, he has really got where he is by crossing the threshold of his London house and becoming the ghost that haunts it. The result of Ralph's attempt to offer a pearl of cheer by explaining what he means is "that appearance for our friend of his companions' helpless failure of any sign of their reading into his solicitous speech an imputable sense, however offhand the imputation" (26:213).

The climax of this small contretemps, which must have lasted a much shorter time than it takes James to tell it and his narrator to offer super-subtle comments on it, or me to recount it in my turn, is that Ralph suc-ceeds, to his own dismay, in turning Molly and the others to inanimate statues or wax figures. This, in a manner of speaking, they are, since they are invented characters in a novel, existing only in words. The blank in-comprehension of the others, says the narrator, speaking by its own tele-pathic knowledge of what is going on in Ralph's mind,

> amounted practically to a rupture of relation with them and presented them to his vision, during a series of moments, well-nigh as an artful, a wonderful trio, some mechanic but consummate imitation of ancient life, staring through the vast plate of a museum. It was for all the world as if his own interpretation grew, under this breath of a crisis, exactly by the lapse of theirs, lasting long enough to suggest that his very care for them had some-how annihilated them, or had at least converted them to the *necessarily* void and soundless state. He could understand that they didn't [understand him, that is], and that this would have made them take him for mad, the chill and dismay of which—felt for that matter by Ralph too—turned them to stone or wood or wax, or whatever it was they momentarily most resem-bled. The chill was a true felt drop of the temperature, a waft across them all of a mortal element, mortal at least to the others and menacing, should it have continued, to himself. (26:213)

Here time momentarily stops altogether. The narrator, meanwhile, takes all the time in the world to tell the reader what goes on during the "series of moments" when all the people in the scene remain poised, motionless. They have been made motionless by amazement at what Ralph has said and by their failure to understand him, also by their grow-ing fear of him as what James himself calls "uncanny" (26:295). What is uncanny about him is "his secret, . . . his queerness" (26:310). This, how-ever, turns them into what they actually are, a "consummate imitation of ancient life," that is, James's imagination of what people in England in 1820 of that class would have been like, how they would have dressed, talked, and behaved. This makes them like statues or wax figures in a mu-seum, behind plate glass, a simulacrum of life.

This perception of their fakery, as cunning imitations, not the real thing, is given the name *interpretation*. As Ralph's "interpretation" grows, they become deader and deader. Interpretation kills, for example, my in-terpretation here, which follows Ralph's. The mortal effect of interpreta-tion is a necessary sequence, as James's odd italicization of the word *necessarily* stresses: "his very care for them [that is, by trying to explain to them how he now understands about Nan, so appeasing their growing fear of him] had somehow annihilated them, or had at least converted them to the *necessarily* void and soundless state." Interpretation is an implacable deathwand or deathbone. It annihilates by an ineluctable necessity, just as, traditionally, a ghost—which is, after all, what Ralph is for them, just as they are ghosts or effigies for him—brings death or is a harbinger of death, as Hamlet's father's ghost presages Hamlet's death. The entire transaction between Ralph and the others brings a mortal chill to the Midmores, just as the grasp of the Commendatore's animated statue's hand, in Mozart / da Ponte's *Don Giovanni*, feels icy cold to Giovanni at the moment of his death. The mortal chill returns, however, on the death-dealing interpreter who has brought it. That chill menaces Ralph too with death. This is the death, one might say, of being permanently absorbed into the now dead and done with past. As Derrida's "spectrology," in *Specters of Marx*, asserts, ghosts always involve death, my death or my unappeasable mourning for the death of another.

This tension, the narrator says, could not have continued "at such a portentous pitch" (26:213) without annihilating Ralph too. The poise of the frozen moment is suddenly broken by the sound of coach wheels on the cobblestones outside in the square. The coach brings Sir Cantopher Bland, the next actor in the drama, onto the scene.

This extraordinary passage recalls Maggie's vision at the end of *The Golden Bowl* of Charlotte and the Prince taking tea as like figures in a wax museum. She and her father have killed them. The passage in *The Sense of the Past* is characteristic of the spectral, hallucinatory, dreamlike quality of the narration throughout. The reader will see what I mean by subdivision of the moment and its representation in a nightmarish slow motion that does not seem to further the action beyond working to inspire the fear of Ralph by the others that will precipitate the dénouement. *The Sense of the Past*, especially the new parts written after 1914, goes on from page to page like the example I have given. The weird narrative lento of this novel gradually inspires fear in the reader, this reader, at least. I helplessly succumb to the genuine "quasi-Turn-of-Screw effect."

Breaking the Spell

Ultimately, however, Molly, her mother, and her brother were, in parts of *The Sense of the Past* James did not live to write, to come to fear Ralph's uncanniness so much that Molly was to break off her engagement to him. This was to happen by way of "the particular effect [James wants] most to catch, that of the crescendo of the malaise" (26:307). Ralph's double living in 1910 was to become more and more dissatisfied with Ralph's behavior. He has wanted to marry Molly and wants ultimately to return to 1820 still free to do so. Or perhaps he expects to find himself already married to Molly by way of his double. Ralph's double was to make several reappearances or "visitations" to Ralph. He was to feel constantly "under observation" by his double. His alter ego was to come rather to like it in 1910. He was to threaten not to change places with him again if he did not play the game. That would have left Ralph forever trapped in an early nineteenth century that he finds more and more distasteful. He develops a tremendous longing to return to his original present, 1910, "of which he now sees only the ripeness, richness, attraction and civilization, the virtual perfection without a flaw" (26:337–38). Analogously, as we read *The Sense of the Past*, we today may conceivably long to return to 2005, to television sets and computer screens, though surely some irony exists in that phrase about "perfection without a flaw."

The "visitations" by Ralph's impatient double mean that, if Ralph is a ghost, another ghost haunts him. The ghost is enghosted, spooked in his turn. Ralph was finally to have confessed his plight to Molly's younger sister, Nan, who now really loves him. She was to have sacrificed herself to make it possible for him to return to 1910. This would have been a characteristically Jamesian act of renunciation, such as generally ends James's fictions: "The 'sacrifice,' the indispensable, unspeakable sacrifice on the girl's part, is involved in her relation to Ralph *as she now knows him*, and the quintessential 'drama' of it, so to speak, is by the same token involved in *his knowing her* as she knows him, and as, above all, she is known *by* him. . . . there is a kind of struggle between them as to who shall give up most" (26:348). James is not entirely clear how Nan's sacrifice liberates Ralph to return to 1910. Presumably it is because her renunciation allows his double to return to 1820 and marry Molly, which otherwise would not have been possible. His double acquiesces now in the re-exchange.

When Ralph returned to 1910, his final union with Aurora Coyne was to have taken place. She would have come to London, "under a tremendous 'psychic' anxiety and distress of her own" (26:293), to seek him out. Her "psychic" anxiety, James makes clear in the "Notes," arises from her telepathic sharing of Ralph's growing malaise: "she, left to the aftersense of what has passed between them, gradually feels her 'state of mind,' state of feeling, state of fancy, say, state of nerves in fine, grow and grow (in a sort of way that is corresponding all the while to the stages of his experience) till the pitch of unsupportable anxiety and wonder is reached for her, and being able no longer to stand it, she comes out to London" (26:352). Ralph has earned the right to marry Aurora by having a "prodigious" adventure. "[N]o prodigious adventure," says James in the "Notes," "of any such figure as she may have had in mind comes within millions of miles of the prodigy of his adventure" (26:352). A prodigy is, etymologically, ominous, full of omens. It is a key word in the "Notes," used repeatedly to describe Ralph's time travel. The "reunion" or "union" of Ralph and Aurora will happen, as I have said, just beyond the last pages of the novel, in a ghostly prolepsis, "so aloof do I feel," James says in the "Notes," "from the possibility of a kind of graceless literality" (26:356). You can say that again! Graceless, or even graceful, literality was not James's forte.

To summarize the action in this way makes it all sound pretty silly, though perhaps many novels would sound silly if baldly given in précis, as I have done with this one. I have said that I believe in *The Sense of the Past*. I must confess that it takes some doing. The alternative is to think James himself or Ralph, his hero, mad, as the Ambassador does think Ralph "demented." One way to think, mistakenly, that you can escape from the aporia of *The Turn of the Screw*, one way to be trapped by the text, is to decide that the governess is mad. Edmund Wilson, followed by many other psychoanalytical critics, notoriously came to that conclusion. To say James or Ralph must be mad is to make a similar futile gesture. I have mimed this response in my own remarks, for example, by saying the plot sounds "silly." Saying this is an apotropaic gesture, to ward off the possibility that some readers of this chapter might say, "What an idiot! He has allowed himself to be taken in by this cunningly contrived representation of paranoia." The Ambassador is the reader's surrogate in the novel for that response: "The Ambassador," says James in the "Notes," "*does* of course think him a curious and interesting case of dementia, feels a kind of superior responsibility about him accordingly, is really in a manner 'fascinated' and mystified too" (26:291). To think Ralph is mad is just another way to be fascinated and mystified, to be caught by that particular turn of the screw.

A Further Twist

What in the world was James up to in this novel?

A number of references to *The Turn of the Screw* punctuate the "Notes" to *The Sense of the Past*. The titular metaphor of James's most famous ghost story is also present in several places. James talks several times about adding another "twist" to the story. The figure is not altogether perspicuous. It has been given contradictory interpretations by critics. The figure of the turn of the screw can refer simply to the twists of a story, as when we say, of *The Turn of the Screw*, "Another twist is given when we realize that the governess is unconsciously in love with the master, or when we see that the governess is molesting the children in the same way she suspects Peter Quint and Miss Jessel to have molested them," or as when James speaks of adding "an effective further twist or two" to *The Sense of the Past* (26:346). That later title, by the way, can be twisted in at least two ways. It can be read as referring to a "feeling for the past" or as referring to "the meaning the past has." Speaking of the way Ralph is "both the other man and not the other man" (26:300), James says this "again strikes me as adding to my action but another admirable twist. Of course I'm afraid of twists, I mean of their multiplying on my hands to the effect of too much lengthening and enlarging and sprawling" (26:299). "I must guard," says James in the "Notes," "guard and all the while intensely guard, myself, none the less—or I shall sprawl out over ever so much more ground than I shall want, or at all need, for my best effect, to cover" (26:307). A new twist is a further addition to the intrigue. Aristotle speaks in chapter 18 of the *Poetics* of what he calls, in Gerald Else's translation, the "tying [*desis*]" of a tragedy, just he calls the ending of a tragedy its "unraveling," "untying [*lusis*]," its untwisting, so to speak.[22] *Lusis* is present in the English word *analysis*. Analysis is interpretation as simultaneous untwisting and twisting, by way of the antithetical prefix *ana-*, which means alongside and against at the same time.

The figure of the turn of the screw, however, also suggests the way James's cunning art screws each part of the novel firmly into place, making a watertight box that resists penetration. He speaks of the invention of the story as "my turning of my present screw" (26:307). Later he says an act of what one might call applying the screws is necessary to force the details of his story to reveal themselves: "Let me figure it out a bit, and under gentle, or rather patiently firm, direct pressure it will come out" (26:311).

A variant of the screw image is used repeatedly in the "Notes" when James speaks of what he calls *clous*, French for "nails," but perhaps also with a pun on "clues." He also calls his *clous* hinges, pivots on which the story turns, recalling Aristotle's term "reversal [*peripeteia*]." James uses silver nails to fasten his story down tight: "The reappearance at home of the second girl, from wherever she has been (expressible in 10 words) at any rate is, as it were, my first clou or hinge" (26:308); "There must be sequences here of the strongest, I make out—the successive driving in of the successive silver-headed nails at the very points and under the very taps that I reserve for them. That's it, the silver nail, the perfection and salience of each, and the trick is played" (26:313). These "clous d'argent" (ibid.) nail down the story at successive points, just as a turn of the screw tightens down a lid, perhaps a coffin lid. Such a lid may be hinged, since James also calls his *clous* hinges, in a not wholly coherent modulation of his figure. The story turns on the succession of silver-headed *clous*. The silver nails in a row made of the successive events of the story, what James calls "every successive link in the chain" (26:327), each nail/hinge/link giving it another twist, expose, however, in the end, a decorative design, salient against a blank background. These nail-heads stand out to make the aesthetic pattern and "tone" of the finished product. James repeatedly uses the term *salience* to name this "standing out."

Another, and final, meaning, however, lurks in the figure of the turn of the screw. This additional meaning is a concluding turn of the screw. In one place in the "Notes," James speaks of "my essential hinges or, as I have called 'em, *clous*, that mark the turns or steps of the action" (26:307). A turn is a twist is a trope, that is, a figure of speech. The word *trope* means "turn," as in "apotropaic," meaning "having the power to turn away." I have already used the word *apotropaic* to name my warding off of those readers who might say I am naïve, or perhaps mad myself, to believe in this absurd story. To say, however, that each twist of the story, each turn of the screw, is another trope, each episode or complication a troping of the episode before, calls attention to the general tropological or even allegorical (in the de Manian sense) dimension of *The Sense of the Past.* Each apparently "realistic" or mimetically represented element stands for something else that is named only indirectly, can be named only indirectly, in catachresis, in a constant displacement from clue to clue or from *clou* to *clou.*

Tropes of What?

It is a priori difficult to say (because by definition it is not directly sayable) just what the ultimate referent of all these tropes or turns of the screw may be. James's phrase "the quasi-Turn-of Screw effect" may, however, come close to naming it, though still in figure. The ultimate referent, it may be, is the uncanny power of words, when used in the way we call "literary," to raise ghosts and thereby to inspire fear. This is, perhaps, the fear, to appropriate a phrase from the novel, of being ourselves no more than "some chapter of some other story" (26:119). This happens as we become inhabited by the ghosts in the stories we read, outside becoming inside once more.

My five Derridean motifs may provide some further clues to follow deeper into this labyrinthine text. Perhaps I had better call them five silver nails with which to pin down my reading. I have spoken already of the way James capitalizes on a Derridean sense that houses are always haunted by the "other." Derrida's "hauntology," in *Specters of Marx*, can help us understand how ghosts are raised by texts that are inheritances from the past. To read an old text, such as *The Sense of the Past*, is to raise ghosts. It is to be forced by the performative effect of the words on the page to see apparitions. The whole of English literature, enshrined there in the books on my shelves, can be said to swarm with ghosts, with the physical books as their houses. The reader will remember James's celebrated phrase, in the preface to *The Portrait of a Lady*, about how "the house of fiction has in short not one window, but a million."[23] It could be shown in detail how James, in a way that recalls "The Jolly Corner," makes Ralph's exploration, at dusk or in the nighttime, of the intricacies of his inherited London house, floor above floor and room behind room, generate the "quasi-Turn-of-Screw effect." The phrase, in this case, means a general fear that houses may be haunted. The description of the house generates that indefinite fear in the reader special to ghost stories. Ralph's exploration of his house leads ultimately to his confrontation with his double. His double inhabits the house in the concrete form of the portrait in an inner room, the inside of the inside, a "small inner retreat" (26:347), a kind of Derridean crypt, such as the one he describes so exuberantly in "*Fors.*" The double in the portrait embodies the generalized fear of the spooky house that the reader, by this time, shares with Ralph.

The reader shares that fear by way of an extravagant version of the telepathy effect. In using this term I am referring to Derrida's essay "Télépathie." I am also thinking of how that essay is brilliantly applied by Nicholas Royle to narrative strategy. "Telepathy": the word means "feeling at a distance." James insists more than once in the "Notes" that the consistency and beauty of *The Sense of the Past* depends on rigorously maintaining the point of view or center of consciousness as always and only Ralph's own. We can see and know and feel only what Ralph sees and knows and feels. The medium of this knowledge, of course, is the narrator. That narrator reports Ralph's thoughts and feelings in the third person, past tense. (The "Notes" are in the present tense. I shall return to the importance of this.) The narrator, whoever he or it is, knows Ralph through and through in an extraordinary experience of telepathy. The reader shares in this telepathy effect. He or she is given, by way of the narrator's words, in the excruciating slow-motion, moment-to-moment notation I have discussed, just that sense of the past that Ralph is said to want, "to be again consciously the creature that *had* been, to breathe as he had breathed and feel the pressure that he had felt." The reader has telepathic knowledge, through the narrator's words, of the narrator's telepathic knowledge of Ralph. This telepathic effect goes in only one direction. Ralph is not shown to be aware that he is known through and through in this way by the narrator, nor is the narrator shown as aware of our knowledge of what he knows. Is the narrator a "he," or perhaps a "she," or an "it"? The narrator is not personified. The narrative voice speaks only, impersonally, of what "we" know. This telepathic effect, though it is the most ordinary thing in the world in novels, seems quite extraordinary if you think about it for a moment. Think what it would be like if your own most secret thoughts and feelings were known by another penetrating impersonal consciousness endowed with telepathic powers. God, in Christian theology, is supposed to have that knowledge of each of us, to have a universal power of telepathy. The Christian God is a telepathic genius.

The "telepathy effect" in *The Sense of the Past* is, however, more complex than this. Ralph Pendrel's surname suggests someone who wields the power of the pen, who drives the pen. *El* is a root meaning "to go," as in Greek *elaunein*, "to drive." Ralph's surname suggests that he is a surrogate for the pen-wielding author. When Ralph Pendrel crosses the threshold of his own house back into the past of 1820, he instantly takes on the personality of his double. He becomes a strange, indeed "uncanny," double personage, a double consciousness. He is both aware of himself as his double and still aware of himself as the Ralph Pendrel of 1910 who is playing the role of his ancestor. "[H]is impression," the narrator says, in a sentence already cited in part, "was that of stepping straight into some chapter of some other story" (26:119). It is not quite certain to Ralph at this point which is the primary story and which is the "other story." His position in relation to the double whom he impersonates is quite like the telepathic relation between narrator and character in the prolonged act of indirect discourse that makes up so much of the novel. The relation between narrator and character is doubled by the relation of Ralph to his double.

Ralph's double has apparently, offstage as it were, before the exchange takes place, given him some hints as to the family situation he is entering and as to the role he will be expected to play as the rich relative from New York come to marry Molly Midmore. Nevertheless, much of the part of

Book Four that James lived to finish writing is made up of an extraordinary account of the way Ralph feels his way into his new self and into his situation in relation to Molly and to the rest of the Midmore family. Inspirations come to him from moment to moment as to what he should say and how he should act. These inspirations come to him by way of a telepathic communication between the person he really is and the person of the past he has magically become. He is also aided by his quite unrealistic telepathic insight into what the Midmores are thinking and feeling. Much of the time he gets it right. This gives him more and more confidence, as when he spontaneously embraces and kisses Molly Midmore the moment he sees her: "That he was to make love, by every propriety, to Molly Midmore, and that he had in fact reached his goal [that is, the goal of the relative from New York who has arrived in 1820] on the very wings of that intention, this foretaste as of something rare had for days and days past hung about him like the scent of a flower persisting in life; but the sweetness of his going straight up to her with an offered embrace hadn't really been disclosed till her recognition, as we have said, breathed upon it with force and filled him at once with an extraordinary wealth of confidence" (26:121). Which "days past" does he mean, those for the man of 1820 or those for the man of 1910? It is impossible to be sure, since when Ralph becomes his double he is suddenly endowed with that double's memory, as well as retaining his own. He has two memories, one superimposed on the other, though he is not often, in the part James lived to write, shown to be explicitly aware of the memories or self-consciousness he had in his 1910 life. Nevertheless, as James says in the "Notes," Ralph is "just sufficiently the other, his prior, his own, self, not to be able to help living in that a bit too" (26:300). This is analogous to the way we never quite fully "lose ourselves" in identification with the protagonist when we read a work of fiction.

"The scent of a flower persisting in life" is a wonderfully apt description of the spectral. If Ralph is a ghost haunting the past, that past can be entered only because it has gone on existing somewhere, like the scent of a flower when the flower is gone. That spectral past remains ready to be entered by someone with Ralph's extraordinary sense of the past. In an analogous way, the narrator dwells in some indefinite future and revivifies the events from some indefinitely distant past. This is indicated only by the use of the conventional past tense in the narration. We readers, in our turn, invoke, convoke, call up, conjure, the ghosts of all these characters when we pick up the novel and read. Reading a novel, as I have said, is a raising of ghosts. The increasingly urgent visitations inflicted on Ralph by his double are embodiments of that telepathic interchange between Ralph and his alter ego.

Ralph's magically appropriated memory, transposed from his double to him, is not, however, perfect. He remembers, by a sudden inspiration, that he has Molly's miniature portrait in his pocket, and there it is. He remembers that he has in his portmanteau tied up in red ribbon Molly's letters. He remembers details from those letters. He does not, however, at first remember the existence of Molly's younger sister, "Sweet Nan." He has to go to great lengths with the others to try to cover up this lapse in memory. He does not remember what he realizes he ought to know. It is these little slips, as much as anything, along with gestures, behavior, and speech that belong to 1910, not 1820, and even little details like his unnaturally good teeth, for 1820, that, as I have said, gradually give him away and cause a profound "malaise" in the Midmore family. It is the malaise of those who have seen a ghost: "he creates malaise, by not being *like* them all" (26:296).

Ralph's painful and not always at first successful attempt to play the role of a historical personage mimes, it can be said, the way a novelist—James, for example—gradually feels his or her way into the plausible and full representation of an invented character and an invented scene in the historical past. *Invention* here, however, as always, has its overtone of "discover" as well as a primary meaning of "to make up freely, by way of the imagination's sovereign authority." Ralph's difficulties mime James's difficulties in trying to imagine, somewhat awkwardly, it must be said, how well-to-do English men and women of 1820 would talk and behave. *The Sense of the Past* is, among other things, a "historical novel." James, it might be said, is trying to carry out the recommendations Ralph Pendrel may be imagined to have made in *An Essay in Aid of the Reading of History.* Though we never get to read that imaginary work, the title gives a clue as to what it must be like.

Where Is the Unfinished Part?

The multidimensional telepathy effect of *The Sense of the Past* has, however, one final dimension, the strangest and most uncanny of all. James died before finishing *The Sense of the Past.* What mode of existence does the unfinished part have? Ordinarily, with unfinished works—say, Schubert's Unfinished Symphony or Shelley's *The Triumph of Life*—the prudent and commonsense answer would be to say that the unfinished part has no sort of existence at all. We have no idea what it would have been, so it is best not to speculate, best not to say anything at all about it. In the case of *The Sense of the Past*, however, we have, as I have said, the full notes that James dictated when he returned in 1914 to the parts written in 1900, that is, after almost fifteen years. These notes track, in considerable detail, James's plan for finishing the novel, right through to the proposed end in the still somewhat postponed union of Ralph and Aurora. In the case of the lengthy notes James wrote for *The Ambassadors*, the finished novel can be compared point by point to the extensive plans, as a building may be compared to the architect's drawings. For *The Sense of the Past*, we have for a large part of the novel only the architect's plans. Only one big wing of the building was actually built.

About the "Notes" for *The Sense of the Past* there would be much to say, and I have already made extensive use of them. I limit myself now to what is essential for my purposes in this concluding section. These notes are a precious account not only of James's sense of the proprieties of literary form but also of the strange process whereby his stories, this one at least, "came to him." What is extraordinary about the "Notes" is that James does not speak in them as if he were making up the action of his novel. He speaks as if that action has somewhere an ideal existence and his problem is to get access to the already-existing story, so he can write it down correctly, thereby transmitting it to his readers. The events of the novel have exactly the same kind of existence for James as the London of 1820 has for Ralph Pendrel, *in* the novel. It both cases, it is an existence that can be, with difficulty, and not always with perfect success, telepathically known. Derrida, in "The Time of a Thesis: Punctuations," speaks of having put officially on record his intention to write a doctoral dissertation on "The Ideality of the Literary Object." He never wrote that thesis, any more than James ever finished *The Sense of the Past*. It exists only as an unrealized "ideality." What Derrida says in "The Time of a Thesis," however, makes clear what he meant by that title:

> It was then for me a matter of bending, more or less violently, the techniques of transcendental phenomenology to the needs of elaborating a new theory of literature, of the very peculiar type of an ideal object that is the literary object, a bound ideality Husserl would have said, bound to so-called "natural" language, a non-mathematical or non-mathematizable object, and yet one that differs from the objects of plastic or musical art, that is to say from all of the examples privileged by Husserl in his analyses of ideal objectivity.[24]

A triangle is for Husserl an ideal mathematical object. It exists independently of its actualization in any triangles in the material world. In a similar way, any work of literature, according to Derrida, would exist somewhere, in a perpetual present, even if it were never to get written down, or even if it has been written down but all copies of it have been destroyed. The latter is the case, for example, with all those lost plays by Sophocles. Copies of them were burned, presumably in the fire in the Library of Alexandria.

James speaks in the "Notes" of *The Sense of the Past* in exactly this way. The notes are all in the present tense. The key expression is *I see*, with many variants. These expressions are repeated again and again to name the act of vision whereby another detail of his unwritten novel becomes clear to James. In a similar way, Ralph Pendrel, in the novel, comes gradually to see who he is and how he should behave when he becomes his double. For James, it is not at all a matter of making up the novel. It is a matter of getting to see clearly something that already exists and to which he alone, apparently, has access, by a species of telepathy: "I have it perfectly before me" (26:292); "I see that he states it to Aurora all sufficiently" (26:294); "It will take more working out, which will come but too abundantly, I seem to apprehend, as I go; but I have the substance of it, I have that still, as I had it of old, in my vision" (26:294); "the more magnificent, upon my word, I seem to see and feel it" (26:295); "I see somehow such beautiful things that I can hardly keep step with myself to expatiate and adumbrate coherently enough" (26:298); "there glimmers out, there floats shyly back to me from afar, the sense of something like *this*, a bit difficult to put, though entirely expressible with patience, and that as I catch hold of the tip of the tail of it yet again strikes me as adding to my action another admirable twist" (26:299); "one sees" (26:300); "Don't I see" (26:301); "At once, withal, I see it in images, which I must put as they come" (26:302); "I seem to make out" (26:303); "I see with a minute's further intensity of focusing" (26:303), and so on and on. A notation of this sort exists on almost every page, on through to such rhapsodic claims of vision as these five more I cannot resist citing: "Yes, yes, yes, I have it, I have it" (26:316); "I feel that my subject contains the exact, the exquisite rightness for this deep in its breast, if only I watch hard enough to see said rightness emerge—emerge as it were of itself and as from the operation of what surrounds it" (26:338); "in short what I see! I have it all, I possess it here, and now must give pause to this long out-ciphering" (26:349); or "There hovers before me a something-or-other in this, a finer twist still, a deeper depth or higher flight of the situation, which seems worth looking into, and which in fact already appears to open out a good bit before me as I consider it" (26:348). This last citation gives yet another meaning to the figure of the twist or turn: the screw goes down into fathomless depths. Here is the last such passage of all in the "Notes," two pages from their end: "I shall see, I shall make up my mind: it will come, in true rightness, it *can* come but so, when I get in close nearness to it" (26:356).

See in these passages has a double meaning. It means "see" in the sense of understanding, as in "I see it all now." It also means *see* as uncanny vision, as in "I am a seer, a visionary. I have seen ghosts." James's "Notes" to *The Sense of the Past* are witness both to the sources of the novel and to its mode of existence. This extraordinary cascade of phrases confirms that James, if his testimony is to be believed, did not concoct the action and characters of *The Sense of the Past* out of thin air. They existed, so it seemed to him, somewhere always already there. They hovered in a perpetual present, waiting to be caught by the tip of the tail, or seen in visionary insight. James was himself haunted by wraiths and visions as he planned out the novel, or, rather, as he let it reveal its plan to him. His vision became then a set of signs that needed to be "out-ciphered," that is, first read, deciphered, and then, in James's neologism, re-ciphered, turned into the words that will make it available to readers. This happens in the irresistible created vision brought about in readers as the quasi-Turn-of-Screw effect. This effect is a performative use of words. It is a speech act that one might call a "conjuration." The *quasi* in James's phrase, I take it, means that *The Sense of the Past*, like *The Turn of the Screw*, makes its readers believe in it. The reader reads personages into its "blanks," including the figured or worded blank that stands for Ralph's ghostly presence in 1820. The difference that justifies *quasi* is the absence of the indefinite, and therefore all the more fearsome, sense of evil that is the center of *The Turn of the Screw*.

Where, after James's death, is the part of the novel he did not live to write down, but of which he had such a clear vision? The "Notes" give the reader a strange glimmer of it, like a faint ghostly presence. In a similar way, Ralph has "glimmers" of things he ought to know if he were his double, but does not quite see or remember clearly. The thing itself, the unwritten part of *The Sense of the Past*, is lost forever. It still exists somewhere as the possibility of the words James did not write. Only James, however, had direct access to that possibility, that virtual reality, that "ideality." With his death, he took his clear vision of *The Sense of the Past* with him to his grave. There it remains encrypted in unrecoverable secrecy, except for the uncanny access without access to it given us by the "Notes."

Conclusion, in Which Nothing Is Concluded

I conclude that *The Sense of the Past*, unfinished as it is, demonstrates admirably, in one example, both how all James's stories are ghost stories and how his ghost stories proper are all, obliquely, about the act of writing fictions and about the performative "quasi-Turn-of-Screw effect" fictions have on their readers. All the chapters in this book have in one way or another explored these features of James's work. I claim also to have demonstrated how Jacques Derrida's work not specifically on literature in English may nevertheless inspire productive questions to be addressed to such literature. I must stop here, and high time, though with a sense that there would be much more to say. As James says, at the end of the preface to *The Portrait of a Lady*, "There is really too much to say" (3:xxi).

NOTES

INTRODUCTION

1. Henry James, *The Golden Bowl*, reprint of the New York Edition of *The Novels and Tales of Henry James*, 26 vols. (Fairfield, N.J.: Augustus M. Kelley, 1971–79), 23:xxiv–xxv. Henceforth in this book citations from James's works will be identified by volume and page number in this edition, which is a reprint of the New York Edition of 1907–9. I have discussed the preface to *The Golden Bowl*, though without explicit reference to speech act theory, in *The Ethics of Reading* (New York: Columbia University Press, 1987), 101–22.

2. J. Hillis Miller, *Speech Acts in Literature* (Stanford: Stanford University Press, 2001).

3. See Stanley Cavell, "Derrida's Austin and the Stake of Positivism," *A Pitch of Philosophy: Autobiographical Exercises* (Cambridge: Harvard University Press, 1994), 77–86.

4. J. L. Austin, *How to Do Things with Words* (Cambridge: Harvard University Press, 1962). A corrected edition is J. L. Austin, *How to Do Things with Words*, 2d ed., ed. J. O. Urmson and Marina Sbisà (Oxford: Oxford University Press, 1980). Further references will be to the latter edition, identified as *HT*.

5. I am thinking, for example, of the shift within *How to Do Things with Words* from the performative/constative distinction to the distinction among locutionary, illocutionary, and perlocutionary acts of language. A final shift introduces yet another nomenclature: Verdictives, Exercitives, Commissives, Behabitives, and Expositives.

6. See, especially, John Searle, *Speech Acts: An Essay in the Philosophy of Language* (Cambridge: Cambridge University Press: 1969), and Jacob Mey, *Pragmatics: An Introduction* (Oxford: Blackwell, 1993).

7. John Searle, "A Classification of Illocutionary Acts," *Proceedings of the Texas Conference on Performatives, Presuppositions, and Implicatures*, ed. Andy Rogers, Bob Wall, and John P. Murphy (Washington, D.C.: Center for Applied Linguistics, 1977), 27–45.

8. See my *Speech Acts in Literature*, 219–20, for a brief bibliography of speech act theory. For further work on speech act theory, see, for example, Shoshana Felman, *The Scandal of the Speaking Body: Don Juan with J. L. Austin,*

or Seduction in Two Languages, trans. Catherine Porter, with a new foreword by Stanley Cavell, and afterword by Judith Butler (Stanford: Stanford University Press, 2003).

9. Derrida's two essays, a summary of Searle's and a new "Afterword," were collected in Jacques Derrida, *Limited Inc* (Evanston, Ill.: Northwestern University Press, 1988).

10. See *HT*, 22: "a performative utterance will, for example, be *in a peculiar way* hollow or void if said by an actor on the stage." That italicized phrase, *in a peculiar way*, is a good example of what is subtle and even enigmatic about Austin's reasoning. Just what is that "peculiar way"? How does it differ from other forms of infelicity, for example, from a marriage performed by someone not authorized to perform marriages? Austin had a great genius for seeing problems and ramifications in his own arguments.

11. To "cock a snook," says the OED, is a "derisive gesture," "of obscure origin." It defines a "snook" as "a projecting point or piece of land; a promontory." To cock a snook, Julian Wolfreys informs me, is to thumb one's nose.

12. Jacques Derrida, "Psyche: Inventions of the Other," *A Derrida Reader*, ed. Peggy Kamuf (New York: Columbia University Press, 1991), 207–8.

13. Paul de Man, "Excuses (*Confessions*)," *Allegories of Reading* (New Haven: Yale University Press, 1979), 296, 299, 300.

14. Jacques Derrida, *Aporias*, trans. Thomas Dutoit (Stanford: Stanford University Press, 1993).

15. See Jacques Derrida, "Déclarations d'indépendance," *Otobiographies* (Paris: Galilée, 1984), 13–32; "Declarations of Independence," trans. Thomas Keenan and Thomas Pepper, *New Political Science* 15 (1986): 15: 7–15.

16. Jacques Derrida, "Fourmis," *Lectures de la différence sexuelle*, ed. Mara Negrón (Paris: Des femmes, 1994), 89, my trans. The passages I cite from Derrida are full of puns and wordplay that are difficult to translate, to say the least. *Appeller* means "call," while *rappeler* means, among other senses, "to call back, to summon up, to restore," and *se rappeler* means "to recollect, to remember, to recall to mind." *Tu* means "you" in the singular, "thou," but it is also the past participle of *taire*, "not to say, to keep hidden."

17. Jacques Derrida, "Deconstruction and the Other," in Richard Kearney, *Dialogues with Contemporary Continental Thinkers: The Phenomenological Heritage* (Manchester: Manchester University Press, 1984), 123.

18. Jacques Derrida, *Aporias*, 22. I have changed Dutoit's "completely" to "wholly."

19. Jacques Derrida, "Psyché: Invention de l'autre," *Psyché: Inventions de l'autre* (Paris: Galilée, 1987), 60, my trans.

20. *Dehisce* is a botanical term meaning "to burst or split open along a line or slit, as do the ripe capsules or pods of some plants," in order to release seeds (*The American Heritage Dictionary*).

21. *Derrida*, "Psyché: Invention de l'autre," 58–59; 60–61, my trans.

22. "L'autre appelle à venir et cela n'arrive qu'à plusieurs voix"; "The other calls [something] to come and that does not arrive except in multiple voices" (*ibid.*, 61, my trans.).

CHAPTER 1: HISTORY, NARRATIVE, RESPONSIBILITY: "THE ASPERN PAPERS"

1. Henry James, "Anthony Trollope," *Literary Criticism: Essays on Literature; American Writers; English Writers* (New York: The Library of America, 1984), 1343. I have discussed this passage in "Narrative and History," *ELH* 41, no. 3 (Fall 1974): 455–73.

2. The sentence reads this way in the revision of the story for the New York Edition. The first version (of 1888) has "When I look at it my chagrin at the loss of the letters becomes almost intolerable" (Henry James, *Complete Stories*, 5 vols. [New York: The Library of America, 1996–99], 3: 320). James made a number of changes in this story for the New York Edition, for example, changing the name of Juliana Bordereau's niece (if she is a niece, rather than her daughter) from Miss Tita to Miss Tina. The changes often add important nuances. I have therefore cited the revised version. The changes act as an implicit reading of the story by its author after its publication, as the prefaces do more overtly. The preface to *The Golden Bowl* discusses the way rereading is both re-vision and revision.

3. See, for example, the preface to *The Portrait of a Lady*, where James speaks of "the anxiety of my provision for the reader's amusement" (1:xvi).

4. Joseph Conrad, *Heart of Darkness*, in *Youth: A Narrative, and Two Other Stories, Works*, 22 vols. (London: Dent, 1923), vols. not numbered, 48. Paul de Man works out the implications of this inside/outside figure for a hermeneutic way of reading in "Semiology and Rhetoric," *Allegories of Reading* (New Haven: Yale University Press, 1979), 3–19. An admirable unpublished paper by Naomi Silver on "The Aspern Papers" called my attention to the relevance of this paradigm for reading the story.

5. James, *Complete Stories*, 3:319.

6. One critic has read the story as a disguised representation of James's feelings about his book on Nathaniel Hawthorne for the English Men of Letters series. That book is in large part biographical. James had tried unsuccessfully to persuade Hawthorne's son Julian (perhaps obliquely referred to in the name *Juliana* in "The Aspern Papers") to give him access to Hawthorne's private papers. Julian later published his father's intimate papers himself and was widely criticized for this as a "publishing scoundrel" (12:118), to cite again the words Juliana Bordereau hisses at the narrator at the climax of the story. See Gary Scharnhorst, "James, 'The Aspern Papers,' and the Ethics of Literary Biography," *Modern Fiction Studies* 36, no. 2 (Summer 1990): 211–17.

7. Friedrich Nietzsche, *Sämtliche Werke: Kritische Studienausgabe*, ed. Giorgio Colli and Mazzino Montinari (Berlin: de Gruyter, 1988), 1:243; "On the Uses and Disadvantages of History for Life," *Untimely Meditations*, trans. R. J. Hollingdale (Cambridge: Cambridge University Press, 1983), 59.

8. Paul de Man, "Kant and Schiller," *Aesthetic Ideology*, ed. A. J. Warminski (Minneapolis: University of Minnesota Press, 1996), 134.

9. *Ibid.*, 132, 133. For materiality in de Man, see the Introduction to the present book.

10. Paul de Man, "The Resistance to Theory," *The Resistance to Theory* (Minneapolis: University of Minnesota Press, 1986), 11.

11. Walter Benjamin, *Illuminationen* (Frankfurt a. M.: Suhrkamp, 1955), 278; *Illuminations*, trans. Harry Zohn (New York: Schocken, 1969), 263.

12. *HT*, 119. See the Introduction to the present book for a discussion of sign acts or gesture acts in Austin's theory.

CHAPTER 2: THE STORY OF A KISS: ISABEL'S DECISIONS IN *THE PORTRAIT OF A LADY*

1. *The Portrait of a Lady* is in volumes 3 and 4 of *The Novels and Tales of Henry James*, 26 vols. (Fairfield, N.J.: Augustus M. Kelley, 1971–79). Page numbers to this edition will be given in the text.

2. See Alastair Hannay, *Kierkegaard: A Biography* (Cambridge: Cambridge University Press, 2001), 158–59. I owe this kiss to Jennifer Williams, who cites it in an admirable dissertation chapter on Kierkegaard.

3. Lydia Maria Child, *The Mother's Book* (Boston: Carter and Hendee, 1831; repr. New York: Arno, 1972), cited in Patricia Crain, *The Story of A: The Alphabetization of America from The New England Primer to The Scarlet Letter* (Stanford: Stanford University Press, 2000), 127.

4. Stephen Owen, ed., *An Anthology of Chinese Literature* (New York: Norton, 1966).

5. James Joyce, *A Portrait of the Artist as a Young Man* (New York: Viking, 1964), 14–15.

6. Sigmund Freud, *The Complete Introductory Lectures on Psychoanalysis*, trans. James Strachey (New York: Norton, 1966), 322, 323. The original German versions of the two sets of lectures were published in 1916–17 and in 1933.

7. Sigmund Freud, *Three Essays on the Theory of Sexuality*, trans. James Strachey (New York: Avon, 1972), 38. This edition reprints the Standard Edition version.

8. William Butler Yeats, *Poems*, Variorium Edition, ed. Peter Allt and Russell K. Alspach (New York: Macmillan, 1977), 513.

9. George Eliot, *Adam Bede*, ed. Stephen Gill (Harmondsworth, Middlesex: Penguin, 1980), 433.

10. James Joyce, *Ulysses* (New York: Modern Library, 1934), 145.

11. James Joyce, *Finnegans Wake* (New York: Viking, 1947), 308.

12. See Marcel Proust, *Remembrance of Things Past*, 3 vols., trans. C. K. Scott Moncrieff, Terence Martin, and Andreas Mayor (New York: Vintage, 1982), 1:33ff.; 2:137, 135; 2:863; 2:1162.

13. Jacques Derrida, *Le toucher, Jean-Luc Nancy* (Paris: Galilée, 2000), 84–85, my trans. here and hereafter. Citations will henceforth be indicated in the text by page numbers only.

14. George Meredith, *The Egoist*, vols. 13 and 14 of *Works*, Memorial Edition, 27 vols. (London: Constable, 1910), 13:29–30; 13:88.

15. Franz Kafka, *Letters to Milena*, trans. T. and J. Stern, ed. W. Hass (New York: Schocken, 1954), 229, trans. slightly altered; for the German original, see *Briefe an Milena*, ed. W. Hass (New York: Schocken, 1952), 260.

16. Thomas De Quincey, *Collected Writings*, ed. David Masson (London: A. & C. Black, 1897), 375–76. Daniel Cottom, in "Kant Comes to His Senses," the last chapter of *Cannibals and Philosophers: Bodies of Enlightenment* (Baltimore: Johns Hopkins University Press, 2001), has discussed this extraordinary Kantian kiss.

17. Heinrich von Kleist, *Sämtliche Werke und Briefe*, ed. Helmut Sembdner (Munich: Carl Hanser, 1984), 1:425, my trans.

18. Barbara Thiering, *Jesus and the Riddle of the Dead Sea Scrolls* (San Francisco: Harper San Francisco, 1992), 87–88. See also, for a slightly different translation, Christopher Knight and Robert Lomas, *The Second Messiah: Templars, the Turin Shroud and the Great Secret of Freemasonry* (Boston: Element Books, Inc., 1997), 91.

19. Paul de Man, "The Return to Philology," *The Resistance to Theory* (Minneapolis: University of Minnesota Press, 1986), 24, 25.

20. Paul de Man, "Shelley Disfigured," *The Rhetoric of Romanticism* (New York: Columbia University Press, 1984), 117–18.

21. Paul de Man, *Allegories of Reading* (New Haven: Yale University Press, 1979), 77, henceforth *AR*, followed by the page number.

22. Nicholas Royle, "The 'Telepathy Effect': Notes toward a Reconsideration of Narrative Fiction," *The Uncanny* (Manchester: Manchester University Press, 2003), 256–76; also available in *Acts of Narrative*, ed. Carol Jacobs and Henry Sussman (Stanford: Stanford University Press, 2003), 93–109.

23. This figure echoes George Eliot's image, in *Middlemarch*, for Casaubon's mistaken belief that because he has delayed marriage he will have stored up large reservoirs of unused passion, like a big balance in a bank account. Of course, James may have come on his own to the same figure, but, added to other details, it is one more small bit of evidence for the large influence of *Middlemarch* on *The Portrait of a Lady*. I shall have more to say later about this influence.

24. See *HT*, 20: "and here I must let some of my cats on the table."

25. Anthony Trollope, *An Autobiography*, ed. David Skilton (London: Penguin, 1996), 119.

26. George Eliot, *Middlemarch*, ed. Rosemary Ashton (London: Penguin, 1994), 195–96.

27. "My attempt to marry by saying 'I will,' " asserts Austin, "is abortive if the woman says 'I will not' " (*HT*, 37). I have discussed Austin's misogyny in *Speech Acts in Literature* (Stanford: Stanford University Press, 2001), 50–51.

28. Gert Buelens, "Henry James's Oblique Possessions: Plottings of Desire and Mastery in *The American Scene*," *PMLA* (March 2001), 309. The only trouble with Buelens's explanation is that the text of the novel does not say anything about a diffuse sexual energy, nor even figure anything of the sort. It has been projected into the text by Buelens. He has disobeyed Brower's Law.

29. George Meredith, *The Ordeal of Richard Feverel* (New York: Modern Library, 1950), 330–31. I refer to this edition because it reprints the original version of 1859 rather than the substantially altered version of 1878.

30. Professor Butler was kind enough to give me a copy of this essay, later published as "Values of Difficulty," *Just Being Difficult? Academic Writing in the Public Arena*, ed. Jonathan Culler and Kevin Lamb (Stanford: Stanford University Press, 2003), 199–215. Here is part of what she says about the impossibility of knowing why Catherine Sloper refuses Morris Townsend at the end of the novella: "we are asked to understand the limits of judgment and to cease judging, paradoxically, in the name of ethics, to cease judging in a way that assumes we already know in advance what there is to be known.

"And this suspension of judgment brings us closer to a different conception of ethics, one that honors what cannot be fully known or captured about the Other. Her action, her nonaction, cannot be easily translated, and this means that she marks the limits of the familiar, the clear, and the common. To honor this moment in which the familiar must become strange or, rather, where it admits the strangeness at its core, this may well be the moment where we come up against the limits of translation, when we undergo what is previously unknown, when we learn something about the limits of our ways of knowing; and in this way we experience as well the anxiety and the promise of what is different, what is possible, what is waiting for us if we do not foreclose it in advance" (208–9).

31. See Jacques Derrida, *Force de Loi: Le "Fondement mystique de l'autorité"* (Paris: Galilée, 1994), 50–63; "Force of Law: The 'Mystical Foundation of Authority,' " trans. Mary Quaintance, in *Deconstruction and the Possibility of Justice*, ed. Drucilla Cornell, Michel Rosenfeld, and David Gray Carlson (New York: Routledge, 1992), 22–29.

32. De Man, "Shelley Disfigured," 122.

33. John Milton, *Paradise Lost*, 4:497, 501–2.

CHAPTER 3: UNWORKED AND UNAVOWABLE: COMMUNITY IN *THE
AWKWARD AGE*

1. See Jean-Luc Nancy, *La Communauté désoeuvrée* (Paris: Christian Bour-
gois, 1986); Jean-Luc Nancy, *The Inoperative Community*, ed. Peter Connor,
trans. Peter Connor, Lisa Garbus, Michael Holland, and Simona Sawhney
(Minneapolis: University of Minnesota Press, 1991), 36–40 . Hereafter cited
in the text as *IC*, followed by page numbers. Maurice Blanchot, *La Communauté inavouable* (Paris: Minuit, 1983), 49–93; Maurice Blanchot, *The Inavowa-
ble Community*, trans. Pierre Joris (Barrytown, N.Y.: Station Hill Press, 1988),
27–60.

2. W. B. Yeats, "A Prayer for My Daughter," *Poems*, Variorum Edition,
ed. Peter Allt and Russell K. Alspach (New York: Macmillan, 1977), 405.

3. Georges Bataille, *L'Apprenti Sorcier du cercle communiste démocratique à
Acéphale: Textes, lettres et documents (1932–1939)*, ed. Marina Galletti, notes
trans. from Italian by Natália Vital (Paris: La Différence, 1999); for Maurice
Blanchot, see footnote 1; Giorgio Agamben, *La comunità che viene* (Turin:
Einaudi, 1990); Giorgio Agamben, The *Coming Community*, trans. Michael
Hardt (Minneapolis: University of Minnesota Press, 1993); Alphonso Lingis,
The Community of Those Who Have Nothing in Common (Bloomington: Indiana
University Press, 1994).

4. Benedict Anderson, *Imagined Communities: Reflections on the Origin and
Spread of Nationalism* (London: Verso, 1991).

5. Phalanstery means "a community of the followers of Charles Fourier,"
from *phalanx* ("any close-knit or compact body of people") plus *monastère*,
"monastery."

6. *Partage* means both "sharing" and "dividing." See Jean-Luc Nancy, *Le
Partage des voix* (Paris: Galilée, 1982); "Sharing Voices," trans. Gayle L. Or-
miston, in *Transforming the Hermeneutic Context: From Nietzsche to Nancy*, ed.
Gayle L. Ormiston and Alan D. Schrift (Albany: State University of New York
Press, 1990), 211–59.

7. Matthew Arnold, *The Poems*, ed. Kenneth Allott (London: Longmans,
1965), 242.

8. See Simon During, "Literary Subjectivity," *Ariel* 31, nos. 1/2 (2000):
33–50.

9. Henry James, "Anthony Trollope," *Literary Criticism: Essays on Literature; American Writers; English Writers* (New York: The Library of America,
1984), 1343.

10. Charles Dickens, *Bleak House*, ed. Nicola Bradbury (Harmondsworth,
Middlesex: Penguin, 1996), 7.

11. *Wise, Witty and Tender Sayings in Prose and Verse, Selected from the Works of George Eliot by Alexander Main*, 6th ed. (Edinburgh: William Blackwood and Sons, 1883); *Wit and Wisdom of George Eliot* (Boston: Roberts Brothers, 1873); *A Moment Each Day with George Eliot; A Quotation for Every Day in the Year Selected from the Works of George Eliot, by Ella Adams Moore and the Students in Her Classes in Literature* (Chicago: Madison Book Co., 1903).

12. See the reviews collected in *Anthony Trollope: The Critical Heritage*, ed. Donald Smalley (London: Routledge and Kegan Paul, 1969), 291–306.

13. Anthony Trollope, *An Autobiography*, ed. David Skilton (London: Penguin, 1996), 177.

14. The phrase "choir invisible" appears in George Eliot's humanist hymn "Oh may I join the choir invisible. . . ."

15. See Dorothea Krook, *"The Awkward Age": The Ordeal of Consciousness in Henry James* (Cambridge: Cambridge University Press, 1967), 135–66; Sheila Teahan, "Representational Awkwardness in *The Awkward Age*," *The Rhetorical Logic of Henry James* (Baton Rouge: Louisiana State University Press, 1995), 143–59; Suzie M. Gibson, "Secrecy and Friendship in *The Awkward Age*," "Dramas of Decision: Ethics and Secrecy in Henry James, Jacques Derrida and Gillian Rose," Ph.D. dissertation submitted to the University of Queensland (2002), 22–71; George Butte, "The Intersubjective Failure of Intersubjectivity: Henry James's *The Awkward Age* and the Shadow of the Body," *I Know That You Know That I Know: Narrating Subjects from Moll Flanders to Marnie* (Columbus: Ohio State University Press, 2004), 163–92.

16. See Paul de Man, foreword to Carol Jacobs, *The Dissimulating Harmony* (Baltimore: Johns Hopkins University Press, 1978), reprinted in Paul de Man, *Critical Writings, 1953–1978*, ed. Lindsay Waters (Minneapolis: University of Minnesota Press, 1989), 221–22.

17. He means in the New York Edition, for which this is one of the prefaces.

18. Friedrich Nietzsche, *Ecce Homo, Sämtliche Werke: Kritische Studienausgabe*, ed. Giorgio Colli and Mazzino Montinari (Berlin: de Gruyter, 1988), 6:285; *Ecce Homo*, trans. Walter Kaufmann, in *The Genealogy of Morals and Ecce Homo*, trans. Walter Kaufmann and R. J. Hollingdale (New York: Vintage, 1967), 243.

19. Gyp, *Le Mariage de Chiffon* (Paris: Calmann Lévy, 1895), 284–86; *A Gallic Girl*, trans. Henri Pène du Bois (New York: Brentano's, 1895), 270–72.

20. For a discussion of this, see J. Hillis Miller, "The Aftermath of Victorian Humanism: Oscar in *The Tragic Muse*," *Renaissance Humanism–Modern Humanism(s): Festschrift for Claus Uhlig*, ed. Walter Göbel and Bianca Ross (Heidelberg: C. Winter, 2001), 231–39.

21. George Butte, in a challenging and penetrating reading of *The Awkward Age*, cited above in note 15, presumes that the reader can correctly infer

quite a bit. Butte's model is the happy "complex intersubjectivity" in which Maurice Merleau-Ponty had confidence. This is the belief that I can know what you know about me, and you can also know that I know. The title of Butte's book, you will note, is *I Know That You Know That I Know*. I am not so confident. However it may be in "real life," in which we are confronted with real bodies, their gestures, and looks, as well as by the words those bodies emit, in a novel we have only the words on the page. I defy any reader, on the basis of the textual evidence, to make a verifiable claim for one exclusive reason why Vanderbank refused Nanda. Nor does the narrator tell the reader the answer.

22. See Sigmund Freud, *Jokes and Their Relation to the Unconscious*, trans. James Strachey (New York: Norton, 1989), 115–16. This is a reprint of the Standard Edition.

23. *The George Eliot Letters*, ed. Gordon Haight (New Haven: Yale University Press, 1955), 5:257.

24. Anthony Trollope, *The Vicar of Bullhampton* (London: Oxford University Press, 1963), v–vi.

25. Henry James, *Letters*, ed. Leon Edel (Cambridge: Harvard University Press, 1984), 4:110.

26. Walter Pater, *The Renaissance* (London: Macmillan, 1910), 238.

27. Henry James, *The Complete Notebooks*, ed. Leon Edel and Lyall H. Powers (New York: Oxford University Press, 1987), 118.

28. Arnold, *The Poems*, 242. See Niklas Luhmann, *Love as Passion: The Codification of Intimacy* (Cambridge: Harvard University Press, 1986; repr. Stanford: Stanford University Press, 1998) for a discussion of how social changes in the West since the eighteenth century have placed increasing weight on intimate love relationships as a symbolic medium of communication, and thus as a support for social systems, as earlier hierarchical forms, such as those of extended family, decay.

29. *The Community of Those Who Have Nothing in Common* is the title of Alphonso Lingis's book. See note 3.

CHAPTER 4: LYING AGAINST DEATH IN *THE WINGS OF THE DOVE*

1. Plato, *Phaedrus*, 275d–e, *The Collected Dialogues*, ed. Edith Hamilton and Huntington Cairns, Bollingen Series 71 (Princeton: Princeton University Press, 1973), 521.

2. Paul Celan, "Ashglory/Aschenglorie," ll. 24–26, *Breathturn/Atemwende*, bilingual ed., trans. Pierre Joris (Los Angeles: Sun and Moon, 1995), 178. Jacques Derrida has commented extensively on this passage in his seminars on witnessing.

3. For the connection between literature and democracy and for the idea that literature is not an intrinsic feature of language but a way of taking any piece of language whatsoever, see Jacques Derrida, " 'This Strange Institution Called Literature': An Interview with Jacques Derrida," *Acts of Literature*, ed. Derek Attridge (New York: Routledge, 1992), 33–73, esp. 37, 44–45; and Jacques Derrida, *Passions* (Paris: Galilée, 1993), 64–68; Jacques Derrida, "Passions: 'An Oblique Offering,' " trans. David Wood, *On the Name*, ed. Thomas Dutoit (Stanford: Stanford University Press, 1995), 28–30.

4. Roland Barthes, "L'Effet du réel," *Communications* (1968), 11:84–89.

5. Sharon Cameron's fine chapter on the novel, the best I know, nevertheless to some degree succumbs to this lure. See Sharon Cameron, "Thinking It Out in *The Wings of the Dove*," *Thinking in Henry James* (Chicago: University of Chicago Press, 1989), 122–68.

6. See J. Hillis Miller, "Re-Reading Re-Vision: James and Benjamin," *The Ethics of Reading* (New York: Columbia University Press, 1987), 110–22.

7. James says exactly the same thing about the preface itself in its last two sentences. He also uses again the figure of a bringing to light of something hidden. It takes him so long to confess to the crime that he commits it again in the act of confessing it: "I become conscious of overstepping my space without having brought the full quantity to light. The failure leaves me with a burden of residuary comment of which I yet boldly hope elsewhere to discharge myself" (19:xxii–xxiii). The preface, like the novel, is a "failure" because not all of it gets said. There is not space enough. The sentences just quoted have the structure of the deferred promise. I have not done it yet and I cannot do it now, but I promise to do it at some point in the future. It is an obligation, a "burden," something important that might be said, something that hovers somewhere as the possibility of being said, of being brought into the open, but that has not yet been said. James, however, never anywhere, so far as I know, discharged himself of the heavy burden of this particular responsibility. He went to his grave keeping the secret of what more he might have said about the "supersubtleties" and "arch-refinements, of tact and taste, of design and instinct, in 'The Wings of the Dove' " (19:xxii).

8. See Jacques Derrida, *Introduction à 'L'Origine de la géométrie de Husserl'* (Paris: Presses Universitaires de France, 1962); Jacques Derrida, *Edmund Husserl's 'The Origin of Geometry': An Introduction*, trans. John P. Leavey, Jr. (Lincoln: University of Nebraska Press, 1989), esp. 94–95 and 90–91n of the English translation. Husserl's treatise is reproduced in translation on pp. 157–80 of the English version. See also Jacques Derrida, "Ponctuations: Le Temps de la thèse," *Du droit à la philosophie* (Paris: Galilée, 1990), 443; Jacques Derrida, "The Time of a Thesis: Punctuations," *Philosophy in France Today*, ed. Alan Montefiore (Cambridge: Cambridge University Press, 1982), 37.

9. See Nicholas Royle, "The 'Telepathy Effect': Notes toward a Reconsideration of Narrative Fiction," *The Uncanny* (Manchester: Manchester University Press, 2003), 256–76.

10. See J. L. Austin, "Conditions for Happy Performatives," *HT*, 12–24.

11. See Walter Pater, "Demeter and Persephone," *Greek Studies* (London: Macmillan, 1910), 100.

12. See my discussion of this aspect of Austin in J. Hillis Miller, *Speech Acts in Literature* (Stanford: Stanford University Press, 2001), 40–49.

13. See Immanuel Kant, *Grundlegung zur Metaphysik der Sitten, Werkausgabe*, ed. Wilhelm Weischedel (Frankfurt a. M.: Suhrkamp, 1982), 7:29–30; Immanuel Kant, *Foundations of the Metaphysics of Morals*, trans. Lewis White Beck (Indianapolis: Bobbs-Merrill, 1978), 21–23. I have discussed this passage in "Reading Telling: Kant," *The Ethics of Reading*, 30–33.

14. See *HT*, 20, 40, 41.

15. See *ibid.*, 9–10.

16. Charles du Bos, "Pauline de Browning: Extraits d'un cours inédit," *Études Anglaises* 7, no. 2 (April 1954): 162–64. The phrase cited is on 164.

17. All that I have to say about lies in *The Wings of the Dove* is deeply indebted to Jacques Derrida's admirable "History of the Lie: Prolegomena," *Without Alibi*, ed. and trans. Peggy Kamuf (Stanford: Stanford University Press, 2002), 28–70.

18. Maurice Blanchot, "La Voix narrative (le 'il,' le neuter)," *L'Entretien infini* (Paris: Gallimard, 1969), 556–67; Maurice Blanchot, "The Narrative Voice (the 'He,' the Neuter)," *The Gaze of Orpheus*, trans. Lydia Davis (Barrytown, N.Y.: Station Hill Press, 1981), 133–43.

19. Jean-Luc Nancy, *The Sense of the World*, trans. Jeffrey S. Librett (Minneapolis: University of Minnesota Press, 1997), 29.

20. http://www.perseus.tufts.edu/cgi-bin/ptext?lookup = Cic. + Catil. + 1.1.

21. W. B. Yeats, *Poems*, Variorum Edition, ed. Peter Allt and Russell K. Alspach (New York: Macmillan, 1977), 408, 445

22. I have discussed this seminar in *Speech Acts in Literature*, 134–39.

23. See Immanuel Kant, "On a Supposed Right to Lie Because of Philanthropic Concerns" ("Über ein vermeintes Recht aus Menschenliebe zu lügen"), in *Grounding for the Metaphysics of Morals*, trans. James Ellington (Indianapolis: Hackett, 1993), 63–67. See also Jacques Derrida's discussion of Kant's little essay in "History of the Lie: Prolegomena," *Without Alibi*, 43–45.

24. See note 5, above.

25. "'I give and bequeath my watch to my brother'—as occurring in a will" (*HT*, 5).

26. The fullest are dated November 3, 1894, and November 7, 1894. See Henry James, *The Complete Notebooks*, ed. Leon Edel and Lyall H. Powers

(New York: Oxford University Press, 1987), 102–7. Another, briefer entry is dated February 14, 1895 (*ibid.*, 114–15). These notebook entries show how far James's first ideas for the characters and the action were from the final "idea," the "virtual reality" that he ultimately, years later, transformed into words.

27. Paul de Man, "Autobiography as De-Facement," *The Rhetoric of Romanticism* (New York: Columbia University Press, 1984), 81.

28. Joseph Conrad, *Heart of Darkness*, in *Youth: A Narrative and Two Other Stories* (London: Dent, 1923), 82. Marlow says: "You know I hate, detest, and can't bear a lie, not because I am straighter than the rest of us, but simply because it appalls me. There is a taint of death, a flavor of mortality in lies— which is exactly what I hate and detest in the world—what I want to forget. It makes me miserable and sick, like biting something rotten would do."

29. Marcel Proust, *À la recherche du temps perdu*, Pléiade ed., ed. Jean-Yves Tadié (Paris: Gallimard, 1987–89), 4:191; Marcel Proust, *Remembrance of Things Past*, trans. C. K. Scott-Moncrieff, Terence Kilmartin, and Andreas Mayor (New York: Vintage, 1982), 3:625.

30. "Matcham" is perhaps an echo of "Matching," Plantaganet Palliser's country house in Anthony Trollope's *Can You Forgive Her?* and the other Palliser novels. If so, it is graceful homage to the elder novelist, about whom James wrote a substantial essay. See Henry James, "Anthony Trollope," *Literary Criticism: Essays on Literature; American Writers; English Writers*, ed. Leon Edel and Mark Wilson (New York: The Library of America, 1984), 1330–54.

31. James writes eloquently of the death of Minny Temple in the concluding section of his second autobiographical volume, *Notes of a Son and Brother* (New York: Scribner, 1914).

32. F. O. Matthiessen, *The James Family* (New York: Knopf, 1947), 61–63. See also the discussion of this letter and the section in *Notes of a Son and Brother* about Minny Temple in Sharon Cameron, "Thinking It Out in *The Wings of the Dove*," *Thinking in Henry James*, 154–55.

33. James uses the latter figure to describe Milly's relation to Kate during their private talks in Venice: "Thus insuperably guarded was the truth about the girl's own conception of her validity; thus was a wondering pitying sister condemned wistfully to look at her from the far side of the moat she had dug round her tower. Certain aspects of the connection of these young women show for us, such is the twilight that gathers about them, in the likeness of some dim scene in a Maeterlinck play; we have positively the image, in the delicate dusk, of the figures so associated and yet so opposed, so mutually watchful: that of the angular pale princess, ostrich-plumed, black-robed, hung about with amulets, reminders, relics, mainly seated, mainly still, and that of the upright restless slow-circling lady of her court who exchanges with her, across the black water streaked with evening gleams, fitful questions and answers" (20:139).

34. Henry James, *Complete Stories: 1892–1898* (New York: The Library of America, 1996), 609–34.

35. Proust, *Recherche*, 4:44; *Remembrance*, 3:470.

36. James, *Notebooks*, 115.

CHAPTER 5: "CONSCIOUS PERJURY": DECLARATIONS OF IGNORANCE IN *THE GOLDEN BOWL*

1. Mark Twain, *The Adventures of Huckleberry Finn*, *Writings*, Author's National Edition (New York, Harper, 1899), 13:15.

2. See Chapter 4, n. 23.

3. Amerigo tells Maggie, before they are married: "It's you yourselves meanwhile . . . who really know nothing. There are two parts of me. . . . One is made up of the history, the doings, the marriages, the crimes, the follies, the boundless *bêtises* of other people—especially of their infamous waste of money that might have come to me. Those things are written—literally in rows of volumes, in libraries; are as public as they're abominable. Everybody can get at them, and you've both of you [Maggie and her father] wonderfully looked them in the face. But there's another part, very much smaller doubtless, which, such as it is, represents my single self, the unknown, unimportant—unimportant save to you—personal quantity. About this you've found out nothing" (23:9). This personal quantity is one opacity. Another is racial, as the Prince is shown meditating about when he asks himself whether he is arrogant and greedy: "Personally, he considered, he hadn't the vices in question—and that was so much to the good. His race, on the other hand, had had them handsomely enough, and he was somehow full of his race. Its presence in him was like the consciousness of some inexpugnable scent in which his clothes, his whole person, his hands and the hair of his head, might have been steeped as in some chemical bath: the effect was nowhere in particular, yet he constantly felt himself at the mercy of the cause" (23:16).

4. *HT*, 5. Authorities I have consulted say that both "I will" and "I do" are used at different times in marriage ceremonies. In the modern Anglican ceremony, which Austin probably had in mind, "I will" is said by the bride and groom, while "I do" is said by the father of the bride in answer to the question "Who brings this woman to be married to this man?" Since Austin was discussing what the bride and groom say, Urmson is right to say Austin made a mistake. The two speech acts have quite different nuances. To say "I do" is a present-tense performative that makes something happen now, whereas "I will" (love her [or him], cherish her, honor and protect her, etc.) is a promise oriented toward the future. "I do" is complete in the moment it is uttered, whereas "I will," like all promises, may or may not be faithfully carried out. Only time will tell. Urmson was therefore perhaps wrong to say that the mis-

take does not matter to the argument Austin is making, since the two performative utterances have such different temporal orientations.

   5. Amerigo cites this cliché in his dialogue with Charlotte before their
escapade in Gloucester: " 'But as to cracks,' the Prince went on—'what did
you tell me the other day you prettily call them in English? "rifts within the
lute"?—risk them as much as you like for yourself, but don't risk them for
me' " (23:360).

   6. Jacques Lacan, "Le Séminaire sur 'La Lettre volée,' " *Écrits* (Paris: Seuil,
1966), 15–16. A translation of this essay plus Derrida's commentary on it ("Le
Facteur de la verité") may be found in *The Purloined Poe: Lacan, Derrida, and
Psychoanalytic Reading*, ed. John P. Muller and William J. Richardson (Baltimore: Johns Hopkins University Press, 1988).

   7. See Chapter 4, n. 3.

   8. Ludwig Wittgenstein, *Philosophical Investigations*, trans. G. E. M. Ans-
combe (Oxford: Basil Blackwell, 1968), paragraphs 2–21, pp. 3e–10e.

   9. See Chapter 4, n. 9.

   10. Edgar Allan Poe, *The Narrative of Arthur Gordon Pym*, *Works* (New
York: Thomas Y. Crowell, 1902), 3:242.

   11. Ovid, *The Metamorphoses*, trans. Mary M. Innes (Harmondsworth,
Middlesex: Penguin, 1976), 45.

   12. See Gerard Manley Hopkins, *Further Letters*, ed. Claude Colleer Ab-
bott, 2d ed. (London: Oxford University Press, 1956), 252–53.

   13. See Gerard Manley Hopkins, *The Journals and Papers*, ed. Humphry
House and Graham Storey (London: Oxford University Press, 1959), 289.

   14. James Joyce, *Ulysses* (New York: Random House, 1942), 112. Brook
Thomas cites and discusses this passage in "History Repeating Itself with a
Difference," *James Joyce's 'Ulysses': A Book of Many Happy Returns* (Baton
Rouge: Louisiana State University Press, 1982), 149–50.

   15. Jacques Derrida, *Spectres de Marx* (Paris: Galilée, 1993), 163.

   16. Jacques Derrida, *Specters of Marx*, trans. Peggy Kamuf (New York:
Routledge, 1994), 99.

   17. Sharon Cameron, "Thinking Speaking: *The Golden Bowl* and the Production of Meaning," *Thinking in Henry James* (Chicago: University of Chicago Press, 1989), 119.

   18. Jacques Derrida, "Déclarations de Indépendance," *Otobiographies*
(Paris: Galilée, 1984), 13–32; Jacques Derrida, "Declarations of Independence," trans. Thomas Keenan and Thomas Pepper, *New Political Science* 15
(1986): 7–15; David deKanter Arndt, "The Declaration of Independence,"
"Ground and Abyss: The Question of *Poiesis* in Heidegger, Arendt, Foucault,
and Stevens," Ph.D. dissertation in Comparative Literature, University of
California, Irvine (Ann Arbor: UMI, 1998), 127–83.

CHAPTER 6: THE "QUASI-TURN-OF-SCREW EFFECT," OR HOW TO RAISE A
GHOST WITH WORDS: *THE SENSE OF THE PAST*

1. Jacques Derrida, "Justices," in *Provocations to Reading: J. Hillis Miller and the Democracy to Come*, ed. Barbara Cohen and Dragan Kujundžić (New York: Fordham University Press, forthcoming).

2. Jacques Derrida, "L'Aphorisme à contretemps," in *Psyché: Inventions de l'autre* (Paris: Galilée, 1987), 519–33; Jacques Derrida, "Aphorism Countertime," trans. Nicholas Royle, *Acts of Literature*, ed. Derek Attridge (New York: Routledge, 1992), 414–33.

3. Jacques Derrida, *Force de loi* (Paris: Galilée, 1994); Jacques Derrida, "Before the Law," trans. Avital Ronell and Christine Roulston, in *Acts of Literature*, 181–220.

4. See Chapter 5, n. 6, above.

5. Jacques Derrida, "The Time of a Thesis: Punctuations," *Philosophy in France Today*, ed. Alan Montefiore (Cambridge: Cambridge University Press, 1982), 37.

6. See Nicholas Royle, "The 'Telepathy Effect': Notes toward a Reconsideration of Narrative Fiction," *The Uncanny* (Manchester: Manchester University Press, 2003), 256–76.

7. Jacques Derrida, *Voyous: Deux essais sur la raison* (Paris: Galilée, 2003), 143; Jacques Derrida, *Rogues: Two Essays on Reason*, trans. Pascale-Anne Brault and Michael Naas (Stanford: Stanford University Press, 2005), 100.

8. Jacques Derrida, "Télépathie," *Furor* 2 (February 1981): 5–41; Jacques Derrida, "Telepathy," trans. Nicholas Royle, *Oxford Literary Review* 10, nos. 1–2 (1988): 3–41, also in *Deconstruction: A Reader*, ed. Martin McQuillan (Edinburgh: Edinburgh University Press, 2000), 496–526; Jacques Derrida, *Spectres de Marx* (Paris: Galilée, 1993); Jacques Derrida, *Specters of Marx*, trans. Peggy Kamuf (New York: Routledge, 1994); Jacques Derrida, "Ponctuations: Le Temps de la these," *Du droit à la philosophie* (Paris: Galilée, 1990), 439–59; Jacques Derrida, "The Time of a Thesis: Punctuations," trans. Kevin McLaughlin, *Philosophy in France Today*, 34–50; Jacques Derrida, "Fors: Les mots anglés de Nicolas Abraham and Maria Torok," in Nicolas Abraham and Maria Torok, *Cryptonymie: Le Verbier de l'Homme aux Loups* (Paris: Aubier Flammarion, 1976), 7–73; Jacques Derrida, "*Fors*: The Anglish Words of Nicolas Abraham and Maria Torok," trans. Barbara Johnson, in Nicolas Abraham and Maria Torok, *The Wolf Man's Magic Word: A Cryptonymy*, trans. Nicholas Rand (Minneapolis: University of Minnesota Press, 1986), xi–xlviii; Jacques Derrida, *Limited Inc*, trans. Samuel Weber and Jeffrey Mehlman (Evanston: Northwestern University Press, 1988). For a more recent discussion of speech acts, see, among many other examples, the final pages of Jacques Derrida, "Psyché: Invention de l'autre," in *Psyché*, 58–61, or Jacques Derrida,

"Déclarations de Indépendance," *Otobiographies* (Paris: Galilée, 1984), 13–32; Jacques Derrida, "Declarations of Independence," trans. Thomas Keenan and Thomas Pepper, *New Political Science* 15 (1986): 7–15

9. For my essays on three of these, see, for "The Time of a Thesis: Punctuations," J. Hillis Miller, "Derrida and Literature," *Jacques Derrida and the Humanities*, ed. Tom Cohen (Cambridge: Cambridge University Press, 2001), 58–81; for "Fors," "Les Topographies de Derrida," trans. Marie-Pierre Baggett, *Le Passage des frontières*, Colloque de Cérisy (Paris: Galilée, 1994), 193–201; for "Telepathy," "Thomas Hardy, Jacques Derrida, and the 'Dislocation of Souls,'" *Taking Chances: Derrida, Psychoanalysis, and Literature*, ed. Joseph H. Smith and William Kerrigan (Baltimore: The Johns Hopkins University Press, 1984), 135–45.

10. Cited in Fred Kaplan, *Henry James: The Imagination of Genius, a Biography* (New York: William Morrow, 1992), 553.

11. See Henry James, *The Turn of the Screw*, Norton Critical Edition, 2d ed., ed. Deborah Esch and Jonathan Warren (New York: Norton, 1999), for a representative sample of critical essays on *The Turn of the Screw*.

12. See Shoshana Felman, "Turning the Screw of Interpretation," *Yale French Studies* 55–56 (1977): 94–207.

13. See Friedrich Schlegel, "Kritische Fragmente," *Kritische Schriften* (Munich: Carl Hanser, 1964), 20–21; Friedrich Schlegel, "Critical Fragments," *Philosophical Fragments*, trans. Peter Firchow (Minneapolis: University of Minnesota Press, 1991), 13. See also Friedrich Schlegel, "Über die Unverständlichkeit," *Kritische Schriften*, 530–42; Friedrich Schlegel, "On Incomprehensibility," in *German Aesthetic and Literary Criticism: The Romantic Ironists and Goethe*, ed. Kathleen Wheeler (Cambridge: Cambridge University Press, 1984), 32–40.

14. Hans-Walter Gabler kindly pointed out to me this resemblance.

15. It is not, however, included among the eighteen stories collected in *The Ghostly Tales of Henry James*, ed. Leon Edel (New Brunswick: Rutgers University Press, 1949), nor among the ten stories collected in Henry James, *Ghost Stories*, ed. Martin Scofield (Ware, Hertfordshire: Wordsworth Classics, 2001).

16. I cite the first version, as reprinted in Henry James, *Complete Stories: 1864–1874*, ed. Jean Strouse (New York: The Library of America, 1999), 543–611. James substantially revised the story for its inclusion in the New York Edition.

17. *Ibid.*, 582.

18. *Ibid.*, 558.

19. Derrida, *Specters of Marx*, 106.

20. Edmund Husserl, *Cartesianische Meditationen*, ed. S. Strasser, *Husserliana*, vol. 1 (The Hague: Martinus Nijhoff, 1950); Edmund Husserl, *Cartesian*

Meditations: An Introduction to Phenomenology, trans. Dorion Cairns (The Hague: Martinus Nijhoff, 1960), 108–11.

21. Henry James, "The Art of Fiction," *Literary Criticism: Essays on Literature; American Writers; English Writers* (New York: The Library of America, 1984), 33.

22. See Aristotle, *Poetics,* trans. Gerald F. Else (Ann Arbor: University of Michigan Press, 1970), 49.

23. Henry James, *The Portrait of a Lady,* 3:x.

24. Derrida, "The Time of a Thesis: Punctuations," 37.